RUSSIAN

INVESTMENT & BUSINESS GUIDE
EVERYTHING YOU NEED TO START AND OPERATE A SUCCESSFUL BUSINESS IN RUSSIA

International Business Publications, USA
Washington, DC- Moscow

- 2 -

RUSSIA
INVESTMENT & BUSINESS GUIDE

Editorial content: International Business Publications, USA

Editor-in-Chief: Dr. Igor S. Oleynik
Editor: Natasha Alexander
Managing Editor: Stas Oliynyk

Published by
International Business Publications, USA
P.O.Box 15343, Washington, DC 20003
Phone: (202) 546-2103, Fax: (202) 546-3275.
E-mail: rusric@erols.com

UPDATED ANNUALLY

We express our sincere appreciation to all government agencies and international organizations which provided information and other materials for this guide

Databases & Information: International Business Publications, USA
Cover Design: International Business Publications, USA

International Business Publications, USA. has used its best efforts in collecting, analyzing and preparing data, information and materials for this unique guide. Due to the dynamic nature and fast development of the economy and business environment, we cannot warrant that all information herein is complete and accurate. IBP does not assume and hereby disclaim any liability to any person for any loss or damage caused by possible errors or omissions in the guide.

This guide is for individual use only. Use this guide for any other purpose, included but not limited to reproducing and storing in a retrieval system by any means, electronic, photocopying or using the addresses or other information contained in this guide for any commercial purposes requires a special written permission from the publisher.

2001 International Business Publications, USA
ISSN 1082-8249   ISBN 0-7397-7288-0
For customer service and information, please contact:

in the USA: International Business Publications, USA
               P.O.Box 15343, Washington, DC 20003
               Phone: (202) 546-2103, Fax: (202) 546-3275.
               E-mail: rusric@erols.com
               Global Markets DataBank on Line: http://world.mirhouse.com

Printed in the USA

RECEIVED

SEP 1 9 2002

Kirstein Business Branch

For additional analytical, business and investment opportunities information, please contact Global Investment & Business Center, USA at (202) 546-2103. Fax: (202) 546-3275. E-mail: rusric@erols.com
Global Business E-Books on Line: http://world.mirhouse.com

For additional analytical, business and investment opportunities information,
please contact Global Investment & Business Center, USA
at (202) 546-2103. Fax: (202) 546-3275. E-mail: rusric@erols.com
Global Business E-Books on Line: http://world.mirhouse.com

**For additional analytical, business and investment opportunities information,
please contact Global Investment & Business Center, USA
at (202) 546-2103. Fax: (202) 546-3275. E-mail: rusric@erols.com
Global Business E-Books on Line: http://world.mirhouse.com**

For additional analytical, business and investment opportunities information,
please contact Global Investment & Business Center, USA
at (202) 546-2103. Fax: (202) 546-3275. E-mail: rusric@erols.com
Global Business E-Books on Line: http://world.mirhouse.com

For additional analytical, business and investment opportunities information,
please contact Global Investment & Business Center, USA
at (202) 546-2103. Fax: (202) 546-3275. E-mail: rusric@erols.com
Global Business E-Books on Line: http://world.mirhouse.com

**For additional analytical, business and investment opportunities information,
please contact Global Investment & Business Center, USA
at (202) 546-2103. Fax: (202) 546-3275. E-mail: rusric@erols.com
Global Business E-Books on Line: http://world.mirhouse.com**

STRATEGIC AND DEVELOPMENT PROFILES

VLADIMIR V. PUTIN PRESIDENT OF THE RUSSIAN FEDERATION

Vladimir Putin was born in Leningrad on October 7, 1952.

In 1975, Putin graduated from the law department of the Leningrad State University. After graduation he worked at the Foreign Intelligence Service. He also worked for a long time in Germany. After his return to Leningrad, Putin became an aide to the vice-president of the Leningrad State University in charge of international issues.

In 1990, he was adviser to chairman of the Leningrad City Council and in 1991-1994 chairman of the committee for foreign relations of the St. Petersburg Mayor's Office.

In 1994-1996, he was first deputy chairman of the city government and chairman of the committee for external relations.

In 1996-1997, he was first deputy presidential business manager.

In 1997-1998, Putin worked as head of the president's Main Audit Directorate and presidential deputy chief of staff.

From July 1998 to March 1999 he was director of the Federal Security Service.

For additional analytical, business and investment opportunities information, please contact Global Investment & Business Center, USA at (202) 546-2103. Fax: (202) 546-3275. E-mail: rusric@erols.com Global Business E-Books on Line: http://world.mirhouse.com

Between March 1999 and August 1999, Putin combined his job as Federal Security Service director with the work as Security Council secretary.

On August 9, 1999, he was appointed first vice-prime minister and later on the same day he became acting prime minister.

On March 26, 2000, he was elected the President of the Russian Federation.

Putin is married with two daughters. His hobbies include sports, particularly wrestling.

CURRENT POLITICAL ENVIRONMENT

BILATERAL RELATIONSHIP WITH THE UNITED STATES

The U.S. relationship with Russia has evolved since the break-up of the Soviet Union through numerous summits and Bilateral Commission meetings that have built a substantial agenda for U.S.-Russian cooperation. The last bilateral summit was held in Moscow in June 2000. In addition to resolution of regional crises, such talks have focused on arms control, non-proliferation of weapons of mass destruction and the means for their delivery, counter-terrorism, organized crime, and the environment.

The United States continues to support Russian efforts to build a democratic society and market economy, with the goal of integrating the country more broadly and firmly into the international community. The United States also continues its support to engage international financial institutions with Russia.

Major Political Issues Affecting Business Climate
Democratic institutions are fragile in Russia. The March 2000 presidential election was the first democratic transfer of power in Russia's 1,000-year history; the election reassured investors about Russia's political stability. Nevertheless, other legal and juridical factors affect the business environment in Russia. Although Russian law now includes a civil code (which contains a commercial code) and a criminal code, key amendments are needed to improve the business environment.

Protectionist elements in the Russian executive and legislative branches have risen in response to the broad belief that free trade and foreign business activity have caused the nation's industrial decline. Some politicians advocate limits on foreign share holdings or property ownership, or an increased tax burden on foreign businesses. Putin and the Russian government have pledged to improve the business climate and increase legal protection for investment.

RUSSIA: STRATEGIC PROFILE

Population: 145.7 million (November 1999, declining), the sixth largest national population after China, India, the United States, Indonesia, and Brazil; 81.5 percent are ethnic Russian; 73.9 percent urban; population of Moscow - 9 million; population of St. Petersburg - 4.8 million. Russia has a 98 percent literacy rate.

Territory: 17,075,200 square kilometers/6.6 million square miles. Russia, covering one-eighth of the world's land surface, is the largest country in the world. Its territory is almost twice the size of the United States. Russia is divided into 89 administrative regions, including provinces (oblasts and krais), metropolitan cities (Moscow and St. Petersburg), 16 autonomous republics with their own independent governments, 5 autonomous regions, and 10 national regions. The autonomous and national regions have less autonomy than the republics.

Economic Significance: Russia is well endowed with natural resources and raw materials such as petroleum, diamonds, gold, copper, rare metals, manganese, bauxite, uranium, silver, graphite, and platinum, all of which are a source of hard currency because of worldwide demand. The country ranks as either the largest or one of the largest worldwide producers of several of the above commodities and products. Although Russia has been a leading international player in select manufacturing sectors, such as chemicals and military aerospace, the country=s manufacturing base remains greatly diminished.

Russia manufactures approximately 62 percent of all the machinery made in the Newly Independent States of the former Soviet Union (NIS) and nearly 60 percent of the NIS= crude steel (Russia is the world's largest steel producer after Japan).

Industrial Profile: Steady growth over the last three years in the trade and service sectors, which were underdeveloped during the years of the USSR=s central planning, has been an increasingly important contributor to Russian GDP. Since the mid-to-late 1990s, *services* have accounted for more than 50 percent of GDP, with *manufacturing* contributing just under 40 percent, and *agricultural output* accounting for just under 10 percent. Overall trends indicate that the portion of GDP accounted for by services and taxes is increasing, while production is decreasing in importance as a contributor to GDP.

- 18 -

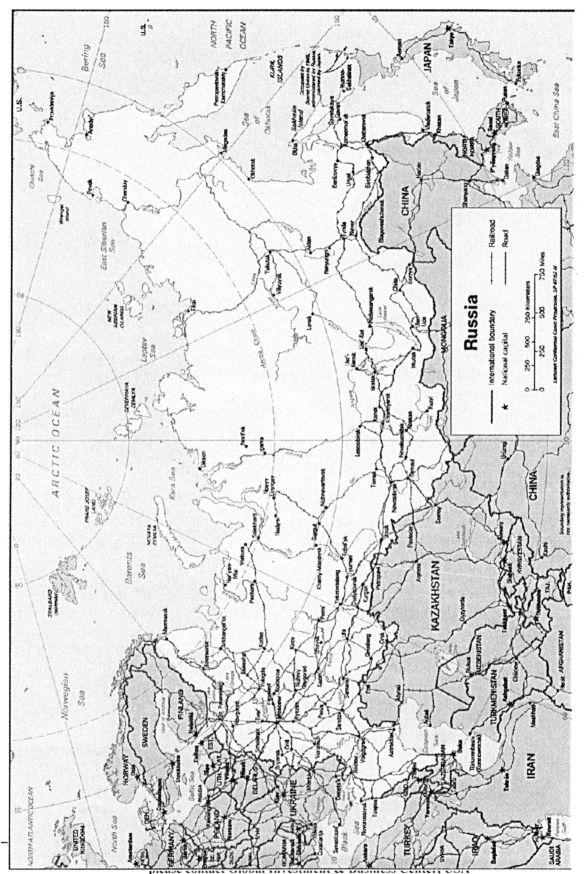

please contact Global Investment & Business Center, USA
at (202) 546-2103. Fax: (202) 546-3275. E-mail: rusric@erols.com
Global Business E-Books on Line: http://world.mirhouse.com

Aside from output related to the above-mentioned petroleum products and minerals/metals, other key Russian industries are chemicals, timber and wood products, including paper, and non-ferrous metals. Nearly 15 percent of Russia's industries are defense related.

MACROECONOMIC INDICATORS

In many areas, Russia showed better performance in 1999 than expected, and improved results compared to 1998. Higher world prices for fuels and metals facilitated improvements, as did the devalued ruble, which rendered Russian products relatively cheaper than imports and contributed to increased domestic purchases and exports. Given Russia's extremely poor performance in 1998, however, a comparison of 1999 performance to 1997 results can provide a a useful frame of reference. On many fronts, a comparison of Russian performance in 1999 vs. 1997 shows small declines in 1999 results.

Goskomstat, the Russian State Statistics Committee (www.gks.ru), is the organization that provides many of Russia=s official statistics. Official Russian statistics indicate improving economic performance in 1999 following initial declines in the first quarter of 1999, with particularly strong recovery in the third quarter.

GDP per capita: According to the European Bank for Reconstruction and Development (EBRD). GDP per capita in Russia climbed steadily from 1991 to 1997 (1997: $1,868; : $2,910; 1997 $3,056), but then dropped sharply in 1998, to $1,867 per capita. For 1999, early estimates suggest that per capita GDP fell to levels on par with the early 1990s.

Industrial production: "Free fall" is a term some used to describe industrial output immediately following the breakup of the Soviet Union. According to the Russian State Statistics Committee (Goskomstat), industrial production has fallen nearly 55 percent since 1990; larger declines are suggested by other sources. The military-industrial complex, suppliers of goods to the state sector, and light industry have been among the hardest hit. However, depending on world prices and ruble stability, some export-oriented industries have fared relatively well during Russia=s transition. One of the effects of the August 1998 crisis was to facilitate, at least temporarily and for some sectors, progress at stimulating local production and import substitution.

Initial Russian government estimates report 8.1 percent growth in industrial output during 1999 over the previous year, reportedly the strongest growth since the early 1990s, but perhaps unsurprising given the challenges and declines of 1998. The finish to the year marks a significant improvement from performance in early 1999—during the first quarter of 1999, industrial output dropped 1.6 percent compared to the same period of 1998. Third quarter performance was particularly strong with year-on-year growth in industrial output of 16.5 percent. Analysts within Russia and abroad assert that Russia achieved this growth as a result of the August 1998 crisis and will not be able to maintain this growth in 2000 without higher levels of consumer spending and investment.

According to official Russian data, most major industry sectors showed an increase in output in 1999 over 1998, as well as compared to 1997 (exception: agribusiness and the power and fuel sectors, which showed improvements over 1998, but declines compared to 1997). Specific subsectors showing declines in output in 1999 over 1998 include heat/oil, machine tools, television, and sausage production. Certain sectors that have otherwise fared poorly in the mid and late 1990s, such as light industry and the pulp/paper, chemical and building materials sector, showed increased output in 1999 over 1998. Sectors that fared the worst in 1998 included light industry, metallurgy, chemicals, and agribusiness.

Despite improvements in 1999, some experts note that a majority of Russian companies remain uncompetitive. Meanwhile, according to Goskomstat, output continues to fall at medium and large Russian enterprises, while small companies and joint ventures are largely responsible for increased output.

Russian production levels face monthly and seasonal fluctuations, as well as wide disparities between industry sectors. Secondary indicators such as freight haulage and energy output can suggest a slightly different scenario than that indicated by official statistics. This mystery is somewhat accounted for by the informal, or shadow, economy, as well as by ongoing tremendous tax avoidance by Russia=s enterprises, despite efforts to improve tax collection. The Russian Federal Security Service has estimated that the **shadow economy** may account for as much as 40-50 percent of GDP, compared with less than 10 percent in most developed economies. In early 1999, the State Statistics Committee reported that on average 20 percent of incomes are concealed from the government, with much higher rates in trade and during the summer months, when individuals are harvesting food from their summer homes.

Inflation: Inflation levels in Russia dropped drastically between 1992, when the annual inflation rate surpassed 2,000 percent, and July 1998, when annualized inflation in Russia dropped to a low of 5-6 percent. The Russian Government was aiming for 5-7 percent inflation in 1998, but the eruption of financial crisis and related developments on and after August 17, 1998 (ruble devaluation, etc.) resulted in a dramatic climb in monthly inflation. Monthly inflation was just 0.2 percent in July 1998, but jumped to 15 percent in August 1998 and 38 percent for September 1998, closing at 84 percent for the year.

Despite concerns that inflation might reach 100 percent in 1999, Russian inflation rates generally showed decline in 1999 over 1998, ending the year at 36.5 percent. The following chart shows the progression of Russian inflation rates between 1994 and early 1999.

TABLE 3: RUSSIAN INFLATION: 1994-1999

Year	January	August	December	Annual Total
1999	8.5%	1.2%	1.3%	36.5%
1998	1.5%	0.2%	11.6%	84.4%
1997	2.3%	-0.1%	1.0%	11%
	4.1%	-0.2%	1.4%	21.8%
1997	18.0%	4.6%	3.0%	131%
1994	22.0%	4.0%	18.0%	215%

Monthly inflation rates have varied depending the time of year under consideration, with recent years indicating a general pattern of relatively higher levels at the beginning and end of the year but lower rates during the summer months. Although inflation rates are usually reported for Russia as a whole, regional variations do occur.

RUBLE / EXCHANGE RATES

Russia has undertaken a number of different approaches to **exchange rate policy** over the past few years, including a currency corridor in 1997 and a crawling band mechanism from 1997-1997. For the most part, these measures were viewed as part of an effort to establish a more >natural= ruble-to-foreign currency rate and have generally been positively received for their perceived contribution to Russian macroeconomic stability. Falling inflation, slow money supply growth, and the effective functioning of Russia=s ruble-dollar mechanisms also contributed to a period of relative ruble stability through early 1998.

In January 1998, with the ruble trading at just over 6 to the dollar, Russia replaced the crawling band mechanism with a more freely floating but still semi-managed ruble. The exchange rate policy allowed the ruble to fluctuate within 15 percent around a central exchange rate, which Russia intended to maintain at between 6.1-6.2 rubles to the U.S. dollar in 1998-2000. In July 1998, the ruble was trading at R6.2 to the dollar. On **August 17, 1998,** Russia widened the band within which the ruble was allowed to fluctuate, resulting in a de facto devaluation of the ruble. In total, the ruble lost 71 percent of its value in 2002, closing the year at R32 to the dollar.

Ruble redenomination: On January 1, 1998, Russia redenominated its ruble, introducing new bills with three fewer zeros than pre-1998 rubles. At the same time, Russia re-introduced the kopek, valued at 1/100th of a ruble.

DEBT / DEFICIT

According to the Russian Government, payments to service domestic and foreign debt accounted for nearly 30 percent of federal budget spending in 1998. Among the measures introduced on **August 17, 1998**, in response to the growing financial crisis, the Russian Government announced a 90-day moratorium on some foreign debt payments. Lacking specific guideline regarding the implementation of the moratorium, banks applied their own interpretation to the measure, with some continuing payments and others stopping them all together.

Budget Deficit: Russia has initially reported a budget deficit for 1999 of 1.4 percent of GDP, lower than the 2.5 percent projected for the year's budget. Revised Russian 1998 figures report a budget deficit of 5.5 percent for 1998. Russian estimates of the country's budget deficit, however, tend to be at least a few percentage points lower than international estimates. In 1997, for example, the Russian Government reported a budget deficit of 3.3 percent of GDP, but other sources, such as the International Monetary Fund (IMF), estimated Russia=s budget deficit to be closer to 7.7 percent; in Russia reported a 3 percent deficit, while many other sources estimated the deficit to be 5 percent. One source of the variance is differing methods used to calculate deficit figures--Russian Government methods do not include debt service payments (interest on debt).

Wage and Pension Arrears: The Russian government continues to name as a top priority paying arrears to state workers, students, and military personnel. Russian wage arrears have reportedly fallen steadily each month since October 1998. Between January 1999 and November 1999, total wage arrears fell from nearly R77 billion to R53 billion. Regional governments are said to account for more than 80% of those wage arrears. According to the Ministry of Economy, in November 1998 pension arrears totaled R30 billion, roughly equal to $1.7 billion at the time.

Foreign Debt: The Russian Government maintains substantial foreign debt. Approximately $100 billion of Russia=s foreign debt was inherited from the Soviet Union -- Russia assumed all of the foreign debt of the Soviet Union in exchange for the other NIS countries abrogating any claims to the FSU=s foreign assets. The remaining amount of foreign debt has accumulated since the break-up. Russian total foreign debt grew approximately $20 billion between and 1998, to roughly $144 billion. Of the total debt, approximately two-thirds is principal, while the remaining amount constitutes interest and payment arrears accumulation.

In June the Russian Government reached a settlement on rescheduling $38.7 billion in old Russian sovereign debt to the *Paris Club* of creditor countries, and in October 1997 Russia was admitted to the Paris Club. In December 1997 Russia signed a closing agreement with the *London Club* of commercial creditors for a program to restructure nearly $32 billion of mostly Soviet-era debt over a period of 25 years.

Russia missed a number of foreign debt payments following the onset of the August 1998 financial crisis and pursued a rescheduling of its foreign debt throughout 1999. The Paris Club agreed to a 20-year restructuring plan in August 1999; enactment of this plan is contingent upon Russia's signing of agreements with each Paris Club member. In February 2000, the London Club agreed to write off $10.6 billion in debt and to restructure the remaining debt over 30 years. Russia is expected to pay roughly $10 billion in foreign debt payments in 2000.

Resolution of the outstanding bad debt between Western government and Russian commercial creditors under the Paris and London clubs opened up the possibility of resolving the estimated $7 billion of unsecured debt owed foreign companies, as well as the recovery by 2004 of up to $12 billion from developing countries with debts to Russia. In 2000, Russia estimated that 51 countries owed Russia a combined total of $30 billion.

In late July 1999, Russia was able to meet the pre-conditions set by the ***International Monetary Fund (IMF)***, including the passage of a number of laws by the Duma, and the IMF agreed to provide a $4.5 billion credit. These funds, to be disbursed in several loan tranches, are to be used to facilitate repayment of the IMF for other funds provided. The release of the loan tranches, however, is contingent upon Russia meeting IMF requirements on structural reform; of three loan tranches to be received in 1999, Russia received only one. The IMF is not expected to release any new funds until after the March 2000 presidential elections. As of early 2000, Russia, the IMF's largest borrower, owed the international lender more than $15 billion.

INCOME AND LABOR

Income/Wages: Developments in 1998 interrupted growth trends for nominal and real income in Russia. Russia=s financial crisis had a severe effect on wages in the country. Many employees were helpless as ruble devaluation and price increases eroded the buying power of their salaries. Meanwhile, both foreign and Russian companies, faced with their own challenges stemming from the crisis, resorted to pay cuts in order to maintain what staff they felt able to keep.

Although nominal wages in Russia continue to climb, real wages in the country continue to fall. The average nominal monthly wage in January 1999 was approximately R1,200; in January 2000, the nominal wage was roughly R1,575 (about $58 at the January 1 exchange rate). According to official figures, real wages and real disposable income had fallen roughly 30 percent by the end of 1999 compared to 1997. Many mid-1999 estimates placed *real incomes* down 35-40 percent or more from August of 1998.

The ***minimum wage*** is currently R83 (equivalent to roughly $3 in early 2000). In December 1999, the average monthly ***subsistence minimum*** was R943 (approximately $36 according to the exchange rate in effect at the time); 30 percent or more of Russia=s population is believed to be living below the subsistence level. As of February 1, 2000, Russian pensions increased 20 percent; the minimum Russian *pension* is R410 per month, but the average pension is R650, still below the subsistence minimum.

Russia's well-educated but relatively inexpensive labor force has been a leading attraction for foreign firms. While in the early 1990s many Western firms initially found it challenging to find employees educated in Western business concepts and practices, there is a growing pool in Russia of individuals with Western business exposure, education, and experience. Russian law requires that wages be paid in rubles.

Unemployment: Although the Russian Government has been using International Labor Organization (United Nations) statistical methods to determine unemployment, officially reported unemployment levels in Russia, as with other official statistics, have often been lower than figures determined by the international community. Russia reported several years of very slowly growing unemployment, which temporarily peaked at 9.6 percent in the spring of 1997 before dropping to a low of 9 percent at the end of 1997. During this time, alternative estimates of unemployment suggested a combined unemployment and underemployment rate of between 12 and 15 percent.

In 1998, unemployment levels resumed their climb. In the wake of Russia=s financial crisis, both Russian and foreign companies resorted to layoffs and salary cuts. In November 1998, when the official unemployment rate was 11.6 percent, the Russian Ministry of Economy predicted that unemployment would grow 70 percent by 2001. In early June 1999, the Russian government reported that unemployment had reached 14.2% of the country=s work force, or 10.4 million people, the highest level ever officially reported by Russia. For much of 1999, the unemployment rate hovered at 12.4 percent, or 9.12 million people. *Russia closed 1999 with an official unemployment level of 11.7 percent.*

A challenge in determining Russian unemployment is that many of Russia=s underemployed have kept their official jobs but have worked reduced hours or have stayed on unpaid leave in order to receive social benefits and also to establish a >cover= for tax purposes, that is, to conceal income made in the informal sector.

ECONOMIC REFORM

Throughout the Yeltsin presidency doubt continued to rise and fall about the speed at which economic reform would proceed in Russia. Key elements of President Yeltsin's reform program were price liberalization, financial stabilization, and privatization. Yeltsin also cited additional economic goals and plans, including: a stronger government role in promoting economic growth, greater transparency in government transactions, and creation of a federal treasury, as well as improved tax collection, decreasing capital flight, and adopting economic legislation necessary to obtain further IMF funding. Four government shuffles, differences between the President=s government and the Russian duma, and Yeltsin=s periodic sidelining due to health problems are among the factors perceived as slowing economic policy developments during his administration.

When Vladimir Putin assumed the position of acting president on December 31, 1999 following Boris Yeltsin's resignation, he had not yet elaborated a precise economic agenda. In subsequent January 2000 statements, he advocated a "moderately liberal" economic policy, involving the strengthening of legal institutions, maintaining state regulation of certain portions of the economy, nonpreferential treatment of organizations, and caution in formulating policy.

Multilateral institutions continue to consult with Russia on the country=s economic reform measures. Lack of progress at implementing structural reforms has been an ongoing sticking point between Russia and groups such as the International Monetary Fund (IMF) and the World Trade Organization (WTO).

Tax collection remains a major priority, and challenge, of the Russian Government, although the country improved its collections in 1999. In 1998 tax collection reached only 78 percent of original target levels for the federal budget, and in 1997 the tax collection rate was only 70 percent of targeted levels. Tax revenues exceeded targets in 1999 and accounted for 8 percent of GDP. According to the Russian State Tax Police, five Russian regions--Moscow City, Moscow Oblast, Khanty-Mansii Autonomous Okrug (4.6 percent), Kemerovo Oblast (4.5 percent), and St. Petersburg City--account for more than 50 percent of Russian tax payments.

Price controls have been lifted on almost 90 percent of wholesale and retail goods. Although there are still price controls on certain sectors, such as housing and telephone services, and some prices remain artificially low, generally these controls are being lifted. Energy costs, for instance, have risen from between 7 and 10 percent of the world energy market price to 75 percent (wholesale domestic fuel oil only). In March 1997, the Russian Government announced that corporate energy rates would be lowered 13 percent, while consumer rates would be allowed to grow. Tariffs on railroad transportation were lowered in 1998 and again in 1999. In the aftermath of the August events, a number of regions established price ceilings for foodstuffs, but enforcing these ceilings proved difficult. In early 2000, Moscow city announced energy prices would rise 20-25 percent.
In mid February, the Russian government approved a 40 percent hike in the minimum price of vodka.

Privatization: As of January 1994, 75 percent of medium- and large-scale enterprises in Russia and approximately 80 percent of small shops and restaurants (establishments with under 200 employees) had been privatized. Since January , the Russian Government has reported that at least 70 percent of Russian GDP is composed of goods and services accounted for by the private sector. Early 1997 Russian Government figures reported that the private sector accounted for 75 percent of manufacturing enterprises, 85 percent of manufacturing, and more than 80 percent of the Russian workforce.

Russia has moved through four phases of privatization. Phase one began on October 1, 1992, and involved the distribution of privatization vouchers to every citizen (a voucher was roughly equivalent to the value of six weeks' worth of wages) and holding voucher auctions. The second phase of privatization, initiated in July 1994, involved the sale of vouchers of Russian companies for cash and privatization of some of the largest Russian enterprises. The third phase, starting in the second half of 1997, involved the controversial "equity-for-loans auctions." The concept behind this model was to raise long-term loans from major Russian banks in exchange for granting bankers controlling stakes in the largest Russian enterprises as collateral, together with voting and management rights. Lastly, since late 1997, Russia has been selling shares--primarily to domestic investors--of approximately 136 enterprises considered the "crown jewels" of Russian industry.

In 1997, President Yeltsin signed a decree on plans for privatization of Russia=s *natural monopolies*, including power and gas enterprises as well as Russian railroads. Privatization of the natural monopolies continues to be a disputed issue. During 1998 the Russian Government planned to begin the process of selling unused Russian military assets and to offer shares in a number of key companies, including Svyazinvest, Lukoil, Rosneft, and Slavneft. However, due to failed tenders, financial turmoil that postponed privatization auctions, and other factors revenues from privatization in both 1998 and 1999 were far less than expected. In 2000 Russia plans to proceed with a number of privatizations, including selling shares of Gazprom, Rosneft, Slavneft, Svyazinvest and others.

Land Reform: Russia does not yet have a land code establishing the framework for overall land reform and sale, and progress in this arena has been slow. In particular, the Russian Duma has resisted passing land reform laws, with many duma members intending to significantly restrict the sale of land, especially agricultural land.
Since Vladimir Putin became Acting President, there has been speculation and mention of land reform as a Russian reform priority for 2000.

A decree on land privatization was issued in January 1992, but it was not until October 1992 that the first private plots were sold at auction. Yeltsin's decree #1767 on land of October 1993 allowed, on paper, the free sale and purchase of land to Russians as well as to joint-ventures with foreign participation. Fully foreign-owned companies are not allowed to purchase land outright. In practice, however, 49 to 99 year leases are allowed on land abundant in natural resources (e.g., forestry). In May the Communist-led duma attempted to enact a land code that included measures prohibiting the sale of privately-held agricultural lands or shares in private farm enterprises (preferential allowances were made for collective farms), but the Federation Council (upper house)

For additional analytical, business and investment opportunities information, please contact Global Investment & Business Center, USA at (202) 546-2103. Fax: (202) 546-3275. E-mail: rusric@erols.com
Global Business E-Books on Line: http://world.mirhouse.com

vetoed the code. A resolution committee has been negotiating differences over the land code since that time, leaving the Presidential Decree still in effect.

Russian legislation is somewhat clearer over the ability of companies to own buildings than it is on allowing buildings' tenants to own the land upon which those buildings rest. In May 1997, Yeltsin signed a land ownership decree for urban real estate (non-agricultural lands), which was designed to make it easier for building owners to buy the land on which their real estate rests.

Russia established the basic foundation for a mortgage system though the above-mentioned Decree 1767, which enabled banks to lend money to farmers. The land/property purchase/sales process has moved slowly because the real estate sector remains undeveloped. The actors that normally play an integral roll in land/home purchasing and sales in the West, i.e., real estate agents, title companies, and law firms, are in their infancy. The lack of a central land registry, which would guarantee title to a land/property purchaser, is another obstacle to the natural development of the real estate sector.

For additional analytical, business and investment opportunities information, please contact Global Investment & Business Center, USA at (202) 546-2103. Fax: (202) 546-3275. E-mail: rusric@erols.com Global Business E-Books on Line: http://world.mirhouse.com

IMPORTANT INFORMATION FOR UNDERSTANDING RUSSIA[1]

Official Name: Russian Federation

PROFILE

GEOGRAPHY

Area: 17 million sq. km. (6.5 million sq. mi.); about 1.8 times the size of the U.S.
Cities: *Capital*--Moscow (pop. 9 million). *Other cities*--St. Petersburg (5 million), Novosibirsk (1.4 million), Nizhniy Novgorod (1.3 million).
Terrain: Broad plain with low hills west of Urals; vast coniferous forest and tundra in Siberia; uplands and mountains (Caucasus range) along southern borders.
Climate: Northern continental, from subarctic to subtropical.

PEOPLE

Nationality: *Noun and adjective*--Russian(s).
Population (1997 est.): 147.5 million.
Annual growth rate: Negative.
Ethnic groups: Russian 81%, Tatar 4%, Ukrainian 3%, other 12%. Religion: Russian Orthodox, Islam, Judaism, Roman Catholicism, Protestant, Buddhist, other.
Language: Russian (official); more than 140 other languages and dialects. Education (total pop.): *Literacy*--98%.
Health: *Life expectancy*--() 58 yrs. men, 72 yrs. women.
Work force (85 million): *Production and economic services*--84%; *government*--16%.

GOVERNMENT

Type: Federation.
Independence: August 24, 1991.
Constitution: December 12, 1993.
Branches: *Executive*--president, prime minister (chairman of the government). *Legislative*--Federal Assembly (Federation Council, State Duma). *Judicial*--Constitutional Court, Supreme Court, Supreme Court of Arbitration, Office of Procurator General.
Political parties: Shifting. The 1999 elections were contested by Conservative Movement of Russia, Russian All-Peoples Union, Women of Russia, Stalin Bloc-For the USSR, Yabloko, Working Russia, Peace-Labor-May, Bloc of Nikolayev and Federov, Spiritual Heritage, Congress of Russian Communities, Peace and Unity Party, Party for the Protection of Women, Unity Interregional Movement, Social Democrats, Movement in Support of the Army, Zhirinovskiy's Bloc, For Civic Dignity, Fatherland-All Russia,

---

[1] US State Department Profile

For additional analytical, business and investment opportunities information,
please contact Global Investment & Business Center, USA
at (202) 546-2103. Fax: (202) 546-3275. E-mail: rusric@erols.com
Global Business E-Books on Line: http://world.mirhouse.com

Communist Party, Russian Cause, All-Russian Political Party of the People, Union of Right Forces, Our Home is Russia, Socialist Party of Russia, Party of Pensioners and the Russian Socialist Party.
Subdivisions: 21 autonomous republics and 68 autonomous territories and regions.
Suffrage: Universal at 18 years.

ECONOMY

GDP: $183 billion.
Growth rate: 3.2%.
Per capita GDP (exchange rate method): $1,241.
Natural resources: Petroleum, natural gas, timber, furs, precious and nonferrous metals.
Agriculture: *Products*--Grain, sugarbeets, sunflower seeds, meat, dairy products.
Industry: *Types*--Complete range of manufactures: automobiles, trucks, trains, agricultural equipment, advanced aircraft, aerospace, machine and equipment products; mining and extractive industry; medical and scientific instruments; construction equipment.
Trade: *Exports* (f.o.b.)--$74 billion: petroleum and petroleum products, natural gas, woods and wood products, metals, chemicals. *Major markets*--EU, NIS, China, Japan. *Imports* (c.i.f.)--$41 billion: machinery and equipment, chemicals, consumer goods, medicines, meat, sugar, semi-finished metal products. *Major partners*--EU, U.S., NIS, Japan, China. *Principal U.S. exports* ($1.85 billion)--meat, machinery, tobacco. *Principal U.S. imports* ($5.81 billion)--aluminum, precious stones and metals, iron, and steel.

PEOPLE

Russia's area is about 17 million sq. km. (6.5 million sq. mi.). It remains the largest country in the world by more than 2.5 million sq. mi. Its population density is about 23 persons per square mile (9 per sq. km.), making it one of the most sparsely populated countries in the world. Its population is predominantly urban.

Most of the roughly 150 million Russians derive from the Eastern Slavic family of peoples, whose original homeland was probably present-day Poland. Russian is the official language of Russia, and an official language in the United Nations. As the language of writers such as Tolstoy, Dostoevsky, Chekov, Pushkin, and Solzhenitsyn, it has great importance in world literature.

Russia's educational system has produced nearly 100% literacy. About 3 million students attend Russia's 519 institutions of higher education and 48 universities. As a result of great emphasis on science and technology in education, Russian medical, mathematical, scientific, and space and aviation research is generally of a high order. The number of doctors in relation to the population is high by American standards, although medical care in Russia, even in major cities, is far below Western standards.

The Russian labor force is undergoing tremendous changes. Although well-educated and skilled, it is largely mismatched to the rapidly changing needs of the Russian economy. Millions of Russian workers are underemployed. Unemployment is highest among women and young people. Many Russian workers compensate by working other part-time jobs. Following the collapse of the Soviet Union and the economic dislocation it engendered, the standard of living fell dramatically, and one third of the population lives on just over $1 a day.

Moscow is the largest city (population 9 million) and is the capital of the Federation. Moscow continues to be the center of Russian Government and is increasingly important as an economic and business center. Its cultural tradition is rich, and there are many museums devoted to art, literature, music, dance, history, and science. It has hundreds of churches and dozens of notable cathedrals; it has become Russia's principal magnet for foreign investment and business presence.

St. Petersburg, established in 1703 by Peter the Great as the capital of the Russian Empire, was called Petrograd during World War I, and Leningrad after 1924. In 1991, as the result of a city referendum, it was renamed St. Petersburg. Under the Tsars, the city was Russia's cultural, intellectual, commercial, financial and industrial center. After the capital was moved back to Moscow in 1918, the city's political significance declined, but it remained a cultural, scientific and military-industrial center. The Hermitage is one of the world's great fine arts museums. Finally, Vladivostok, located in the Russian Far East, is becoming an important center for trade with the Pacific Rim countries.

HISTORY

Human experience on the territory of present-day Russia dates back to Paleolithic times. Greek traders conducted extensive commerce with Scythian tribes around the shores of the Black Sea and the Crimean region. In the third century B.C., Scythians were displaced by Sarmatians, who in turn were overrun by waves of Germanic Goths. In the third century A.D., Asiatic Huns replaced the Goths and were in turn conquered by Turkic Avars in the sixth century. By the ninth century, Eastern Slavs began to settle in what is now Ukraine, Belarus and the Novgorod and Smolensk regions.

In 862, the political entity known as Kievan Rus was established in what is now Ukraine and lasted until the 12th century. In the 10th century, Christianity became the state religion under Vladimir, who adopted Greek Orthodox rites. Consequently, Byzantine culture predominated, as is evident in much of Russia's architectural, musical, and artistic heritage. Over the next centuries, various invaders assaulted the Kievan state and, finally, Mongols under Batu Khan destroyed the main population centers except for Novgorod and Pskov and prevailed over the region until 1480.

In the post-Mongol period, Muscovy gradually became the dominant principality and was able, through diplomacy and conquest, to establish suzerainty over European Russia. Ivan III (1462-1505) was able to refer to his empire as "the Third Rome" and heir to the Byzantine tradition, and a century later the Romanov dynasty was established under Tsar Mikhail in 1613.

During Peter the Great's reign (1689-1725), Russia began modernizing, and European influences spread in Russia. Peter created Western-style military forces, subordinated the Russian Orthodox Church hierarchy to the Tsar, reformed the entire governmental structure, and established the beginnings of a Western-style education system. His introduction of European customs generated nationalistic resentments in society and spawned the philosophical rivalry between "Westernizers" and nationalistic "Slavophiles" that remains a key dynamic of current Russian social and political thought.

Peter's expansionist policies were continued by Catherine the Great, who established Russia as a continental power. During her reign (1762-96), power was centralized in the monarchy and administrative reforms concentrated great wealth and privilege in the hands of the Russian nobility.

Napoleon failed in his attempt in 1812 to conquer Russia after occupying Moscow; his defeat and the continental order that emerged following the Congress of Vienna (1814-15) set the stage for Russia and Austria-Hungary to dominate the affairs of eastern Europe for the next century.

During the 19th century, the Russian Government sought to suppress repeated attempts at reform from within. Its economy failed to compete with those of Western countries. Russian cities were growing without an industrial base to generate employment, although emancipation of the serfs in 1861 foreshadowed urbanization and rapid industrialization late in the century. At the same time, Russia expanded across Siberia until the port of Vladivostok was opened on the Pacific coast in 1860. The Trans-Siberian Railroad opened vast frontiers to development late in the century. In the 19th century, Russian culture flourished as Russian artists made significant contributions to world literature, visual arts, dance, and music.

Imperial decline was evident in Russia's defeat in the unpopular Russo-Japanese war in 1905. Subsequent civic disturbances forced Tsar Nicholas II to grant a constitution and introduce limited democratic reforms. The government suppressed opposition and manipulated popular anger into anti-Semitic pogroms. Attempts at economic reform, such as land reform, were incomplete.

1917 REVOLUTION AND THE U.S.S.R.

The ruinous effects of World War I, combined with internal pressures, sparked the March 1917 uprising, which led Tsar Nicholas II to abdicate the throne. A provisional government came to power, headed by Aleksandr Kerenskiy. On November 7, 1917, the Bolshevik Party, led by Vladimir Lenin, seized control and established the Russian Soviet Federated Socialist Republic. Civil war broke out in 1918 between Lenin's "Red" army and various "White" forces and lasted until 1920, when, despite foreign interventions, the Bolsheviks triumphed. After the Red army conquered Ukraine, Belorussia, Azerbaijan, Georgia, and Armenia, a new nation was formed in 1922, the Union of Soviet Socialist Republics.

The U.S.S.R. lasted 69 years. In the 1930s, tens of millions of its citizens were collectivized under state agricultural and industrial enterprises. Millions died in political purges, the vast penal and labor system, or in state-created famines. During World War II, as many as 20 million Soviet citizens died. In 1949, the U.S.S.R. developed its own nuclear arsenal.

First among its political figures was Lenin, leader of the Bolshevik Party and head of the first Soviet Government, who died in 1924. In the late 1920s, Josif Stalin emerged as General Secretary of the Communist Party of the Soviet Union (CPSU) amidst intraparty rivalries; he maintained complete control over Soviet domestic and international policy until his death in 1953. His successor, Nikita Khrushchev, served as Communist Party leader until he was ousted in 1964. Aleksey Kosygin became Chairman of the Council of Ministers, and Leonid Brezhnev was made First Secretary of the CPSU Central Committee in 1964, but in 1971, Brezhnev rose to become "first among equals" in a collective leadership. Brezhnev died in 1982 and was succeeded by Yuriy Andropov (1982-84), Konstantin Chernenko (1984-85), and Mikhail Gorbachev, who resigned as Soviet President on December 25, 1991. On December 26, 1991, the U.S.S.R. was formally dissolved.

THE RUSSIAN FEDERATION

After the December 1991 dissolution of the Soviet Union, the Russian Federation became its largest successor state, inheriting its permanent seat on the United Nations Security Council, as well as the bulk of its foreign assets and debt.

Boris Yeltsin was elected President of Russia by popular vote in June 1991. By the fall of 1993, politics in Russia reached a stalemate between President Yeltsin and the parliament. The parliament had succeeded in blocking, overturning, or ignoring the President's initiatives on drafting a new constitution, conducting new elections, and making further progress on democratic and economic reforms.

In a dramatic speech in September 1993, President Yeltsin dissolved the Russian parliament and called for new national elections and a new constitution. The standoff between the executive branch and opponents in the legislature turned violent in October after supporters of the parliament tried to instigate an armed insurrection. Yeltsin ordered the army to respond with force to capture the parliament building (known as the White House).

In December 1993, voters elected a new parliament and approved a new constitution that had been drafted by the Yeltsin government. Yeltsin has remained the dominant political figure, although a broad array of parties, including ultra-nationalists, liberals, agrarians, and communists, have substantial representation in the parliament and compete actively in elections at all levels of government.

In late 1994, the Russian security forces launched a brutal operation in the Republic of Chechnya against rebels who were intent on separation from Russia. Along with their opponents, Russian forces committed numerous violations of human rights. The Russian Army used heavy weapons against civilians. Tens of thousands of them were killed and more than 500,000 displaced during the course of the war. The protracted conflict, which received close scrutiny in the Russian media, raised serious human rights and humanitarian concerns abroad as well as within Russia.

After numerous unsuccessful attempts to institute a cease-fire, in August the Russian and Chechen authorities negotiated a settlement that resulted in a complete withdrawal of Russian troops and the holding of elections in January 1997. The Organization for Security and Cooperation in Europe (OSCE) played a major role in facilitating the negotiation. A peace treaty was concluded in May 1997. Following an August 1999 attack into Dagestan by Chechan separatists and the September 1999 bombings of two apartment buildings in Moscow, the federal government launched a military campaign into Chechnya. Russian authorities accused the Chechan government of failing to stop the growth of the rebels activities and failure to curb widespread banditry and hostage taking in the republic. By spring 2000, federal forces claimed control over Chechan territory, but fighting continues as rebel fighters regularly ambush Russian forces in the region.

GOVERNMENT AND POLITICAL CONDITIONS

In the political system established by the 1993 constitution, the president wields considerable executive power. There is no vice president, and the legislative is far weaker than the executive. The president nominates the highest state officials, including the prime minister, who must be approved by the Duma. The president can pass decrees without consent from the Duma. He also is head of the armed forces and of the national security council.

Duma elections were on December 19, 1999 and presidential elections March 26, 2000. While the Communist Party won a narrow plurality of seats in the Duma, the pro-government party Unity and the centrist Fatherland-All Russia also won substantial numbers of seats in the legislature. In the presidential election, Vladimir Putin, named Acting President following the December 31 resignation of Boris Yeltsin, was elected in the first round with 53% of the vote. Both the presidential and parliamentary elections were judged generally free and fair by international observers.

Russia is a federation, but the precise distribution of powers between the central government and the regional and local authorities is still evolving. The Russian Federation consists of 89 components, including two federal cities, Moscow and St. Petersburg. The constitution explicitly defines the federal government's exclusive powers, but it also describes most key regional issues as the joint responsibility of the federal government and the Federation components.

JUDICIAL SYSTEM

Russia's judiciary and justice system are weak. Numerous matters which are dealt with by administrative authority in European countries remain subject to political influence in Russia. The Constitutional Court was reconvened in March 1997 following its suspension by President Yeltsin in October 1993. The 1993 constitution empowers the court to arbitrate disputes between the executive and legislative branches and between Moscow and the regional and local governments. The court is also authorized to rule on violations of constitutional rights, to examine appeals from various bodies, and to participate in impeachment proceedings against the president. The July 1994 Law on the Constitutional Court prohibits the court from examining cases on its own initiative and limits the scope of issues the court can hear.

In the past 3 years, the Russian Government has begun to reform the criminal justice system and judicial institutions, including the reintroduction of jury trials in certain criminal cases. Despite these efforts, judges are only beginning to assert their constitutionally mandated independence from other branches of government.

HUMAN RIGHTS

Russia's human rights record remains uneven and worsened in some areas. Despite significant improvements in conditions following the end of the Soviet Union, problem areas remain. In particular, the Russian government's military policy in Chechnya is a cause for international concern. Government forces have killed numerous civilians through the use of indiscriminate force in Chechnya. There have been credible allegations of violations of international human rights and humanitarian law by Russian forces. Chechen groups also have committed abuses.

Although the government has made progress in recognizing the legitimacy of international human rights standards, the institutionalization of procedures to safeguard these rights has lagged. Implementation of the constitutional provisions for due process and timely trials, for example, has made little progress. There are indications that the law is becoming an increasingly important tool for those seeking to protect human rights; after a lengthy trial and eight separate indictments, environmental whistleblower Alexander Nikitin was acquitted of espionage charges relating to publication of material exposing hazards posed by the Russian Navy's aging nuclear fleet earlier this year. Nonetheless, serious problems remain. The judiciary is often subject to manipulation by political authorities and is plagued by large case backlogs and trial delays. Lengthy pretrial detention remains a serious problem. There are credible reports of beating and torturing of inmates and detainees by law enforcement and correctional officials. Prison conditions fall well below international standards and, according to human rights groups, in between 10,000 and 20,000 prisoners and detainees died, most because of overcrowding, disease, and lack of medical care.

Efforts to institutionalize official human rights bodies have been mixed. In , human rights activist Sergey Kovalev resigned as chairman of the Presidential Human Rights Commission to protest the government's record, particularly the war in Chechnya. Parliament in 1997 passed a law establishing a "human rights ombudsman," a position that is provided for in Russia's constitution and is required of members of the Council of Europe, to which Russia was admitted in February . The Duma finally selected Duma deputy Oleg Mironov in May 1998. A member of the Communist Party, Mironov resigned from both the Party and the Duma after the vote, citing the law's stipulation that the Ombudsman be nonpartisan. Because of his party affiliation, and because Mironov had no evident expertise in the field of human rights, his appointment was widely criticized at the time by human rights activists. International human rights groups operate freely in Russia, although the government has hindered the movements and access to information of some individuals investigating the war in Chechnya.

The Russian Constitution provides for freedom of religion and the equality of all religions before the law as well as the separation of church and state. Although Jews and Muslims continue to encounter prejudice and societal discrimination, they have not been inhibited by the government in the free practice of their religion. High-ranking federal officials have condemned anti-Semitic hate crimes, but law enforcement bodies have not effectively prosecuted those responsible. The influx of missionaries over the past several years has led to pressure by groups in Russia, specifically nationalists and the Russian Orthodox Church, to limit the activities of these "nontraditional" religious groups. In response, the Duma passed a new, restrictive, and potentially discriminatory law in October 1997. The law is very complex, with many ambiguous and contradictory provisions. The law's most controversial provisions separates religious "groups" and "organizations" and introduce a 15-year rule, which allows groups that have been in existence for 15 years or longer to obtain accredited status. Senior Russian officials have pledged to implement the 1997 law on religion in a manner that is not in conflict with Russia's international human rights obligations. Some local officials, however, have used the law as a pretext to restrict religious liberty.

The constitution guarantees citizens the right to choose their place of residence and to travel abroad. Some big-city governments, however, have restricted this right through residential registration rules that closely resemble the Soviet-era "propiska" regulations. Although the rules were touted as a notification device rather than a control system, their implementation has produced many of the same results as the propiska system. The freedom to travel abroad and emigrate is respected although restrictions may apply to those who have had access to state secrets. Recognizing this progress, since 1994, President Clinton has found Russia to be in full compliance with the provisions of the Jackson-Vanik amendment.

PRINCIPAL GOVERNMENT OFFICIALS

President--Vladimir Putin
Prime Minister--Mikhail Kasyanov

(A list of other government officials is not available at this time)

The Russian Federation maintains an embassy at 2650 Wisconsin Ave. NW, Washington, DC 20007 (tel. 202-298-5700) and a consular section at 2641 Tunlaw Road, Washington DC (tel. 202-939-8907/8913/8918). Russian consulates also are located in New York, San Francisco, and Seattle.

ECONOMY

The Russian economy has undergone tremendous stress as it has moved from a centrally planned economy toward a free market system. Difficulties in implementing fiscal reforms aimed at raising government revenues and a dependence on short term borrowing to finance budget deficits led to a serious financial crisis in 1998. Lower prices for Russia's major export earners (oil and minerals) and a loss of investor confidence due to the Asian financial crisis exacerbated financial problems. The result was a rapid decline in the value of the ruble, flight of foreign investment, delayed payments on sovereign and private debts, a breakdown of commercial transactions through the banking system and the threat of runaway inflation.

However, Russia appears to have weathered the crisis relatively well. Real GDP increased by the highest percentage since the fall of the Soviet Union, the ruble stabilized, inflation was moderate, and investment began to increase again. Russia is making progress in meeting its foreign debts obligations. In 1999, with limited access to financing from international financial institutions or bilateral sources, the GOR serviced around half its external debt payments due, and sought delays in servicing Soviet-era debt pending negotiations in the Paris and London Clubs. In early 2000 Russia negotiated a 35% write off of its commercial debt with the London Club. Russia's current Paris Club agreement expires at the end of 2000.

GROSS DOMESTIC PRODUCT

Russia's GDP, estimated at $183 billion at exchange rates current in 1999, increased by 3.2% in 1999 compared to 1998. The major factors behind this strong growth were the earlier devaluation of the ruble (spurring production of Russian products as substitutes for more expensive imports); record high commodity prices on international markets, particularly oil (Russia's principal export); low inflation; and strict government budget discipline. For 1999 the unemployment rate was 12.6% (using International Labor Organization methodology). Combined unemployment and underemployment may exceed that figure. Industrial output in 1999 was up sharply (to 8.1%) compared to 1998, aided by the devalued ruble.

MONETARY POLICY

The exchange rate stabilized in 1999 -- after falling from 6.5 rubles/dollar in August 1998 to approximately 25 rubles/dollar by April 1999, one year later it had further depreciated only to approximately 28.5 rubles/dollar. After some large spikes in inflation following the August 1998 economic crisis, inflation declined steadily throughout 1999, with an overall figure of 36.5 percent; inflation for the first quarter of 2000 was an estimated 4.1 percent. Factors dampening price increases include weak domestic demand, a relatively stable ruble, and the absence to date of a federal budget deficit for the Central Bank of Russia to monetize.

GOVERNMENT SPENDING/TAXATION

Fiscal policy has been very disciplined in 1999 and early 2000. The overall budget deficit for 1999 was 1.7 percent of GDP, with a primary surplus of 2 percent; 1999 was the first year the federal budget was fully implemented. The primary surplus during the first quarter of 2000 was 3.5 percent of GDP. The GOR estimates that it will exceed budgeted revenue forecasts for 2000 by about 100 billion rubles, collecting 897.2 billion rubles. In part, the increase in cash revenues reflects increased receipts from large taxpayers, e.g. oil companies and natural monopolies, as well as growing economic activity.

LAW

Lack of legislation in many areas of economic activity is a pressing issue. Taxation and business regulations are unpredictable, and legal enforcement of private business agreements is weak. Government decisions affecting business have often been arbitrary and inconsistent. Crime has increased costs for both local and foreign businesses. On the positive side, Russian businesses are increasingly turning to the courts to resolve disputes. The passage of an improved bankruptcy code in January 1998 was a positive step; the government is advocating further improvements to this legislation.

NATURAL RESOURCES

The mineral-packed Ural mountains and the vast oil, gas, coal and timber reserves of Siberia and the Russian Far East make Russia rich in natural resources. However, most such resources are located in remote and climactically unfavorable areas that are difficult to develop and far from Russian ports. Oil and gas exports continue to be the main source of hard currency, but declining energy prices have hit Russia hard. Russia is a leading producer and exporter of minerals, gold and all major fuels. The Russian fishing industry is the world's fourth-largest, behind Japan, the U.S. and China. Russia accounts for one-quarter of the world's production of fresh and frozen fish and about one-third of world output of canned fish.

For additional analytical, business and investment opportunities information, please contact Global Investment & Business Center, USA at (202) 546-2103. Fax: (202) 546-3275. E-mail: rusric@erols.com Global Business E-Books on Line: http://world.mirhouse.com

INDUSTRY

Russia is one of the most industrialized of the former Soviet republics. However, much of its industry is antiquated and highly inefficient. Besides its resource-based industries, it has developed large manufacturing capacities, notably in machinery. Russia inherited most of the defense industrial base of the Soviet Union. Efforts have been made with varying success over the past few years to convert defense industries to civilian use.

AGRICULTURE

Russia comprises roughly three-quarters of the territory of the former Soviet Union, but has relatively little area suited for agriculture because of its arid climate and inconsistent rainfall. Northern areas concentrate mainly on livestock, and the southern parts and western Siberia produce grain. Restructuring of former state farms has been an extremely slow process, partially due to the lack of a land code allowing for the free sale, purchase and mortgage of agricultural land. Private farms and garden plots of individuals account for over one-half of all agricultural production.

INVESTMENT

In 1999, investment increased by 4.5 percent, the first such growth since 1990. The increase came in the last half of 1999, and has continued in the opening months of 2000, up 5.9 percent year-on-year in the first quarter. Higher retained earnings, increased cash transactions, the positive outlook for sales and political stability have contributed to these favorable trends. Over the medium-to-long term, Russian companies that do not invest to increase their competitiveness will find it harder either to expand exports or protect their recent domestic market gains from higher quality imports.

Foreign direct investment rose slightly in 1999, but remains small. Foreign direct investment in Russia in 1999 was USD 2.9 billion, up from USD2.8 billion in 1998, but still well below the USD6.6 billion of FDI received in 1997.

A significant drawback for investment is the banking sector, which has neither the resources, capability, nor the trust of the population to attract substantial savings and intermediate them to productive investments. While ruble lending has doubled since the October 1998 financial crisis, loans are still only 28 percent of total bank assets, the same percentage as before the crisis. The CBR has reduced its refinancing rate three times in 2000, to 33 percent, signaling its interest in lower lending rates. Banks still perceive commercial lending as risky, and some banks are inexperienced with assessing credit risk.

TRADE

The major factor contributing to Russia's significant economic growth in 1999 was trade performance. Exports were up slightly to USD74.3 billion, while imports slumped by 30.5

percent to USD41.1 billion. As a consequence, the trade surplus ballooned to USD33.2 billion, more than double the previous year's level. After a weak start, both imports and exports recovered somewhat in the second half of the year, as the economy began to stabilize. The effect of higher oil prices had a major effect on export performance, particularly in the latter half of the year. Even though volumes of crude oil exports (to non-CIS countries) were down by 2.9 percent, prices jumped up 45.9 percent. Fuels and energy comprise 42 percent of Russian exports. Other exports performed better in 1999: fertilizer exports were up 16.7 percent, forestry products up 38 percent, copper up 17.6 percent, and aluminum up 10.5 percent. On the import side, food and consumer goods suffered especially, with food imports dropping by 28 percent.

Most analysts predict these trade trends will continue to some extent in 2000. The GOR forecasts export increases of about 4 percent and, as the ruble strengthens in real terms and purchasing power slowly recovers, a slightly larger recovery in imports of about 8 percent. However, imports in the first quarter remained flat at USD9.4 billion, compared to USD9.5 billion in the same period in 1999. The devaluation of the ruble and difficulties in completing transactions through the Russian banking system continue to depress imports. The combination of import duties, a 20% value-added tax and excise taxes on imported goods (especially automobiles, alcoholic beverages, and aircraft) and an import licensing regime for alcohol further restrain demand for imports. Frequent changes in customs regulations also have created problems for foreign and domestic traders and investors. Exports have continued to benefit from higher oil prices, bolstered by higher natural gas prices. In the first quarter of 2000, exports were up USD6 billion, driving the trade surplus to USD12.1 billion from USD6.1 billion higher than the same period last year.

FOREIGN RELATIONS

Russia has taken important steps to become a full partner in the world's principal political groupings. On December 27, 1991, Russia assumed the seat formerly held by the Soviet Union in the UN Security Council. Russia also is a member of the Organization for Security and Cooperation in Europe (OSCE) and the North Atlantic Cooperation Council (NACC). It signed the NATO Partnership for Peace initiative on June 22, 1994. On May 27, 1997, NATO and Russia signed the NATO-Russia Founding Act, which provides the basis for an enduring and robust partnership between the Alliance and Russia--one that can make an important contribution to European security architecture in the 21st century. On June 24, 1994, Russia and the European Union (EU) signed a partnership and cooperation agreement.

Russia has played an important role in helping mediate international conflicts and has been particularly actively engaged in trying to promote a peace following the conflict in Kosovo. Russia is a co-sponsor of the Middle East peace process and supports UN and multilateral initiatives in the Persian Gulf, Cambodia, Angola, the former Yugoslavia, and Haiti. Russia is a founding member of the Contact Group and (since the Denver Summit in June 1997) a member of the G-8. In November 1998, Russia joined APEC. Russia

For additional analytical, business and investment opportunities information, please contact Global Investment & Business Center, USA at (202) 546-2103. Fax: (202) 546-3275. E-mail: rusric@erols.com Global Business E-Books on Line: http://world.mirhouse.com

has contributed troops to the NATO-led stabilization force in Bosnia and has affirmed its respect for international law and OSCE principles. It has accepted UN and/or OSCE involvement in instances of regional conflict in neighboring countries, including the dispatch of observers to Georgia, Moldova, Tajikistan, and Nagorno-Karabakh.

DEFENSE

Since the breakup of the U.S.S.R., the Russians have discussed rebuilding a viable, cohesive fighting force out of the remaining parts of the former Soviet armed forces. A new Russian military doctrine, promulgated in November 1993, implicitly acknowledges the contraction of the old Soviet military into a regional military power without global imperial ambitions. In keeping with its emphasis on the threat of regional conflicts, the doctrine calls for a Russian military that is smaller, lighter, and more mobile, with a higher degree of professionalism and with greater rapid deployment capability. Such a transformation has proven difficult.

The challenge of this task has been magnified by difficult economic conditions in Russia, which have resulted in reduced defense spending. This has led to training cutbacks, wage arrears, and severe shortages of housing and other social amenities for military personnel, with a consequent lowering of morale, cohesion, and fighting effectiveness. The poor combat performance of the Russian armed forces in the Chechen conflict in part reflects these breakdowns.

The actual strength of the Russian armed forces probably falls between 1.4 and 1.6 million and is scheduled to fall to 1.2 million by the end of 1999. Weapons production in Russia has fallen dramatically over the past few years; between 1988 and 1993, it fell by at least 50% for virtually every major weapons system. Weapons spending in 1992 was approximately 75% less than in 1988. Almost all of Russia's arms production is for sales to foreign governments, and procurement of major end items by the Russian military has all but stopped.

About 70% of the former Soviet Union's defense industries are located in the Russian Federation. A large number of state-owned defense enterprises are on the brink of collapse as a result of cuts in weapons orders and insufficient funding to shift to production of civilian goods, while at the same time trying to meet payrolls. Many defense firms have been privatized; some have developed significant partnerships with U.S. firms.

U.S.- RUSSIA RELATIONS

The United States remains committed to maintaining a constructive relationship with Russia in which we seek to expand areas of cooperation and effectively work through differences. The United States continues to support Russia's political and economic transformation and its integration into major international organizations. These steps, in

For additional analytical, business and investment opportunities information, please contact Global Investment & Business Center, USA at (202) 546-2103. Fax: (202) 546-3275. E-mail: rusric@erols.com Global Business E-Books on Line: http://world.mirhouse.com

conjunction with achievements in considerably reducing nuclear weapons, have greatly enhanced the security of the United States.

The intensity and frequency of contacts between President Yeltsin and President Clinton, most recently the Moscow Summit in August 1998, are indicative of the strong commitment to working together on a broad range of issues. These include European security, reducing the threat to our countries posed by weapons of mass destruction, and economic cooperation, especially American investment in Russia.

ECONOMIC RELATIONS

U.S.- Russia Joint Commission on Economic and Technological Cooperation. Under the leadership of Vice President Gore and the Russian Prime Minister, the U.S. and Russia are working to advance bilateral cooperation through nine working committees and several working groups known collectively as the U.S.-Russian Joint Commission on Economic and Technological Cooperation. Committees address issues in the fields of science and technology, business development, space, energy policy, environmental protection, health, defense conversion, capital markets, and agriculture. In addition, the commission provides a forum for high-level discussions of priority security and economic issues. The commission held its 10th session in Washington in March 1998 and an executive session in Washington in July 1999.

Trade and Investment. In 1999, the U.S. trade deficit with Russia was $3.96 billion, up $1.76 billion over 1998. U.S. merchandise exports to Russia were nearly $1.85 billion in 1999. Russia was the United States' 41st largest export market in 1999. U.S. imports from Russia were $5.81 billion in 1999, making Russia the 28th largest supplier of U.S. imports. The 1992 U.S.-Russia trade agreement provides mutual most-favored-nation status and includes commitments on intellectual property rights protection. In 1992, the two countries also signed treaties on the avoidance of double taxation and on bilateral investment. In 1992, the two countries also signed treaties on the avoidance of double taxation and on bilateral investment. As of spring 2000, however, the Russian parliament has not ratified the bilateral investment treaty. It has been ratified by the U.S. Senate.

The U.S. actively supports Russia's efforts to join the World Trade Organization on commercially viable terms. Russia is currently in the process of negotiating terms of accession to the WTO. By the end of 1999 it had completed ten working party meetings. It tables its initial services market access offer in October 1999 and has conducted negotiations on its goods market access offer. These offers contain Russia's proposed commitments to maximum tariff rates and opening of its markets to foreign providers of services. The U.S. actively supported Russian membership in the Asia-Pacific Economic Cooperation (APEC) forum. Russia became a member of APEC in November 1998.

For additional analytical, business and investment opportunities information, please contact Global Investment & Business Center, USA at (202) 546-2103. Fax: (202) 546-3275. E-mail: rusric@erols.com Global Business E-Books on Line: http://world.mirhouse.com

SECURITY COOPERATION

NATO/Russia Founding Act. Russia signed the NATO Partnership for Peace initiative in June 1994. U.S. and Russian troops are serving together in the Implementation Force in Bosnia and its successor, the Stabilization Force. Building on these steps, NATO and Russia signed the NATO-Russia Founding Act on May 27, 1997, in Paris. The act defines the terms of a fundamentally new and sustained relationship in which NATO and Russia will consult and coordinate regularly, and where appropriate, act jointly. Cooperation between NATO and Russia exists in scientific and technical fields.

Agreements/Cooperation/Nuclear Arms. The U.S. and Russia signed a memorandum of understanding on defense cooperation in September 1993 that institutionalized and expanded relations between defense ministries, including establishing a broad range of military-to-military and scientist to scientist contacts. The U.S. and Russia carried out a joint peacekeeping training exercise in Totskoye, Russia, in September 1994. Based on the January 14, 1994, agreement between Presidents Clinton and Yeltsin, the two nations stopped targeting their strategic nuclear missiles at each other as of May 30, 1994. U.S. and Russian security cooperation emphasizes strategic stability, nuclear safety, dismantling nuclear weapons, preventing proliferation of weapons of mass destruction and their delivery systems, and enhancing military-to-military contacts. The START I Treaty was signed by the United States and the Soviet Union on July 31, 1991. Five months later, the Soviet Union dissolved, and in May 1992, Belarus, Kazakhstan, Russia and Ukraine signed the Lisbon Protocol to the START I Treaty, making them Parties to the START I Treaty. Belarus, Kazakhstan and Ukraine have also fulfilled their commitment to accede to the Nuclear Non-Proliferation Treaty (NPT) as non-nuclear weapon states in the shortest possible time, and to return all nuclear weapons on their territory to Russia for dismantlement. The START I Treaty entered into force on December 5, 1994. START I requires reductions in strategic offensive arms to 6,000 accountable warheads on each side as of December 4, 2001. All Parties to the Treaty have been successful in meeting the Treaty's reduction requirements.

START II. The START II Treaty was signed by the United States and Russia on January 3, 1993. START II builds on the START I Treaty, requiring reductions in two phases to 3,000-3,500 deployed strategic nuclear warheads on each side, a two-thirds reduction from Cold War levels. At the September 1994 summit, the two nations agreed to begin removing nuclear warheads due to be scrapped under START II immediately, once START I takes effect and the START II Treaty is ratified by both countries, instead of taking the 9 years allowed. At their May 1997 summit, Presidents Clinton and Yeltsin agreed on a set of principles that would guide further discussion in the field of demarcation between anti-ballistic missile systems and theater missile defenses. They also agreed on steps to increase the transparency and irreversibility of nuclear arms reduction and committed not to use newly produced fissile materials or to reuse the fissile materials removed from nuclear weapons being eliminated and excess to national security requirements in nuclear weapons. Since that time, all strategic nuclear weapons have been removed from Ukraine, Belarus, and Kazakhstan to Russia. Under

START II, all heavy ICBMs and MIRVed ICBMs must be eliminated from each side's deployed forces. In January , the U.S. Senate provided its advice and consent to ratification of the START II Treaty.

The deadline for START II reductions was extended to December 2007 by the START II Protocol signed by the United States and Russia on September 26, 1997. The Protocol has not been submitted to the U.S. Senate for ratification. On April 14, 2000, the Russian Duma approved the START II Treaty and the START II Protocol, and on May 5, President Putin signed the ratification document. In ratifying the START II Treaty, the Russian Duma passed a federal law containing a number of conditions. Among them is a requirement that the United States ratify the START II Protocol before the START II Treaty can enter into force. The Duma's ratification law and the relationship between the 1997 agreements, including those related to the ABM Treaty, and START III and changes to the ABM Treaty, will be considered before the START II Protocol is submitted to the Senate for approval.

In March 1997, in Helsinki, Finland, Presidents Clinton and Yeltsin agreed that a START III agreement would include the following basic elements, among others:

- Lower aggregate levels of 2,000-2,500 strategic nuclear warheads -- 80 percent below the Cold War peak -- for each of the parties

- Transparency measures related to strategic nuclear warheads inventories and the destruction of strategic nuclear warheads

- Resolving issues related to the goal of making the current START treaties of unlimited duration

- Exploration of possible measures relating to nuclear long-range sea-launched cruise missiles and tactical nuclear systems, including confidence-building and transparency measures

- Early deactivation of all strategic nuclear delivery vehicles to be eliminated under START II by December 31, 2003, by removing their nuclear warheads or taking other jointly agreed steps.

In June 1999, in Cologne, Germany, Presidents Clinton and Yeltsin reaffirmed their readiness to conduct new negotiations on strategic offensive arms aimed at further reducing the level of strategic nuclear warheads on each side, elaborating measures of transparency concerning existing strategic nuclear warheads and their elimination, as well as other agreed technical and organizational measures. Presidents Clinton and Yeltsin also agreed at this Summit to begin discussions on START III and the ABM Treaty.

START III. As agreed at Cologne, the United States and Russia began discussions on both START III and ABM issues during the summer of 1999. Since then extensive discussions have been held on these matters at senior levels of both governments. On

July 23, 1999, the President signed into law H.R. 4, the National Missile Defense (NMD) Act of 1999. We are continuing substantive discussions with Russia on START III, in parallel with discussions on changes to the ABM Treaty. These discussions are continuing and, with Russia's ratification of START II, are expected to intensify.

CFE. Following ratification by Russia and the other NIS, the Conventional Armed Forces in Europe Treaty entered into force on November 9, 1992. This treaty establishes comprehensive limits on key categories of military equipment--tanks, artillery, armored combat vehicles, combat aircraft, and combat helicopters--and provides for the destruction of weaponry in excess of these limits. An adapted CFE Treaty was adopted at the November 1999 Istanbul Summit. The adapted Treaty takes account of the changes in Europe since CFE was signed. Politically, the process of adaptation has played a pivotal role in managing Russian concerns and expectations regarding NATO enlargement, through both the Madrid and Washington NATO Summits. NATO Allies addressed deeply-held Russian concerns by accepting provisions in CFE which demonstrated that NATO did not contemplate a massive eastward shift in peacetime military potential as a result of enlargement. But this remains a very NATO-friendly Treaty.

Cooperative Threat Reduction (CTR). Often called Nunn-Lugar assistance, this type of assistance is provided to Russia (as well as Belarus, Kazakhstan and Ukraine) to aid in the dismantling of weapons of mass destruction and to prevent the proliferation of such weapons. More than $730 million has been allocated for assistance to Russia during fiscal years 1997 and 1998 under this program, and 13 implementing agreements have been signed. Key projects have included assistance in the elimination of strategic offensive arms ($184 million), design and construction of a fissile material storage facility ($127 million), provision of fissile material containers ($45 million), material control and accounting and physical protection of nuclear materials ($51 million), and development of a chemical weapons destruction facility and provision of equipment for a pilot laboratory for the safe and secure destruction of chemical weapons ($106 million).

Under the highly enriched uranium agreement, the U.S. is purchasing uranium from Russian weapons for use in power reactors. Also, both the U.S. and Russia will cooperate to dispose of excess military plutonium. The U.S. also is assisting Russia in the development of export controls, providing emergency response equipment and training to enhance Russia's ability to respond to accidents involving nuclear weapons, providing increased military-to-military contacts.

In a multilateral effort (the European Union, Japan, and Canada also are involved), the U.S. also has provided over $60 million to establish and support the International Science and Technology Center (ISTC), which provides alternative peaceful civilian employment opportunities to scientists and engineers of the former Soviet Union involved with weapons of mass destruction and their delivery systems.

U.S. ASSISTANCE TO RUSSIA

Cumulative U.S. Assistance Figures. Since 1992, the U.S. Government has allocated more than $8.2 billion in grant assistance to Russia, funding a variety of programs in four key areas: security programs, humanitarian assistance, economic reform and democratic reform. The U.S. Government is also providing assistance in such areas as nuclear reactor safety and the environment. The grant assistance provided by the U.S. Government to date can be broken down as follows: almost $3.3 billion in security assistance (weapons dismantlement and nonproliferation), over $2.2 billion in humanitarian assistance, over $1.4 billion in economic reform programs, almost $650 million in democratic reform programs, and $615 million in cross-sectoral and other programs. The U.S. Government has also supported approximately $8.9 billion in commercial financing and insurance for Russia. Nearly 40,000 Russians have traveled to the United States under U.S. Government-funded training and exchange programs. The annual level of FREEDOM Support Act-funded assistance for Russia, which declined from a peak of $1.6 billion in FY 1994 to $95 million in FY 1997, is about $178 million in FY 2000. For more detailed information on these programs, please see the FY 1999 Annual Report to Congress on U.S. Government Assistance to and Cooperative Activities with the New Independent States of the Former Soviet Union, which is available on the State Department's website at the following address: http://www.state.gov/www/regions/nis/nis_assist_index.html

How U.S. Assistance Has Evolved. The U.S. Government's strategy for assistance to Russia is based on the premise that Russia's transition to democracy and free markets will be a long-term process. The U.S. will need to remain engaged throughout this process, and therefore U.S. assistance emphasizes activities that promote the establishment of lasting ties between Russians and Americans at all levels of society. Over the past three years, the U.S. assistance program has moved away from technical assistance to the central government, although such assistance is still provided when it is appropriate and will help to advance reform. An increasing proportion of U.S. assistance is focussed at the regional and municipal level, where programs are helping to build the infrastructure of a market economy, remove impediments to trade and investment, and strengthen civil society.

In general, U.S. assistance programs in Russia are working at the grassroots level by bolstering small business through training and enhanced availability of credit; expanding exchanges so that more Russian citizens can learn about America's market democracy on a first-hand basis; and increasing the number of partnerships between Russian and U.S. cities, universities, hospitals, business associations, charities, and other civic groups. In FY 1999, humanitarian assistance accounted for approximately 60% of U.S. assistance to Russia, in response to the increased need for such assistance in the aftermath of Russia's August 1998 financial crisis. However, in FY 2000, security and nonproliferation programs represent over two-thirds of U.S assistance to Russia.

Security programs help demilitarize facilities; eliminate weapons of mass destruction and prevent their proliferation, as well as the proliferation of weapons materials, delivery systems, technology and weapons expertise; and enable compliance with arms accords.

U.S. Government-funded humanitarian assistance consists mainly of food assistance provided by the U.S. Department of Agriculture (see below). The U.S. Government also transports food, medical equipment and other humanitarian assistance donated by U.S. private voluntary organizations (PVOs), as well as Defense Department excess commodities.

Increasingly, U.S. Government-funded economic reform programs are focused in Russia's regions. A limited amount of assistance is targeted at promoting reforms at the national level, particularly with regard to tax administration and Russia's efforts to accede to the World Trade Organization (WTO).

Democratic reform programs are helping Russians develop the building blocks of a democratic society based on the rule of law by providing support to non-governmental organizations (NGOs), independent media the judiciary and other key institutions. To support this long-term generational transition, the U.S. Government is increasingly promoting links between U.S. and Russian communities and institutions, including universities, hospitals and professional associations, and is establishing public-access Internet sites throughout Russia. The U.S. Government will also be awarding a grant to support a curriculum development program for the Institute of Public Administration and Social Studies at Moscow State University. In addition, the U.S. Government is helping Russia combat crime and corruption through cooperation with U.S. law enforcement agencies and community-based groups.

Regional Initiative (RI). The RI concentrates an array of U.S. government technical assistance, business development, and exchange programs in a small group of progressive Russian regions, with the goal of helping to create successful models of economic and political development at the regional level. Over time, it is hoped that these regions will achieve broad-based economic growth, attract outside investment, and build a strong civil society, and that they will participate in efforts to disseminate their experience to other regions of Russia. Three RI sites are up and running, in Novgorod, Samara, and Khabarovsk/Sakhalin in the Russian Far East, and a new site is currently being established in Tomsk.

COOPERATIVE THREAT REDUCTION (CTR) PROGRAM

The Defense Department's (DoD) CTR or "Nunn-Lugar" Program was initiated in FY 1992 to reduce the threat posed to the United States by the weapons of mass destruction (WMD) remaining on the territory of the former Soviet Union. CTR promotes denuclearization and demilitarization, and seeks to prevent WMD proliferation.

Through FY 1999, DoD has notified the U.S. Congress of over $1.6 billion in CTR assistance to Russia, of which over $1.2 billion has been obligated through FY 1999 and over $790 million disbursed. Cooperation has evolved and strengthened over the years in DoD's interaction with the Russian ministries administering the CTR program, including the Ministry of Defense (MoD), the Ministry of Atomic Energy (MinAtom), the now-disbanded Ministry for Defense Industry (MDI), and the Ministry of Economy (MinEcon). In June 1999, the U.S. and Russian Governments extended the CTR Umbrella Agreement through 2006.

Since FY 1997, the CTR Program has focused increasingly on Russia. About $383 million of the $440.4 million appropriated for CTR in FY 1999 was earmarked for Russia. To position Russia to reduce its force structure to START II or potential START III levels, DoD, MoD and MinEcon agreed in December 1997 on new CTR projects to support the required missile systems dismantlement, strategic submarine elimination, and enhance nuclear weapons and fissile material security. Several of these projects are underway. In 1999, projects were being developed to help the Russians process and package fissile material in the post-dismantlement stage and to prevent the proliferation of biological weapons (BW) expertise and technology.

The CTR Program is providing Russia equipment, training, services and logistical support to expedite the elimination of strategic offensive arms pursuant to the START Treaties. This includes assistance with liquid rocket-fuel disposition, SLBM launcher and associated submarine elimination, solid rocket-motor elimination, SS-18 and heavy-bomber dismantlement, and other projects. This also includes provision of equipment for emergency support in case of an accident involving the transport or elimination of missiles. Under the CTR Program, the U.S. is helping Russia destroy its CW stockpile and associated infrastructure. Efforts have focused on designing a CW destruction facility at Shchuchye that the U.S. Government plans to help construct. Construction is under way on a Central Analytical Laboratory (CAL) that will enhance Russia's ability to conduct chemical-agent monitoring at CW storage and destruction sites. The U.S. Government procured and delivered three mobile analytical laboratories to support Russian CW destruction projects. U.S. Government-funded efforts also continued to eliminate CW infrastructure at the KhimProm Volgograd and Novocheboksarsk chemical complexes.

Construction continues on a facility for the storage of fissile material derived from dismantled Russian weapons at Mayak in the Southern Urals. DoD is providing design assistance, construction support and equipment, and facility equipment. The U.S. Government is also providing Russia's Ministry of Atomic Energy (MinAtom) with containers for the transport and storage of fissile materials from dismantled weapons. Production of the containers began in October 1997, and initial shipments to Russia began in December 1997. Through FY 1999, more than 32,000 fissile material containers have been produced and delivered.

For additional analytical, business and investment opportunities information,
please contact Global Investment & Business Center, USA
at (202) 546-2103. Fax: (202) 546-3275. E-mail: rusric@erols.com
Global Business E-Books on Line: http://world.mirhouse.com

CTR Weapons Protection Control and Accounting (WPC&A) Program. This program is improving security of nuclear weapons during transportation and interim storage. The project was started in April 1997 under two CTR implementing agreements with Russia. Assistance provided includes supercontainers, railcar upgrades, emergency support equipment, automated inventory control and management systems, computer modeling, a personnel reliability program, 50 sets of "quick-fix" fencing and sensors for storage sites, and the development of a Security Assessment and Training Center to test and evaluate new security systems for storage sites. This project is planned to expand to protect over 70 additional storage sites.

CTR Materials Protection, Control and Accounting Program. Since 1993, the United States and Russia have worked together to prevent the theft or loss of nuclear material by improving nuclear materials protection, control, and accounting (MPC&A). MPC&A improvements are designed to keep nuclear materials secured in the facilities that are authorized to contain them, and are the first line of defense against nuclear smuggling that could lead to nuclear proliferation and/or nuclear terrorism. DOE took over the program from DOD and is seeking to enhance the security of weapons-grade fissile materials at more than 40 sites in Russia.

In addition, under the highly enriched uranium agreement, the U.S. is purchasing uranium from Russian weapons for use in power reactors. Also, both the U.S. and Russia will cooperate to dispose of excess military plutonium.

Export Control Assistance. Since the early 1990s, the U.S. has provided assistance to Russia to help it develop more effective export control systems and capabilities in order to prevent, deter and detect the potential proliferation of weapons of mass destruction (WMD) and associated materials. The objective is to help Russia build export control institutions, infrastructure and legislation to help prevent weapons proliferation. Initial funding from the CTR program has been augmented by funds from the Departments of Commerce, Energy, State and Treasury (Customs Service).

In FY , overall responsibility for export control assistance shifted to the Department of State, which provides policy direction and coordinates all agencies providing export control and border security assistance, capitalizing in particular on the unique capabilities of the U.S. Coast Guard to support export control and border security assistance programs. Recent State Department funded programs with Russia include supporting the Russian Center for Export Controls (CEC) work with the Department of Commerce to install internal compliance programs (ICPs) in key Russian defense and high-technology enterprises and facilitating the adoption of a new, comprehensive export control law and other legal/regulatory changes in Russia.

DOE export control efforts in Russia include traditional activities such as workshops, studies and regulatory development. DOE also initiated the Second Line of Defense program for Russia to combat the trafficking of illicit nuclear materials across border and control points to strengthen its overall capability to prevent nuclear materials, equipment and technology from getting into the hands of would-be proliferators. This program entails procuring Russian-manufactured detection equipment for key border crossings and training programs for Russian Customs officials.

International Science and Technology Center (ISTC). In a multilateral effort involving the European Union, Japan, and Canada, the U.S. has provided over $100 million to the Moscow-based ISTC for redirection activities in Russia in addition to millions of dollars in contributions from the EU, Canada, Norway, Japan and South Korea. The ISTC provides alternative peaceful civilian employment opportunities to scientists and engineers of the former Soviet Union involved with weapons of mass destruction and their delivery systems. To date, the ISTC has funded more than 500 projects involving more than 20,000 Russian scientists.

Biotechnical Redirection Program. In FY 1999, the U.S. Government implemented a State Department-led pilot project aimed at increasing transparency in former Soviet biological weapons (BW) facilities and redirecting their scientists to civilian commercial, agricultural and public health activities. All activity under this project is subject to strict oversight by an interagency working group. Facilities and government officials in countries where the U.S. Government is pursuing redirection activities are explicitly informed that any cooperation with countries of proliferation concern or terrorist entities, or any behavior inconsistent with the Biological and Toxin Weapons Convention (BWC), would have an immediate and negative impact on U.S. Government assistance.

The majority of U.S. Government-funded redirection activities are taking place under the auspices of the International Science and Technology Center (ISTC), which has access to facilities, provides tax-exempt assistance directly to scientists, and can engage multilateral funding. Agencies involved in these efforts include the U.S. Departments of State, Energy (DOE), Defense (DoD), Agriculture (USDA) and Health and Human Services (HHS). Most of these activities are oriented toward Russian institutes and scientists.

The State Department has allocated over $22 million since FY 1998 for these activities. DoD also has initiated a CTR program to fund collaborative biotechnical research with former biological weapons scientists to prevent the proliferation of biological weapons expertise and technology, increase access to Russian scientists, and to enhance the transparency of their work. CTR also is enhancing the security of Russian biotechnical facilities through initiation in FY 1999 of a Biological Material Protection, Control and Accountability Program.

IMPLEMENTING AGENCIES

U.S. Agency for International Development (USAID). USAID has implemented the lion's share of U.S. Government-funded technical assistance to Russia--over $1.8 billion since 1992. USAID has devoted its assistance efforts to helping Russia develop democratic institutions and transform its state-controlled economy to one based on market principles. USAID has been active in the areas of privatization and private-sector development, agriculture, energy, housing reform, health, environmental protection, economic restructuring, independent media, and the rule of law.

U.S. Department of State--Public Diplomacy Exchanges (formerly the U.S. Information Agency). Approximately 27,000 Russians have traveled to the United States on USIA-funded exchanges since 1992. Public diplomacy exchanges promote the growth of democracy and civil society, encourage economic reform and growth of a market economy in Russia. USIA's professional and academic exchanges cover such diverse fields as journalism, public administration, local government, business management, education, political science, and civic education.

Library of Congress. In FY 2000, the Russian Leadership Program will bring 1,800 Russians from throughout Russia to the United States for short-term study tours, including up to 150 members of the Russian Parliament for meetings with their counterparts in the U.S. Congress.

U.S. Department of Commerce. The Special American Business Internship Training (SABIT) Program places Russian managers for short-term internships with U.S. companies. To date, over 1,000 Russians have participated in the SABIT Program. The Commerce Department also operates the Business Information Service for the New Independent States (BISNIS), which provides market information, trade leads, and partnering services to U.S. companies interested in the Russian market.

U.S. Export-Import Bank (Eximbank). Eximbank has approved more than $3.6 billion in loans, loan guarantees, and insurance for transactions in Russia since 1991. Of this total, more than $1 billion was approved under its Oil and Gas Framework Agreement.

U.S. Overseas Private Investment Corporation (OPIC). OPIC has provided more than $4.0 billion in loans, loan guarantees, and political investment insurance to American companies investing in Russia.

Trade and Development Agency (TDA). TDA has approved approximately $55 million in funding for feasibility studies on more than 135 investment projects.

U.S. Department of Agriculture (USDA). In FY 1999, in response to a request by the Russian Government, USDA provided more than 3.7 million metric tons of food valued at more than $1 billion, including 100,000 metric tons of nonperishable food donated through U.S. private voluntary organizations (PVOs), 1.7 million tons of wheat on a grant basis, and 1.55 million tons of commodities (including beef, pork, poultry, corn, rice, wheat and soybeans) on a concessional basis under USDA's P.L. 480, Title I Program. USDA also donated 15,000 tons of corn and vegetable seeds to the Russian Government for the 1999 planting season. In FY 2000, USDA will be providing approximately $225 million in food assistance to Russia, which will consist of approximately 300,000 metric tons of government-to-government commodities targeted at institutions such as orphanages and hospitals, and approximately 200,000 metric tons of commodities provided by U.S. PVOs. In addition, USDA provides training to

Russian agriculturists and agricultural faculty through its Cochran Fellowship and Faculty Exchange Programs, with the goal of helping to familiarize the Russian agricultural sector with Western-style agribusiness management, marketing, and other issues, while at the same time increasing U.S. agricultural exports to Russia. Since 1992, over 500 Russians have traveled to the U.S. under these two programs.

U.S. Department of Defense (DoD). DoD implements the majority of the U.S. Government's security-related assistance programs through its Cooperative Threat Reduction (CTR) Program (see above). DoD also implements the Foreign Military Financing (FMF) and International Military Education and Training (IMET) programs in support of the Partnership for Peace.

U.S. Department of Energy (DOE). DOE funds and implements a wide range of programs in the security area, including the provision of Material Protection Control and Accounting (MPC& A) assistance to secure and prevent proliferation of nuclear materials and plutonium disposition assistance. DOE is also focusing on preventing proliferation of weapons expertise, facilitating the downsizing of Russia's nuclear cities, and improving the safety of Russia's nuclear reactors.

- **Initiatives for Proliferation Prevention (IPP).** DOE's IPP Program provides meaningful, sustainable, non-weapons-related work for former Soviet weapons-of-mass-destruction (WMD) scientists, engineers and technicians in the NIS through commercially viable market opportunities. IPP provides seed funds for the identification and maturation of technology and facilitates interactions between U.S. industry and NIS institutes for developing industrial partnerships, joint ventures and other mutually beneficial arrangements. Since 1994, IPP has funded over 440 projects involving more than 7,000 former Soviet weapons scientists at over 170 NIS institutes. Since establishing the IPP program, DOE has allocated over $100 million to support IPP projects in Russia.

- **Nuclear Cities Initiative (NCI).** NCI was established by DOE in late FY 1998 to help Russia provide new employment opportunities to the workers who are displaced through downsizing of the Russian nuclear weapons complex. DOE has initially concentrated its efforts on three focus cities of Sarov, Snezhinsk and Zheleznogorsk, which house the two Russian weapons-design laboratories and a plutonium production enterprise. NCI is helping create the conditions under which new jobs can be created through economic diversification in these closed cities. DOE has allocated $20 million through FY 2000 for this program.

Eurasia Foundation. The Eurasia Foundation, a private, non-profit, grant-making organization supported by the U.S. Government and private foundations, has awarded more than 1,600 grants totaling more than $40 million to Russian non-governmental organizations (NGOs) and U.S.-Russian NGO partnerships since 1993. The Foundation's grants have been targeted in three main programmatic areas: economic reform, governmental reform and the non-profit sector, and media and communications.

The Foundation has also implemented targeted grant initiatives to address specific issues, such as the rule of law and alternative dispute resolution.

PRINCIPAL U.S. EMBASSY OFFICIALS

EMABSSY IN MOSCOW

AMB: Alexander Vershbow
DCM: Paul Smith
AMB EXEC ASST: Cynthia Doell
ADM: Robert McAnney
CON: James Warlick
ECON: Mary Warlick
EST: Deborah Linde
IMO: Lawrence Krause
LAB: Karen Enstrom
LES: Karen Aguilar
PAO: Anne Chermak
POL: George Krol
RSO: John Gaddis
AGR: Geoffrey Wiggin
AID: Carol Peasley
COM: Stephan Wasylko
DAO: Col. Kevin Ryan
DOE: Cynthia Lersten
DOJ (LEGAT) vacant
FAA: Dennis Cooper (Resident in Brussels)
INS: Donald Monica
IRS: Margaret Lullo (Resident in Bonn)
NASA: Dennis McSweeny, Acting
PC: Timothy Douglas
TREAS: Brian Cox
VOA: Sonja Pace

U.S. Foreign Commercial Service, American Embassy Moscow, 23/38 Bolshaya Moltchanovka, 121069
Moscow, Russian Federation, Tel [7] (095) Tel 737-5030, Fax 737-5033, e-mail moscow.office.box@mail.doc.gov

CONSULATES

St. Petersburg [CG], Furshtadtskaya Ulitsa 15, 191028, St. Petersburg, Russia • PSC 78, Box L, APO AE

09723, Tel [7] (812) 275-1701, after hours Tel 274-8692, Fax 110-7022; GSO Fax 275-3295; ADM Fax
275-4735. E-mail address: usa.consulate@cltele.com

CG: vacant
DPO: Michael Klecheski
CGSEC: Caryn Solomon
ADM: James Doty
BPAO: David Siefkin
COM: Michael Richardson

CON: Robin Morritz
GSO: Vangala S. Ram
IM - IPO: Harry Chamberlain
POL/ECON: Kathleen Morenski
RSO: David Hall

U.S. Foreign Commercial Service, American Consulate General, 25 Nevskiy Prospect, St. Petersburg,
191186 Russia, Tel [7] (812) 326-2560, Fax 326-2561

PAO- The American Center, Millionnaya Ulitsa 5/1, 191186 St. Petersburg, Tel [7] (812) 311-8905 or
325-8050, Fax 325-8052

Vladivostok [CG],Ulitsa Pushkinskaya 32, Vladivostok, Russia, 690001 • Pouch address: AmConGen
Vladivostok, Dept. of State, Washington, D.C. 20521-5880, Tel [7] (4232) 30–00–70 (Note: if calling from the
U.S., and the U.K., dial 7-501-4232), 30–00–72, Fax (7) (4232) 26-02-48 (if faxing from the U.S. or U.K.:
(7-501) (4232) 26-02-48); CON Fax 30–00–91 (if faxing from the U.S. or U.K.: (7-501) (4232) 30–00–91);
COM Tel 30-00-93, Fax 30-00-92; PAO Tel 26–70–17, Fax 30–00–95 (if faxing from the U.S. or U.K., (7-501)
(4232) 30–00–95); FCS Tel. 30–00–93, Fax 30–00–92; Peace Corps Tel 22-11-31, Fax 49-69-23

CG: vacant
ADM: Andrew Graves
BPAO: vacant
CON: Elizabeth K. Thompson
POL/ECON: Joseph Hamilton

PC: Valerie Ann Ibaan
RSO: Karen R. Schaeffer

Yekaterinburg [CG],Ulitsa Gogolya 15A • P.O. Box 400, 620151 Yekaterinburg, AmConGen Yekaterinburg, Dept. of State, Wash., D.C., 20521-5890, Tel [7] (3432) 564-619, 564-691, 629-888; COM 564-736; CON 564-744; PAO 564-760; Fax [7] (3432) 564-515. E-mail: uscgyekat@gin.ru; website: www.uscgyekat.ur.ru

CG: Dale Eppler
ADM: vacant
BPAO: vacant
CON: Andrew Flashberg
POL/ECO/COM: Scott Hamilton

THE RUSSIAN FEDERATION TODAY: NEW BUSINESS OPPORTUNITIES AND CHALLENGES

The development of the private sector is a key factor in the transformation of formerly centrally planned economies. Direct foreign investment (DFI) plays an important role in this regard because it provides capital, market access, technology and management skills. DFI can be a significant contributor to the transformation of these economies. Unfortunately, the positive influence of foreign investment on the Russian economy is still years away.

Several factors have prevented direct foreign investment in Russia from reaching the levels anticipated only a few years ago. Most notably, economic instability and ambiguities with respect to future policies and economic reform have all created an uncertain investment environment.

The government's implementation of its macro-economic stabilization program will be central to providing a favorable investment climate. If economic stabilization is successfully carried forward into and the momentum of liberalization is maintained, the Russian economy could enter a period of growth. According to numerous estimates, Russian GNP and other economic indicators continued to fall in 1997 but could begin to recover - perhaps strongly in 1997 - if proper policies are in place. With a stable economic environment, one would anticipate a considerable increase in foreign investment flows compared to levels seen in the past. On the other hand, if inflation remains high and variable, or if structural policies do not encourage resources to move toward more productive uses, then the upturn could falter, and recorded output could fall in . Under such a scenario, DFI would likely be maintained at the more modest levels experienced to date.

The lack of a transparent and stable legal structure has also been a serious impediment to direct foreign investment. Bureaucratic obstacles to licensing and registration ought to be removed; and the tax system should ensure the equitable treatment of foreign investors. The weak business practices of many Russian enterprises (e.g., inadequate accounting procedures, insufficient marketing and strategic planning capabilities) may make foreign investors reluctant to take on enterprise restructuring. Finally, the privatization program has often given preferential treatment to the employees of state-owned enterprises over foreign investors.

For additional analytical, business and investment opportunities information, please contact Global Investment & Business Center, USA at (202) 546-2103. Fax: (202) 546-3275. E-mail: rusric@erols.com Global Business E-Books on Line: http://world.mirhouse.com

BUSINESS AND INVESTMENT CLIMATE IN RUSSIA (GENERAL OVERVIEW)

During the past five years the Russian political and economic systems went through the painful and very deep process of transformation. As a result, the Russian economic and industrial system as well as the rules of the game have been changed completely. From a highly politically and economically centralized society, Russia, as a country, made a gigantic step toward becoming a modern developed society with a multi-party, democratic political system and market economy. Despite the fact that the process of transition in Russia is far from completion, we have to recognize that the whole investment and business climate in that country became much more promising than five years ago.

The main purpose of this guide is to analyze current changes in the Russian economic, political and legislative systems and present, in a condensed fashion, a set of information and data necessary for the understanding of the current situation in Russia. We hope that this guide will be a useful source of information for any business executive who is already doing or wants to do business in Russia.

Anyone who may want to do business in the modern Russia ought to know about several important topics.

DIVISION OF POWER AMONG FEDERAL, REGIONAL AND MUNICIPAL LEVELS IN THE RUSSIAN FEDERATION

The division of power among the various levels of government in the Russian Federation is a complex and sensitive issue. The Russian Federation today consists of 21 republics, 6 krays (territories), 49 *oblasts* (provinces), 1 autonomous oblast, 10 autonomous *okrugs* (ethnic districts) and two federal cities (Moscow and St. Petersburg). Each of these 89 federal jurisdictions has its own administration and has varying approaches to foreign investment.

The existing division of power is determined by the Federation Agreement of 1992, the Constitution adopted by a national referendum on December 12, 1993, and bilateral agreements of the Federation with certain jurisdictions. There is no clear rule as to the exact distinction of law and decision making and the implementing authority between each level. Using their right to introduce their own economic legislation, regions have already adopted a number of local laws and regulations affecting foreign investment. As the Federation has little direct power to ensure implementation of its regulations or decisions, regions often do not feel obliged to implement federal acts.

Important issues are land ownership, taxation, privatization and privileges for foreign investors. Understanding the regional structure of the country as well as the administrative structure of local authorities is a necessity for foreign investors. Local support may be particularly helpful in promoting a project. Foreign investors are advised to gain support from the key players at the regional and local levels, down to the management and the workers' collective of the enterprise connected to the investment.

ENTREPRENEURIAL ACTIVITY AND CORPORATE LAW

Like other areas of Russian law, commercial and corporate law is in a period of rapid transition as outdated Soviet-era legislation is replaced by legislation that better reflects the country's evolving market economy system.

Although neither the Russian Constitution nor the First Part of the new Civil Code adopted in October 1994 contains any specific provision relating to direct foreign investment, together they establish general principles which lay the foundation for foreign investment and the conduct of entrepreneurial activity. In addition, the First Part of the Civil Code defines a broad range of permissible legal forms for engaging in commercial activity, including various forms of partnerships and limited liability corporate entities, and establishes general norms for contractual and other civil relations and obligations.

Despite notable progress, legislation in many key areas remains inconsistent, incomplete or in need of substantial revision. Legislation on limited liability and joint-stock companies, on banking and securities activities, among many other areas, is in the process of being drafted or pending before the Russian Parliament (Duma).

PRIVATE PROPERTY

Private property, in general, is protected by law. The ownership of real or immovable property, such as buildings, structures or other fixtures, is distinct under Russian law and is governed by a separate and less restrictive legal regime than the one for land. Currently a draft of a comprehensive law on land ownership rights is being considered. Until this legislation is enacted, however, there are a number of unresolved issues in the regulation of land ownership rights. This creates uncertainty for owners of privatized enterprises and also limits the ability to secure financing the land on which the enterprise stands.

PRIVATIZATION

Privatization in the Russian Federation has resulted in tens of thousands of state-owned enterprises having been transformed to privately owned companies. According to official statistics, more than 70 percent of the Russian work force is now employed by private businesses.

As of May 1997, two privatization programs had been adopted: the State Program for the Privatization of State and Municipal Enterprises, known as the 1992 Program, and the 1994-1997 Program. The privatization programs separate privatization on different administrative levels (federal, regional, municipal). At the federal level, two major bodies are involved in the privatization process: the Federal Committee for the Management of State Property - or in Russian -- *Goskomimushchestvo* -- (commonly known as GKI) -, and the Russian Federal Property Fund.

From the outset, the Russian Government has attempted to encourage participation in the privatization process. Legislation concerning privatization contains remarkably few restrictions on foreign participation. It does not, however, cover the privatization of land.

FOREIGN INVESTMENT LEGISLATION

The main law governing direct foreign investment in Russia - "On Foreign Investments in the RSFSR" - was adopted in July 1991. It provides definitions that qualifies somebody as a foreign investor, what forms foreign investment can take, and what constitutes an enterprise with foreign investment. The law is based primarily on Soviet legal principles and was subsequently modified by the adoption of a number of legislative acts. Currently, the Duma is considering another legislative draft for foreign investment regulation.

GUARANTEES FOR FOREIGN INVESTMENT

Investment guarantees are provided by the Law "On Foreign Investments in RSFSR", by some more recent Presidential decrees and by sector oriented legislation (especially in energy and mining). Guarantees for foreign investment are further granted under both domestic law and international treaties. They, in principle, encompass the transfer of investment related funds, expropriation, national treatment and recourse to judicial dispute resolution and arbitration. Some twelve bilateral investment protection treaties (BITs) are in force, and an additional four have been signed and await ratification. Other such treaties are currently being negotiated.

Guarantees under domestic law and international treaties overlap to some extent. As a rule, international treaty protection can be invoked through ultimate recourse to international arbitration whereas guarantees under domestic legislate must usually be pursued in the domestic courts.

FINANCIAL SECTOR

Since 1992, a large number of commercial banks have been established in the Russian Federation either as new banks or as spin-offs of former industrial sectors banks. The banking system has evolved mainly in a spontaneous way under liberal and poorly enforced regulations. Lately, however, implementation of financial sector reform has begun and consolidation of the banking sector is underway. Foreign investors should be attentive to the financial strength and solvency of their banking partners.

The capital markets of the Russian Federation are underdeveloped but growing quickly. The Russian Federation lacks a comprehensive system of securities market regulation. In order for markets to develop, a number of issues need to be addressed: reliable information on which to base investment decisions; settlement and registration procedures; custodial arrangements; rules on corporate governance; and tax treatment of portfolio investment.

TAXATION

Russian tax laws are evolving and are subject to continuous change. This has caused and continues to pose considerable difficulties for the foreign investor who is constantly faced with a changing tax regime.

Under the Law "Concerning the Fundamental Principles of the Taxation System in the Russian Federation," adopted in December 1991, taxes are divided into three categories: federal taxes; taxes of the constituent republics of the Russian Federation and taxes of territories, provinces, autonomous provinces and autonomous districts; and local taxes.

Russian legal entities with foreign ownership and foreign legal entities with a taxable presence in Russia are subject to a Russian profits tax. While Russian legal entities are taxed on their worldwide income, foreign legal entities with a taxable presence in Russia are only taxed on profits earned through their permanent representation in the Russian Federation. Foreign legal entities without such a taxable presence in Russia may, nevertheless, be subject to Russian withholding on certain types of Russian source income.

Income of foreign legal entities which is taxed in Russia may also be taxed in the home country of the foreign legal entity. Tax treaties eliminate or reduce the impact of double taxation through special rates of tax on certain types of income. Many double tax treaties provide for either reduced rates of withholding or a complete exemption from withholding on Russian source income.

ACCOUNTING

Russian accounting retains a very different orientation from the accounting systems used in Western countries. New regulations on accounting adopted in 1992 establish the basic framework for the present Russian accounting system. The new Russian accounting rules are applicable to all Russian legal entities including enterprises with foreign investment.

Many enterprises with foreign investment operate with dual accounting systems. Their financial statements are prepared under both Russian and Western accounting rules in order to satisfy domestic Russian reporting requirements and the requirements of foreign investors.

For additional analytical, business and investment opportunities information, please contact Global Investment & Business Center, USA at (202) 546-2103. Fax: (202) 546-3275. E-mail: rusric@erols.com Global Business E-Books on Line: http://world.mirhouse.com

FOREIGN TRADE AND CUSTOMS REGULATIONS

Domestic shortages of certain goods along with high inflation have led the Russian government to require import and export licenses for specific commodities. Licenses are issued by the Russian Ministry of Foreign Economic Relations through its authorized representatives.

Most export quotas have been abolished since July 1, 1994. The only remaining ones are those imposed pursuant to international obligations of the Russian Federation to prevent unfair trade practices such as dumping. There are no import quotas at the present time.

Customs duties apply depending on the country where the goods originated. A number of goods may be imported to Russia duty-free. Right now, goods in transit move freely over the territory of the Russian Federation except for a customs fee of 0.1 percent of their customs value. In addition to import customs duties, an importer must pay a fee for customs clearance of the goods. The Russian Federation has set goals for gradually reducing customs duties for most goods.

LABOR REGULATIONS

Employees of enterprises with foreign investment are subject to Russian labor law. The principle Russian legislation governing labor relations is the Russian Federation Code of Labor Laws (the Labor Code). In addition to this core legislation, the 1990 RSFSR Law on Employment of the Population, the 1990 Law on Trade Unions, the Russian legislation on minimum wages, and the 1991 Law of the USSR on the Resolution of Labor Disputes are also applicable to labor regulations.

ANTI-MONOPOLY REGULATIONS

The March 1991 **Law on Competition and Restriction of Monopolistic Activities on Markets of Goods**, as amended, introduced regulations governing competition and monopolistic activities. Restrictions of competition through agreements or coordinated action between economic units such as the fixing of prices or sharing of markets are forbidden. Activities of economic units with a dominant market position are not allowed if they interfere, to a substantial degree, with free competition or the interests of other economic units.   Furthermore, State bodies are not allowed to interfere with the independence of economic units without due reason. Unfair competition, such as the dissemination of misleading information to consumers about competitors or goods as well as unauthorized use of trade-marks, names and business secrets, is prohibited.

An Anti-Monopoly Committee has been established in order to implement the law. For the foundation or merger of an Organization or company, the approval of the Committee or notification to the Committee may be required.

ENVIRONMENTAL PROTECTION

Current Russian environmental legislation is in a developmental stage and its interpretation is complicated by the ill-defined relationship between various levels of governments. The basic legislation on environment, "On the Protection of the Environment" was adopted in December 1991 and provides a framework for the regulation and subordinate legislation largely yet to be drafted. Nevertheless, the foreign investor must pay close attention to existing environmental norms and standards which may be strictly enforced.

GOVERNMENT INVESTMENT PROGRAM

The Russian Ministry of Economy has designed a program to promote direct foreign investment. The objectives of the program include stabilizing output in key areas, accelerating the modernization of obsolete equipment, introducing energy-saving technologies and developing infrastructure. In order to facilitate investment, the Government will offer tax breaks and other incentives. The Government is also considering offering special financing facilities for specified large investment projects. In addition, investment insurance may be available. Because the status of special incentives frequently changes, careful checking of existing incentives is necessary.

FREE ECONOMIC ZONES (FEZ)

About 15 FEZs have been established in various regions of the Russian Federation. However, despite some progress the FEZs have not been substantially developed yet. Potential foreign investors are advised to confirm the existence and validity of FEZ regimes and benefits with both local and federal authorities.

OIL AND GAS SECTORS

The current structure of the Russian oil and gas sectors can in large part be explained by Soviet-era industrial policy. Large vertically integrated companies dominate the oil sectors and a single enterprise largely controls the gas sector. There is a constant tension between the need for foreign investment and the desire of the various state bodies (both at the Federal and local levels) and domestic Russian enterprises to remain in control of the development of the country's natural resources. Foreign investments in the oil sector remains subject to case-by-case governmental review and, in most cases, licensing. Although export licensing and quotas have recently been significantly reduced, restrictions remain in many sectors. Benefits for foreign investment in the natural resources sector are limited and currently provide little incentive for foreign investors.

There have been important legislative changes recently clarifying the rules for developing the country's natural resources. These include the March 1997 amendment to the **Law on Subsoil Resources** and the December 1997 **Law on Production Sharing Agreements**. The new Law on Production Sharing Agreements sets the framework for contracts between the state and investors, both domestic and foreign, for the development of energy and mineral resources. In its current state the law contains a number of provisions which may be perceived as creating particular disadvantages for foreign investors in the Russian oil, gas and mineral sectors. Still pending, however, is the new **Oil and Gas Law**, which should deal more specifically with the procedures and conditions related to hydrocarbon production, pricing and transport. Considerable uncertainty will therefore remain until these laws are finalized, adopted and reconciled.

DISPUTE RESOLUTION

The Russian Federation is not yet a party to the International **Center for Settlement of Investment Disputes** (ICSID) Convention which provides facilities for conciliation and arbitration on investment disputes between Contracting States and nationals of other Contracting States.

In accordance with Article 9 of the foreign investment law, so-called "investment disputes" are to be settled by the Supreme Court or by the Supreme Arbitration Court of the Russian Federation if no other methods of settlement are stipulated by international agreements. As to "other disputes" in which a foreign interest is involved, these are usually considered under Russian law as disputes of an international character, which means that the jurisdiction of the Russian Courts can be avoided upon the parties' agreement to submit the dispute to arbitration. The parties are free to choose *"ad hoc"* or "institutional" arbitration, the country where arbitration should take place and, under certain circumstances, the substantive law to be applied. Therefore, foreign investors are advised to pay particular attention to the adoption and wording of an appropriate arbitration clause. The Russian Federation is bound by the 1958 New York Convention on the Recognition and Enforcement of Foreign Arbitrage Awards and by the 1961 European Convention on International Commercial Arbitration. In addition, the Rules of Conciliation and Arbitration of the **International Chamber of Commerce (ICC)** are being increasingly used in disputes connected with foreign investment in Russia.

BASIC CONCLUSION

Provided that heightened political or economic uncertainty does not cause foreign companies to abandon or postpone their projects, direct foreign investment is likely to expand in Russia. Substantial inflows of direct foreign investment, however, are likely to raise a number of new policy issues for the Russian Government. In particular, the Investment Guide identifies a number of issues which need to be urgently addressed.

The legislative framework. More stability and predictability is needed. The Civil Code and related laws on entrepreneurial activity need to be fully expressed in regulation and practice. For instance, the limited liability of shareholders in limited liability companies remains in question. The rights of minority shareholders in joint-stock companies are given little protection, although some of these concerns are addressed in the new law on Joint-Stock Companies adopted in December 1997. Forthcoming legislation should address the rights and liabilities of shareholder in other forms of legal entities. The right to own land should also be established.

Foreign investment legislation. The upcoming enactment of the Foreign Investment Law should provide greater transparency and move towards an investment regime that provides national treatment of foreign investors in both the pre- and post-establishment phase of investment; recognize international commercial standards such as those for accounting and taxation; adopt recognized standards for the protection of foreign investors; and remove the administrative obstacles to the registration and implementation of foreign investment on all administrative levels.

The oil and gas sector. Major impediments to foreign investment include the lack of a comprehensive legal and regulatory framework covering oil and gas production, pricing and transportation; ill-defined property rights and physical access rights to mineral resources; a tax system that is complicated, burdensome and targets revenue instead of profits; export controls that restrict access to international markets; and pricing polices that maintain disparities between internal and external prices. In addition, the new Law on Production Sharing Agreements contains, in its current state, a number of provisions which may be perceived as creating particular disadvantages for foreign investors in the Russian oil, gas and mineral sectors. One hopes that any futures amendments to the Law on Production Sharing Agreements will address these concerns and establish a more transparent and conductive legal regime for foreign investment in the natural resource sector.

Corporate governance. Effective laws on corporate governance and accountability to shareholders are needed. For instance, codes of conduct for corporate officers and directors, such as rules on duty of care, duty of loyalty, and the corporate opportunity doctrine, need to be established.

Capital Market Regulation. Russia's capital markets are underdeveloped but are growing quickly. Russia requires a comprehensive system of securities market regulation. For capital markets to develop, a number of issues need to be addressed, notably: access to reliable price and market information; settlement and registration procedures; custodial arrangements; rules on corporate governance; and tax treatment of portfolio investment.

Taxation. The government should provide a clear and stable tax framework. The lack of such a framework limits the ability of investors to predict the tax consequences of their investments. This issue is particularly important for the development of long-term capital investments. Apart from this, the present system contains unusual burdens.

Personal security. While not a traditional economic issue, crime and corruption continue to affect the day-to-day business operations of foreign firms. In order to ensure the personal and material safety of investors, the Government should undertake further initiatives to prevent crime in vulnerable spheres of the economy and in regions of Russia with a high level of crime.

In essence, Russia is making considerable progress as it enacts new legislation favorable to the development of a market economy, and thus to foreign investors. At the present time, there are still many risks and uncertainties associated with investing in Russia, but there is also much potential to be tapped. Many of the difficulties associated with investing in Russia are neither unique to this country nor are they likely to be resolved in a short period of time. At an early stage in the process of economic transition, few countries of the former Communist bloc have a clear, efficient policy on direct foreign investment. It is encouraging to note that initial *"trial and error"* implementation of laws and regulations is giving way to more carefully thought-out policies.

For additional analytical, business and investment opportunities information,
please contact Global Investment & Business Center, USA
at (202) 546-2103. Fax: (202) 546-3275. E-mail: rusric@erols.com
Global Business E-Books on Line: http://world.mirhouse.com

INTERNATIONAL ASSISTANCE TO RUSSIA

US ASSISTANCE

	FY 1998 Actual	FY 1999 Estimate	FY 2000 Request
FREEDOM Support Act	$133,181,000	$172,360,000	$295,000,000

Russia's evolution toward free-market democracy remains crucial to U.S. national security and its political and commercial interests. In supporting and hastening that evolution, the U.S. seeks to build and consolidate new relationships with Russia, first as a full partner on a wide array of global issues --ranging from the maintenance of regional and international peace to the reduction of environmental threats-- and second, as an active partner in trade and investment. USAID assistance has contributed significantly to the broad U.S. reform agenda by working with Russians in many sectors. While the economic crisis of August, 1998 caused USAID to reexamine its strategy, the Agency is convinced that continued engagement is critical to U.S. national interests despite the many uncertainties.

THE DEVELOPMENT CHALLENGE.

Russia is experiencing a severe macroeconomic and financial crisis reflecting in large part the Government's failure to implement the comprehensive economic reform measures needed to foster economic growth, generate revenues and maintain fiscal discipline. Russia's inability to provide the environment for private sector-led growth and increasing levels of foreign direct investment has seriously delayed the modernization of Russian industry while keeping revenues woefully inadequate to cover minimal government spending and foreign debt obligations. Instead, the Government of Russia (GOR) resorted to heavy borrowing to fund current Government expenses.

This unsustainable position combined with the spreading financial crisis in emerging markets came to a head in August, 1998. The ruble plummeted sharply from six to over fifteen to the dollar depleting Russia's foreign exchange reserves in the process. The GOR failed to meet its domestic and foreign debt obligations. Russia's vulnerable banking system collapsed, disrupting the payments system. GDP is now estimated to decline by 4 percent in 1998 and estimates for 1999 are unclear given the uncertain economic environment. Inflation projections for 1999 are currently over 80%, which is optimistic given the continued sharp decline of the ruble and the growing budget deficit. Direct foreign investment levels are down about 50% from a year ago, well below levels required to revitalize and expand Russia's productive capacity.

The change of government brought about by the economic turmoil has exacerbated economic and political uncertainties. The most significant obstacle to Russia's transition to a market economy is the lack of political consensus to move ahead with comprehensive economic reforms. This suggests there is no near-term solution to resolving the fiscal and financial crisis, as evidenced by the inability of the government since August to adopt a realistic economic program which the IMF can support.

Corruption and organized crime are a major impediment to fundamental change, reflecting a lack of effective and comprehensive systems to maintain the rule of law under transparent and democratic principles. Foreign and domestic investors continue to be cautious in the light of a still unclear tax and legal regime. Independent media outlets are struggling as a result of falling revenues from private sector advertisers. While the non-governmental sector is growing, it is still in its early stages of development and not firmly rooted.

NGOs still need to strengthen their management practices and diversify their funding base. Production of greenhouse gases and other environmentally harmful industrial practices persist and an enforceable environmental legal structure has not yet been developed. Health risks from infectious diseases and environmental factors are undermining the human resources necessary to tackle future problems.

In an atmosphere as described above, the assistance challenge is to support those areas of the economy and society that can keep economic and democratic reform alive during these difficult times. These remain the private sector and civil society where USAID has already had a significant impact. For example, electoral commissions assisted by USAID are working to ensure that elections scheduled for 1999 and 2000 are free and fair, and partnerships between U.S. and Russian entities continue without direct USAID assistance. As a result of USAID small business programs, thousands of small businesses are changing their product mix and marketing approaches to respond to problems generated by the financial crisis.

The development of infrastructure for the Russian capital markets system proceeds in Moscow and 15 regions. Tens of thousands of non-governmental organizations (NGOs) still operate, while independent local TV stations and newspapers seek ways to ensure their financial independence. Russian hospitals, in partnership with U.S. hospitals, continue to provide more cost effective health care and new techniques for combating infectious diseases, particularly tuberculosis (TB) and HIV/AIDS.

New and environmentally friendly industrial processes are being implemented throughout the country; and, international accounting standards are being adopted by a growing number of businesses. All of these efforts provide the grassroots support and know how for implementation of reform in their respective areas. When the macro-level situation stabilizes, USAID stands ready to use its policy reform expertise to work on that level in concert with other donors.

OTHER DONORS.

A key objective of U.S. assistance to Russia is to serve as a catalyst for other assistance providers, both bilateral donors and international financial institutions. Russia's ability to attract significant multilateral assistance is presently stymied by its failure to meet IMF conditions and the consequent suspension of the IMF program. In the past, USAID has leveraged World Bank funding for housing, community services, legal reform, urban development and local infrastructure development.

In FY's 1999 and 2000, USAID funding will complement the World Bank and other international donors if a comprehensive plan to restructure the Russian banking system can be developed. In sectors less directly affected by the macroeconomic crisis there remain areas for fruitful collaboration. USAID continues to coordinate with the EU-TACIS in business development and environmental policy reform.

U.S. foundations, including Mott, MacArthur, Ford and the Open Society Institute, meet regularly with USAID and forge complementary strategies in areas such as health care and rule of law. Other donors with which USAID works include UNICEF, UNAIDS, the Red Cross and Medecins Sans Frontieres in health care, the Council of Europe and the Organization for Economic Cooperation and Development in legal and tax reform, and bilateral donors and other USG agencies in media, violence against women, crime and corruption, political party development, and electoral reform.

FY 2000 PROGRAM.

USAID-Implemented Programs: USAID's program is part of the Partnership for Freedom (PFF) and the companion Regional Investment Initiative which target funds to the regions away from Moscow, and emphasizes the creation and strengthening of sustainable partnerships between U.S. and Russian organizations in all sectors. In FY 2000 USAID will continue to target funds away from the Government and from Moscow towards reform-minded regions, including the Russian Far East.

Economic reform, democratic reform, and health and social sector reform will continue to provide the broad framework for all USAID activities. Under economic reform, activities will include small and medium enterprises development, establishment of alternative credit sources and loan guarantees for small and micro enterprise, assistance to local and regional governments interested in developing investor friendly regulations, and implementation of environmentally sound business practices. USAID will continue to work with other donors in banking and tax reform. In the democratic reform area, USAID will support the further strengthening of civil society and human rights, highlighted by funding for free and fair elections and political party development, particularly in preparation for the upcoming parliamentary elections in late 1999 and the Presidential elections in June, 2000. Increased strengthening of NGOs, support to the independent media, establishing U.S.-Russia partnerships and more work on the rule of law will also be key components.

In the health and social sector area, assistance will work to stem the spread of infectious diseases, primarily HIV/AIDS and TB, increase access to and quality of health care, including maternal and child health, and support reform for Russian orphanages. Under cross-cutting and special initiatives, FY 2000 funding will support a number of programs. Training and exchanges will offer a variety of Russians an opportunity to travel to the United States to see systems functioning in a free market democracy. The broad program of the Eurasia Foundation and activities combating violence against women will continue.

Other U.S. Agency Programs: Included also with this request are programs implemented by other U.S. Government agencies. The request for cross-cutting and special initiatives, in particular, reflects expanded emphasis on the need to reduce the risks of proliferation of weapons of mass destruction through programs which enhance our mutual security, such as export controls, science centers and efforts designed to employ Russian scientists in non-military areas. In addition, other USG agencies participating in technical cooperation programs with Russia through inter-agency transfers from USAID include the Environmental Protection Agency, Health and Human Services, U.S. Forest Service, Departments of Justice, Treasury, Energy, Agriculture and Commerce, and U.S. Peace Corps. In addition, exchange programs run by the U.S. Information Agency are critical in fostering support in the next generation of Russians for democratic and free market reforms.

RUSSIA FY 2000 PROGRAM SUMMARY* (in Thousands of Dollars)

Strategic Objectives	Economic Restructuring	Democratic Transition	Social Stabilization	Cross-cutting / Special Initiatives	Total
Privatization	--	--	--	--	--
Fiscal Reform	--	--	--	--	--
Private Enterprise	59,925	--	--	--	59,925
Financial Reform	8,675	--	--	--	8,675
Energy	--	--	--	--	--
Environmental Management	3,700	--	--	--	3,700
Citizens' Participation	--	13,000	--	--	13,000
Legal Systems	--	3,450	--	--	3,450
Local Government	--	--	--	--	--

For additional analytical, business and investment opportunities information, please contact Global Investment & Business Center, USA at (202) 546-2103. Fax: (202) 546-3275. E-mail: rusric@erols.com Global Business E-Books on Line: http://world.mirhouse.com

Crises	--	--	--	--	--
Social Benefits	--	--	7,750	--	7,750
Environmental Health	--	--	--	--	--
Cross-cutting / Special Initiatives	--	--	--	198,500	198,500
TOTAL	72,300	16,450	7,750	198,500	295,000
*Freedom Support Act (FSA) funds					
USAID Mission Director: Janet Ballantyne					

SELECTED PROJECT

ACCELERATED DEVELOPMENT AND GROWTH OF PRIVATE ENTERPRISE, 110-S001.3

STATUS: Continuing
PROPOSED OBLIGATION AND FUNDING SOURCE: FY 2000: $59,925,000
FREEDOM Support Act
INITIAL OBLIGATION: FY 1992; **ESTIMATED COMPLETION DATE:** FY 2002

Summary: Russian GDP and productivity continue to decline and official unemployment continues to grow. More successful businesses will provide new jobs and new incomes, leading to further growth and stability of the Russian economy. Under this strategic objective, U.S. assistance providers work with a wide variety of Russian organizations throughout the country to accelerate the development and growth of private enterprise based on individual initiative and the operation of market forces.

Activities under this objective respond to the tremendous unmet needs of small and medium enterprises in Russia to stimulate economic development and to guarantee income and employment. Activities include business training for individual entrepreneurs in marketing and western management practices; on-site client focused business consulting services; the formation of sustainable business associations, trade organizations and business support centers; improving access to credit for micro and small businesses from non-commercial bank sources; and work on land and real estate privatization to increase availability of real collateral. Beneficiaries include Russians from all regions of the country.

Key Results: Four intermediate results are necessary for achievement of this objective: (1) policies, legislation and regulations conducive to broad-based competition and private sector growth are adopted; (2) land and real estate market mechanisms are operating, accessible and used by businesses; (3) successful models of private business ownership and modern management are widely replicated; and (4) a sustainable network of business support institutions are rendering services to entrepreneurs and enterprises.

Performance and Prospects: Since inception, over 200,000 Russian entrepreneurs (of which 104,000 are women) have received business training and consulting assistance, over 50,000 jobs have been created directly as a result of USAID funding, and over 5,000 continuing new businesses have been created. 71% of USAID business clients report increases in production, 81% report increases in sales, 89% increased customer base, and 82% increased net profit. Five of ten institutions established with USAID support to provide financing for small and micro entrepreneurs continue to operate without USAID assistance; over 3,200 loans have been provided to micro and small entrepreneurs; membership in the Russian Guild of Realtors has increased from five to over 800; and local boards have been established in 25 regions.

These efforts help build grassroots support for implementation of land reform and private property laws. Over the next few years USAID will continue to fund small and medium business training and consulting and increase coverage of indigenous business support institutions, supplying them with the tools to weather the economic crisis and grow. With matching funds from the Global Bureau, USAID plans to expand micro credit programs, strengthen the real estate profession and land privatization efforts. USAID will also launch a Development Credit Authority Project to provide large infrastructure credit guarantees to encourage banks to make loans in support of telecommunications and port and energy infrastructure projects.

Demand for business services continues throughout the country. Last year thousands of entrepreneurs were trained, business support centers were able to provide services without USAID funding, micro entrepreneurs paid back loans at a 99% rate, Regional Investment Initiative business support including work on legal and regulatory systems in regions continued, and environmentally friendly methods of doing business were adopted. Normal project implementation problems were encountered, but, even in the face of the economic crisis, demand for USAID business services continued.

Possible Adjustment to Plans: USAID continues to focus its programs. This will result in fewer separate activities under this strategic objective. Also, given the inevitable turmoil in Russia's road to reform, USAID will continue to be flexible and make appropriate adjustments to ensure that funds are utilized to achieve the highest impact.

Host Country and Other Donors: USAID works with private Russian institutions, the managers and owners of private enterprises and associations of private businesses, and with various Ministries and agencies of the government at both national and local levels. USAID collaborates with other donors seeking to support private sector growth, especially the British Know-How Fund, the European Bank for Reconstruction and Development (EBRD), the International Finance Corporation, and the World Bank. EU-TACIS funds complementary support projects as do both private and public representatives of European governments.

For additional analytical, business and investment opportunities information, please contact Global Investment & Business Center, USA at (202) 546-2103. Fax: (202) 546-3275. E-mail: rusric@erols.com Global Business E-Books on Line: http://world.mirhouse.com

Principal Contractors, Grantees, or Agencies: USAID works with dozens of U.S. nongovernmental organizations as well as for-profit contractors in implementing a broad program of support to private sector growth.

Selected Performance Measures:

	Baseline	Target
Private sector production as % of GDP	20% (1997)	45% (2000)
New businesses created	5,000 (1998)	25,000 (2000)
New jobs created	50,000 (1998)	150,000 (2000)

IMPROVED ECONOMIC INFRASTRUCTURE TO SUPPORT ECONOMIC GROWTH, 110-S001.4

STATUS: Continuing
PROPOSED OBLIGATION AND FUNDING SOURCE: FY 2000: $8,675,000
FREEDOM Support Act
INITIAL OBLIGATION: FY 1992; **ESTIMATED COMPLETION DATE:** FY 2002

Summary: The development of a middle class in Russia requires sustainable economic growth, which in turn requires an improved economic infrastructure. However, USAID is limited in its ability to fund activities which directly fund the Government of Russia. It is in this strategic objective where the bulk of government-related funds are disbursed. Representative activities include assistance to the Government, the Duma, the State Tax Service, and selected regional and local governments to analyze the potential impacts of different tax regimes on the government budget, draft legislation, and implement new taxes. In the banking sector, USAID has trained examiners in bank supervision, providing advisory services, and has developed loan guarantee protocols. Under the Regional Investment Initiative, USAID has helped improve open markets by assisting regional governments to design investment policies that promote more liberal trade and investment regimes. USAID funds also help strengthen the capability of key think tanks to conduct quality economic analysis to support sound policy formulation, and promoting the adoption and use of international accounting standards. Beneficiaries include Russian businesses, foreign and domestic investors, the Russian public, government agencies, and think tank institutions.

Key Results: To help develop an improved economic infrastructure, USAID supports activities in tax reform, banking reform, adoption of international accounting standards, and institutional strengthening of policy think tanks. Previously, funds were used to establish the Russian Securities and Exchange commission in Moscow and the regions.

Performance and Prospects: The transition from a centrally planned economy with a strong central government to a market economy continues to face difficult obstacles, although progress has been made in many areas. Economic and legal guidance has been provided to the Russian Government and Duma to evaluate strengths and weaknesses of the proposed tax code, including amendments. Economic analysis has been provided to the Ministry of Finance, showing impacts of changes in taxes, particularly personal income tax, on the hypothetical taxpayer. The State Tax Service's unit for collecting from large enterprises has been strengthened. A property tax system is being implemented in the cities of Tver and Novgorod.

The Securities Commission, National Association of Broker Dealers, Depository Clearing Company and other regulatory bodies have been established and institutionalized to strengthen investor protection. USAID has helped establish commercial bank training institutes outside of Moscow in order to increase Russian financial services to small and medium sized businesses. Over 30 banks have begun housing and commercial mortgage lending, and, International Accounting Standards have been published in Russian, accepted by the Russian Ministry of Finance, and are being adopted by business.

The establishment of the Russian Securities and Exchange Commission provides a solid infrastructure for securities trading in the country. Once the economic situation stabilizes and investor confidence returns, this exchange will play a major part in mobilizing finance. While the Government has consistently indicated a strong demand for USAID assistance in the tax reform area, these efforts have met with significant obstacles in the implementation stage, including differing views by groups in the Duma of how the tax system should be reformed. USAID will work with the World Bank to develop a bank restructuring plan and also to strengthen think tanks which can offer high quality economic analysis to decision-makers.

Possible Adjustments to Plans: For FY 1999, USAID decreased the numbers of components it was working on in tax reform. Depending on the progress in tax reform and changes from the 1999 Duma elections, further refinement may be necessary. As in other strategic objectives, USAID will need to be flexible and ensure that its activities support reform in ways that can be replicated and continued after bilateral assistance ceases.

Other Donor Programs: USAID plays a critical role in the financial sector. Activities are used as practical laboratories for future funding by the World Bank, the EU, and other donors. Of particular import will be the collaboration between USAID and the World Bank in banking restructuring. USAID works closely with bilateral donors and the International Committee for Accounting reform in its international accounting standards project. USAID hopes to strengthen Russian think tanks abilities to provide high quality economic analyses.

Principal Contractors, Grantees, or Agencies: USAID implementers include: Georgia State University, Financial Services Volunteer Corps (FSVC), the Gaidar Institute, the International Committee for Accounting Reform, and executive ministries of the Russian Government working on tax reform.

Selected Performance Measures:

	Baseline	Target
Legislative authority for bank restructuring agency (ARCO) passed	No (1998)	Yes (2000)
Fixed capital formation (% increase from previous year)	87 (1997)	100 (2000)

INCREASED ENVIRONMENTAL CAPACITY TO SUPPORT SUSTAINABLE ECONOMIC GROWTH, 110-S001.6

STATUS: Continuing
PROPOSED OBLIGATION AND FUNDING SOURCE: FY 2000: $3,700,000
FREEDOM Support Act
INITIAL OBLIGATION: FY 1992; **ESTIMATED COMPLETION DATE:** FY 2002

Summary: The acuteness of environmental problems in Russia, deepened by the difficult socio-economic conditions, have led to significant losses in economic productivity. To help address this situation, USAID activities in the environmental sector respond to Russia's need to achieve sustainable economic growth. This growth is dependent on improved capacity in environmental and natural resources management. USAID activities also respond to the needs of local environmental non-governmental organizations who require technical assistance to achieve financial and technical sustainability. Current activities include strengthening partnerships among institutions throughout Russia to promote exchange of practical lessons gathered from ground-breaking work in pollution prevention, risk assessment, and land-use planning, reforestation and other successful activities.

Activities also include reducing the negative impact of global climate change through programs targeted at fire prevention, pest control, reforestation, forest policy, and the phase-out of ozone depleting substances production. The entire population of Russia will benefit if USAID-supported and other donor programs in this area have their intended impact. The Russian Far East in particular will benefit from improved forestry practices and new ecology-based businesses.

Key Results: Three intermediate results are necessary for achievement of this objective: (1) increased capacity to deal with environmental pollution as a threat to public health; (2) improved management of natural resources and biodiversity protection; and (3) improved economic mechanisms for natural resources management, environmental protection and emissions trading.

Performance and Prospects: Significant progress has been achieved, with results of pilot projects in six regions now replicated and disseminated in more than 50 regions in the Russian Federation. In pollution prevention, private industry and municipal utilities in four industrial regions have reduced air and water pollution and demonstrated significant cost savings. A new health risk assessment methodology has been tested in seven cities and a Federal Working Group was established to utilize this methodology nationally.

Non-governmental organizations have reduced local pollution by conducting city clean-up days, developing solid waste collection programs, and constructing new drinking water wells for small villages. In natural resource management and biodiversity protection, the first ever comprehensive reforestation program was introduced in the Russian Far East, resulting in a 60 fold increase in the production of seedlings. The Regional Forestry Service and governments in the Russian Far East drafted the first Regional Forestry Code to ensure regional management of forest resources, and the endangered Siberian Tiger population stabilized at approximately 400 animals.

USAID assistance has also helped generate funding for the environment. Private enterprises and municipalities have financed environmental projects through domestic and international financial institutions, and regional eco-funds in three municipalities leveraged environmental loans for drinking water improvements. The municipal government in Nizhnii Tagil, an industrial city in the Urals, secured World Bank funding to improve its drinking water system. Gagarin and Smolensk are candidates for similar financing for municipal water improvements. Zapovedniks (nature reserves) in the Russian Far East are generating new revenue to fund protective programs through eco-tourism.

The Replication of Lessons Learned Project is USAID's flagship environmental project and applications for small grants in the environment continue to overwhelm the selection committees. Regional forestry departments are appreciative of USAID assistance in forestry matters and USAID is looking forward to seeing the results of new projects in non-forest timber product development and marketing. The key to the success of activities in this strategic objective is the focus on grassroots level work.

Possible Adjustments: As with all of its strategic objectives, USAID will continue to monitor work in this area to ensure that appropriate activities are designed and implemented. Demand continues to be very high for the services offered, especially at the local level.

Host Country and Other Donors: USAID closely coordinates with host country government, non-government, and private sector counterparts at the national, regional, and local levels. USAID programs work with other donors and international financial institutions, particularly the World Bank and EBRD, to coordinate activities and to leverage additional resources. To date, environmental assistance projects in Russia have leveraged at least $370 million in environmental investments, with the potential for a total of $400-500 million before the assistance program comes to an end.

Principal Contractors, Grantees, or Agencies: USAID is working with the following partners: U.S. Environmental Protection Agency, U.S. Forest Service, U.S. Department of Interior, ISAR, Institute for Sustainable Communities, Ecologically Sustainable

Development, World Wildlife Fund/U.S., Center for International Environmental Law, and the Department of Energy.

Selected Performance Measures:

	Baseline	Target
Environment-related business plans developed and implemented	0 (1993)	8 (2000)
Number of self-sustaining environmental NGOs	5 (1993)	25 (2000)
Environmental grants provided to local entities throughout Russia	0 (1993)	50(2000)

INCREASED BETTER INFORMED CITIZENS' PARTICIPATION IN POLITICAL AND ECONOMIC DECISION-MAKING, 110-S002.1

STATUS: Continuing
PROPOSED OBLIGATION AND FUNDING SOURCE: FY 2000: $13,000,000
FREEDOM Support Act
INITIAL OBLIGATION: FY 1992; ESTIMATED COMPLETION DATE: FY 2002

Summary: This strategic objective will ensure that citizens have the opportunity to express their opinions and influence decision-makers. USAID targets citizens, communities, NGOs, public officials, independent media, and various political party officials in order to expand public outreach efforts and to increase participation.

The National Democratic Institute (NDI) and the International Republican Institute (IRI) work in political party building at the national, regional, and local levels and in strengthening political institutions essential to democracy. NGO support networks covering two-thirds of the Russian Federation support thousands of active local NGOs. Major grant programs, administered through umbrella grants to U.S. and Russian NGOs, such as the Sustaining Partnerships into the Next Century (SPAN) program, provide funding to sustain dozens of partnership activities between Russian and American organizations in the areas of civil society, rule of law, tax reform, financial sector, business development, environment, and health.

The Eurasia Foundation is a major grass-roots grant making institution assisting economic and social reform. Sixteen media partnerships and most newspaper partnerships have achieved progress toward self-sustainability. Media partnerships promote business development of selected media, upgrade professional standards and expand access to independent sources of information. Under the Regional Investment Initiative (RII), NGO, local government, and private sector elements are brought together in selected communities to simultaneously address two principal elements of the Partnership for Freedom: reducing impediments to trade and investment and increasing citizens' participation in civil society.

The entire citizenry stands to gain as a direct result of USAID programs under this strategic objective. The political process activities are of greatest importance to voters and public officials at the national and regional level. Both independent media and NGOs reach a large portion of the Russian population. Independent media provides more objective news coverage essential for informed debate while NGOs offer an avenue for citizen participation in economic, social and political decision making.

Key Results: Three intermediate results are pursued in support of this objective: (1) free and fair elections are administered nationally and locally; (2) increased public access to information informs political and economic choices; and (3) NGO sector provides opportunities for citizen participation in economic and political speres of society.

Performance and Prospects: Given that democratic development can take decades, even generations, USAID must be realistic about program expectations. However, there have been impressive results to date. Some 65,000 local NGOs now contribute to the building of civil society in Russia. USAID training programs have reached over 13,500 activists from non-governmental organizations. Over 300 new independent television stations exist. A Russian non-governmental organization provides long-term services for Russian regional newspapers. Most recent elections were considered free and fair. Approximately 6,500 political party activists have been trained in party development. Twenty-four partnerships are receiving assistance to sustain and increase Russian - U.S. cooperation.

The increasing involvement of Russians in all activities has helped strengthen work in this strategic objective. Most impressive is the continuing work to strengthen NGOs around the country with the establishment of regional NGO Support Centers. Observers consider the SPAN Partnership Project an excellent model for the creation and strengthening of enduring partnerships between U.S. and Russian entities. All media assistance goes through Russian organizations. Civil society strengthening will continue to be a crucial element of U.S. assistance to Russia.

Possible Adjustments to Plans: USAID will continue to monitor this strategic objective to ensure that activities continue to have results and that they respond appropriately to NGO, media, partnerships, and political party needs.

Other Donor Programs: Russia has dozens of political parties. USAID has emphasized responding to requests for technical advice and training services from those parties viewed as "reform-oriented." Work with citizens' groups has generally been carried out through NGOs and in concert with local institutions, including municipal governments. Other donors have been active in electoral process issues; USAID has coordinated regularly with them in all election run-up periods and will continue to do so. USAID also works cooperatively with other bilateral donors providing assistance to the media and, increasingly, to Russian civil society.

Principal Contractors, Grantees, or Agencies: USAID is working with the following: International Republican Institute (IRI), National Democratic Institute (NDI), International Foundation for Electoral Systems (IFES), ISAR, World Learning, Inc., American Center for International Labor Solidarity (ACILS), Internews, National Press Institute (formerly RAPIC), the Helsinki Group, IREX, the Eurasia Foundation, and the Moscow School of Political Studies.

Selected Performance Measures:

	Baseline	Target
Percentage of viewers with access to independent TV	12% (1997)	21% (2000)
Increased and strengthened party identification among voters	22% (1994)	25% (2000)
Number of media partnerships that are fully self-sustaining	0 (1997)	3 (2000)
Share of assisted NGOs showing increased domestic funding	15% (1997)	40% (2000)

STRENGTHENED RULE OF LAW AND RESPECT FOR HUMAN RIGHTS, 110-S002.2

STATUS: Continuing
PROPOSED OBLIGATION AND FUNDING SOURCE: FY 2000: $3,450,000
FREEDOM Support Act
INITIAL OBLIGATION: FY 1992; **ESTIMATED COMPLETION DATE:** FY 2001

Summary: This strategic objective will strengthen the legal systems that better support democratic processes and market reforms. USAID's Rule of Law program now focuses on two principal aspects of legal reform in Russia: judicial reform (including enforcement of judgments and alternative dispute resolution), and legal education and training.

Partnerships between U.S. and Russian legal entities are encouraged. USAID has worked with the Rule of Law Consortium to ensure that all Russian Commercial Court judges are familiar with new legislation, including the Civil Code. In , Russia moved to strengthen the independence of its judiciary, creating a Judicial Department to put administration of the courts of general jurisdiction into the hands of judges.

USAID funds the National Judicial College in Reno, Nevada to work in partnership to ensure that this department fulfills its role. USAID has started to work on improving enforcement of judgments, and is providing assistance as Russia sets up a Russian equivalent of the U.S. Marshall's Service, which in addition to handling court security will enforce civil judgments. The American Bar Association (ABA/CEELI) supports commercial law training for lawyers, legal advocacy for women involved with domestic violence, continuing legal education, and law clinics. USAID also addresses corruption with activities promoting judicial ethics and discipline and improved government auditing. Another important USAID-supported effort is the work with many local NGOs to improve advocacy and outreach, helping Russians become more aware of their rights in such areas as housing, property, civil rights, and environmental protection.

The American Center for International Labor Solidarity (ACILS) works with local legal groups to provide citizens with the resources to seek enforcement of their labor rights and to organize into effective, independent labor unions. USAID continues to support the Sakharov Center and the Moscow Helsinki Group to increase human rights awareness.

Beneficiaries include investors, both foreign and Russian, Russian citizens desiring an open, transparent civil and commercial legal system, and the judicial and legal professions. They all stand to benefit from activities that increase transparency and the soundness of new laws, and that ensure their even-handed application and enforcement.

Key Results: Two intermediate results are pursued in support of this objective: (1) better administration, application and enforcement of law; and (2) higher standards and competence in the legal profession.

Performance and Prospects: Recent USAID support has assured that all 1600 commercial court judges in the country received Part 1 and 2 of the new civil code and other laws recently enacted; over 40% of these judges received training on substantive, Russian commercial law topics. USAID training and technical assistance produced several reforms.

The legal framework for property rights was improved to promote more private property transactions. Over 2000 Russian judges and lawyers received training on Russian laws to ensure that court process and judgments are transparent and consistent with written law. Twenty exchanges of top Russian judges led to the formation of the new Judicial Department, which is modeled on the Administrative Office of the U.S. Courts.

Continuing legal education is available in eight more cities. Numerous law schools instituted trial advocacy and other practice-based curricula. Partnerships have been established between U.S. institutions and Russian judicial training institutions at all levels, and 18 training programs were conducted to improve judges' decision-making skills. Thirty human rights groups in the regions now monitor abuses throughout the Russian Federation. Over 3,300 legal consultations were provided to trade unions in FY 1998 alone.

USAID will continue its dual focus on creating the requisite legal and regulatory environment to promote trade and investment and the rule of law while combating crime and corruption and supporting human rights. Activities will include continuing support for judicial partnerships, the new judicial department, enforcement of judgments, legal education, and legal rights advocacy by NGOs, especially related to domestic violence.

Possible Adjustments to Plans: Projects will be monitored to ensure results and modified if necessary.

Other Donor Programs: The World Bank, the EU, and several bilateral donors are involved in Rule of Law activities for Russia. An active donor coordination group meets quarterly. USAID also works closely with the Russian government, local governments, legal associations, and NGOs such as the Sakharov Center and the Moscow Helsinki Group.

Principle Contractors, Grantees, or Agencies: In addition to DOJ technical assistance and training, USAID works with ABA/CEELI, Chemonics and the National Judicial College, the Sakharov Center and Museum, Moscow Helsinki Group, and the Organization for Economic Cooperation and Development.

Selected Performance Measures:

	Baseline	Target
Judges have electronic access to laws and judicial decisions	No (1997)	Yes (2000)
Judicial decisions are viewed as uniform and predictable by commercial lawyers (annual survey of commercial lawyers taking CLE seminar)	10 (1998)	20 (2000)
Increased number of regions with human rights monitors	0 (1998)	32 (2000)

IMPROVED EFFECTIVENESS OF SELECTED SOCIAL SERVICES AND BENEFITS, 110-S003.2

STATUS: Continuing
PROPOSED OBLIGATION AND FUNDING SOURCE: FY 2000: $7,750,000
FREEDOM Support Act
INITIAL OBLIGATION: FY 1992; **ESTIMATED COMPLETION DATE:** FY 2002

Summary: This strategic objective will improve the delivery of selected social services and benefits, primarily health care services at the community level. Funds have been disbursed to assure the sustainability of basic social services and benefits target users of the health care system, low-income populations, and members of recently privatized state farms.

Projects have included technical assistance, training, and advice in several areas, successfully demonstrating the benefits of a restructured, more market-oriented health system. Sustainable models for cost efficient health care have been implemented in several oblasts and cities in Siberia. Increased health care efficiency also means rational pharmaceutical use. As the health care model evolves, USAID will put the majority of its funds into medical partnerships, women and infant care, and into the fight against HIV/AIDS and tuberculosis. Achievement of this objective will result in more efficient and sustainable delivery of quality basic health, and of communal services, such as heating, to those who cannot afford it.

Key Results: Three intermediate results have been pursued in support of this objective: (1) new approached to service delivery adopted; (2) new approaches to resource allocation and alternative financing of service delivery adopted; and (3) relevant policies, laws and regulations are drafted and submitted to the Duma.

Performance and Prospects: In view of the enormity and complexity of the social services delivery system, the precipitous decline in local resources available for social services over the past decade, and the current economic crisis, USAID's ability to significantly improve the overall health and well being of Russia's citizens is limited. Nonetheless, there have been some significant results to date.

Fourteen model family planning centers have been established in six regions and serve over three million women of reproductive age; overall abortion rates in these areas decreased by 11 percent between and 1997, almost twice the national average. Twelve partnerships between U.S. medical institutions and Russian hospitals have been established.

The Russian Medical Association is now responsible for accrediting physicians and distributed a Code of Ethics for Nurses. In three pilot regions, hospitals have developed clinical guidelines for five major illnesses, generating significant financial savings. In another pilot district the number of hospital beds has been reduced by almost half and, together with other cost saving measures, the district has saved $700,000 per year, one fourth of the entire budget for health care services.

Other discrete activities in support of the Gore-Chernomyrdin Commission Health Committee included: blood-lead screening for over 1200 children; national conferences on micronutrient malnutrition; and seminars on the early detection, prevention and control of major infectious and non-communicable diseases.

"Means tested" housing allowance programs coupled with gradual increases in rents and utilities charges have been adopted by over 90 percent of Russian communities. Housing was constructed for 4,569 returned Russian officers; this program served as the prototype for the Russian Government's efforts to house Russian officers as the military was downsized.

USAID is scaling back it's efforts for comprehensive health reform with the central government due to limited progress at that level. Russian counterparts have expressed consistent high demand for work in infectious diseases and hospital partnerships are producing good results. With high infant mortality rates, the mother and infant health care project is timely.

Possible Adjustments to Plans: USAID's priorities will be in fighting infectious diseases (AIDS and TB), women and infant health care, and medical partnerships in support of these priorities. Health finance, pharmaceutical policy, and work on discrete topics such as cardiovascular and mental health are of lower priority. USAID will continue to play an important role in supporting the U.S. - Russia bi-lateral commission in health care.

Other Donor Programs: Activities are closely coordinated with the World Bank, UNAIDS, the Soros Foundation, the British Know-How Fund and other donors. USAID normally pilot tests activities which are later embraced and expanded by other donors. The World Bank has made a $64 million loan for the health sector and is considering an additional $500 million over three years. The Soros Foundation is considering a $100 million contribution over three years. The Ministry of Health considers USAID activities to be most important and are working closely with USAID in formulating policy.

Principal Contractors, Grantees, or Agencies: American International Health Alliance, Boston University, Lutheran Hospital, LaCrosse, American Medical Association, U.S. Department of Health and Human Services, AVSC, and others.

Selected Performance Measures:

	Baseline	Target
Abortion rates in USAID-supported areas decrease more than the national average	7% (nationally)	10% (assisted areas)
Number of facilities using modern cost accounting and financial systems in pilot oblasts	0 (1994)	40 (2000)
Infectious disease protocols initiated	0 (1999)	4 (2000)

THE WORLD BANK IN RUSSIA

The Russian Federation, the largest of the Commonwealth of Independent States with an area of 17 million square kilometers, has a population of 146 million people and a 2001 GDP per capita of US$2,270[1].

In 1992, the Russian Federation embarked on the long and difficult path of transition towards a market economy. This process has resulted in a profound change in Russia's economy, even though the transition is far from complete and has often been accompanied by disappointment and setbacks. Nevertheless, recent economic developments are encouraging, the recovery from the financial crisis of 1998 may be an indication that reforms implemented prior to the crisis are beginning to bear fruit. The World Bank's role is to remain a steadfast partner of the Russian government and people in seeing that the transition process is completed and the basis for sustainable growth in the years to come is established.

After an initial period of macroeconomic instability and high inflation, the economic situation appeared to stabilize in 1997 with a substantial reduction in inflation and the first signs of positive GDP growth. However, the financial crisis of 1998 showed that these developments were not based on a sustainable foundation for economic growth. The principal reason was an unsustainable fiscal and public debt situation combined with continuing structural weakness. These fundamental problems also reflected weak implementation of fiscal and structural reforms stemming in part from insufficient involvement of legislative bodies in the design of reforms.

The macroeconomic situation in the Russian Federation deteriorated following contagion from the East Asian financial crisis, which initially spilled over in November 1997. So did the terms-of-trade, as world commodity prices fell. The consequent rise in macro instability and interest rates contributed further to the rapidly worsening fiscal situation, leading to an unsustainable accumulation of public debt with a large short-term component. The rise in real interest rates choked off growth, highlighting the Russian Federation's vulnerability to changing sentiment in the international capital markets.

During this period, the Russian Federation experienced several episodes of exchange market instability as investors sought to flee from ruble-denominated assets, including government securities, into hard currency, depleting foreign exchange reserves in the process. Following the first episode in November 1997, two others soon followed in 1998. The first occurred in late January 1998, when investor concerns focussed on Russian risk associated with the fiscal deficit and structural impediments to private sector development.

The second, and eventually decisive episode, began in mid-May, abating only temporarily with the announcement on July 13, 1998, of the US$22.6 billion dollar

International Monetary Fund (IMF), World Bank, and Japanese enhanced assistance package to support the government's anti-crisis Economic and Financial Stabilization Plan. However, the Ruble remained under sustained attack, depleting reserves and eventually triggering the August 17, 1998, meltdown.

The meltdown is traceable to three fundamental factors: (i) an inability to close the gap between public resources and spending, resulting in incomplete stabilization, unsustainable debt accumulation, and financial collapse; (ii) an inability to push forward systematically with effective implementation of structural reforms, resulting in a lack of effective restructuring in the industrial and agricultural sectors and a lack of new investment and growth; and (iii) the absence of broad-based political support for government initiatives.

All this led to disappointing economic results in 1998. Real GDP contracted by 4.9 percent, and industrial output decreased by 5.2 percent. December-on-December inflation reached 84.5 percent, compared to a target of 8 percent. The Ruble exchange rate skyrocketed to 20.65 rubles per U.S. dollar by year-end, compared to 5.96 at the beginning of the year. Real disposable income dropped 28 percent in the fourth quarter of 1998 relative to the same period of 1997, substantially increasing the number of people living below the subsistence level.

Initial expectations were that the recession would deepen in 1999, but the large real devaluation, the rise in oil prices, and the insulation from the financial sector crisis provided to the real sector by barter and other non cash settlements have led to much better short-run results than expected. Buoyed by the devaluation and a 40 percent increase in average oil export prices over 1999, real GDP grew by 3.2 percent. Likewise, fiscal performance was strong, with cash revenues of the federal budget increasing from 9 percent of GDP in 1998 to 13.4 percent in 1999. Once again, this can be explained almost entirely by the devaluation, higher oil prices, and changes in tax-sharing rules with the regions. In like vein, in spite of a sizable US$30 billion trade surplus, Central Bank reserves barely budged, indicating that exporters prefer to keep their money abroad.

Industrial production grew by over 8 percent in 1999. None of the principal industrial sectors surveyed by Goskomstat registered a decline. The industrial recovery has been broad-based, and economic growth continues in 2000. Real GDP has been estimated to grow by 8.1 percent, and industrial production by 8.5 percent in the first half of the year. The Russian stock market has been rebounding from its post-crisis level. Yet, it's still significantly below the 1997 levels

As a result of the devaluation and higher oil prices, the trade surplus was of the order of US$36 billion; but reserves grew only by US$0.2 billion during 1999, indicating that the trade surplus was largely consumed by debt service and by continuing capital flight. Reserves stood at US$12.5 billion at end-1999, of which currency reserves were US$8.5 billion, and the rest was gold.

For additional analytical, business and investment opportunities information,
please contact Global Investment & Business Center, USA
at (202) 546-2103. Fax: (202) 546-3275. E-mail: rusric@erols.com
Global Business E-Books on Line: http://world.mirhouse.com

The situation has radically changed in 2000. Primarily due to a continuing increase in export prices, the trade surplus reached US$29 billion already during the first six months of the year. With capital flight still consuming about half of export proceeds, this allowed central bank reserves to almost double during this period, reaching an unprecedented US$23 billion by end-July. With budgeted foreign debt service for 2000 of US$10.2 billion, this gives the government certain comfort at a time of limited access to new foreign borrowing. However, rapid build-up in reserves has had its price, pushing the Ruble to appreciate in real terms, and thus reducing competitiveness of domestic goods.

The increase in industrial production has noticeably affected the unemployment rate in 1999, which decreased from 13.8 percent at the beginning of the year to 11.7 percent by year-end. The unemployment rate further decreased in 2000, and had reached 11.3 percent by June. The improvement in the labor market was accompanied by a rise in real wages and personal income. The average real wage and real income per capita fell by 23 percent and 15 percent, respectively, between 1998 and 1999). In 2000, real growth in monthly wages has continued, bringing growth in household's real disposable income to 9.3 percent during the first six months of the year.

At the same time, a large share of the population of the Russian Federation still lives below the poverty line-26.3 percent at end-1999-and the social assistance provided by the government has not been sufficient and targeted to the poor. The general quality of the government's services has deteriorated since 1991, and the poor were the most affected. The government is currently working to improve targeting of social transfers. For example, potential savings from the elimination of implicit subsidies could be channeled to better finance the social safety net in the country.

Despite the generally positive economic developments, the government still faces a number of key challenges in building the foundation for sustainable growth. While in the short-run the real devaluation of the Ruble has helped engineer a rebound in economic activity, translating this into sustainable economic growth is another major challenge that requires addressing structural issues, most notably the non-payments problem. A related challenge is to improve the investment climate by increasing transparency and addressing corruption and bureaucratic red tape, while, at the same time, strengthening property rights and contract enforcement.

On December 31, 1999, the sudden resignation of Boris Yeltsin, was followed by the appointment of Vladimir Putin as acting president of the Russian Federation. Shortly thereafter, in accordance with the Russian constitution, new presidential elections were held on March 26, 2000, and Mr. Putin was elected president.

The new Russian government, formed after the major reorganization of ministries in May-June 2000, has embarked on a course of reforms unparalleled since the initial launch of reform in early 1992. Deregulation and increased transparency of the business environment; comprehensive administrative, judicial and public service reforms; hardening of budget constraints at the enterprise level; changing nature of the social welfare system-these are just a few major components of the new, ten-year government program, and the program of priority measures for 2000 and 2001. Challenges are vast, and so are the government's plans. Only time will allow to judge the actual breakthrough the government is able to achieve.

RUSSIAN FEDERATION AND THE WORLD BANK

Since the Russian Federation joined the World Bank in 1992, the Bank has approved more than US$11 billion in loans for 45 operations. As of today, 33 of these operations are under implementation, and due to some cancellations total commitments equal US$10.4 billion. Cumulative disbursements to the Russian Federation as of June 30, 2000, amounted to US$7.2 billion (US$2.5 billion for investment loans and US$4.7 billion for adjustment loans).

The Bank's assistance since 1992 initially emphasized the vital role of the emerging private sector and the importance of maintaining financial stability during the transition. The operational objectives (i.e., development of a market economy based on private sector initiative, institutional development, protection of the most vulnerable during transition) underpinning the Bank's program have not changed appreciably since 1992. During the early years, the lending program emphasized rehabilitation-particularly in energy-infrastructure and environment, and institutional development. A substantial technical assistance and training effort was also mounted to support institutional development in partnership with other donors. Because of the volatile economic, political, and administrative environment of the early-to-mid 1990's, policy reform was pursued largely through analytical work and dialogue: quick disbursing operations-apart from Rehabilitation I and II-did not feature in the Bank's program until .

Following the elections of July and the political and economic developments of the ensuing twelve months, the Bank believed that the conditions for a concerted reform effort-while far from the assured-were as favorable as could be envisaged. At the policy level, support for reforms appeared particularly strong. The Bank's fiscal[2] 1998-99 strategy took advantage of this perceived "window of opportunity" to support a comprehensive, accelerated program of structural reform. The strategy envisaged-and delivered-a substantial volume of adjustment lending in support of a comprehensive program of structural reform.

At the time of the August 1998 crisis, the World Bank had three on-going structural adjustment operations: a second Coal Sector Adjustment Loan, a Social Protection Adjustment Loan, as well as the US$1.5 billion SAL3-the Bank's largest loan to the Russian Federation-which was initially part of a US$22.6 billion lending package from the IMF, the World Bank, and the Japanese government. Following the crisis, all three operations were restructuring during 1999 and were still being implemented as of June 2000.

In December 1999, the Bank's Board of Executive Directors approved the new Country Assistance Strategy (CAS) for the Russian Federation. Overall, the planned strategy envisages a further shift in emphasis to deepen structural reform and address more directly the need for systemic reforms. In particular, the CAS: (i) increased emphasis on reform of systemic policies and institutions intended to improve the performance of the public sector, critical for public administration and for the development of an environment attractive to investors-domestic and foreign alike-and conducive to efficient private sector development; (ii) reduces emphasis on sector-and/or region-specific interventions, particularly in energy and infrastructure. In the social area, the CAS emphasizes pilot projects testing approaches to increase service delivery efficiency and crisis interventions. Regarding social protection, the Bank would focus more narrowly on more equitable distribution of the social costs of transition, with special emphasis on segments of the population that appear to be the hardest hit and most vulnerable-single parent families, pensioners, and children.

Since August 1998, only three projects have been added to the World Bank's portfolio in the Russian Federation: the State Statistical System Project (US$30 million) to enhance quality of official statistics; the Regional Fiscal Technical Assistance Project (US$30 million) to help build government institution capacity to reform inter-governmental fiscal relations and improve fiscal performance at the sub-national level; and the Sustainable Forestry Pilot Project (US$60 million) that aims at improving public sector management of the country's forests through policy reform, protecting and regenerating forested areas, and supporting the development of a more favorable environment for private investment in the sector.

The financial-economic crisis of August 1998 also affected the Bank's investment loan portfolio. Persisting difficult macroeconomic conditions, decreasing creditworthiness of regions and other project beneficiaries, and continuous changes in government, disrupted project implementation, delayed decision-making on key project issues, and led to a substantial decline in the performance of the Bank's lending portfolio in the Russian Federation. Initially, the percentage of projects rated as satisfactory declined from 74 percent in June 1998 to 33 percent by July 1999. The effects of the crisis have also made it apparent that some projects, as originally designed, could not accommodate the effects of devaluation, and that others are not sufficiently reform-oriented to be sustained. While some serious issues, such as frozen special accounts, have been successfully resolved, the pace of project implementation has significantly slowed down. In fiscal 1999, only US$359 million was disbursed for the investment portfolio, compared to US$722 million for fiscal 1998.

In July 1999 the Bank and government agreed on specific targets to be achieved for each problem project so that these projects could achieve satisfactory implementation progress, including through urgent restructuring, where needed. Achieving a significant improvement in the quality of the loan portfolio, however, required the government and the Bank to take an aggressive approach in monitoring the portfolio, following up with appropriate action.

The implementation of portfolio improve-ment measures were reviewed jointly by the government and the Bank in September 1999 and February 2000, when a progress assessment of agreed actions was made and further key actions were proposed for the Russian government's approval. The results of the Country Portfolio Performance Review (CPPR) held in February 2000 proved that the overall portfolio performance had dramatically improved with 60 percent of projects rated as satisfactory, up from 33 percent recorded by the July 1999 CPPR. Further progress was made during the remaining months of fiscal 2000 to improve the share of projects with satisfactory rating to 76 percent. The Bank and the government agreed that vigorous efforts, both by the government and the Bank, are still required to ensure improvement and sustainability of the active portfolio.

LOANS COMMITTED SINCE THE RUSSIAN FEDERATION JOINED THE WORLD BANK

...

DATE APPROVED	LOAN	AMOUNT (million US$)
August 6, 1992	Rehabilitation	600.00
November 24, 1992	Employment Services and Social Protection	70.00
December 17, 1992	Privatization Implementation Assistance	90.00
June 17, 1993	Oil Rehabilitation I	610.00
February 17, 1994	Highway Rehabilitation and Maintenance	300.00
May 19, 1994	Financial Institution Development	200.00
June 16, 1994	Land Reform Implementation	80.00
June 16, 1994	Agricultural Reform Implementation	240.00
June 21, 1994	Enterprise Support	200.00
June 29, 1994	Oil Rehabilitation II	500.00
November 8, 1994	Environment Management	110.00
December 15, 1994	Management and Financial Training	40.00
February 16, 1997	Portfolio Development	40.00
March 7, 1997	Housing	400.00
March 9, 1997	Tax Administration Modernization	16.80
April 25, 1997	Emergency Oil Spill Recovery and Mitigation	99.00
May 2, 1997	Energy Efficiency	70.00

Date	Project	Amount
May 16, 1997	Urban Transport	329.00
June 6, 1997	Second Rehabilitation	600.00
November 30, 1997	Standards Development	24.00
March 28,	Bridge Rehabilitation	350.00
April 30,	Community Social Infrastructure	200.00
May 7,	Enterprise Housing Divestiture	300.00
May 30,	Capital Markets Development	89.00
June 4,	Medical Equipment	270.00
June 13,	Legal Reform	58.00
June 27,	Coal Sector Adjustment	500.00
June 27,	Coal Sector Restructuring Implementation	25.00
March 27, 1997	St. Petersburg Center City Rehabilitation	31.00
May 29, 1997	Sea Launch Project Guarantees	100.00
June 5, 1997	Structural Adjustment	600.00
June 5, 1997	Education Innovation	71.00
June 5, 1997	Health Reform Pilot Project	66.00
June 5, 1997	Bureau of Economic Analysis	22.60
June 5, 1997	Enterprise Restructuring Services	85.00
June 5, 1997	Electricity Sector Reform Support	40.00
June 25, 1997	Social Protection Adjustment	800.00
October 7, 1997	Social Protection Implementation	28.60
December 18, 1997	Structural Adjustment II	800.00
December 18, 1997	Coal Sector Adjustment II	800.00
August 6, 1998	Structural Adjustment III	1,500.00
December 22, 1998	Second Highway Rehabilitation and Maintenance Project	400.00
May 13, 1999	State Statistical System Project	30.00
December 22, 1999	Regional Fiscal Technical Assistance Project	30.00
May 24, 2000	Sustainable Forestry Pilot Project	60.00
TOTAL	45 Projects	11,875.00*

For additional analytical, business and investment opportunities information, please contact Global Investment & Business Center, USA at (202) 546-2103. Fax: (202) 546-3275. E-mail: rusric@erols.com
Global Business E-Books on Line: http://world.mirhouse.com

...

GLOBAL ENVIRONMENTAL FACILITY (GEF) GRANTS

FISCAL YEAR (July 1 to June 30)	GRANTS	AMOUNT (million US$)
1997	Green House Gas Reduction Project	3.20
	Ozone Depleting Substances Phase-Out Project	60.00
	Biodiversity Conservation Project	20.10
TOTAL	3 Grants	83.30

* The actual net commitments total may be slightly different due to the regular portfolio reviews. The total in this table is based on the original loan amounts.

STRATEGIC INFORMATION FOR CONDUCTING BUSINESS

BASIC DATA

GEOGRAPHY AND CLIMATE

The Russian Federation has a surface area of 17 million square kilometers. It occupies the largest part of Eastern Europe and North Asia. The country extends 9,000 km from West to East and 2,500 to 4,000 km from North to South. The Russian Federation borders Norway and Finland to the North-West; Estonia, Latvia, Lithuania, Belarus, Ukraine and Poland to the West; Georgia, Azerbaijan, Kazakhstan to the South; and China, Mongolia and North Korea to the South-East. Russia's longest coastlines run along the Arctic and Pacific Oceans.

70 percent of Russia's land-mass is composed of large plains. The East European Plain stretches to the Ural Mountains - traditionally considered the eastern edge of Europe. East of the Urals lies the West Siberian Plain. Between the Yenisei and Lena rivers is the high Middle Siberian Plateau, which meets the Central Yakutian Plain to the East.

Mountains are found in Eastern and Southern Russia. The North Slope of the Big Caucasus Range is located to the South - in the European part. The range includes Elbrus - the country's highest mountain peak culminating at 5,642 m. A belt of mountain ranges stretches through Southern Siberia (the Altay, the Kuznetsky Alatau, the West Sayan, the East Sayan, the Pribaikalye, Zabaikalye, Tuva, and Stanovoy). The mountains of Kamchatka and the Kuril Islands feature active volcanoes.

Russia has about 120,000 rivers, whose total length exceeds 2.3 million km. The longest ones are the Amur (4,400 km), the Volga (3,530 km), the Yenisei (4,102 km), the Ob (5,410 km) and the Lena (4 440 km). There are about two million lakes and seas, the largest of which are Baikal, Ladoga, Onega and the Caspian Sea.

Because of its vastness and geographical location, Russia is subject to different kinds of climate: maritime, continental, monsoon, etc. North-Western Russia has a maritime climate. Siberia has a sharp continental one. The Far East has a monsoon climate. Most of the country, however, enjoys a moderate continental climate, with cold winters and rather warm summers. The average temperature in January ranges from zero to minus five degrees C in the West and around the Caucasus, to -40 to -50 degrees C in Yakutia. Snow covers the land for 60 to 80 days in the South and 260 to 280 days in the far North. The average temperature in July is 24 to 25 degrees C near the Caspian lowland and one degree C in northern Siberia. Precipitation in the West comes primarily from the Atlantic Ocean. The Pacific Ocean is the primary irrigation "device" in the Far

For additional analytical, business and investment opportunities information,
please contact Global Investment & Business Center, USA
at (202) 546-2103. Fax: (202) 546-3275. E-mail: rusric@erols.com
Global Business E-Books on Line: http://world.mirhouse.com

East. Precipitation ranges from 100 mm a year in semi-desert areas near the Caspian Sea to 2,000 mm in the Caucasus and Altai Mountains.

ADMINISTRATIVE STRUCTURE OF RUSSIA

When the Russian Federation emerged as a sovereign country at the end of 1991, its former unitary structure was replaced by a loose federation of 89 *federation subjects.* These are composed of twenty-one republics, six *krays (territories)* , forty-nine *oblasts,* one autonomous oblast, ten autonomous (ethnic) *okrugs,* and two federal cities (Moscow and St. Petersburg). As far as their relations with the federal government are concerned, all of these jurisdictions have, *equal political* status - since the adoption of the new constitution in 1993. In practice however, these relations are governed by bilateral arrangements where the degree of autonomy, particularly for the republics, can be considerable. All Russian jurisdictions unofficially united into 11 economic regions.[2]

REPUBLICS

Regardless of their various sizes and population, Russia's 21 republics are the most politically developed and active jurisdictions of the Federation. The boundaries of Russia's republics were drawn in the 1920s to give political recognition to important ethnic groups. Their governmental structures is composed of a parliament - called either the Supreme Soviet, the Duma or the Council of Representatives - which represents both the legislative and executive branches. According to the Constitution, the parliaments of these republics have the right to adopt their own economic regulations even if they differ from federal ones (see below). Taking advantage of these legislative powers, the representative bodies in the republics have adopted more than 10,000 local laws and resolutions since 1993.

OBLASTS

Oblasts have primarily been administrative subdivisions of Russia with little power of their own. Meanwhile, since the new constitution gives them equal status with the other jurisdictions, they have become increasingly more important both politically and economically. Since the 1994 local elections, each oblast government acquired both a Council of Representatives and an Executive Administration with elected and appointed officials. These legislators will have a dominating role in local political and economic development and play a part in policy-making at the federal level.

KRAYS (TERRITORIES)

Krays were unique administrative entities, a combination of republic and *oblast,* whose boundaries were drawn primarily for administrative purposes. Political subdivisions - autonomous *oblasts* or *okrugs* - was their distinguishing feature. Under the new Constitution, the distinction between *kray* and *oblast* should gradually disappear.

---

[2] The description of each economic region is provided in the Supllement 6

For additional analytical, business and investment opportunities information,
please contact Global Investment & Business Center, USA
at (202) 546-2103. Fax: (202) 546-3275. E-mail: rusric@erols.com
Global Business E-Books on Line: http://world.mirhouse.com

AUTONOMOUS OBLASTS AND OKRUGS (ETHNIC DISTRICTS)

Autonomous oblasts *and okrugs* were created to give political recognition to relatively small ethnic groups. They are sparsely populated regions located in Siberia, the Far East and the northern regions of Russia. Because of their small populations, the role of autonomous *oblasts and okrugs* at the federal level has been limited. Under the new Constitution, however, their importance will gradually increase as officials from these jurisdictions obtain more independence from the federal government in solving their economic problems - especially when it comes to the exploitation of mineral and other natural resources concentrated in their territories.

LOCAL GOVERNMENTS

Republics, *oblasts, krays and okrugs* are divided into *rayons* - which can be compared to counties in the United States. Each of the 1,857 *rayons* in Russia has an administrative center, a local council of representatives, and an executive administration, consisting of appointed officials. Small cities and settlements are under the jurisdiction of *rayons.*

RELATIONS BETWEEN FEDERAL AND LOCAL GOVERNMENTS

The basic framework of federal-regional relations was initially defined in the Federation Treaty of 1992. The existing division of power determined by the Treaty allows regions of the Russian Federation to "form and pursue their own policy." The relative confusion reigning in Russia over the division of decision making authority among each level of government allows for the vagueness of this statement. It was, nevertheless, indispensable to be agreed upon by all regions and added to the Federation Treaty.

The new Constitution adopted in 1993 defined more broadly than the Federation Treaty the division of authority between the Federation and its subjects. (The provisions in the Federation Treaty remain valid as long as they do not contradict the Constitution.) According to the Constitution, all 89 regional jurisdictions are equal when it comes to their relations with the federal government. In reality, these relations are governed by bilateral arrangements between the federal authorities and the regional governments.

The degree of autonomy stated in the constitutions of the different Russian republics varies significantly. The Chechen Autonomous Republic claimed the greatest degree of autonomy of any region in Russia. Its proclaimed independence from the Russian Federation led to an armed rebellion against the central authority. Other republics, such as Komi and Tartarstan, enjoy a large degree of autonomy but do not claim to be sovereign states.

Following the adoption of the Constitution, some jurisdictions managed to bargain for special rights and had some degree of success. From 1992 to 1994, 18 presidential decrees and four resolutions of the federal government granted special rights and powers to 14 republics and three *oblasts* (Murmansk, Kamchatka and Tula). In most cases, these decrees and resolutions pertain to regional jurisdiction over specific export quotas and licenses. In a few cases, however, special property rights pertaining to natural resources were granted to autonomous republics. These include the Buryatia, Komi and Tuva Republics.

The "Unity of Economic Space" is guaranteed by the 1993 Constitution. Articles 8 and 27 allow for the free movement of goods, capital and labor. Article 74 explicitly prohibits any regional barriers preventing the free flows of goods, services and financial resources. Exemptions may only be introduced by specific federal legislation. Although a common economic space was created by the Constitution, many provinces adopted laws and administrative measures creating trade barriers. Some local administrations prohibit the exports of certain goods from their territories. The City of Moscow, for instance, required residence permits to be obtained. Similar measures are being considered by other *oblasts* such as Voronezh and Yaroslavl. It is interesting to note that regional laws and decrees violating free movement as stated in the Constitution are usually poorly enforced.

REGIONAL LEGISLATION AFFECTING FOREIGN INVESTMENT

The regions are in the process of developing their own legislative systems. Using the right to introduce their own economic legislation, a number of jurisdictions have been adopting laws and regulations that should improve both the commercial environment in the region and attract direct foreign investment. The most common features of such regional legislation are discussed below.

PROPERTY LAWS AND REGULATIONS

Private property has been affected by a number of legislation adopted by some of the regions - notably the autonomous republics. These legislation declare, in most cases, that state entities and resources on a given territory belong to the republican authorities. Other republics have stipulated that state property ought to be divided between federal and regional jurisdictions and be subjected to negotiation among the governmental bodies. Some republics have adopted privatization laws that reflect similar federal legislation but differ at the technical or procedural level.

Property in the *Oblasts* and *okrugs* is being regulated by legislation adopted by the jurisdictions. In general, these jurisdictions do not have as much legislative power over property as the republics. A notable exception is, however, the City of Moscow. According to a special presidential decree, Moscow is authorized to adopt its own program in the second "non-voucher" stage of privatization.

PRIVATIZATION

Federal legislation on privatization does not clearly establish minority rights. The main points of dispute are usually related to the extent of effective control an investor

For additional analytical, business and investment opportunities information,
please contact Global Investment & Business Center, USA
at (202) 546-2103. Fax: (202) 546-3275. E-mail: rusric@erols.com
Global Business E-Books on Line: http://world.mirhouse.com

may actually have over an enterprise. The local authorities responsible for privatization - i.e., the Administration on Privatization and the State Property Committee (GKI- make the decisions on key terms of investment tenders.

Local authorities, if so inclined, can take a number of measures to make foreign investment more difficult. Excessive delays on decision making about minor matters could be one example of the kind of mild measures that could be taken. Extreme measures could involve the **Federal Counter-Intelligence Service** - responsible for checking the authenticity of the information supplied by an investor. Disputes involving a foreign investor's right to own particular shares can be taken to local courts. Local courts, however, are subordinated to the local administration. The key to ensuring a good relationship between a foreign investor and the local authorities is to make wise choices in the selection of local partners.

TAXATION

There are three different levels of taxation in Russia: local, regional and federal. Revenues from each level go to the treasury of that particular government. The Tax Service and Tax Police are federal organizations with local branches. Even though the local and regional offices are officially not subordinate to federal authorities, they are under considerable pressure from those jurisdictions. Taxes are collected locally and then allotted proportionally - the result of a lot of bargaining. Republics are able to withhold tax revenues more easily than provinces due to the regional branches of the Central Bank of Russia - unlike their counterparts in *krays* and *oblasts* which are subordinate to both the government of the republic and the federal authorities.

Taxation is supervised by the local tax inspection and by the local tax police. Depending on the attitude they have toward a given investment, local authorities may either increase or weaken the pressures exerted by the local tax police. It should be noted, however, that depending on the stand taken by the local authorities in each case, the various provisions regarding taxation may be interpreted differently.

According to the Constitution of the Russian Federation, the establishment of tax legislation and regulations and its collection is in the mutual competence of the Federation and its subjects. Taxation laws and regulations were among the first regional laws adopted after the establishment of the new legislative bodies in 1994.

BANKING AND SECURITIES MARKETS

A number of republics - such as the republics of Bashkortostan and Sakha and the city of Moscow - have adopted a number of regulations regarding banks and banking services. These regulations are generally similar to federal legislation.

Regional and local governments have started to issue their own municipal and regional government securities. These are generally traded at the local level, but some are traded throughout Russia. Cities and *oblasts* which have issued bonds include

Moscow, St. Petersburg, Nizhniy Novgorod, and Yaroslavl. These securities are usually backed by real estate owned by the issuer. Money received from the sale of these securities has often been invested in large housing and infrastructure projects. In some cases, bonds are paid back in kind - e.g., housing facilities.

RUSSIAN POLITICAL STRUCTURE: LEGISLATIVE, EXECUTIVE AND JUDICIAL SYSTEMS[3]

FEDERAL LEGISLATIVE INSTITUTIONS

Russia is a federal state with a republican form of government. A new constitution was adopted in a national vote on December 12, 1993. The legislative branch of government established by the Constitution is composed of: a lower house - State Duma - composed of 450 deputies elected on a territorial basis; and, a upper house - Federation Council - with 178 deputies - two from each of Russia's 89 jurisdictions (see below). The electoral system is the direct universal suffrage. Every Russian over the age of 18 has the right to vote. Two-thirds of the State Duma candidates are in a simple majority contest with the other one-third elected from party lists (requiring at least 5 percent of the total vote). The Federation Council is elected directly. The last elections were held on December 17, 1997.

THE PRESIDENCY

The President of Russia, currently Boris Yeltsin, was elected to a five-year term in June 1991. The next elections are scheduled for June . The new Constitution gives the President considerable power. The President's main function is to establish and maintain the political, legislative and economic stability of the country as a whole. The President and his staff are responsible for the overall functioning of the executive branch. Under the Constitution, the chief executive has the right to issue Decrees that will affect the economic life of the country. The president chairs the Security Council - an entity responsible for the preservation of state security, political stability, and the defense of the basic human rights and liberties of Russia's citizens.

The President's administration is composed of political, military and economic counselors and their staffs, advisory committees, and numerous functional departments. They are responsible for the development and the implementation of a general political and economic strategy.

FEDERAL EXECUTIVE GOVERNMENT

The federal government of the Russian Federation is composed of the Federal Executive Government (formerly the Council of Ministers), the Ministries, the State Committees, and other government agencies. The Government is appointed by

[3] For obtaining detailed information on the Russian government, please acquire our Russian Government Encyclopedic directories. For details, please contact Russian Info&Business Center, Inc. or visit our Russian Database on Line at http://www.rusline.com

the Prime Minister, currently Mr. **Victor Chernomyrdin,** and was formed in December 1992. Major cabinet reshuffles took place in November 1994 and January .

The prime minister, or the chairman of the Federal Executive Government, is nominated by the president. The nominee may take office only after being approved by Parliament. Nevertheless, he may carry out his duties as an acting prime minister for a certain period of time before his confirmation by the legislative body. If Parliament refuses to approve the nominee or demands the resignation of the cabinet, the president may dissolve the Parliament and call for new elections. The prime minister currently has three first deputy prime ministers and five deputy prime ministers appointed by him in agreement with Parliament and the President. The prime minister has a large staff - called the Executive Administration of the Prime Minister - which is responsible for the development and implementation of economic reforms. The functional departments of the administration are responsible for different sectors of the economy. These officials are in charge of creating and administrating programs for each industry.

FEDERAL EXECUTIVE GOVERNMENT: MINISTRIES, STATE COMMITTEES AND AGENCIES

According to the new governmental structure which was approved by the president in January 1994, the executive branch of the Russian federal government comprises 23 ministries, 10 state committees, 15 federal committees, and more than 24 various federal agencies, commissions, and other bodies. Officials of these bodies are nominated by the president or chairman but must be approved by Parliament. Each of these bodies is responsible for regulating certain fields of industrial or economic activity. Ministries, State Committees, and Agencies continue to participate in the running of the remaining state-owned enterprises.

Federal ministries and state agencies can be divided into four groups. The first group includes traditional government ministries such as the Ministries of Finance, Justice, Defense and Education. The second group consists of ministries and state agencies responsible for managing and administrating different branches of the economy. For instance, the Ministry of Fuel and Energy manages and controls this industry as a whole; the Ministry of Transportation administers the development of state transportation systems; and the Committee of Land Reform manages the privatization of land. The third group is composed of state committees, which have the same status as ministries - their top officials are ministers. Compared to ministries, state committees have a broader purview and are responsible for the development and implementation of multi-sector programs approved by the president. The fourth group consists of all the other federal committees, agencies and bodies that are charged with specific functions such as geological research, support for the Olympic Games, professional training of state officials, and statistics.

For additional analytical, business and investment opportunities information, please contact Global Investment & Business Center, USA at (202) 546-2103. Fax: (202) 546-3275. E-mail: rusric@erols.com Global Business E-Books on Line: http://world.mirhouse.com

LOCAL GOVERNMENTS

When the Russian Federation emerged as a sovereign country at the end of 1991, its former unitary structure was replaced by a loose federation of 89 *federation subjects.* These consist of twenty-one republics, six *krays,* forty-nine *oblasts, one* autonomous oblast, ten autonomous *okrugs,* and two federal cities - Moscow and St. Petersburg[4].

All federation subjects, or jurisdictions, have their own government, with a legislature and an executive branch. The legislature consists of an elected body headed by a chairman that drafts and adopts local laws and regulations. All *oblasts, okrugs, rayons,* cities, and towns have a local executive body of elected and appointed officials headed by a governor. The local legislature or governor may appoint officials. The administration is responsible for all matters related to the economic development of the locality. The situation is approximately the same in the republics. However, they are governed by an elected President. The executive branch of a republic is usually made up of a council of ministers, ministries, and agencies.

All federation subjects have a specially appointed Presidential Representative, located in the region, and an official representatives under the Administration of the President, located in Moscow. The Presidential Representatives can be powerful and important regional officials, given that they are personally responsible for implementing presidential programs - most often political and economic reforms - in their jurisdictions.

THE JUDICIAL SYSTEM

The judicial branch has two levels, federal and local. The Constitutional Court, the Supreme Court and the Supreme Arbitration Court are part of the federal level. The Constitutional Court implements the Constitution in political, economic and civil matters and ensures that all political parties as well as the highest legislative and executive bodies in the country abide by the Constitution. The Supreme Court is the highest court in Russia and provides legal guarantees and protects the legal rights of Russian citizens. The Supreme Arbitration Court holds economic and business proceedings.

Judges serving in federal courts are nominated by the president and approved by the Federation Council (upper house of Parliament). Judges to the Constitutional Court serve for life, while judges of the Supreme Court and Supreme Arbitration Court serve for ten years.

At the local level, each jurisdiction - republic, kray, oblast, etc. - has its own criminal court. Citizens may appeal decisions to a higher court. Local judges are elected for five years and can be re-elected.

---

[4] For obtaining detailed information on the Russian geography, political and economic structure, please acquire our Russian Regional Explorer, CD-ROM or Russian Regional Economic & Business Atlas. For Additional information please contact Russian Info&Business Center, Inc. at (202) 546-2103

For additional analytical, business and investment opportunities information,
please contact Global Investment & Business Center, USA
at (202) 546-2103. Fax: (202) 546-3275. E-mail: rusric@erols.com
Global Business E-Books on Line: http://world.mirhouse.com

Current reform of the judicial system makes the activities of the Supreme Court very complicated. The judicial branch in Russia will be considerably changed in the near future as criminal and commercial legislation are modernized.

RUSSIA: DEMOGRAPHY AND POPULATION

The population of Russia is 148 million - 73 percent of which live in urban areas. The average population density is 8.7 inhabitants per square kilometer (sq.km), well below the European average of 67 (sq.km),. More than four-fifths of the population are concentrated in the European part of Russia. The population has declined in recent years. The number of inhabitants decreased by 124,000, following a decline of 300,000 in 1993. The reductions are due to both socio-economic conditions and peculiarities in the current demographic pattern. In 1994, the number of births per 1000 increased slightly from 9.2 in 1993 to 9.4. The number of deaths also increased. The figures went from 14.6 per 1000 in 1993 to 15.6 in 1994. Thus, the number of deaths exceeded births by a factor of 1.7. This trend is being partly, but not fully, offset by immigration, which totaled 796,000 in 1993. Twelve Russian cities have more than one million inhabitants. The largest are Moscow (8.9 million), St. Petersburg (4.9 million), and Nizhny Novgorod, Novosibirsk, and Yekaterinburg, each with approximately 1.4 million people. Life expectancy in Russia was 64 years in 1994. Russia experiences a huge difference in the life expectancy of its male and female population - a difference that is very unusual for a developed country. According to 1994 statistics, male were expected to live, on average, 59 years, while female were expected to reach 72 years.

ETHNIC COMPOSITION AND LANGUAGES

Russia has more than 100 nationalities or ethnic groups. Ethnic Russians comprise 81.5 percent of the total population, according to the 1989 census. Ethnic Russians are usually the largest ethnic group, even in national areas and autonomous regions. Tatars are a distant second with 3.8 percent of the population. The Tatars mainly live in Tatarstan, but large groups also reside in Bashkortostan, Siberia, and the Far East. Ukrainians make up three percent of the population - the largest groups are located in the areas adjoining Ukraine, in the North Caucasus, and in the southern regions of the Urals and Siberia. The Chuvash are the fourth most populous ethnic group in Russia with 1.2 percent. Beside the Chuvash Republic, Chuvash live in small groups in the Urals, Siberia, and the Far East.

With Russians, Ukrainians, Ossets, Carachaevs, Balkars, Kalmyks, Nogaits, Kabardians, Adygeits, Cirkassians, Abkhazians, Chechens, Ingushs, Avars, Dargians, Lesghins and Lucks, the North Caucasus is the most heterogeneous region of Russia. The comparatively small native populations living in Siberia and the Far East - the Yakuts, Dolgans, Khakas, Tuvinians, Nenets, Evenks, etc. - spread out over vast distances, in territories often exceeding the size of large European states. Russian, an

For additional analytical, business and investment opportunities information, please contact Global Investment & Business Center, USA at (202) 546-2103. Fax: (202) 546-3275. E-mail: rusric@erols.com Global Business E-Books on Line: http://world.mirhouse.com

East Slavonic language, has become the common language of the country's various ethnic groups. Languages of the Finno-Ugrian, Turkish, Mongolian, Iranian, Tungus-Manchurian and Chuckchee-Kamchatka groups are also spoken in Russia.

EDUCATION SYSTEM

Primary, secondary, and higher education, as well as a system of professional advancement and refresher courses are widespread in Russia. The most formal education takes place within the state sector and is free of charge. In 1993, more than 35 million people, or 23.6 percent of the population, were enrolled in all levels of education. More than two million people worked while pursuing their studies.

During the 1994-1997 academic year, 21.1 million students attended classes at 68, 200 full-time primary and secondary state schools. Russia has 822 gymnasiums and 505 private schools - which can both be classified as advanced secondary institutions. They totaled 659, 000 and 345,000 students, respectively.

There are 553 institutions of higher learning in Russia, including 52 universities, and 2,591 professional secondary schools. In 1994 these advanced education facilities taught 4.4 million students and graduated 938,000.

A system of private education is emerging in Russia. In the 1994 -1997 academic year, a total of 39,500 students attended 447 primary and secondary private schools. There were at that time also 157 private high schools being the learning centers to 110,600 students.

EMPLOYMENT: LOCAL SPECIFICS

Traditional enterprises in Russia function as collectives, thus differing in a fundamental way from their western counterparts. Collectives are an organizational form of business activity unique to Russia and rooted in centuries of cultural tradition - which can be traced back to the medieval village of the ninth century. Collectives are closely-knit work groups bound together by shared values and mutual support. The "corporate behavior" in post-communist Russia can be explained by comparing Russian enterprises to collectives.

Each employee of an enterprise, regardless of his position - is considered a member of the worker's collective and is treated equally. Because of this, workers want to be able to be part of the decision-making process of an enterprise. Collectives, in the face of persistent shortages of goods and services, have traditionally been expected to be concerned about the well-being of their employees. These values remain especially strong today in hundreds of medium-sized towns all over Russia where the economic life depends on the survival of only one or two local enterprises.

For additional analytical, business and investment opportunities information,
please contact Global Investment & Business Center, USA
at (202) 546-2103. Fax: (202) 546-3275. E-mail: rusric@erols.com
Global Business E-Books on Line: http://world.mirhouse.com

Workers in enterprises continue to consider their managers as benefactors, rather than their union leaders. This support gives the senior management political leverage with the regional and federal government. It also accounts for their ability to lobby successfully for the survival of their enterprises by securing "soft" credits.

In spite of adverse job conditions affecting most enterprises, workers still consider the prospect of losing their jobs as a dramatic event. Thus, the preservation of these jobs remains one of the top priorities of traditional Russian managers. The resilience of collectivism in Russian enterprises is exemplified in the low unemployment figure of today's Russia. These values will be put to the test as competitive market forces emerge in the Russian economy. Managers will have to choose between the interest of the members of the worker's collective and the need for reducing costs, which may require the elimination of jobs.

The preservation of collectives was also evident in the voucher privatization program. Managers and workers were granted preferential term, under Option 2, which allowed them to secure a majority ownership in their enterprise.

In conclusion, collectivism in Russian enterprises is a consideration that foreign investors should factor into their decision-making and planning. If ignored it could act as a potent obstacle, but when acknowledged it should facilitate the implementation of investment.

For additional analytical, business and investment opportunities information,
please contact Global Investment & Business Center, USA
at (202) 546-2103. Fax: (202) 546-3275. E-mail: rusric@erols.com
Global Business E-Books on Line: http://world.mirhouse.com

RUSSIAN ECONOMY IN TRANSITION (TRENDS & RESULTS)

Since the break-up of the Soviet Union, the Russian economy has been changing rapidly. The intention of the Russian government to move toward a stable economic system has rarely been in doubt. On the other hand, the ability of the authorities to bring this about has not always been clear.

MAJOR TRENDS

The Russian economy is increasingly producing good news: strong GDP growth, burgeoning foreign exchange reserves and trade surpluses. Inflation is moderate by earlier standards, the currency is stable, reform of the tax code is well advanced and beginning to show early positive results, and the regulatory framework is improving. The effects of the 1998 crisis are fading and there are signs of a sustained recovery, including in the regions. Each economic success enhances the standing and confidence of President Putin's team, and paves the way for further reform.

By mid 2001 Russia showed strong signs of continuing its economic growth for the third consecutive year. GDP for 2000 was around USD 251 billion, and official estimates cite GDP growth of 3-4 percent for 2001. Although down from 2000's 8.3 percent surge, a 3 or 4 percent growth rate appears to be sustainable through 2002. These rates compare favorably with negative growth rates experienced throughout most of the 1990's. While high oil prices have played a significant role, the broader economy is accounting for an increasing part of GDP growth. Industrial output increased by a healthy 9 percent in 2000, up from 8.1 percent growth in 1999. However, current GDP per capita is just USD 1,707 well below the potential of a country which boasts a highly educated population and abundant natural resources.

Policy makers are keenly aware of the risks on the horizon, most notably inflation. By mid 2001, inflation was running at 23.7% year-on-year, well above the government's target rate of 14% for 2001, and continuing to erode the competitiveness of the ruble. The large devaluation of the ruble in 1998, had enhanced the competitiveness of Russian manufacturers, despite the relatively low level of operational efficiency of many.

Rough estimates put the total of cumulative foreign investment in Russia at a mere USD 32 billion. The United States remains the largest foreign investor in Russia, followed closely by Germany. However, America's investments amount to around USD 7 billion dollars, about the same as its investments in Costa Rica. Still, there are hopeful signs for improvement. Many of those U.S. firms with a long-term presence in Russia, are beginning to report healthy returns, and are planning to expand operations. In the first half of 2001, relatively large direct investments were announced by major U.S. corporations, such as General Motors and Ford. The flow of investment funds from

Cyprus has grown dramatically, and Cyprus is now the fourth largest investor in terms of accumulated investment. In the first half of 2001, Cyprus was the leading source of investment flows. Since these are considered by experts to be largely Russian offshore capital returning home, this might demonstrate a growing confidence on the part of some Russians in their country's improving investment climate. Most investment remaind direct investment. Foreign portfolio investment has been miniscule since 1998, but there are preliminary signs of renewed interest among portfolio investors.

The GoR's credit rating improved in July 2001, to the modest level it had enjoyed prior to the 1998 crisis. Standard & Poor's upgraded Russia's long-term sovereign debt from "B-" to "B", and short-term debt from "C" to "B." S&P based its decision on Russia's "high rate of economic growth." Nonetheless, the Russian government's limits on sovereign guarantees, and the weakness of local banking institutions have restricted lending by the U.S. Export Import Bank.

The weakness of Russia's banking sector continues severely to constrain business development, particularly for small to medium sized firms. There is a lingering distrust of banks by potential small depositors, and an apparent lack of both interest and expertise in the banking community for the provision of small loans. The difficulty and cost of loan financing from Russian banks is an almost universal complaint.

Growth in consumer purchasing power is accelerating, following a drop of 30% in personal incomes in the aftermath of the 1998 crisis. The use of barter, once estimated to account for 70-80 percent of transactions in Russia, appears to have declined significantly, as liquidity returns to the system.

TRADE

Russia's trade turnover increased by 33 percent in 2000, led by a 25 percent increase in her exports. This growth in 2000 interrupts declines in both exports and imports for 1999 and 1998. The value of Russian exports in 2000 was, at USD 103 billion (per the State Customs Committee), the highest level achieved since the early 1990s, while the level of imports (USD 33.8 bn.) remained lower than for each year from 1995 to 1998. Trade between Russia and the European Union totaled 58 billion euros in 2000, soaring 42.5 percent compared to 1999. Russian exports to the EU increased by 58.3 percent, while imports increased by only 14.9 percent. Oil, fuel and gas accounted for 54 percent of Russia's exports, followed by iron and steel, aluminum, precious metals and stones, and machinery/equipment. Russia's leading import was of machinery, followed by electrical equipment, inorganic chemicals and pharmaceuticals.

On balance, the 2001-2002 period could renew the intensity of U.S. business interest in Russia. In the wake of the economic crisis, U.S. exports fell by about half to $1.85 billion in 1999, but there have been signs of moderate recovery with U.S, exports increasing by 25 percent in 2000. However, Russia still only plays a very small role in overall U.S. trade—around one percent of our combined imports and exports.

For additional analytical, business and investment opportunities information, please contact Global Investment & Business Center, USA at (202) 546-2103. Fax: (202) 546-3275. E-mail: rusric@erols.com Global Business E-Books on Line: http://world.mirhouse.com

PRINCIPAL GROWTH SECTORS

The oil and gas industry is expected to remain the leading sector both in size of market and potential growth not simply because of continuing high oil prices but also because of new sources of financing, slowly advancing Western investment projects and evolving pipeline projects. Telecommunications is the next strongest sales and investment prospect, as Russia shows a strong demand for modernized communications infrastructure, and the industry is opening up through privatization, intensified competition and entry of foreign investors. There is a large pent-up demand from consumers for computers and related technology. However, the low levels of disposable income, means that American computer hardware will be limited primarily to corporate customers for some time. Should incomes continue to rise, demand for a whole range of consumer products can be expected to increase exponentially, although competition from European and domestic sources will be steep.

There are likely to be substantial sales in such areas as a mining and construction equipment, automotive equipment, aircraft, and agricultural and food processing equipment—areas affected by the difficulty of financing for Russia from export credit agencies and, in some cases, government regulatory barriers.

Given reform and moderate growth, Russia has the potential to become a major market for U.S. industrial equipment and engineering services which are vitally needed to upgrade its industry and agriculture. In the near term, industries such as aluminum, steel, transportation equipment, food processing and forestry products seem to have sufficient cash flow and organization to be potential prospects for trade or investment. In the longer term, there should be great demand in such sectors as electric power and agricultural equipment for U.S. products and services.

An interesting recent trend has been the growth of the offshore services sector. Much of Russia's existing large pool of scientific and engineering talent remains underutilized. Some foreign investors are beginning to harness these inexpensive human resources by opening in Russia such enterprises as engineering design bureaus and offshore software development shops. Projects of this type are proving to be particularly successful, and are embraced Russian authorities, worried by a brain drain of Russia's best talent overseas.

Russia could potentially be a major market for agricultural equipment and food processing technology, especially when such issues as land reform are resolved. In the short term, there is demand for food products including poultry, frozen and processed red meats primarily for further processing, fresh fruit (apples), fish and sea-food items, and pet foods. It is also expected that, with promotion built upon the recent U.S. food aid program in Russia, the following bulk and intermediate agricultural products have good export potential: wheat, wheat flour, soybeans, soybean meal and cake, animal feed corn, and planting seeds.

For additional analytical, business and investment opportunities information, please contact Global Investment & Business Center, USA at (202) 546-2103. Fax: (202) 546-3275. E-mail: rusric@erols.com Global Business E-Books on Line: http://world.mirhouse.com

U.S. PRESENCE AND THIRD-COUNTRY COMPETITION

Many U.S. companies already active in the Russian market are planning expansions. However, fewer new U.S. companies are exploring the Russia market and the level of U.S. participation in major trade shows is relatively low. In contrast, European companies, appear to be aggressively marketing their goods in Russia, establishing distribution channels, and taking over market share as Russian demand rebounds. Of these, German and Italian companies continued to build upon strong ties with Russia, which date back many years, aided by the fact that Germany is Russia's best market for gas exports, and Italy for her oil exports.

Western European firms are active throughout Russia in most industrial sectors and are particularly strong in consumer goods. In the Far East, Urals and Siberia, Asian firms are marketing aggressively, notably in autos and lower-cost consumer goods. In the northwest, Scandinavian and Finnish firms are prevalent in infrastructure development. Turkish firms are strong in the construction industry in many areas and are increasingly successful in retailing. Russian firms offer low-cost competition in most sectors, helped by the ruble's depreciation in 1998-1999.

THE GOVERNMENT'S ROLE IN THE ECONOMY

BUDGET

Russia is running a surplus estimated at 280 billion rubles ($9.6 billion) on its 2001 budget of 1.93 trillion rubles (USD 40 billion). Russia's oil producers are major sources of tax revenues, and high world oil prices have permitted these firms to make windfall profits and consequently pay higher taxes. Current estimates are that the budget will grow to USD 49.7 billion in 2002, and USD 54.86 billion in 2003. Russia is living within her means, with no deficit spending in 2000 and 2001.

Approximately USD 14 billion, or 35 percent of the 2001 budget, is allocated to service Russia's USD 144 billion in foreign debt. This includes USD 48 billion in Paris Club debt. Russia had originally hoped for a postponement of some part of its Paris Club debt service obligation of $3.8 billion in 2001, but the country's healthy budget surpluses caused creditors to reject the bid. The budget was consequently amended so that the first 41 billion rubles in surplus will go to make foreign debt repayments, with the excess split 50-50 between debt service and other spending.

REFORM

The reform process is very much a work in progress, and hopes for an acceleration of the process under the Putin administration have been partially realized. After a successful drive to push through tax reform, efforts are now focused on reforming the three big "natural monopolies," which dominate the Russian economy—the railroad system, the giant gas utility Gazprom, and national electric utility Unified Energy Systems.

Real reform of the natural monopolies should remove many artificial cost distortions in the economy, such as uneconomically-low domestic energy prices, and make these industries better able to finance the large-scale equipment purchase needed for their renovation. In August 2001, President Putin approved the creation of a Unified Tariff Agency using the structure of the Federal Energy Commission as a model, to set tariffs on electricity, railroads and oil. The tariff issue is sensitive, as many poor Russians have come to rely on subsidized energy.

TAX REFORM

Russia is deeply involved in creating a tax system which is comparable with those of advanced, market economies, and in bringing some relief from levels of taxation which throw out of balance the government's needs for revenue and businesses' needs to grow. The reform process is both well advanced and sweeping in its scope, impacting government funding at all levels. Significantly, the driving force behind tax reform now comes from within the government and from Russian entrepreneurs, rather than from the international financial community and foreign consultants. Much of the progress is due to the determination and pragmatism of the Putin Administration, and to the constructive engagement of the Duma.

In view of the enormity of the task, and in recognition of the on-going and sometimes heated debate in the legislature, the new Tax Code has been adopted in stages. Part One of the Tax Code, implemented in 1999 dealt largely with administrative issues. Part Two, which came into effect in January 2001, covered Value Added Tax, Excise Duties, and Personal Income Tax, among others. Personal Income Tax was reduced from rates as high as 30 percent to a flat rate of 13 percent, in a bold move designed to improve compliance and thus tax revenues. With personal income tax collections in the first half of 2001 exceeding expectations, the strategy appears to be successful. Similar success is hoped for in the all-important Profits Tax Bill, passed in July 2001, which reduces tax on corporate profits from 35% to 24%, one of the lowest rates in Europe.

With the bulk of tax reform legislation now passed into law, and as the uncertainties become resolved, attention is focusing on implementation. Much work still lies ahead in gearing up the tax authorities, and the accounting profession to operate within the new legal structure.

Reform of the 'Natural Monopolies:
The process of reform of the 'natural monopolies' – electrical power generation and distribution, gas extraction and distribution, and rail transportation – moved forward in May 2001. The GOR approved plans to restructure the electricity monopoly, Unified Energy Systems (UES), and the Railway Ministry. In the same month the long-time Chairman of Gazprom, the gas monopoly, was replaced with a man viewed as more

open to reform, who has moved quickly to open the company's finances to closer outside scrutiny. While UES and Gazprom are privatized, the GOR is a major shareholder in each.

Together these natural monopolies account for around 13% of Russia's GDP. However, they play a much larger role in the economy in terms of price setting and overall asset allocation. They have traditionally delivered energy and transportation to Russian businesses and consumers at uneconomically low prices, which has distorted the economic landscape. Implementation of the reform plans in the natural monopolies, and the end of unrealistically cheap energy and transportation, should act as a catalyst for widespread enterprise restructuring throughout Russia, and increase the country's long-term growth potential.

Under the electricity and railway restructuring plans, the government will retain control of these unified infrastructure networks, while creating competition by opening access to them on an equal basis to competitors (independent rail operators or electricity generators) in return for an access fee.

JUDICIAL REFORM

While the trend towards a more independent, transparent and impartial judicial system is generally positive, it cannot be taken for granted that several regional or local courts will deliver judgements free from financial or political persuasion. President Putin, whose package of judicial reform proposals is working its way through the government, has repeatedly stressed that enforcement of the rule of law is a high priority of his administration, and at the federal level the record is good. It may still be some time, however, before some regional and local courts fall into line with Putin's desired "dictatorship of the law."

LABOR CODE REFORM

In a significant step forward in reforming Russia's Soviet-era Labor Code, the Duma approved the first reading of a new compromise Labor Code, after heated debate, in July 2001. The current Labor Code, enacted in 1971, is clearly inappropriate for a market economy and an evolving pattern of labor relations. The draft new Labor Code appears to establish greater flexibility in defining labor relations while retaining some basic guarantees for workers. If enacted, it would give private employers the right to fire employees without prior approval of trade unions, and would limit trade union participation in collective bargaining negotiations to those unions representing at least 51 percent of the employees at an enterprise. The draft Code would also establish a minimum monthly wage at the official subsistence level – currently RUR 1,400 ($48) per month, would retain the 40-hour working week with special provisions for overtime work, and would allow for the payment of wages in-kind. However, the draft Code is a highly contentious issue, and many modifications can be expected before it passes its final reading in the Duma.

PENSION REFORM

Russia's current state pension system, created in the early 1990s, in essence transfers funds from existing workers to retirees. It is deemed inadequate to meet the requirements of those existing workers upon retirement, especially in light of Russia's changing demographics (see below). Plans are currently under consideration, which will more closely identify individuals' contributions with their benefits upon retirement. The probable outcome will be a pension system with three component; a basic guaranteed state pension for all citizens, a second 'accumulated pension rights" portion, and a third amount accumulated in private, personal accounts. Final decisions on the structure of the reformed pension system are expected by early 2002, and offer the prospect of a more sustainable system and of a source of funds accumulated over time, which would be available for investment.

FOREIGN CURRENCY LIBERALIZATION

For some time the GoR has used currency controls as a mechanism to control capital flight. Russian firms operating overseas are required to convert 75 percent of the foreign currency they generate to Russian rubles with the Central Bank, even if held for a short time. Many observers view this as too cumbersome and costly for legitimate Russian businesses involved in international trade. It may also be counterproductive, as it encourages Russian firms to deal through related entities registered overseas. In July 2001, a draft law was sent to the Duma which would reduce the mandatory sale to the Central Bank of exporters' currency revenues from 75% to 50%. There are further plans, which if adopted would reduce the surrender requirement to 25% in 2003, and abolish it completely in 2004.

DE-BUREAUCRATIZATION

The Ministry of Economic Development and Trade has drafted a package of three laws which it hopes will reduce bureaucratic barriers to entrepreneurship. Of these three laws, a new licensing law, which drastically reduces the number of activities licensed by the government, was passed by the Duma and Federation Council in summer 2001 and signed by the President in August. A law to simplify business registration procedures, and a law to limit the number of inspections state agencies can conduct on businesses have received first readings, and will be taken up by
the Duma again in its fall session.

INVESTMENT PRIORITIES

Infrastructure renewal (see below) is a priority for government spending. There still appears to be some ambivalence on the part of government officials, particularly in the regions, to the value of some forms of foreign direct investment in the private sector. There is universal support for direct investment that takes the form of construction of physical plant, or capital equipment, while investment in intangibles, such as research and development or management training, often receives little official recognition. Stated government priorities, in which foreign investments are particularly encouraged, include the automotive and aerospace industries, and the development of small and medium-sized businesses.

The GoR has announced plans to revive Russia's automobile industry as a national priority, prompting bureaucrats to declare that the auto sector will be the "engine of the Russian economy." The recent spectacular growth rate in car ownership in Russia is expected to continue into the foreseeable future, and the GoR seems anxious that the demand be met largely by domestic car plants. In support of this goal, tariffs will be significantly increased on imports of used cars over 7 years old, which have been a main source of competition to Russia's car manufacturers. With higher EU environmental standards about to be applied to vehicles operating in Western Europe, Russian planners are seeking to protect domestic producers from a projected flood of inexpensive used European cars, unable to meet the new standards.

In June 2001, General Motors and the giant Russian auto manufacturer Avtovaz, signed a joint venture agreement to build a USD 332 million plant. The plant will produce a SUV based on a Russian design. This is the second largest U.S. investment ever in Russia (after the Caspian Pipeline project) and the largest in the manufacturing field. In addition, Ford is constructing a USD 221 million plant near St. Petersburg to assemble the Ford Focus, a mid-priced car by Russian standards, with an initial volume of 27,000 per year. Volkswagen is also reported to be in negotiations to construct 100% foreign owned auto plant.

In the aerospace sector, both Boeing and the European EADS are among those actively developing cooperative arrangements with Russian aerospace firms. Boeing has invested upwards of $1 billion to date in various ventures in Russia, and is studying the feasibility of developing a regional jet aircraft in Russia.

BALANCE OF PAYMENTS

Russia's current account balance in 2000 was USD 46.3 billion, a significant increase over 1999's USD 24.6 billion, itself a record for recent years. Estimates for 2001, indicate a decrease to USD 32.2 bullion.

ADEQUACY OF THE INFRASTRUCTURE SYSTEM

Across the board, Russia's infrastructure is in a state of general decay. While difficult to quantify, official guestimates show that 25% of equipment in the public sector is operating well past its service life, and that 60 percent of capital stock is worn out. However, after a decade of general neglect, there are a number of plans both developed and under development to begin to address the numerous problems. As ever, funding is the major constraint, but more stable and growing tax revenues and more responsible fiscal management are bringing many projects within the realm of the feasible.

TELECOMMUNICATIONS

The telecommunications infrastructure is of inconsistent quality and accessibility throughout Russia. While major population centers are quite well served, large areas of this vast country have extremely poor access, or none at all. In rural areas there are 54,000 villages with no telephone access whatsoever. In the country as a whole, there are a mere 21 phone lines per 100 people, and the waiting list for basic services currently has 6 million names. The development of e-commerce is greatly impeded by the lack of telecommunications infrastructure. The number of cellular phone subscribers is growing rapidly in the main population centers where it is available. Cellular service providers are moving quite rapidly to increase coverage, but there are likely to remain large, sparsely populated areas where coverage is uneconomical.

The Ministry of Communications estimates that the country will need USD 33 billion in telecommunications investment over the next 10 years to bring the country to European standards, and it is hoped that some part of this would be provided by foreign investors.

Internet penetration is currently at just 2% of the population, but growing fast. In July 2001, the GOR approved a USD 2.6 billion plan to boost e-commerce and internet use through the year 2010. Part of the plan is aimed at transferring much of the government's work online, and it is hoped that much of the cost of the plan may be met by savings in such areas as government procurements via the net. Another area of interest for the GOR is e-education, and its potential to give equal access to first rate education to a geographically widely dispersed student body.

There is almost no broadband infrastructure in Russia, although several projects to develop it in major population centers are under consideration. However, the low level of average disposable incomes in Russia places the viability of most projects in doubt. Outside of Moscow, average monthly income levels are around $100. Although they are rising, it will be some time before disposable incomes will be sufficiently large to allow the average Russian to contemplate subscribing to any service delivered via broadband.

TRANSPORTATION

Russia has a road network of 948,000 km, a little more than half of what experts claim is needed, given the country's geographic expanse, population size, rate of growth of car ownership, and shifting economy. However, only 336,000 km of roads are paved. Apart from Moscow and several other major cities, the quality of roads is quite poor. Some cities are not even connected to the federal highway system. Ten years ago just 7% of the country's (then) 150 million people owned cars, but that number is expected to quadruple by 2010. Adding to individual demand is that of a changing economy. During

Soviet times, industrial production was concentrated in huge plants, each with its own railhead, and the majority of cargo was transported in large volumes by rail. As the economy shifts towards smaller scale private enterprises located near customers, road haulage is projected to increase in importance. Roads currently carry only 10 percent of total cargo traffic.

The Russian Ministry of Transportation in June 2001, announced a USD 75 billion public works program aimed at overhauling the country's highway system. The program, which is to be funded from federal and local budgets, envisages constructing an additional 80,000 km of highways and improving the circulation around major transport hubs. However, there is some skepticism over the state's ability to fund this ambitious program in full.

Railway transport is the leading means of transportation in Russia, carrying 81% of the country's freight turnover and 43% of the country's passenger turnover. The Russian railway network includes 17 regional railways and covers approximately 86,000 kilometers of track. There is an additional 63,000 km of track serving specific industries, and not available for common carrier use. Most industrial goods and raw materials such as coal, coke, ores, ferrous metals, chemical and mineral fertilizers, and grain and milling products are transported by railroads.

The Russian railway system (MPS) is one of the country's most conservative organizations, centrally controlled and 100 percent state owned. MPS develops its own budget and policies and is responsible for coordinating railway operations, determining rail policy and the legal framework governing railway operations, and planning and allocating investments, including the construction of new railways. As a coordinating agency, MPS defines technical standards, sets tariffs, collects and apportions revenue among the regional railways, sets train schedules, and serves as the interface between the central government and the railway system However, the GOR in May 2001 presented a new three stage concept for the restructuring of railways, to be carried out during 2001-2010, which provides for separation of the regulatory and commercial operations and creation of a competitive environment in the railway sector

Russia boasts 530 airports, 62 of which have 'international' status. While most are serviceable, almost all need upgrading. However, only Moscow's main airports and one or two others have been able to sustain the traffic levels of 10 years ago. The remainder have suffered a significant decline. In 1991, Russia's airports handled a total of 120 million passengers, but by 1999 this had declined to 21.5 million passengers. Since then, however, there has been modest growth in passenger volumes, which should reach 23 million in 2001. This increase occurred despite large increases in fuel prices during the same period, which account for 30% of airlines' expenses, and must be attributed to Russia's improving economy.

INVESTOR CONFIDENCE

A recent Economist Intelligence Unit survey of 75 multinationals operating in Russia revealed a generally positive view of the country's current business environment. Of the companies surveyed, over 80 percent reported making a profit in 2000; more than 60 percent were operating at pre-crisis (1998) levels; more than half expected sales to grow between 10 percent and 25 percent in 2001; and more than 70 percent hired new personnel in 2000 and expect to continue hiring. No company surveyed believed that political risk is worsening, while 82 percent believed it was improving. Half of the companies believed that Russia is a favorable opportunity. These expectation of attractive business prospects in Russia have begun to spark renewed interest among many foreign firms, which had backed away from the Russian market in response to gloomy portrayals of Russian conditions. A list of familiar complaints also emerged from the survey including the lack of corporate transparency, and the high level of crime and corruption. However, the majority of companies rated the issue of crime and corruption as manageable or better.

EMERGENCE OF SMES

Having spent the last decade in the shadows, small and medium-sized enterprises (SMEs) are just beginning to emerge as an economic and political force throughout Russia. The collapse of the command economy closed off career paths in state-owned enterprises for large numbers of Russia's graduates, many of whom turned instead to small entrepreneurial endeavors. In a business environment that was not supportive and often obstructive to small business development, those entrepreneurs who were successful tried to avoid the unwelcome attention of government authorities.

In recent years, however, several have run successfully for seats in the parliament and are becoming increasingly active and supportive participants in the reform process. The continuing overall improvement in the business environment of the last year, most particularly the lowering of corporate and personal income tax rates, is encouraging SMEs to become more visible and more organized players in the economy. Nevertheless, the large, former state-owned industries are still dominant, accounting for some 80 percent of GDP by some estimates. Currently, there are only 5-7 small enterprises per 1000 people in Russia, compared to an average of 45-50 in developed countries. Big is still regarded as beautiful by many Russians, and the perception of SMEs as the dynamic engines of job and wealth creation has yet to take hold.

EDUCATION

The true wealth of the Russian economy lies in its highly educated human resources, particularly in the large number of scientists, engineers and technicians. The Soviet system delivered excellent basic education free to its citizens, achieving literacy rates higher than those of the United States. However, since the collapse of the Soviet Union, investment in education has been inadequate and teachers, along with other public sector employees, have seen their real salary levels drastically eroded by inflation. Public sector workers, including some highly educated professionals, earn 50-60 percent of the average national wage. Education standards in many institutions are dropping, as some of the best educators leave the system for the private sector, while others focus on students whose parents are able to pay the teachers directly. Consequently, the teaching profession is failing to attract young graduates, and poor bright students may not achieve their full potential. Unless the trend can be reversed, the negative long-term economic consequences of declining education standards could be significant. In the mean time Russian planners are considering innovations, such as education delivered over the internet, as a way to address the problem, which is particularly acute in Russia's vast regions.

DEMOGRAPHICS

The Russian population of 145 million is shrinking. Russia's birth rate is among the lowest in the world, at around half the replacement rate, while life expectancy - at age 60 for men -- has fallen since Soviet times. The primary reason for the falling birth rate is the level of poverty to which many Russians have been reduced, and lack of confidence in an improvement in the near future. At the current rate, the population could drop to around 100 million over the next 50 years. Among many long-term negative implications for Russia, if this demographic trend is not reversed, is the immense financial burden that an aging population will likely place on a dwindling number of young taxpayers.

REGIONAL ECONOMIC INTEGRATION

Russia more resembles a continent than a country. Across its vast territories there are major variances in terms of natural resources, economic and social condition, business and investment climate, industry sector mix, and receptivity to the reform process. The main population centers of Moscow and St. Petersburg were sufficiently large to developed relatively mixed economies. However, under the former Soviet centrally-planned economy, Russia's regions were perhaps too interdependent. There was little, if any internal competition and little trading with the world outside of the closed Soviet system. With the collapse of the Soviet Union, many regions, and newly-created former Soviet states, found themselves uncompetitive, with significantly reduced markets domestic markets and little experience in developing overseas markets.

RUSSIAN REGIONS: STRATEGIC ECONOMIC INFORMATION

CENTRAL RUSSIA REGION

THE CITY OF MOSCOW

(Population: 10 million):

Moscow's population, when combined with that of the surrounding oblast (region), makes up over ten percent of Russia's total population. Together, the city and the oblast represent the largest and wealthiest metropolitan consumer market. The purchasing power of residents of Moscow at the end of 2000 was 3.3 times higher than the Russian average. Only 8, of Russia's 89 regions, have income levels higher than the national median. The annual retail trade turnover in Moscow is around $20 billion, or about 30 percent of national retail turnover, even though the city accounts for only 7 percent of the national population. Moscow is Russia's undisputed political and financial center; it has superb infrastructure (by Russia's standards) and a strong industrial base. During the first quarter of year 2000, industrial growth in Moscow reached 14 percent.

The city of Moscow is also the leading international partner with the highest amount of cumulative foreign investment of $13 billion (direct, portfolio, and other.) In the first quarter 2001, Moscow received over $1 billion, or 40% of all foreign investments in Russia during that period, which amounted to $2.7 billion. Furthermore, 70 percent of Russian small businesses operate in Moscow.

The Moscow City Government is active in facilitating business development. It emphasizes the importance of such sectors as high technologies, pharmaceuticals, tourism, food processing industry and retail trade.

Moscow Oblast (Population: 6.7 million):

Moscow Oblast offers a unique mix of opportunities to local companies and foreign investors. Foreign companies in the oblast enjoy proximity to Moscow's consumer market while retaining reduced production and overhead costs. Moscow Oblast offers a well-developed business infrastructure including a transportation network, telecommunications, and a services market. The Moscow Oblast Customs Department oversees seven customs posts and processes one-third of Russia's trade turnover.

Although the city of Moscow is the capital of the Moscow Oblast, the oblast and the city are two separate administrative entities. Since 1997 the Moscow Oblast Administration adopted several laws that provide foreign investors with significant tax privileges and guarantees.

Moscow Oblast has tremendous industrial potential. It specializes in machine building (represented mainly by electronics, instrumentation, and aerospace), metal processing, chemical production, construction materials, and textiles. It also possesses a well-developed agricultural sector. From 1992 to 2000, Moscow Oblast reportedly attracted more than $3 billion of foreign investment. U.S. companies are among the five major foreign partners. Recently, it received more foreign investment due to projects in the dairy, automotive, chemical, furniture, and other sectors. A dozen U.S. companies are resident in the region.

For the year 2001 the Moscow Oblast's exports amounted to $1,748 million. The retail trade turnover of Moscow region in 2000 was $ 3.3 billion

Moscow Oblast ranks among Central Russia's regions with the lowest investment risk. In both the city and oblast of Moscow, companies generally do not face the liquidity problems endemic in other Russian regions.

KALUGA OBLAST

(Population: 1.1 million):

Kaluga is located in Central Russia, adjacent to Moscow Oblast and 180 kilometers south of the national capital. Major industries include machinery and metallurgy, food processing, wood and paper, and electrical engineering. Kaluga's industrial sector faces challenges common to all of Russia's 89 regions: lack of investment for reconstruction and modernization, government cutbacks in orders to former defense enterprises, and a disrupted distribution network. Currently, 200 companies with foreign capital are operating in Kaluga Oblast, including 48 representative offices of foreign companies.

Both domestic and foreign investors are eligible for tax breaks from the Kaluga Oblast administration under a number of legislative acts adopted to improve the investment climate in the region. The Kaluga Regional Administration offers tax cuts to companies reinvesting their profit in local production or lending funds to scientific research centers for development of new technologies. The Kaluga Administration can participate in investment projects and will consider providing guarantees for investments.

TULA OBLAST

(Population: 1 million):

Covering an area of 25,700 square kilometers, Tula is 100 miles south of Moscow. The region has attracted some well-known foreign companies through tax and investment incentives. The most developed industries include the machinery, metallurgy, chemical and woodworking sectors, as well as food processing and power generation. Tula is the only Russian region boasting completely digitized telecommunication. Among Central Russian regions, Tula is third (behind Moscow and the Moscow Oblast) in exports to non-NIS countries.

Dozens of foreign companies find Tula attractive. However, although over 100 companies, including 22 with direct foreign participation, have started operations in Tula, it still has the smallest foreign business community in Central Russia. Tula's investors produce a quarter of the region's industrial output. The presence of large American corporations in Tula may make it more accessible to American companies. Compared to other Central Russia regions beyond Moscow and Moscow Oblast, Tula is the largest foreign investment recipient.

TVER OBLAST

(Population: 1.6 million):

Tver is rich with forests and water and is the source of fresh water for Central Russia and the city of Moscow. The oblast has an excellent location in terms of access to the two largest metropolitan areas in Russia: Moscow and St. Petersburg.

Tver industry is concentrated in electrical energy, machine building, food processing, light industry and textiles, and wood processing. Agribusiness in Tver Oblast is mainly concentrated in flax harvesting and dairy and meat processing. Tver Oblast used to produce up to 40% of all flax in Russia. Despite 35 textile plants, not all flax is processed locally; the majority of the local mills work with resources purchased elsewhere. One reason for using imported materials is the region's lack of processing equipment. New, contemporary technologies are needed. The timber and wood processing industries also hold potential for development as the region refocuses from exports of raw materials to increased local processing. In 2000, the foreign trade turnover of the Tver region reached $186 million, after having declined to $149.9 million in 1999 as a result of the financial crisis of 1998., and reached $ 186 million. Imports to Tver totaled $85 million, of which 50% came from machine building industry, 26% from food exports, 12% from textiles and 10% from chemical industry. Foreign direct investment in the Tver region was $33.2 million in 1998-2000.

Ryazan Oblast (Population: 1.5 million):
Foreign investors have only started to take notice of Ryazan. Due to its high concentration of defense enterprises, the region had been closed to foreign visitors during the Soviet era. The region acquired the reputation of being "red zone" and this has impacted economic development. However, the situation is rapidly changing.

The energy, oil refining, machine building, construction and food-processing sectors are viewed as the strongest and most important sectors for the regional economy. The U.S. Export-Import Bank (EXIM) currently provides partial financing for reconstruction of the Ryazan Oil Refinery. Wood processing and food processing are among the best investment prospects as regional enterprises lack equipment.

YAROSLAVL OBLAST

(Population: 1.4million):

East of Moscow, Yaroslavl is a hub of important highways, railroads, inland waterways, and air routes. The oblast is famous for heavy machinery (diesel engines, electrical equipment), refined petroleum, textiles, aviation, synthetic rubber and tires. Yaroslavl is increasing its regional output. Recently, the Yaroslavl Motor Plant, the sole surviving manufacturer of diesel engines in the former Soviet Union, and Rybinsk Motors, producing aircraft engines, showed significant growth. A number of U.S. companies have participated in investment projects in these industry sectors.

Furthermore, oil reserves have been discovered in Yaroslavl Oblast, although significant geologic and economic research needs to be completed before commercial production can be launched.

ST. PETERSBURG AND NORTHWEST RUSSIA REGION

Northwest Russia, including St. Petersburg, Leningrad Oblast, Archangelsk, Kaliningrad, Karelia, Murmansk, Novgorod, Pskov, and Vologda, covers a vast area comparable in size to Alaska. The region is home to 13 million people. St. Petersburg, Russia's second largest city and the fourth largest in Europe, boasts a population of approximately 5 million, and is a major commercial, educational, research, industrial, and financial hub. Its factories produce everything from heavy machinery and electronics to a wide variety of consumer goods. St. Petersburg's ports and railways comprise a major transportation center, tying Russia to the Baltics, Scandinavia and the rest of Europe. Surrounding the city, Leningrad Oblast contains 1.8 million people in an area comparable to Ireland. Combined, St. Petersburg and Leningrad Oblast form a substantial market for consumer and industrial goods.

INVESTMENT IN NORTHWEST RUSSIA:

During the last several years, Northwest Russia has attracted a large portion of total U.S. investment in Russia, and U.S. companies such as Caterpillar, Coca-Cola, Ford, Gillette, International Paper, Lucent, Otis Elevator, Philip Morris, RJ Reynolds and Wrigley have all established production facilities. Following the 1998 economic downturn, regional authorities were forced to become more competitive, and local and regional governments became more willing to grant tax and other concessions in order to encourage foreign investment. To varying degrees, the regional governments have taken the right steps toward attracting such investment through the creation of foreign investment laws, tax abatements, and the creation of foreign investment advisory councils. Several oblasts have been especially successful at creating commercial environments conducive to investment. St. Petersburg, Leningrad Oblast and Novgorod are the best examples, accounting for over $1.4 billion in U.S. direct investment.

With their proximity to European shipping routes, St. Petersburg and Leningrad Oblast comprise a natural transportation hub; in fact, Northwest Russia is Russia's leading export region. In 1999, the Northwest Customs Department handled $12.8 billion in trade, with the U.S. ranked as the number one trade partner (11% of trade turnover to the region). The Port of St. Petersburg is Russia's largest commercial seaport by volume, handling roughly a third of Russia's imports. Commercial seaports are also located in Murmansk, Kaliningrad, and Arkhangelsk, and several additional cargo port projects are currently being developed in Leningrad Oblast. For the most part, Russian ports are not sufficiently equipped to provide modern services, and commercial opportunities exist for U.S. firms in modernizing port handling facilities, developing modern freight forwarding systems and constructing cargo-processing terminals in the ports. The St. Petersburg area also has an extensive rail network connecting it to Europe, Moscow and other Russian regions.

TOURISM:

According to UNESCO, St. Petersburg is the only Russian city ranked among the world's top 10 cities in "tourism appeal," and its developing tourism infrastructure helped the city attract 3.3 million foreign tourists to Northwest Russia in 1999. Tourism is expected to grow five to seven percent annually over the next five years, adding additional demand on the city's hotels and infrastructure. Moreover, St. Petersburg has few mid-range hotels, and is in dire need of international-standard two and three star hotels. The city administration is attempting to cultivate joint ventures with foreign investors and hotel chains and to conclude management contracts with international chains that can invest in hotel renovation.

Best Prospects in Northwest Russia:

In addition to several of the best prospects listed elsewhere in this report, Northwest Russia offers commercial opportunities in other key sectors. The region produces 35% of Russia's output in the forestry and wood working industry (more than any other Russian region), with a majority of production exported to Finland. This production creates demand for U.S. equipment related to logging, wood processing, and pulp and paper production. The domestic food processing, packaging and textile industries are gaining strength and consequently demand is also growing for such equipment. The region's growing tourism market provides opportunities in hotel and restaurant development, as well as products and equipment. As one of Russia's major academic centers, St. Petersburg possesses extensive intellectual resources and is quickly developing into a significant player in offshore software programming. Pollution control equipment and services (especially related to water resources) fill an important niche market, and financing may be available from neighboring Scandinavian countries that are funding environmental programs here.

THE URALS AND WESTERN SIBERIA REGION

The Urals Region and Western Siberia territories cover an area larger than the United States east of the Mississippi and are home to over 40 million people. They possess some of Russia's most valuable resources, with minerals, fossil fuels and vast forests. During the Soviet period, the Urals became a leading center of heavy industry (metallurgy and machine building), as well as defense and aerospace plants. Today, those industries remain concentrated in Sverdlovsk, Chelyabinsk, and Perm Oblasts. In Western Siberia, Tyumen Oblast is known for its prolific gas and oil reserves.

In addition to fossil fuels and heavy industry, the telecommunications and food processing industries offer opportunities for U.S. firms. The telecommunications infrastructure around urban centers has developed rapidly over the past five years. Local landline services are concentrating on data communications and digital switching upgrades. Cellular telephone services are now available in most of the region's major cities. Food processing also has been expanding. The region is home to over 6,000 food processing firms, many of which seek imported processing and packaging lines to meet the increasing demand for high quality, competitively priced foodstuffs.

SVERDLOVSK OBLAST

(Population: 4.6 million):

The Sverdlovsk Oblast is one of Russia's most urbanized areas. Eighty-seven percent of the population lives in cities. Its capital, Yekaterinburg (1.6 million inhabitants), is Russia's fourth largest city. Sverdlovsk Oblast has the largest GDP of any oblast in the Urals, producing five percent of Russia's industrial output and ranking second only to Moscow Oblast in that category. Of 89 Russian regions, Sverdlovsk Oblast is one of only nine net contributors to the federal budget. Ferrous metallurgy and machine building form a large portion of Sverdlovsk's economy, much of it defense-related. Services have grown to 40 percent of regional GDP. Yekaterinburg is a major road and rail hub and also has regular air service to several European cities. Its banking infrastructure is the best in the Urals, with 31 banks and 17 branches of commercial banks from other regions. Sverdlovsk Oblast leads the Urals in attracting investment, and several large U.S. firms have substantial investments here. The United States is the major investor in Sverdlovsk Oblast with 47 percent of total investments. Sverdlovsk's top exports are steel, copper, chemicals, aluminum, titanium and radioisotopes. According to oblast statistics, 1999 foreign trade was valued at $2.28 billion. Non-ferrous metallurgy remains a growth sector, and VSMPO, the world's second-largest titanium producer and a supplier to Boeing, is located here.

PERM OBLAST

(Population: 3.1 million):

Heavy industry, primarily metallurgy and machine building, constitute a large sector of Perm's economy. Much of this industry is defense-related, including production of aircraft engines, Proton rockets, and space control systems. Perm produces 30 percent of Russia's paper and 98 percent of its potassium-based fertilizers. The oblast is also a regional center for electricity generation. The city of Perm, the oblast capital, is a major river port, has two airports and is situated on the Trans-Siberian railway. Perm's top exports are refined oil and petrochemical products, fertilizers and metals. Perm has over 100 known deposits of oil and gas and two oil refineries. Annual extraction exceeds 9 million metric tons of oil and 500 million cubic meters of gas. Fifty percent of Russia's magnesium and most of its titanium ore come from Perm.

CHELYABINSK OBLAST

(Population: 3.6 million):

The Chelyabinsk Oblast, situated on the Trans-Siberian railway, ranks fifth in Russian industrial output. Ferrous metallurgy and machine building play a key role in the oblast's economy. Metals account for 85 percent of the oblast's exports and over 40 percent of total output. The oblast is rich in iron ore, copper, bauxite and gold. Over 70 percent of Chelyabinsk Oblast's ferrous metal exports originate from the giant Magnitogorsk Metallurgical Works.

TYUMEN OBLAST

(Population: 3 million):

Tyumen is Russia's third largest oblast in terms of territory, and includes two autonomous districts, Khanty-Mansiysk and Yamalo-Nenets. Tyumen is rich in oil and gas: its combined output of both exceeds seven percent of Russia's GDP (including over 90 percent of Russia's natural gas and 60 percent of its oil). Gazprom dominates the gas industry in Yamalo-Nenets, while Lukoil, Yukos, Sibneft and Tyumen Oil Company are the oil leaders in Khanty-Mansiysk. Several U.S. and European firms have established joint ventures in the region for production and sale of crude oil. Southern Tyumen Oblast is predominantly agricultural. Tyumen is an important electric power producer, accounting for seven percent of Russia's electricity. It also produces a third of Russia's automobile batteries.

VOLGA

The Nizhny Novgorod Oblast ranks seventh in Russia in terms of industrial output, and industry accounts for 83 percent of the oblast's gross domestic product. Key industrial sectors include automotive, aviation, machine-tool manufacture, chemicals and petrochemicals, lumber and paper production, and woodworking. In addition, the region has a number of companies engaged in radio electronics, light manufacturing, the production of building materials, and agribusiness and food processing. The huge Gorky Automobile Plant (GAZ), a manufacturer of cars and trucks is located in Nizhny Novgorod, as is the SOKOL aircraft plant, which produces MIG fighters and commercial jet planes. The oblast has a population of 3.72 million, of which 1.5 million live in the capital city of Nizhny Novgorod. It boasts an extensive, integrated and heavily-used transportation system, connecting it with the rest of Russia and beyond by rail, waterway, road, and air. The investment climate of Nizhny Novgorod is among the most favorable in Russian, and has attracted over 500 joint ventures to the region, including major U.S. and European firms.

For additional analytical, business and investment opportunities information, please contact Global Investment & Business Center, USA at (202) 546-2103. Fax: (202) 546-3275. E-mail: rusric@erols.com
Global Business E-Books on Line: http://world.mirhouse.com

Samara Oblast: The Samara region is quite unique in Russia in that it has two major industrial centers - Samara City and Togliatti. During the Soviet era the city of Samara was a center for military development and was closed to foreigners. The former city of Stavropol was renamed Togliatti, in honor of an Italian communist leader, when the immense Volga Automobile Plant (VAZ) was completed in 1964 as a joint venture with Fiat. The Samara Oblast has successfully applied its industrial heritage to the market economy and has attracted significant foreign direct investments. In 2001 General Motors announced a $330 million joint venture with AutoVAZ to produce a 4WD vehicle. The region also has tremendous agricultural potential, and is considered one of the top areas of petroleum by-product and machinery production in Russia. The region is home to 3.3 million, who represent the third wealthiest population in the country after Moscow City, St. Petersburg and the Moscow Region.

CENTRAL SIBERIA

Novosibirsk, with a population of 1.5 million is Siberia's largest city and Russia's fourth largest. It stands at Russia's crossroads, geographically, politically and economically, and represents one of the most important commercial centers outside of European Russia. It does not boast the mineral wealth found in neighboring regions, but serves as the processing and handling center for much of those regions' resources. The capital city, around which the Novosibirsk region of 2.8 million gravitates, came to prominence during World War II and derives its economic-strategic position largely from its location on main rail, road, water and air routes. A center of research, it boasts 28 scientific institutes and 3 universities. Its primary industries are heavy machinery, chemicals, electrical equipment, metals, and timber.

The Omsk Oblast: The City of Omsk ranks 4th among the industrially developed cities of Russia after Moscow, St-Petersburg and Yekaterinburg. It accounts for more than 90 percent of the oblast's total industrial output and is home to one million of the region's 2.18 million population. As much as 70-80 percent of its engineering capacity remains concentrated in the defense sector. Aerospace is a prominent industrial sector, and the region is Russia's largest hub of oil refining and the petrochemical industry.

The Tomsk Oblast's distinctive feature is a favorable combination of natural, industrial and intellectual resources. Its natural environment includes the famous Siberian cedar forests, which cover most of the region's territory, and there are abundant reserves of other natural resources, such as oil, gas, and non-ferrous ores. It is also a scientific and educational center, and scientists from its 50 institutions conduct research in physics, chemistry, technology, and medicine. The Region has a highly developed defense complex, focusing on the manufacture of high technology products, which potentially represent natural incubators for innovative and high-tech enterprises. Nearly half of the region's one million population live in the city of Tomsk

SOUTHERN FEDERAL DISTRICT

Rostov is the capital of the Russian Southern Federal District, the second largest Russian producer of agricultural products and home to the country's major manufacturers of agricultural machinery, electric locomotives and helicopters. The region's natural resources include coal and anthracite, oil and gas, and raw construction materials. The most important resource, however, is Rostov's fertile black soil, which produces high-value crops on an area under cultivation which is twice as large as Denmark. The region ranks sixth in Russia by population. The Port of Rostov-on-Don is accessible from five seas and Russian river-to-sea vessels make regular runs from Rostov to many Mediterranean ports. The reform-minded government and relatively favorable investment climate have attracted strategic investments from several large international corporations, such as Coca-Cola, Citroen, Russian Aluminum Holding and others.

Krasnodar Krai: Five million people inhabit Krasnodar Krai, which includes the cities of Krasnodar, Novorossiisk, and Sochi. The krai (region) contains transportation infrastructure vital to Russian and Caspian Basin oil and gas exports, and transportation routes crossing the krai connect Russia and Central Asia to the Mediterranean, Europe, and the Middle East. Agriculture is the largest sector of the Krasnodar economy, and much of the region's 75,500 square kilometers lies in Russia's fertile Black Earth zone. Other important sectors include oil and gas, power engineering, and metal working. Machine tools, agricultural equipment, machinery for the petroleum industry, food-processing equipment, and textiles dominate local manufacturing. The extraction minerals - crude oil, gas, manganese, iron, and phosphates - is a major component of Krasnodar's economy, and raw materials comprise three-fourths of Krasnodar exports. The krai's Black Sea coast, often called the "Russian Riviera," includes the resort city of Sochi, which attracts over one million tourists each year.

RUSSIAN FAR EAST REGION

Separated from the world market for most of its history, the Russian Far East (RFE) has lagged behind Western Russia in integrating itself into international trade and investment. This presents unique opportunities and challenges for the U.S. export community. The RFE market covers four time zones and has a population of 8 million people spread over 6.2 million square kilometers (roughly two-thirds the size of the continental United States). It is rich in natural resources, including oil, natural gas, gold, timber, fish, coal, diamonds, and metals and minerals. Of the ten regions contained in the RFE, the leading regions for U.S. exports are Primorskiy and Khabarovskiy Krais and Sakhalin Oblast.

Though the regional economy is still depressed, it is recovering, with the strongest opportunities existing in the wood processing, food processing, and oil and gas equipment/services. Additionally, according to *Goskomstat*, personal income levels in the regions of the Far East and Siberia, where extraction industries dominate, are higher than the Russian national average. This may provide opportunities for U.S. consumer products if they can be price competitive with Asian imports.

PROMISING REGIONS

Commercial activity in Primorskiy Krai is centered in its capital, Vladivostok, the largest city in the RFE and one of its leading trading, manufacturing, and financial centers. Fishing and fish processing provide one-third of the region's budget income, and much of its local employment (the Primorskiy fishing fleet catches two-thirds of all fish in the RFE and one-third of all fish in Russia.) It is the eastern terminus of the Trans-Siberian railway, a major port city, and the principal base of the Russian Pacific Navy Fleet. In addition to Vladivostok's ports, numerous large and small commercial ports, including the ports of neighboring Nakhodka and Vostochny, make Primorye the leading transportation center in the RFE. After Vladivostok was opened to foreigners, it was thought that the city might develop into Russia's version of Hong Kong. The regions' continued political problems, however, have portrayed a poor picture in the western media and little investment has poured into the region.

SAKHALIN OBLAST:

Sakhalin, located in the Sea of Okhotsk, is positioned to become one of the most important centers in the RFE for commercial and investment activity. ExxonMobil, Shell, British Petroleum and Texaco are a few of the energy companies that have had some level of activity in the region, preparing to invest some $30-45 billion into offshore oil and gas development. Yuzhno-Sakhalinsk could soon have one of the largest expatriate communities in Russia, and already has the highest concentration of American citizens per capita in Russia. According to 1999 data of the Shelf Department and Committee for Natural Resources, proven reserves of hydrocarbons in four offshore projects total 1,400 mmt oil and 2.3 bcm gas, with another 2.6 billion barrels oil equivalent estimated in areas yet to be leased. Discovered onshore reserves are 60-70% depleted, though opportunities exist for secondary/tertiary recovery and work-over. Until these oil projects come on-line, the Sakhalin economy will remain largely based on the fish, fish processing, and forestry industries.

KHABAROVSK:

Khabarovsk is the leading industrial region in the RFE, and many consider it to be the unofficial capital (President Putin's federal representative to the RFE, Konstantin Pulikovsky, is based here). Unlike the other regions in the far east, which rely on extraction industries, Khabarovsk has a strong manufacturing and processing base, the result of the former Soviet Union's burgeoning defense industry. This manufacturing base, combined with the krai's close location to Sakhalin (especially the port at Vanino), should provide the region with an opportunity to assist in the development of Sakhalin's oil and gas industry. Key industries include machine building, oil-refining and metallurgy.

Khabarovsk also accounts for more than one-third of the total timber output of the Russian Far East. Although rising production and transportation costs have reduced output in recent years, the region's vast timber resources and geographical proximity to Asia/Pacific markets make it a promising area for future development. However, logging is accompanied by immense losses of raw materials - as much as 25% of the felled timber. To cut these losses, it is essential to introduce more advanced processing technologies, which could be done only with the help of foreign investment.

BEST PROSPECTS IN THE RUSSIAN FAR EAST

In addition to several of the best prospects listed elsewhere in this report, the RFE offers commercial opportunities in other key sectors. U.S. manufacturers of equipment involved in the extraction or processing of natural resources can find opportunities in oil and gas exploration/production, forestry, mining, and fish processing. The domestic food processing and packaging industries are gaining strength, and demand is also increasing for such equipment. Environmental and pollution control equipment and services fill a growing niche market, and financing may be available through the USAID-funded program EcoLinks. Companies involved in transportation services or manufacturing port equipment may find export opportunities in the many ports located in the RFE.

FINANCIAL MARKETS DEVELOPMENT

Financial market[5] is a new and rapidly growing phenomenon in Russia. There are currently four separate but closely linked financial markets: the foreign exchange market, the inter-bank money market, the government bond market and the stock market.

The official exchange rate is determined by the outcome of daily auctions on the Moscow Inter-bank Currency Exchange. Trade on the foreign exchange market can amount to $500 million a day. Although the volume of the exchange is large, there is anecdotal evidence that the number of participants is restricted. This does not, however, appear to impede flexible adjustments of the rate.

A genuine inter-bank money market has developed. Banks trade short-term credit with interest rates freely determined by market conditions. This market, however, can be illiquid and prone to rapid change. A crisis in the Moscow inter-bank money market in August 1997 raised rates over night by a factor of ten. In the aftermath of this crisis, considerable consolidation in the banking sector has taken place.

---

[5] For additional information on the current situation in the Russian securities market, please contact the Russian info&Business Center, Inc. at (202) 546-2103 or our WWW site at http://www.rusline.com

The Russian government has also made available short and medium-term credit through the issuance of bonds. The government bond market is small but has steadily grown. Two government debt instruments are most widely traded, short-term ruble denominated debt (known as GKOs) and medium-term dollar denominated debt (known as Tiaga Bonds).

An active stock market is taking shape in Russia. Shares are available in thousands of open-ended joint-stock companies, many of which were formerly state-owned enterprises. The market is illiquid, however, with about 200 companies widely traded. Portfolio investment is technically possible in all trade companies, though there are limits to the percentages of shares that foreigners may hold.

The only substantial legislation aimed at reducing the tax burden for some entrepreneurs was a law entitled "In Support of Small Businesses" adopted on July 24, 1997. Among the many benefits, the legislation was to protect small businesses from future changes in taxation that would worsen their position for a number of years. It is noteworthy that, so far, not a single small business has figured out a way to register for the benefits. Subsequent legislation, as mentioned above, has increased taxes on small businesses by eliminating exemptions.

CURRENCY EXCHANGE OPERATIONS

The Law on Currency Regulation and Currency Control provide the fundamental basis of currency regulation in Russia. The regulations pertaining to money transfers in or out of the Russian Federation are relatively complex and change frequently. Most of the critical details are contained in "Instructions and Letters of the Central Bank". After an initial period of comparative freedom in 1991, the general trend over the past two years has been to gradually narrow down the scope of hard currency's permissible transactions on the Russian territory.

Russian enterprises, private citizens and legal foreign entities and citizens are currently permitted to maintain hard currency accounts at Russian banks and to hold hard currency, but there are restrictions on their use. Russian enterprises may pay for foreign goods purchased abroad in hard currency and pay for foreign business travel within a (rather low) per diem limit. Hard currency may not be used by resident Russian entities to compensate Russian or foreign employees in Russia. All other hard-currency transactions within the Russian Federation require Central Bank approval.

For foreign companies located outside the Russian Federation, hard-currency payments for Russian goods can be transferred into the Russian Federation without restriction. Rubles obtained outside of Russia cannot legally be transferred into the Federation.

For hard currency transactions connected with the movement of capital in or out of Russia, a central bank license is generally required. This includes any hard currency loans to a Russian entity. In recent practice, the Central Bank has begun requiring licenses for cash (hard currency) contribution to the Charter capital of Russian enterprises. This practice, however, is not uniformly followed.

Rules affecting currency dealings of entities located within the Russian Federation depend to a large extent on the identity of the entities engaged in such dealings. Payments between legal entities are to be carried out via authorized banks, those possessing a central bank license. Though there are certain limited exceptions, transactions within the Russian Federation between Russian resident entities are to be carried out in rubles. In practice, prices are often quoted in other currencies such as dollars. For transactions between legal entities valued at more than two million rubles, the monetary transfer must be done through the banking system - it may not be carried out in cash. Cash payments in dollars between legal entities in the Russian Federation are prohibited.

A Russian resident entity receiving hard currency as export income from outside Russia must convert 50 percent of hard currency receipts into rubles within 14 days.

FINANCIAL SECTOR DEVELOPMENT

During the early years of economic transition, the banking sector presented a sharp contrast to much of the rest of the economy. It grew very quickly and showed very high relative profits. Bank stocks proved to be the most popular financial securities in Russia, even before state bonds became effectively marketable. In March of 1997, 2558 banks were officially active in Russia. 1997 has proven to be an extremely difficult period for most commercial banks though and has marked the beginning of what is commonly referred to as a crisis in the banking sector. This so-called crisis will, in the coming years, most likely lead to major structural change in the banking sector.

The changes in the fortunes of most banks reflect major changes in the economy as a whole. In earlier years, the regulatory environment for banks was very slack. Capital and reserve requirements were fixed in nominal terms long enough for very rapid inflation to eat them away, leading to a proliferation of small, poorly capitalized commercial banks. While severe information problems, unstable, high inflation, and low profitability in the real economy essentially kept banks out of financing investment projects, important sources of profits did exist.

In past years, the RCB operated with negative real refinance rates and targeted credits to special firms and sectors of the economy, typically those which employed a large amount of workers and had no income to pay wages. Commercial Banks operated as intermediaries, administering these loans, typically rolling them over, and lobbying the central bank for refinance. But the availability of such credit was curtailed considerably in 1993, and virtually cut off in 1994, as refinancing rates of the RCB were increased to near market levels, and the few remaining special (below market rate) loans to industry were mostly removed from commercial bank inter-mediation.

For a long time, hard currency operations were the greatest source of profits for banks. First, for those banks that could successfully obtain credit and deposits at negative real interest rates, significant profits could be made by just holding a large portion of assets in dollars. Many banks also made significant profits from servicing currency exchange. In the presence of rapid inflation and devaluation, the demand for currency exchange was very high. Some banks made close to 100 percent of their profits this way. Other banks reportedly operated with inside information on currency markets and made a significant amount of money through speculation. But banks no longer have access to credit or deposits at low interest rates. Furthermore, the stabilization of 1997 and the significant decrease in the purchasing power of the dollar lowered profitability substantially.

In addition, the RCB policy became very restrictive in 1997. Net credit expansion to banks is estimated at -17 percent for the first half of the year. In March, reserve requirements were increased, and were not, as in the past, subsequently eaten away by rapid inflation. As inflation decreased by more than was expected, those banks that made initial attempts to meet the new challenges by extending credits for a duration of more than six-month found themselves with riskier portfolios than they had planned for (i.e. lower-than-expected inflation increased the burden on debtors and the probability of default).

As banks struggled to adapt to this environment, they began to experience greater and greater problems in liquidity. Defaults on loans to the real economy increased. In this context, more and more banks began to rely on the inter-bank loans market to provide them with the liquidity for day-to-day operations. Some banks started to fall deeper and deeper into debts, the inter-bank loans market thus began to be used to pay back obligations on the inter-bank loans market, thus creating a spiral of indebtedness.

In the past, banks could expect the RCB to refinance or re-capitalize their assets in the event of a crisis. But the inter-bank loans crisis of August 1997 in Russia demonstrates a change. The population is starting to believe that the state is serious about permitting large-scale economic failure and bankruptcy. Banks began to worry and started to ration credit on the inter-bank loans market according to what they estimated was the financial position of other banks.

In mid-August, it was already clear that two large banks, Mezhregionbank and Natsionalnyi Bank, were experiencing serious problems with growing indebtedness on the inter-bank loans market. Annual rates rose overnight from 80 to 300 percent on August 23. Unable to obtain credit under "reasonable" conditions, these banks defaulted on the repayments of their loans. This event set off a panic and a chain reaction. On August 24, annual rates were pushed up to a record breaking 2000 percent, and 150 banks could not close. This essentially had the effect of temporarily shutting down the inter-bank loans market. Since this time, the market has been fragmented and restricted, with small groups of banks carrying out mutual lending among themselves. Interest rates are back to reasonable levels, but credit is closely monitored.

The RCB intervened only moderately to contain the crisis. It was actually quite a successful move. The RCB marginally improved liquidity by injecting about 1.75 trillion rubles into the banking sector, both through direct credit and through purchases of a number of state bonds. This was enough to contain the crisis and prevent a potential situation in which bad banks could drag down good banks in a spiral of mass failure. But it was not enough to generate expectations that the RCB will rescue different Russian banks from the overall difficult situation in the financial sector. Approximately 100 smaller banks were forced out of business following the events of August. As the banking sector works to rebuild itself according to new principles, more failures and mergers are expected in the future. On the negative side, it is interesting to note that the current events serve to further discourage banks from tying up funds in long-term investment projects. Due to lower-than-expected inflation and high default rates, the banks that pursued active long-term investment strategies were often precisely those that encountered the most troubles.

This crisis may have had the effect of further delaying the more active role of banks in the investment sphere. Perhaps the recent events in the banking sector are a sign of maturity for the Russian market economy. One thing is certain, the crisis demonstrated important incentive changes that could potentially alleviate the chronic problem of inter-indebtedness between Russian economic organizations. In 1997, the sum of all delinquent debt still exceeds the Russian GDP by about 10 percent. (Defaults by the Federal Government in 1997 served as the catalyst for the escalation of this problem.). As opposed to the continual partial administrative measures that have been used to contain this situation, the basic problem will remain until other economic organizations, in addition to banks, begin to worry seriously about the solvency of those whose debts they are accepting. This major qualitative change in incentives is essential to the economic success in Russia.

For additional analytical, business and investment opportunities information,
please contact Global Investment & Business Center, USA
at (202) 546-2103. Fax: (202) 546-3275. E-mail: rusric@erols.com
Global Business E-Books on Line: http://world.mirhouse.com

TRADE AND ECONOMIC POLICY

1. GENERAL POLICY FRAMEWORK

The Russian economy rebounded somewhat in 1999 from the economic and financial crisis of 1998, based on higher oil prices and import substitution resulting from the devaluation of the ruble. However, in the absence of substantial progress toward the reforms necessary to underpin a vigorous market economy and attract domestic and foreign investment, the Russian economy remains fragile and vulnerable to external and internal shocks. Industrial production in October was up 10.3 percent from the depressed levels of October 1998. The IMF is forecasting year on year inflation at end-December of 45 percent, compared to more than 80 percent in 1998. Unemployment has eased and the demand for cash transactions continued to rise as barter deals declined.

Despite estimates for real GDP growth in 1999 ranging from 0 to 3 percent, the economic boost from devaluation of the ruble and increased revenues from oil exports is unlikely to be repeated in the coming year. In the near term, sustainable growth in Russia will depend importantly on domestic demand, consumption and investment, all of which are running well below last year's levels. The lack of significant progress on structural reforms and the difficult investment climate contribute to continued net capital outflow. Surveys suggest that a main constraint to production is the absence of working capital, but the banking sector has not stabilized from its collapse in 1998 and is not in a position to effectively intermediate savings to productive investments on a large scale.

Fiscal policy for the first half of the year was moderately disciplined, with an overall deficit of 3.8 percent compared with a budget target of 2.5 percent for the year. Following low cash collections in the beginning of the year, revenue collections increased substantially, topping 13.2 percent of GDP during the first half of the year, compared with 10.5 percent over the same period in 1998. The GOR expects revenues of R551 billion for the year, about 16 percent over budget. Monetary policy was moderately tight. Base money increased 22 percent during the first half of the year, in part due to indirect central bank financing of the federal deficit, specifically assisting in servicing the GOR's external debt. The ruble remained relatively stable between March and August in a more tightly controlled foreign exchange environment than before. In these conditions, the Central Bank has sought to avoid exchange rate volatility through selective interventions to smooth the trend. The Central Bank's reserves have not significantly increased, partially due to external debt payments, changes in accounting and unauthorized capital exports.

The cost of Russia's 1998 financial collapse was significant. GDP measured in USD terms declined from around USD 422 billion in 1997 to USD 132 billion at the end of 1998, about the level of GDP in 1993. While nominal ruble revenues have increased this year to date, they are still about half those of last year, as measured in USD terms.

Similarly in the banking sector, assets in USD fell by 50 percent to around USD 50 billion. As with other emerging markets that have suffered sharp setbacks, rebuilding will take time.

Government economic policy has been largely static this year. While the three successive post-August-1998 governments have not adopted policies that would have exacerbated an already fragile situation, none have adopted aggressive policies to address fundamental challenges faced by the country. With upcoming parliamentary elections in December and presidential elections in June, the consensus of observers is that major movement on reforms or major policy changes are unlikely until the new Duma and new President are in place.

2. EXCHANGE RATE POLICY

The objective of the Central Bank of Russia's (CBR) exchange rate policy is to ensure the stability and predictability of the ruble exchange rate and prevent abrupt fluctuations, in the context of a floating exchange rate regime. After slipping at the beginning of the year, the nominal ruble/dollar rate held steady at around 24.5 from May through August, then drifted down to about 26.8 in December. High ruble liquidity, as reflected by the approximately R70 billion in banks' correspondent accounts at the CBR, supported the decline late in the year. From September through mid-November, the ruble has depreciated approximately 4.5 percent in nominal terms.

The ruble's tentative stability can be explained in part by new market conditions. The CBR has tightened foreign exchange controls by imposing restrictions on foreign exchange for import contracts, requiring 75 percent of repatriated export proceeds to be sold on authorized exchanges, not allowing banks to trade on their own accounts, limiting the conversion of funds in S-accounts from the GKO restructuring, and banning the conversion of ruble funds from non-resident banks' correspondent accounts. The latter was repealed, but replaced by requiring banks to deposit amounts equivalent to those it holds in S-accounts of non-residents. These exchange controls are only marginally effective at controlling capital flight, which reportedly increased to nearly $3.0 billion per month in late 1999, but they presumably have helped CBR to manage exchange rate volatility.

3. STRUCTURAL POLICIES

The economic crisis of 1998 overshadowed structural issues for the most part throughout 1999. The share of GDP produced by private companies reached 74 percent by the end of 1999 according to official figures. The share of barter in the economy appears to be declining, although it still accounts for roughly half of all transactions according to most estimates. External barter trade sharply declined in 1999 as well. Government arrears dropped dramatically as payment of pensions and salaries in nominal terms became cheaper in light of the drastic ruble devaluation after August 1998. Even though personal incomes dropped precipitously over the last year, industrial production has increased as a result of import substitution. Without investment, however, the up-tick in production is not expected to be sustainable, and little has been done to improve the investment climate. Indeed, several cases involving foreign investment suggest that many issues remain to be addressed.

Repeated changes in government have exacerbated the problems of inadequate structural policies by obscuring economic policy overall. With three Prime Ministers in the first 8 months of 1999, articulation, much less implementation of a coherent structural policy has proven elusive. In addition, the end of the current legislative period carried forward the effective policy stalemate in the economic sphere that has plagued the reform process. The election of a new State Duma in December 1999 will produce a new opportunity for legislative initiatives. However, economic policy is effectively on hold for now, and may well remain so until after the presidential election in July 2000.

Meanwhile, privatization continues, with sales of shares of the government's stakes in oil and gas companies. At the same time, a debate about the benefits of past privatizations has become an element in the Duma election campaign with a number of leading politicians suggesting that de-privatization of some enterprises could be considered. The privatization of the Lomonosov porcelain factory, partly owned by U.S. investors, was reversed by a St. Petersburg court. Court appeals continue. Prime Minister Putin has opposed wholesale reversal of privatization but has suggested that mistakes made in the privatization process should be identified and corrected within the framework of existing legislation. The government has worked to prevent passage of legislative initiatives that would inhibit foreign investment, for example in the insurance sector, but with mixed results. One potentially important achievement has been the adoption of an ambitious action plan for reducing the regulatory burden on small business, along with tax reduction. Overall however, there has been little progress in the structural policy area over the last year, a development that can only delay Russia's recovery from its financial crisis.

4. DEBT MANAGEMENT POLICIES

Following the August 1998 financial crisis, the Government of Russia has sought to restructure much of its internal debt and the Soviet-era portion of its external debt. The Russian government has reached a Framework Agreement with its Paris Club official creditors in July 1999, but final bilateral agreements are not expected until early in 2000. The Government of Russia is actively negotiating with its London Club commercial creditors on an agreement to restructure and/or reduce its commercial debt inherited from the Soviet government.

In March, the Russian government announced its GKO (Russian T-bill) restructuring proposal, which offered foreign GKO holders a choice between receiving a basket of securities or having their investments placed in a frozen account. Funds received in the restructuring, including from the securities, must be held in investors' S-accounts. The Central Bank of Russia prohibits conversion of S-account rubles into foreign currency, although it held six foreign exchange auctions for S-account holders, of USD 50 million each, all of which were heavily oversubscribed. Investors also may invest restricted S-account rubles in certain securities. In November, the Government of Russia announced it would permit S-account holders to make direct investments in projects approved by the government, and is reopening its offer to restructure GKO's to those investors who did not take advantage of the first offer. On December 15, the Government of Russia allowed a one-time change in S-account ownership. As of November 15, there were approximately USD 350-400 million, and another USD 2 billion in OFZ bonds, in restricted S-accounts.

The Government of Russia is continuing with its IMF program, although a second tranche release in 1999 has been delayed. The World Bank's Structural Adjustment Loan (SAL) is on hold due to lack of progress on structural reform legislation.

5. SIGNIFICANT BARRIERS TO U.S. EXPORTS

At the end of 1999, the most significant impediments to U.S. exports were not statutory but were instead results of the difficult economic situation in Russia. The devaluation in August 1998 and the reduced purchasing power of Russians played the greatest role, as Russia's overall imports slumped by over 50 percent. U.S. exports to Russia have decreased by an even larger margin in 1999, although one-time sales of aircraft in 1998 exaggerated the overall decline somewhat. Many exporters remain cautious about entering the Russian market due to reduced availability of trade finance, and bad experience with payment/clearance problems in the past. These problems have become less common in 1999, perhaps partially due to the lower volume of trade.

Since 1997, Russian tariffs have generally ranged from five to thirty percent, with a trade-weighted average in the 13-15 percent range. In addition, excise and Value-Added Tax (VAT) is applied to selected imports. The VAT, which is applied on the import price plus tariff, is currently 20 percent with the exception of some food products. Throughout 1999, some revision of tariffs occurred, with in some cases tariffs dropping for inputs needed by Russian producers in the electronics and furniture businesses. On the other hand, there have been sharp hikes in tariffs for sugar and for pharmaceuticals, including high seasonal tariffs on raw and processed sugar. In particular, compound duties with minimum levels of tariffs enacted in 1998 on poultry had the effect of increasing percentage duties after the fall in poultry prices in 1998-99. The Ministry of Trade, supported by the State Customs Committee, has proposed reducing some of Russia's higher tariffs, recognizing that very high tariffs only lead to evasion. However, the government has been reluctant to approve an across-the-board reduction in tariffs given acute revenue concerns, as customs duties account for a larger percentage of state revenues than in most other countries.

Other Russian tariffs that have stood out as particular hindrances to U.S. exports to Russia include those on autos (where combined tariffs and engine displacement-weighted excise duties can raise prices of larger U.S.-made passenger cars and sport utility vehicles by over 70 percent); some semiconductor products; and aircraft and certain aircraft components (for which tariffs are set at 30 percent). The Russian government continues to make waivers on aircraft import tariffs for purchases by Russian airlines contingent on those airlines' purchases of Russian-made aircraft.

Throughout 1999, Russia introduced a number of export duties (for exports to non-CIS countries) as a revenue measure. Initially, these duties were imposed on oil and gas, but have since been expanded to include many export commodities, including fertilizers, paper and cardboard, some ferrous and non-ferrous metals, and agricultural products, including oilseeds raw hides, and hardwoods, all ranging from 5 to 30 percent. Import licenses are required for importation of various goods, including ethyl alcohol and vodka, color TVs, sugar, combat and sporting weapons, self-defense articles, explosives, military and ciphering equipment, encryption software and related equipment, radioactive materials and waste including uranium, strong poisons and narcotics, and precious metals, alloys and stones. In 1999, new import license requirements were added for raw and processed sugar. Most import licenses are issued by the Russian Ministry of Trade or its regional branches, and controlled by the State Customs Committee. Import licenses for sporting weapons and self-defense articles are issued by the Ministry of Internal Affairs.

Throughout 1999, the government has continued tight controls on alcohol production, including import restrictions, export duties, and increased excise taxes. Many of these controls are in order to increase budget revenues.

In spring 1998, Russia passed the Law on Protective Trade Measures, which provides the government authority to undertake antidumping, countervailing duty and safeguard investigations, under certain conditions. Although Russian companies have filed several petitions for protection in 1999 under this new law, no petition has yet been approved, due to substantive or procedural insufficiencies of the petitions.

The June 1993 Customs Code standardized Russian customs procedures generally in accordance with international norms. However, customs regulations change frequently, (often without sufficient notice), are subject to arbitrary application, and can be quite burdensome. In addition, Russia's use of minimum customs values is not consistent with international norms. In November 1999, the State Customs Committee imposed a restriction that forced U.S. poultry importers to ship directly through Russian ports, rather than through warehouses in the Baltic States, as had been their practice. On the positive side, Russian customs is implementing the "ClearPac" program in the Russian Far East that facilitates customs clearance from the U.S., and is considering extending this program to other regions.

U.S. companies continue to report that Russian procedures for certifying imported products and equipment are non-transparent, expensive and beset by redundancies. Russian regulatory bodies also generally refuse to accept foreign testing centers' data or certificates. U.S. firms active in Russia have complained of limited opportunity to comment on proposed changes in standards or certification requirements before the changes are implemented, although the Russian standards and certifications bodies have begun to work closely with the American Chamber of Commerce in Russia to provide additional information. Occasional jurisdictional overlap and disputes between different government regulatory bodies compound certification problems.

A January 1998 revision to State Tax Service Instruction #34, now being enforced, makes it more difficult for expatriate employees of U.S. entities to benefit from the U.S.-Russia bilateral treaty on avoidance of double-taxation. A wide range of U.S. companies selling goods and services in Russia, who formerly could receive advance exemptions from withholding taxes for salaries, are now required to apply for a refund of tax withheld.

Although little of Russia's legislation in the services sector is overtly protectionist, the domestic banking, securities and insurance industries have secured concessions in the form of Presidential Decrees, and a draft law before the parliament will soon codify restrictions and bans on foreign investment in many services sectors. Foreign participation in banking, for example, is limited to 12 percent of total paid-in banking capital. As of mid 1998 foreign banks' capitalization only accounted for around 4 percent of the total. However, as foreign banks recapitalized following the financial crisis and Russian banks' capital shrank, the share of foreign banks' grew to 12.8 percent as of September 1. The Central Bank of Russia has indicated it will seek a higher quota so as not to impede foreign bank entry. Foreign investment is also limited in other sectors, such as electricity generation. In October 1999, a new law took effect, which implicitly allows majority-foreign-owned insurance companies to operate in Russia for the first time, but restricts their share of total market capitalization and prohibits them from selling life insurance or obligatory types of insurance. The law contains a "grandfather clause" exempting the four foreign companies currently licensed in Russia from these restrictions. In practice, foreign companies are often disadvantaged vis-a-vis their Russian counterparts in obtaining contracts, approvals, licenses, registration, and certification, and in paying taxes and fees.

Despite the passage of a new law regulating foreign investment in June 1999, Russian foreign investment regulations and notification requirements can be confusing and contradictory. The Law on Foreign Investments provides that a single agency (still undesignated) will register foreign investments, and that all branches of foreign firms must be registered. The law does codify the principle of national treatment for foreign investors, including the right to purchase securities, transfer property rights, protect rights in Russian courts, repatriate funds abroad after payment of duties, and to receive compensation for nationalizations or illegal acts of Russian government bodies.

However, the law goes on to state that Federal law may provide for a number of exceptions, including those necessary for "the protection of the constitution, public morals and health, and the rights and lawful interest of other persons and the defense of the state." The potentially large number of exceptions thus gives considerable discretion to the Russian government.

The law also provides a "grandfather clause" that protects existing "priority" foreign investment projects with a foreign participation over 25 percent be protected from unfavorable changes in the tax regime or new limitations on the foreign investment. The definition of "priority" projects is not fully clear, but it appears that projects with a foreign charter capital of over $4.1 million and with a total investment of over $41 million will qualify. In addition, foreigners encounter significant restrictions on ownership of real estate in some cities and regions in Russia, although the situation has improved over the past few years.

The government maintains a monopoly on the sale of precious and several rare-earth metals, conducts centralized sales of diamonds, and conducts centralized purchases for export of military technology. Throughout 1999, the government has sharply restricted exports of platinum group metals, based on new legislation. An August 1997 series of Presidential Decrees on military exports remain in effect. These decrees established tighter control over military exports by the state enterprise Rosvooruzheniye, enabled two additional state firms to sell military goods and technology, and opened the door to future direct sales by arms manufacturers, if licensed and approved by the Ministry of Foreign Economic Relations.

Most of these issues are the subject of discussion, as Russia continues to negotiate its accession to the World Trade Organization (WTO). By the end of 1999, the government had completed ten working party meetings. It tabled its initial market access offer for services in October 1999 and has conducted negotiations on its goods market access offer throughout the year. The Russian Ministry of Trade has stated it plans to revise its goods market access offer early in 2000. Russia is not yet a signatory of the WTO Government Procurement or Civil Aircraft codes.

6. EXPORT SUBSIDIES POLICIES

The government has not instituted export subsidies, although a executive decree allows for provision of soft credits for exporters and government guarantees for foreign loans. The government does provide some subsidies for the production of coal, but coal exports are minimal. Soft credits are at times provided to small enterprises for specific projects.

7. PROTECTION OF U.S. INTELLECTUAL PROPERTY

Russia is in the process of accession to the World Trade Organization (WTO), and as a new member, it will be required to meet obligations under the WTO's Agreement on Trade-Related Aspects of Intellectual Property Rights (TRIPs) immediately upon accession. Russia belongs to the World Intellectual Property Organization (WIPO), and has acceded to the obligations of the former Soviet Union under the Paris Convention for the Protection of Industrial Property (patent, trademark and related industrial property), and the Madrid Agreement Concerning the International Registration of Marks, and the Patent Cooperation Treaty. Russia has also become a signatory to the

Berne Convention for the Protection of Literary and Artistic Works (copyright) as well as the Geneva Phonograms Convention. In 1999, the U.S. Trade Representative retained Russia on the "Special 301" Priority Watch List for a third year due to a number of concerns over weak enforcement of intellectual property laws and regulations and lack of retroactive copyright protection for U.S. works in Russia.

In 1992-93 Russia enacted laws strengthening the protection of patents, trademarks and appellations of origins, and copyright of semiconductors, computer programs, literary, artistic and scientific works, and audio/visual recordings. Legal enforcement of intellectual property rights (IPR) improved somewhat with a series of raids on manufacturing facilities, and on wholesale and retail outlets of pirated goods. A new Criminal Code took effect January 1, 1997, which contains considerably stronger penalties for IPR infringements. However, there are still disappointingly few cases in which these penalties have been applied. Widespread sales of pirated U.S. video cassettes, recordings, books, computer software, clothes, toys, foods and beverages continue. The formal abolition of the Russian Patent and Trademark Agency this year and the assumption of its responsibilities by the Justice Ministry have raised some concerns, but the practical effect of this change remains to be seen.

Russia's Patent Law includes a grace period, procedures for deferred examination, protection for chemical and pharmaceutical products, and national treatment for foreign patent holders. Inventions are protected for 20 years, industrial designs for ten years, and utility models for five years. The Law on Trademarks and Appellation of Origins introduces for the first time in Russia protection of appellation of origins. The Law on Copyright and Associated Rights, enacted in August 1993, protects all forms of artistic creation, including audio/visual recordings and computer programs as literary works for the lifetime of the author plus 50 years. The September 1992 Law on Topography of Integrated Microcircuits, which also protects computer programs, protects semiconductor topographies for 10 years from the date of registration.

Under the U.S.- Russian Bilateral Investment Treaty (signed in 1992 but waiting ratification by the Russian Parliament), Russia undertook to protect investors' intellectual property rights. The 1990 U.S. Russia bilateral trade agreement stipulates protection of the normal range of literary, scientific and artistic works through legislation and enforcement. Bilateral consultations on IPR were held in March 1999.

8.WORKER RIGHTS

a. The Right of Association: The law provides workers with the right to form and join trade unions, but practical limitations on the exercise of this right arise from governmental policy and the dominant position of the formerly governmental Federation of Independent Trade Unions of Russia (FNPR). As the successor organization to the governmental trade unions of the Soviet period and claiming to represent 80 per cent of all workers, the FNPR occupies a privileged position that inhibits the formation of new unions. In some cases, FNPR local unions have worked with management to destroy new unions. Recent court decisions have limited the right of association by mandating that unions include management as members. Justice Ministry officials have used new re-registration requirements to deny legal status to independent unions.

b. The Right to Organize and Bargain Collectively: Although the law recognizes collective bargaining, and requires employers to negotiate with unions, in practice employers often refuse to negotiate and agreements are not implemented. Court rulings have established the principle that non-payment of wages -- by far the predominant grievance -- is an individual dispute and cannot be addressed collectively by unions. As a result, a collective action based on non-payment of wages would not be recognized as a strike, and individuals would not be protected by the Labor Law's guarantees against being fired for participation. The right to strike is difficult to exercise. Most strikes are technically illegal, and courts have the right to order the confiscation of union property to settle damages and losses to an employer, resulting from an illegal strike. Reprisals for strikes are common, although strictly prohibited by law.

c. Prohibition of Forced or Compulsory Labor: The Labor Code prohibits forced or compulsory labor by adults and children. There are documented cases of soldiers being sent by their superior officers to perform work for private citizens or organizations. Such labor may violate military regulations and, if performed by conscripts, would be an apparent violation of ILO convention 29 on forced labor.

d. Minimum Age for Employment of Children: The Labor Code prohibits regular employment for children under the age of 16 and also regulates the working conditions of children under the age of 18, including banning dangerous, nighttime and overtime work. Children may, under certain specific conditions, work in apprenticeship or internship programs at the ages of 14 and 15. Accepted social prohibitions against the employment of children and the availability of adult workers at low wage rates combine to prevent widespread abuse of child labor legislation. The government prohibits forced and bonded labor by children, and there have been no reports that it occurred.

e. Acceptable Conditions of Work: The Labor Code provides for a standard workweek of 40 hours, with at least one 24-hour rest period. The law requires premium pay for overtime work or work on holidays. Workers have complained of being required to work well beyond the normal week, that is, 10 to 12-hour days, and of forced transfers. As of June 30, workers were owed roughly 2.5 billion US dollars, for periods generally between 3 to 9 months. Although this is less than the $12.5 billion arrears owed in August 1998, workers have lost significant purchasing power since the devaluation. Workers' freedom to move in search of new employment is virtually eliminated by the system of residency permits. The law establishes minimal conditions of workplace safety and worker health, but these standards are not effectively enforced.

f. Rights in Sectors with U.S. Investment: Observance of worker rights in sectors with significant U.S. investment (petroleum, telecommunications, food, aerospace, construction machinery, and pharmaceuticals) did not significantly differ from observance in other sectors. There are no export processing zones. Worker rights in the special economic zones/free trade zones are fully covered by the Labor Code.

U.S. INVESTMENT IN SELECTED INDUSTRIES

(Millions of U.S. Dollars)

Category	Amount
Petroleum	513
Total Manufacturing	269
Food & Kindred Products	243
Chemicals & Allied Products	11
Primary & Fabricated Metals	(1)
Industrial Machinery and Equipment	2
Electric & Electronic Equipment	(1)
Transportation Equipment	0
Other Manufacturing	1
Wholesale Trade	-76
Banking	-346
Finance/Insurance/Real Estate	653
Services	-102
Other Industries	190
Total All Industries	1,101

(1) Suppressed to avoid disclosing data of individual companies.

Source: U.S. Department of Commerce, Bureau of Economic Analysis.

TAX REFORM AND RELATIONSHIPS WITH THE REGIONS.

For a time in 1997, a momentum was underway for major tax reform, including the replacement of the Fundamental Tax Law of 1991. This Law specifies the principles of fiscal federalism for the Federation as a whole, prescribing a division of fiscal authority between three levels of government: federal, regional, and local. It should be noted, however, that there is no corresponding clear division of responsibility for expenditures. Ambiguities in the Tax Law itself, as well as complicated political realities, have led to a practice of separate bilateral negotiations between the center of power and the regions on the division of authority. A few regions, in fact, have negotiated deals with Moscow that guarantee complete fiscal independence.

A new draft law, "On the Fundamentals of the Tax System of the Russian Federation was passed by the Duma and sent to the Council of the Federation for ratification. Unfortunately, it might not be approved for a long period of time. The Draft Law introduces an increase in both equal treatment for regions, conforming to a single set of regulations, and restrictions on the scope of fiscal policy at all levels of government. One provision, for example, significantly reduces the power to set taxes at regional and local levels, cutting the current plethora of such taxes to a maximum of 2 and 4, respectively. Other restrictions are concerned with the levels of those taxes and the permissible range of the division of authority between the center of power and the regions. Some regions have resented and even opposed the Law. It is interesting to note that it has also become an explosive issue in the current election campaign. Chernomyrdinhas been actively campaigning against the Draft law and the equal-treatment-for-all-regions platform.

One major law was adopted on August 12, 1997: "On the General Principles of Local Self-Governance in the Russian Federation." One of the goals of this law was to define the difference between municipal, regional, and federal property in details, and to grant each level of government full ownership rights over the property in its domain. Although the economic and legal interpretations of much of this Law are difficult, at least one provision could be important. The legislation proposes a stable division of revenue between various levels of government. -1998 appears to be the first period in which all rules pertaining to the division of revenue are to remain rigidly fixed.

Before this Law was adopted, the Federal Government was legally free to change revenue sharing rules, or at least negotiate those changes, at any moment in time. But the fate of the provision is questionable due to the general instability of Russian Law and its implementation. As is usually the case in Russia every year, several new tax laws and amendments to old tax laws are introduced and approved. As of October 1997, many of the effective tax laws and instructions for remain unclear. Two somewhat contradictory tax reform themes this year were an increase in tax revenue for the central government and a decrease in the tax burden on economic organizations.

For additional analytical, business and investment opportunities information,
please contact Global Investment & Business Center, USA
at (202) 546-2103. Fax: (202) 546-3275. E-mail: rusric@erols.com
Global Business E-Books on Line: http://world.mirhouse.com

As political constraints largely prevent the victimization of regional and local budgets for this purpose, the latter goal seems to have been sacrificed for the former by the Fall of 1997. The tax system is to be made more transparent and effective. The number of taxes are to be reduced marginally, but made more significant. Numerous exemptions are to be eliminated. Furthermore, registration and enforcement are to be more effective and carried out according to a new set of basic principles.

The Duma agreed this year to eliminate the tax on "excess wages" for . But there is no consensus within the government on this issue. The government tied aid to the agro-industrial complex in to revenue from this tax, thus winning an important political lobby. It appears now that either the tax will remain in effect for , or it will be replaced by another tax that restricts wage growth according to average wages in the economy and a consumer price index. This tax will probably replace the existing one if the Duma insists on its earlier decision.

Some marginal changes will occur in tax rates and the way that taxes are calculated - with the aim of increasing revenue. A number of exemptions will be eliminated, most notably those for small businesses, construction (exemptions for the VAT and profit tax), and some tax heavens for special offshore zones (another example of a tax benefit to promote investment suddenly being revoked.) Investment tax credits in the form of the reduction of profit taxes will be decreased from 50 percent to a smaller number that is being debated. The - **"30 percent rule,"** introduced in 1997, which grants firms the right to deduct 30 percent of their pretax income for wages is to be eliminated. This rule is blamed for some shortfalls in revenue, and is already being gradually phased out at the end of 1997 (20 percent in October, 10 percent in December). Gasoline excise taxes were raised from 25 to 30 percent on September 1, 1997. A new plan to increase taxes and reduce exemptions for the huge gas monopoly, Gazprom, is also under way.

FEDERAL BUDGET

The budget, first submitted by the executive government to the Duma in October 1997, was approved by the Federation Council in December 1997 and signed by the President on January 19, . Critics suggest that the budget is deliberately set up in such a way as to maximize the executive government's discretionary authority to make necessary adjustments later in the year. The budget forecasts an inflation of 1.9 percent per month. According to this estimate, planned nominal expenditures and tax revenue are fixed, something that will automatically decrease real expenditures and increase revenue in the very likely event that inflation is higher. Inflation will likely be in the 3-5 percent a month range.

The budget assumes that the Federal Government will be much more successful in procuring revenue. Revenue is to rise to 15 percent of the GDP as part of the plan to reduce the budget deficit to 3.8 percent of the GDP, while at the same time increasing state expenditures. But even a highly successful privatization and revenue-procurement campaign in late 1997 could hardly bring the share of revenue above 14 percent in the

1997 GDP. It is not clear whether the marginal tax reform measures for (see below) are sufficient to warrant such optimism.

According to the budget, the average value of the dollar is to be 5,500 rubles, a figure well above the current boundary of 5,150. This could be the premise for allowing some nominal depreciation of the ruble next year. These two financial actions depends on the cooperation of the RCB.

The RCB seems to have adapted its plans for in accordance with the budgetary plans. Although credit expansion to commercial banks will be eased slightly in , the RCB is apparently committed to cut out any credit financing of the federal deficit.

ECONOMIC OVERVIEW

Continuing political uncertainties, rapid institutional change, and instability in expectations, make projecting future economic variables in Russia quite difficult. On the basis of current trends, GDP growth could very well be positive in . But continuing structural problems and the cumulative effect of very low investment for several years will most likely keep the growth to modest levels in the very near future. If progress in economic reform continues at its present pace, some of the enormous economic potential of the Russian Federation could be unleashed by the end of the century, and growth rates could accelerate into double-digits.

Table 10. Basic Economic Data

	1993	1994	1997		1999
Real GDP, % change 1	-7.1	-11.6	-4	2	4
CPI, % change 2	840	226	140	60	30
Unemployment 3	5.5	6	8	9	10
Trade balance ($ billion)	10.8	13	13	10	8
Current account ($ billion)	2.1	0.6	-4.4	-5	-5
Consolidated government budget deficit (% of GDP)	7.6	10.1	4	4	3.5

Note: 1993-94 represent actual estimates, 1997-97 are projections.
1. 1993 and 1994 are a Goskomstat recalculation of previously reported growth rates according to a new methodology.
2. December-on-December.
3. Percentage of economically active population.

Given the strong determination of the government and the RCB, with the encouragement of the IMF, to build on the 1997 progress in stabilization, significant reductions in inflation rates are likely in the next few years. Even though political reactions from the opposition could delay this process - and produce spurts of accelerated inflation along the way, economic realities will force the government back on the stabilization track rather quickly. The same can be said with the progress that has been made this year in controlling the Federal Deficit.

There is a definite upward dynamic in unemployment. As a large portion of employed workers will become redundant with the development of competitive markets, an increase in unemployment can be expected. A significant amount of managers have indicated their intentions to downsize in the near future.

The trade balance and the current account should deteriorate somewhat with the real appreciation of the ruble. Other transition economies are familiar with that process as well. As adverse expectations concerning stabilization caused part of the huge devaluation of the ruble since 1991, more positive expectations concerning stabilization, together with growing capital inflows, may continue to put upward pressure on the exchange rate. At the same time, exports of oil and fuels should remain strong. One has to keep in mind that adverse political intervention is still possible. Gradual progress in restructuring should also continually increase productivity and competitiveness. Whether the strong upward trends of late 1994 and early 1997 in the export-oriented sectors can be sustained in such an environment remains an important question.

PRIVATIZATION IN RUSSIA: TRENDS AND RESULTS

When measured in political or absolute terms, the Russian privatization program can be considered a success. Over 70 percent of state-owned small-scale retail trade and consumer services have been placed in private hands. In addition, over 15,000 medium- and large-scale enterprises have been privatized. Beyond the nominal transfer of ownership right, it is unclear whether privatization changed Russia's corporate culture. Incentives and behavior ought to change in Russian enterprises. Privatization needs to be supported by the development of capital markets as well as the ability to transfer corporate control and the emergence of a managerial labor pool.

1997 represented a continuum in the privatization drive in Russia. Compared to the earlier mass voucher-based program, the explicit goal of privatization since mid-1994 has been the procurement of revenue at various levels of government. Planned revenue from privatization in 1997 was 24 trillion ruble with 9.3 trillion going to the federal level. But, as of August 1997, the Institute of Economic Problems of the Transition Period in Moscow estimates that only 162 million (2 percent of the plan) has been collected by the Federal Government. Given the liquidity shortage, demand estimates proved much too optimistic. The spectrum of the upcoming elections, discussed below, may have played a role here. Typically, the required starting bid in the privatization auctions was higher than any willingness to pay.

In light of this situation, combined with the tax revenue problems discussed above, the Federal Government has been stepping up efforts in privatization toward the end of the year. Some very desirable, large, and profitable companies were included in a special mid-year August privatization list for September-December. These firms are to be partly sold (usually 10-40 percent of the stock). They include the giant oil-processing companies LUKoil (17 percent) and Yukos (15 percent), which increased their production by 16 and 22 percent respectively in the first five months of 1997.

One of the most interesting moves, this year, as far as privatization is concerned is a program, announced by a presidential decree in August 1997, to put up rights for the privatization (sale) of federal stock holdings as collateral for commercial credit to finance the deficit. The blocks of stock will be of highly-desirable oil and telecommunication companies. This scheme represents a watered-down variant of a proposal made by a Consortium of commercial banks in April 1997. The Federal Government expects to receive roughly 4-5 trillion rubles this way.

Rights will be auctioned off in the following way. Investors (banks) will bid amounts of "credit," corresponding to particular blocks of stock. If at least two bidders are present, then the highest bidder wins. That particular bidder essentially wins the right to make a loan to the Federal Government that is collateralized by the corresponding block of stock.

The Federal Government will pay market interest plus a premium on the loan until the end of 1997. At that point, the government will decide whether to pay back the loan or allow the creditor the right to sell the stock and receive a sum up to the value of the loan, plus 30 percent of all additional proceeds. Presumably, as long as the bids are reasonably high, the government will not pay back the loans. But the ability to pay back the loan provides the government with some kind of insurance in case the bids are too low. According to the original documents, 136 firms were to be auctioned off this way. The program seems to have failed as only 27 firms are still currently on the list. In fact, a few metals firms that were placed on the list have subsequently been taken off.

As a result of privatization in Russia, tens of thousands of state-owned enterprises - from small retail shops to major industrial enterprises - have been transformed into privately owned companies. More than 70 percent of the Russian work force is now employed by private businesses, according to official statistics.

Mass privatization in the Russian Federation was officially launched on October 1, 1992. On that particular date, 150 million individuals were issued with their first privatization vouchers. Each voucher had a nominal value of 10,000 rubles and gave the bearer the right to purchase shares in state-owned enterprises that were being transformed into joint stock companies. Simultaneously, between 5,000 and 7,000 state-owned enterprises, representing approximately 70 percent of the country's production capacity, were drawing up plans for their privatization. These plans were submitted to the State Committee for the Management of State Property on October 1, 1992. The legislative framework for privatization is complex. It consists of a number of laws, decrees and regulations issued during 1992-1994. Privatization of large state-owned enterprises generally involves:

1. incorporation of state-owned enterprises,
2. distribution of privatization vouchers and
3. selling shares of the newly created joint stock companies or assets of state-owned enterprises.

GOVERNMENT INVOLVEMENT

The privatization program operates on three different administrative levels: federal, regional, and municipal. The authorities on any given level have the right to privatize only the assets that have been transferred to their ownership. On the federal level, two major bodies are involved in the privatization process: 1. the State Committee for the Management of State Property (Goskomimushchestvo or GKI), and 2. the Russian Federal State Property Fund, referred to as the Property Fund.

STATE COMMITTEE ON STATE PROPERTY MANAGEMENT (GKI

GKI is the main Russian privatization agency. It operates mainly through branches called management committees. GKI drafts, coordinates, and controls the implementation of the privatization program. In addition, its role is also to draft other laws and normative acts of privatization. Among its numerous powers, GKI is authorized to take decisions on privatized federally owned enterprises, set up commissions within the enterprises responsible for their privatization, effect the necessary restructuring in their legal and organizational form, and hand over their ownership certificates to the Property Fund. GKI is empowered to take legal action against anyone who violates federal legislation on privatization.

THE STATE PROPERTY FUND

The Property Fund has the power to execute the legal instruments necessary to implement the privatization of federally owned enterprises. The Fund and its duly appointed representatives are the only sellers of state enterprises and of shares or stocks of enterprises being privatized. Accordingly, it organizes auctions and tenders at which shares are sold, holds the shares of privatized state enterprises, and ensures that incentives and advantages given to employees regarding privatization are observed. The Fund represents the interests of the state at general meetings of shareholders - no more than 20 percent of the shares held by the Property Fund may carry voting rights. The Property Fund has the duty to sell the shares for which the voting restriction disappears - all shares have voting rights. The Property Fund receives the proceeds from the sales and transfers them to the state as set forth in Russia's budget and privatization program.

OTHER INSTITUTIONS INVOLVED IN PRIVATIZATION

Regional privatization committees and property funds have been established with structures and authority mirroring those of GKI and the Property Fund.

For additional analytical, business and investment opportunities information,
please contact Global Investment & Business Center, USA
at (202) 546-2103. Fax: (202) 546-3275. E-mail: rusric@erols.com
Global Business E-Books on Line: http://world.mirhouse.com

PROCEDURES AND REGULATIONS EFFECTING PRIVATIZATION

Once the management committee has authorized the privatization of an enterprise, the regional privatization committee prepares a privatization plan within six months. GKI may offer a six-month extension

The privatization plan determines: 1. the method of privatization, 2. option selected by the employees (see below); 3. the time-period; 4. the initial price enterprise; and, 5. the amount of the joint stock partnership's authorized capital after incorporation.

The plan requires the approval of the appropriate management committee, local authorities and workers' collective - all of which will have participated in preparing the plan. The privatization of enterprises included in the State Register of Associations and Monopolistic Enterprises must be implemented in coordination with the **State Anti-Monopoly Committee**.

Once a privatization plan is approved, a nominated management committee transforms the enterprise into a joint stock company. Once created, the shares of the ISC are transferred to the appropriate property fund. A standard form charter, which must comply with the appropriate regulation, must be adopted by all state enterprises transformed into joint-stock companies.

Joint-stock companies arising from the privatization process are subject to existing legislation on joint stock companies, which provides for three different categories of shares:

COMMON SHARES

Type A preferred shares, which may not comprise more than 25 percent of share capital and which are used exclusively for free distribution to employees who have chosen Option 1 (see below). These shares have voting rights but pay a fixed two percent dividend, and remain preferential even after being transferred to new owners.

Type B preferred shares, may be held only by the Property Fund, which acts as the seller in privatization transactions. Type B shares have no voting rights, but give the holder a fixed five percent dividend. When type B shares are transferred, they are automatically converted into common shares. The Property Fund may not hold voting common shares in an amount greater than 20 percent of the total preferred and common shares of the company. The balance of the shares held by the Property Fund will be type B preferred shares.

PRIVATIZATION METHODS

There are two main privatization methods. The privatization program makes a distinction between small and big enterprises. Small enterprises with a fixed capital of

For additional analytical, business and investment opportunities information,
please contact Global Investment & Business Center, USA
at (202) 546-2103. Fax: (202) 546-3275. E-mail: rusric@erols.com
Global Business E-Books on Line: http://world.mirhouse.com

no more than one million rubles - book value as of January 1, 1992 - may, without first being transformed into joint-stock companies, be sold at auctions or at investment tenders. All other enterprises may be privatized through:

- *the sale of shares in open-type joint-stock companies created during the privatization process;*
- *the sale of enterprises, which are not joint-stock companies, at auctions;*
- *the sale of enterprises, which are not joint stock companies, by commercial tender;*
- *the sale of blocks of shares in joint-stock companies by commercial tender;*
- *the sale, at auctions or by tender, of property of operating enterprises, of enterprises being liquidated, of liquidated enterprises, or of facilities whose construction is incomplete;*
- *the sale of leased property;*
- *the sale of share-holdings in state or municipal property by auction and commercial tender.*

Employees and managers in privatized enterprises transformed into joint stock companies, enjoy the benefit of choosing between three different privatization options.

Option 1. Twenty-five percent of the shares are allocated free of charge to employees - these shares are preferred nonvoting. Employees may purchase a further 10 percent of shares at 30 percent less than the nominal value. They may pay in installments over a period of three years - the first installment must not be less than 15 percent of the nominal value. The managers of the company are entitled to purchase five percent of the shares at 0.7 percent of the share's book value, as determined by state auditors. Additional shares purchased by both the employees and the management will be common shares.

Option 2. Employees are offered 51 percent of shares at 1.7 percent of the share's book value. Such shares are common shares.

Option 3. This option is only for companies with more than 200 employees and whose assets are between one and fifty million rubles. Employees and managers may form a group to restructure the company. This group is required to sign a contract stating the terms of the re-structuring. The group has the right to acquire 30 percent of the common shares at their nominal value upon expiration of the contract. During the validity of the contract, the group has the right to vote for all the shares held by the state. All employees, including those who are members of the restructuring group, have the right to purchase 20 percent of the common shares at their nominal value less 30 percent. Payment can be made by installments over a period not exceeding three years. The first installment must be at least 20 percent of the nominal value of the shares.

For additional analytical, business and investment opportunities information, please contact Global Investment & Business Center, USA at (202) 546-2103. Fax: (202) 546-3275. E-mail: rusric@erols.com Global Business E-Books on Line: http://world.mirhouse.com

The employees must vote for one of the different options and present their decision to the regional privatization committee. Decisions require a two-third majority of all the employees. If, for some reason, a decision is not reached collectively by the employees, then the first option is used. Furthermore, the employees of each company are entitled to 10 percent of the proceeds from the sale of the shares of that particular company - excluding proceeds from shares sold to the employees themselves. The proceeds are transferred to individual privatization accounts to be kept by the company in question.

In practice, the employees of most large state enterprises choose Option 2. That option enables them to acquire 51 percent of the shares and thus obtain control of the privatized enterprise. The least popular option so far has been Option 3.

POSSIBILITIES FOR FOREIGN INVESTORS TO PARTICIPATE IN PRIVATIZATION

Since the start of the Russian privatization process, the government has attempted to encourage foreign participation. Privatization legislation contains remarkably few restrictions on foreign participation. Section 10 of the privatization program allows foreign investors to participate in auctions, tenders and investment tenders with prior notification of the Ministry of Finance. No permission from any Russian authority is required. If a transaction is completed with foreign investors, the sole vendor of state and municipal property is the corresponding Property Fund. If foreign investors are the only participants in an auction, tender or investment tender, enterprises may be sold to them.

The privatization program contains three restrictions concerning foreign participation: 1. government approval is required for the privatization of enterprises in the defense industry, the gas and oil industry, of transport and communication enterprises, and of enterprises extracting and processing strategic ores, precious and semi-precious stones, radioactive and rare elements; 2. foreign investors are not allowed to participate in the privatization of enterprises located in restricted areas; and 3. following an auction or tender, the concerned privatization bodies must submit information on successful foreign bidders to the Federal counterintelligence Service, which has the right, within one month, to advise the Russian Government to stop the transaction.

It is interesting to note that despite the facilities that foreign investments are experiencing, foreign participation in the Russian privatization process has been relatively limited. One explanation may be the heavy emphasis on voucher auctions during the earlier stages of privatization, which in practice, kept foreign companies from participating. Foreign investors were allowed to acquire privatization vouchers but currency procedures made this task difficult.

The program put an end to privatization through voucher auctions after July 1, 1994. All auctions must now be conducted on a cash basis. The rules and regulations applicable to voucher auctions are also applicable to cash auctions, with some minor amendments.

The government hopes that cash auctions will increase the participation of foreign investors in the privatization process, particularly since the program allows for the sale of shares held by the state in joint-stock companies and since a number of state enterprises being privatized are joint ventures with foreign partners.

INVESTMENT TENDERS

Investment tenders may be an attractive way for foreign companies to participate in the privatization process. Although many state-owned enterprises are in the process of being privatized and a large portion of their shares have already been distributed (to managers, workers, etc.) and sold at voucher auctions, the remaining shares have to be sold through investment tenders.

The provisions contained in the program regarding investment tender contain several features of interest to foreign investors. One provision is that the enterprise's debts are considered as part of the investment in the enterprise. This opens up interesting possibilities for Western companies to acquire Russian debt at reduced rates and use it in connection with the investment tender procedure.

GKI recently detailed the formerly sketchy procedures for submitting an investment tender with the enactment of Ordinance No. 342 and its Regulations (the Regulations) on February 15, 1994.

Under the Regulations, the first step in the investment tender calls for an enterprise to prepare a proposal based on its investment needs - the proposal needs to meet "mandatory investment conditions." According to these conditions, the proposal must state the minimum bid amounts to be paid by the winner of the tender in cash or in a combination of cash and other forms of payment. The cash portion may not, however, constitute less than 20 percent of the total investment and must be paid within one month of the tender. The investment proposal must further specify the time period in which the investment is to be made. An investor needs to keep in mind that he has a maximum of three years between the signature of the sales contract and the carrying out of the operation. Finally, the proposal must require that the winner of the tender purchase the shares at their nominal value.

Once the proposal is approved by the appropriate management committee, an announcement describing the terms and conditions of the tender must be published in a public newspaper. The proposal may also appear in the official journal of the Property Fund depending on the size of the share capital or the market share of the enterprise. Bids may be submitted at any time up to the deadline stated in the announcement.

The bids are evaluated by a tender commission formed by the Property Fund. The commission is composed of three members representing: the Property Fund, the management committee and the relevant federal or regional authority.

For additional analytical, business and investment opportunities information,
please contact Global Investment & Business Center, USA
at (202) 546-2103. Fax: (202) 546-3275. E-mail: rusric@erols.com
Global Business E-Books on Line: http://world.mirhouse.com

All bids are submitted to the tender commission in sealed envelopes. These envelopes may only be opened on the day of the tender. All participants in the tender are entitled to be present at the time this takes place. The bids are reviewed for compliance with the terms of the adopted tender proposal. The commission shall then determine the highest bid among the qualifying ones. Regardless of the monetary denomination of the bid, the Regulations specify a formula for establishing the bid's ruble value that accounts for the duration of the investment. According to the Regulations, the only criterion for determining the winner is the size of the investment, calculated according to the formula.

Immediately upon determining the winner, the tender commission shall finalize a protocol. Within three days, the seller and the winner will execute a sales agreement for the block of shares that are to be sold at the nominal value. The sum of money must be transferred in cash to the appropriate Property Fund within ten days of the tender. The winner will have full ownership right to the shares only after such payment has been made. In the event that the sales agreement is not executed in a timely manner by the winner, the shares will be offered to the second highest bidder.

If the winning bidder does not fulfill his obligations, the overseeing Property Fund has the right to nullify the agreement. The regulations neither specify such procedures nor their outcome. There may be a risk that the purchaser will lose the nominal value of the shares transferred by the seller. It is unclear whether investments may be returned. Therefore, winning bidders should include provisions for this contingency in their sales agreements.

CASH AUCTIONS AND LOAN FOR SHARES

As mentioned above, the voucher auctions have, as of July 1, 1994, been replaced by cash auctions. However, for a number of reasons the Government did not conduct cash auctions in 1994. The Moscow Property Fund launched the first of these at the beginning of 1997. The procedure for conducting cash auctions largely corresponds to the one employed in voucher auctions. The voucher has been replaced by "lots," representing each 10,000 rubles. So-called agents perform a great deal of the practical work in connection with cash auctions. They act according to a contract with the relevant property fund.

To participate in a cash auction, a participant must submit a number of corporate documents evidencing the ownership structure of the potential bidder. In addition, the participant is required to advance a deposit equal to the entire amount of the proposed bid. The agent determines the initial price for the shares sold at cash auctions. In the past, the initial price did not usually exceed 20 times the nominal value of the shares. However, the Government of the City of Moscow now has the right to determine the initial price - according to the balance sheet of the enterprise in question. Two types of bids are used in cash auctions: *competitive* and *non-competitive*. The first type of bid implies that the bidder will purchase shares at the price established in the auction. The second type implies that the bidder will indicate the highest price per share at which he is prepared to purchase them. If the price eventually reached in the auction is above the potential buyer's limit, the bid is disregarded and the advance deposit returned to the bidder.

The agent typically accepts the bids and transfers them to the property fund once the bidding period is completed. It is then up to the property fund to determine the actual price of the shares and the winner of the auction.

Cash auctions were originally intended to be the second wave in the Russian privatization effort. For a number of reasons, however, the speed of privatization slowed down since the conclusion of the voucher auctions. In September 1997, the Russian Government engaged in a "new" wave of privatization based on loan scheme originally proposed by a group of Russian banks.

In accordance with this "new" wave, investors will have the opportunity to manage the Russian Government's shares in state enterprises in exchange of loans - this plan is based on two presidential decrees. The highest bidder at an auction will be given the right to manage the shares of an enterprise. In return, the successful bidder has to make a loan to the Government - the loan is thus guaranteed by the shares. The successful bidder has the right to sell the shares in a time period of six months to three years after the loan has been granted. At this point, the successful bidder will not only have its loan repaid in full but a moderate fixed interest rate will be added. In addition, the successful bidder will receive 30 percent of the share price appreciation between the time of the loan and the sale of the shares. This implies that the government will receive 70 percent of any share price appreciation.

Whether or not this scheme will be of interest to investors very much depend on the extent to which the successful bidder has the possibility to exercise rate control during the loan period. The presidential decrees stipulate that the successful bidder cannot vote independently on matters concerning: 1) the liquidation and reorganization of the enterprise; 2) changes to and amendments of the chart including the size of the share capital; 3) the sale, mortgage or lease of many assets or the confirmation of the annual amounts and issuing securities. The prior written approval of GKI is necessary concerning such matters.

It is important to note that foreign investors will only be able to bid for the enterprise that the government is in the process of privatizing under the loan-for-shares scheme. The Russian government has published a list of 29 enterprises auctioned this way in 1997. Referring to the Russian economy's strategic security interest, the Government has announced that foreign investors will not be able to bid for a number of enterprises including: Lukoil, Sidanko, Yukos (all three major oil companies), Norilsk Nickel, Novorossiisk Shipping Company and the progressive aviation company. It should be noted, however, that foreign investors are not excluded from bidding on Surgutneftegas which is another major oil company.

PRIVATIZATION OF LAND

The different legislation do not refer or include the privatization of land. This fact is explicitly stated in Article 26 of the privatization law, and repeated in the 1994 privatization program

On March 25, 1992, President Yeltsin, in Decree No. 301 allowed the privatization of land in connection with the privatization of enterprises that occupy it. However, no detailed provisions or procedures were laid down in this decree. On June 14, 1992, President Yeltsin adopted Decree No. 631 outlining the procedures for the purchase of land for commercial and industrial purposes in connection with privatization. Investors have to keep in mind that according to restrictions mentioned in the decree, they will not be able to privatize national parks, public gardens and parks, river embankments, beaches, etc. It should be noted that rights to land containing mineral deposits will continue to be regulated by the law on sub-surface resources.

Decree No. 631 outlines two types of procedures concerning the purchase of land: those connected with the privatization of an enterprise and those having to do with the expansion of the business activities of a privatized enterprise. According to those procedures, the privatization plan for an enterprise must contain a site plan, including, among other things, the location of the buildings, the boundaries of the tract, and the mental and geological conditions. Furthermore, the price of the land is to be determined according to Russian law, which presumably is a reference to the law on payment for land adopted on October 11, 1991, as amended, and the instruction on the application of the law on payment for land adopted on April 17, 1992, as amended. However, since these legislative acts primarily deal with agricultural land, the procedure for determining the value of land remains largely undefined.

According to Section 6 of Decree No. 631, the right to purchase land is a "mandatory condition" when conducting auctions or tenders for the sale of an enterprise. Although it is not entirely clear how this wording is supposed to be understood, it seems to mean that the sale of the land is to be a separate entity from the privatization of the enterprise itself. The starting price for the enterprise announced at an auction or in a tender is not to include the price of the land, which is to be listed separately in the privatization documents.

The assumption is that the owner of the privatized enterprise that has the right to purchase the land is another troublesome aspect of Decree No. 631. According to the decree, the enterprise itself, rather than the owner, will own the land. The problem arises when one considers that the land is usually owned by several persons and not only one. Administering multi-party ownership of one piece of land will be impractical and legally difficult, if not impossible.

A subsequent Presidential Decree - Decree No. 1229 - adopted on October 14, 1992, takes a different approach. Section 2 stipulates that once the required number of shares in a joint-stock company is sold for privatization vouchers, the company has the right to purchase the land on which it stands. In other words, the company itself and not its owners (the shareholders) will have the possibility to acquire the land. This approach is both legally and practically better than its predecessor.

Notwithstanding the fact that President Yeltsin has issued additional decrees in May and July 1994 - further relining the privatization of land, - only a minimum amount of such privatization have taken place so far. The relatively high price of the land is probably one of the reasons. The main factor, however, is that the regulations are neither comprehensive nor transparent. This situation will likely continue until the Russian Duma passes the new Land Code, now under preparation. Until that happens, the provisions of the new Civil Code dealing with private ownership will not take effect.

For additional analytical, business and investment opportunities information,
please contact Global Investment & Business Center, USA
at (202) 546-2103. Fax: (202) 546-3275. E-mail: rusric@erols.com
Global Business E-Books on Line: http://world.mirhouse.com

SECURITIES MARKET AND SECURITIES MARKET REGULATIONS

Despite the passage of more than 50 legislative acts aimed at the licensing and control of stock market activities since 1991, the regulation of the Russian securities market is still in its early stages of development. At the present time, investors in Russian securities can rely on few of the legal or administrative safeguards familiar to Western counterparts. The pace of development is rapid however, and Russian securities firms are becoming increasingly sophisticated. It is interesting to note that a number of western firms have begun operations. However, entry into effect of a new, comprehensive, securities law is not expected before - at the earliest.

Because of the level of risk and the lack of effective regulatory supervision, small retail investors will not find the Russian securities market attractive. At the present time, the rights of shareholder are best defended by both the continual monitoring of the issuer's affairs and the contact with the issuer itself. As of right now, there is no effective system of share custody in effect in Russia. Government securities denominated in rubles offer very high yields but their convertibility is less then transparent.

RUSSIAN SECURITIES MARKET: BASIC TRENDS OF DEVELOPMENT

In the autumn of 1992 Russia issued privatization vouchers to its 148 million citizens, instantly creating the same number of securities holders. That was only a start. Now the capital an securities market in Russia is really taking off. According to the existing forecasts, the Russian Stock Exchange will be the most dynamic and rapidly developing exchanges in the world. The Russian Info&Business Center and the Russian-American Chamber of Commerce (Washington, DC) will be updating their customers and members on new development in the Russian capital market. For additional information and updates, please contact us directly or visit our Russian DataBank on-Line WWW site.[6]

Russia continues along the path of normalizing its economy, the process of establishing and opening a capital and securities markets. The current Russian Trading System reflects a commitment on the part of leading brokers to make a market in 21 stocks whose market capitalization is about 80 percent of all public companies, thus affording investors liquidity. And the first mutual funds are now in the start-up process.

Americans who hold shares in US public companies have grown accustomed to a steady diet of disclosure in the form of annual reports (SEC Form 10-K), quarterly reports (Form 10-Q) and news releases (Form 8-K). Under the new Russian securities

---

[6] Russian Info&Business Center, Inc. (202)546-2103, Fax: (202)546-3275.

law[7], the country's *Commission on Securities and Exchanges* will oversee a reporting and disclosure system very much like the American current reporting disclosure system. 10-Q-like quarterly reports, 10-K-like annual reports, 8K-like material event reports, proxy statements for annual meetings, prospectuses for new issues, and disclosure points reflective of standard American accounting conventions and concepts are all characters in a familiar drama. How Russian companies will respond and comply remains to be seen.

Currently, most Russian companies are skittish about even rudimentary financial disclosures. What enforcement tools will the federal Commission on Securities and Exchanges have? How effectively will it wield these tools? Presumably when a new-to-market issuer files a registration statement for purposes of issuing new equity, the commission will exact full compliance. Article 51 of the new law provides for civil liability for damages resulting from failures in compliance, and provisions have been added to the *Criminal Code* (effective January 1 1997) covering violations of capital markets laws and regulations. But whether companies will seek new shareholders is problematic.

NEW ISSUES OF SECURITIES MARKET DEVELOPMENT

Under Article 20, a completed application, including the form of prospectus and evidence of the issuer's board approval, is required to make a registration for an equity offering effective. A state registration number is then assigned. Article 21 requires that the prospectus include three years of financial statements (accounting standards are to be developed jointly with the Ministry of Finance).

Previously, a prospectus was required even when a small amount of stock was issued, but this requirement was generally not observed. The new securities law requires a prospectus only where the number of investors will exceed 500, or the value of the securities will be in excess of 50 million minimum wages (almost $800,000). Information required to be set forth in the prospectus, in addition to three years' financial information, includes the names of persons owning more than 5 percent of the charter capital of the issuer, names of directors, and overdue indebtedness of the issuer (this last requirement should produce some interesting year-end and quarter-end refunding schemes).

Current Reports & Inside Information. Under Article 23, a quarterly report must be filed within 30 days of the end of the fiscal quarter, and must contain a balance sheet, an income statement, and if appropriate, a description of any material development affecting 20 percent or more of the value of the company's assets or profits. The quarterly report must be approved by the governing board.

Trading based on inside information is prohibited. "Inside information" is defined as any information not generally available. An "insider" is defined as an officer or other

[7] Russian Federation Law No. 39, On the Securities Market, adopted by the State Duma March 20 and effective as of April 25

individual, such as a lawyer or printer, whose work-related responsibilities or contractual relations expose him or her to such information. In addition, the securities law prohibits depositories or custodians from trading in securities, and companies from trading in their own securities. A company may not project expected rates of return on its stock in its advertisements, an may make no guarantees.

COMMISSION ON SECURITIES AND EXCHANGES

This new agency has been patterned after the US Securities and Exchange Commission. Created by presidential decree on March 9, 1993, this federal commission has been administering the licensing of market professionals and the filing of prospectuses for new issues, and has generally been assisting in the organization and surveillance of the securities markets. Under recent decrees governing new mutual funds (Presidential Decree No. 765, July 26, 1997), the commission will also register new funds and their prospectuses and license their investment managers and depositories for fund shares.

SECURITIES MARKER REGULATION IN 1991-

The regulatory infrastructure in Russia lags behind the market's development. Securities regulation is still divided among several agencies: the Ministry of Finance (MinFin), the Central Bank, the State Property Committee, the State Anti-Monopoly Committee (which must approve stock purchases constituting a change of control). The establishment of the Commission on Securities and Exchanges, made up of six full-time members, represents an attempt at a more coordinated approach. The creation of this type of independent agency is unusual in a civil law country, where such licensing and regulatory functions are normally subordinate to a line ministry, such as justice or finance; it is a very promising development indeed in Russia. As a recent World Bank study shows, a legal and regulatory framework, and a pattern of required financial disclosure to the financial markets, are the most important dimensions for the development of substantial, robust capital markets in formerly communist countries.

Yet the future shape of the capital markets themselves is unclear. Russian bankers evidently favor a German-Japanese market infrastructure model based on bank-centered groups of companies with industrial and other financially linked affiliates. Securities trading would take place infrequently among large stockholders. The Russian Central Bank seems to favor this model. The other model is the

SECURITIES IN RUSSIA: CURRENT STAGE OF DEVELOPMENT

The definition of an *"issued security"* contained in Russia's securities law goes beyond the definition of "security" in the Civil Code (which limits a security to an instrument or document) by including "non-documentary" securities *(Law on the Securities Market, Article 2)*. Article 16 provides that securities may be issued in registered documentary form, where share interests may be set forth in one or several certificates stating the total number of shares represented by the certificate, the category of shares, and the face value of the aggregate number of shares; in registered non-documentary form; or in bearer form, which can only be in the form of a document. The securities low also provides that a security issued in documentary form may be represented by either a share certificate or, in case the certificates ore held by a custodian, by appropriate entries in the custodian's register (Article 2). In addition, since the early 1990s, various agencies of the Russian government, namely the Ministry of Finance, the State Property Committee, the Russian Central Bank, and the Commission on Securities and Exchanges, have enacted a number of regulatory measures that currently govern the issuance and circulation of Russian securities (primarily shares of joint-stock companies). These regulations contemplate a broader definition of security than that provided in the Civil Code.

In addition to the newly enacted definition of securities, one of the major pieces of Russian securities regulation, *Decree No 78 (December 28, 1991)*, provides that securities in Russia may exist "as separate documents or as book entries" (Article 1, Paragraph 1), that is, they may be certified or not. In practice today, very few Russian companies issue share certificates, and the vast majority of corporate securities are un-certified, existing in book entry form only.

Under the Law on Joint-Stock Companies, Russian joint-stock companies are allowed to issue the following types of securities: common stocks, preferred stocks, bonds, and other types of securities allowed by Russian law (Articles 25 and 33). These securities may be issued by both open and closed joint-stock companies. The difference between the securities issued by these two types of joint-stock companies lies in their transferability. Under Article 7, and as described above, shares of open joint-stock companies are freely transferable (but see "Special Restrictions," p. 41), while shares of closed joint-stock companies are transferable subject to the existing shareholders' rights of first refusal and, if so provided in the company's charter, the company's right of first refusal.

Russian joint-stock companies may also issue bonds. These bonds may be secured bonds, "collateralized" by a pledge of the company's or a third party's assets, or unsecured bonds. The latter may be issued only by companies that have existed for at least three years and have at least two duly approved annual reports. Under the Law on Joint-Stock Companies, bonds may be inscribed or bearer (Article 33). Inscribed bonds, which may be certified or uncertified, must be registered in the company's register. This law deals largely with the procedures applicable to the transfer and pledge of securities, and does not contain specific rules on the keeping of a register for owners of corporate bonds. The registration of inscribed bond transfers is governed by regulations issued by the Federal Commission on Securities and Exchanges.

SHARES: SPECIAL RESTRICTIONS
The shares of certain open joint-stock companies established in the course of privatization are subject to restrictions on transfer. For instance, the charter and other

constitutive documents of RAO Gazprom, an open joint-stock company, contain provisions that allow shareholders to sell their shares only after offering these securities to the company itself. Gazprom's board of directors has the right either to purchase the shares or allow the transferring shareholder to sell them. Generally, these provisions do not comply with current Russian legislation, nor were they in compliance with the previous wave of corporate legislation in force when Gazprom's charter was adopted. However, since Gazprom's charter was adopted by presidential Decree, certain Russian legal scholars take the position that Gazprom and other major Russian companies whose charters were also adopted in this fashion are exempt from the application of Russian corporate laws.

British-American, more open capital-markets model, where large institutional holders participate through, and depend upon, the liquidity afforded by public capital markets (the exchanges and over-the-counter markets). The new commission favors this second model. Russian banks and their affiliates currently lack the financial strength to impose the first model. A hybrid institutional market model probably will develop in Russia, assuring substantial capital markets activity.

FEDERAL MINISTRY OF FINANCE AND THE CENTRAL BANK

In December 1991, the Russian government adopted the basic scheme of securities regulation that MinFin had worked out with the Central Bank (Decree No. 78). The decree set forth a comprehensive, if skeletal, scheme of securities regulations that includes: oversight by the Ministry of Finance (MinFin) -- with the Central Bank playing the same role for the banks -- disclosure by prospectus in the public offering of securities; licensing and regulation of non-bank broker-dealers, investment advisers, stock exchanges and the over-the-counter market; qualification of securities professionals; disclosure and consent of the antimonopoly committee to acquisitions of control; and prohibition of insider trading.

Pursuant to the decree, MinFin promulgated a series of implementing regulations covering prospectuses (No. 2, March 3, 1992), stock exchange licensing and operations (No. 20, April 13, 1992; No. 1-5-06, August 31, 1992), and broker-dealer qualification and secondary trading (No. 53, July 6, 1992, and No. 91, September 22, 1992). More recently, MinFin has begun to require that issuers file their annual reports with it (Regulation No. 59, May 5, 1994), except for banks, which must file with the Central Bank.

ROLE OF THE FEDERAL REGISTRAR

Article 8 of the new securities law governs registry activities. Registrars must maintain individual accounts for the legal owners of securities or their nominees containing, as of a given date, the name, face value, and amount and type of securities. The new law requires the registrar to charge the same fee for transaction services to all clients, and makes registrars liable for losses caused by their failure to perform their duties properly, including the maintenance of complete and accurate extracts. Any person or entity registered as an owner, nominal holder, or *pledgee* of shares of a company may, at any time, request that the registrar issue an extract from the shareholders' or pledgees' register.

Under Russian law, an extract from the shareholders' register is a document that confirms the status of an owner or pledgee of the shares, but (as opposed to a share certificate) is not a security itself. An extract from the shareholders' register is thus a snapshot of the status of the shareholder's personal account in the company's register as of that date, and must contain all information included in the personal account, including the name of the account holder, the number of securities registered to his name, and any data on encumbrances. The new law thus clearly provides for the duty of a registrar to issue extracts in respect of pledges. Article 8 also contains an interesting provision that any shareholder owning more than one percent of shares is entitled to a complete list of the other shareholders from the registrar, a useful acquisition tool.

Under the Law on Joint-Stock Companies, every Russian joint-stock company must maintain a register of its shareholders. Smaller companies may keep the register themselves, while companies with more than 500 shareholders must appoint as a registrar an independent company licensed by the Commission on Securities and Exchanges. Russian publicly traded (open joint-stock) companies generally comply with these requirements. However, the majority of closed joint-stock companies, especially those with only a few shareholders, do not keep shareholders' registers, and the names of shareholders and the number of shares they own are reflected only in the shareholders' agreements and charters of such companies.

The Statute on Shareholders' Registers also provides that a company's share register must include information on the securities issued by the company, its shareholders, and also on possible liens and encumbrances against the securities. Again, the company's registrar must open separate accounts in the name of every owner and nominal holder (nominee) of the company's securities. The statute further provides (Article 2, Paragraph 2.6) that the following information must be included in a personal account:

Account number

Name of the owner or nominal holder of the shares

Address of the owner or nominal holder, and information allowing the company to transfer dividends and other payments to the owner or nominal holder

Amount of accrued and paid dividends

Number and types of shares owned or held by the person in whose name the account was opened

Encumbrances against the shares, including any pledges of the shares and the number of the personal account of the pledge-holder

Stock certificate number(s), if the company issues stock certificates

For additional analytical, business and investment opportunities information,
please contact Global Investment & Business Center, USA
at (202) 546-2103. Fax: (202) 546-3275. E-mail: rusric@erols.com
Global Business E-Books on Line: http://world.mirhouse.com

THE STATE COMMITTEE ON STATE PROPERTY MANAGEMENT

In the Fall of 1992 Russia issued privatization vouchers to its 148 million citizens, instantly creating the same number of securities holders, who were then entitled to exchange their vouchers for shares in state-owned enterprises. At the close of the voucher privatization program on July 1, 1994, the State Property Committee (abbreviated "GKI" in Russian), the country's securities regulator, had supervised the first step "corporatization" of 15,000 state enterprises, and had privatized half of Russian industry.

By making vouchers tradable, the State Property Committee had also spawned Russia's most active securities market. And by permitting closed-end voucher investment funds to issue fund shares in exchange for vouchers, the State Property Committee, with the help of television commercials claiming returns of 2000 to 3000 percent, had also spawned 650 funds. Some were little more than pyramid schemes, and the collapse of several of them provided Russia with its most spectacular securities scandals to date.

Not surprisingly, the State Property Committee immediately recognized the need to police these voucher funds created at the beginning of the state privatization effort, and contemporaneously with Russia's issuance of privatization vouchers a decree was issued by President Boris Yeltsin providing for the registration and regulation of voucher funds (No. 1186, October 7, 1992).

But the State Property Committee soon found its role as a securities regulator expanded in unexpected ways. As the midwife to the birth of thousands of public companies through privatization, and charged by a political agenda to make sure that Russia's new shareholders did not feel duped, the committee entered through the back door of corporate governance and began the regulation of the stock market and its development. Within weeks of the first voucher auction, the committee found itself up against recalcitrant corporate managers who, having enjoyed steadily increasing autonomy since the beginning of *perestroika*, were in no mood to recognize shareholders other than themselves and their easily-manipulated employees.

The State Property Committee responded in two ways. It fashioned a presidential decree on shareholder rights (No. 1769, October 27, 1993), and followed up with detailed implementing rules for share registries five months later (No. 840-r, April 18, 1994). Second, with little in the way of an enforcement mechanism at its disposal, the committee sought foreign assistance to introduce the technology and organization necessary to foster independent share registrars and clearance and settlement organizations, hoping thereby to break the hold of enterprise managers on the mechanisms for enfranchising new shareholders (GKI No. 859-1, April 20,1994).

In June of 1994, President Yeltsin issued two decrees. One (No. 1200, June 11, 1994), anticipating new issues of stocks and bonds by privatized companies, restated and revised the requirements for registering offerings (including minimum charter capital requirements for companies distributing their shares), and imposed periodic reporting requirements, including publication in newspapers by large issuers. The decree also barred companies with less than three years of operation from issuing bonds. The other decree (No. 1182, June 10, 1994), responding in part to the voucher fund scams, sought to curb blatant fraud in the sale of voucher fund shares by prohibiting unsubstantiated claims on returns. For example, it mandates disclosure of actual performance data and directs MinFin and the Central Bank to review advertising, publish lists of companies that provide financial services without a license, and prohibit such companies from advertising.

NOMINEE ACCOUNTS AND OFFSHORE TRADING

Securities trading in Russia is complicated by the requirement that any transfer of securities be recorded in the issuing company's register of shareholders. This requirement has led to the use of a nominee system by a majority of foreign investors. This system involves an arrangement in which an onshore financial institution, often a bank or a broker-dealer, is recorded in the issuer's register of shareholders as the nominal holder of securities (beneficially owned by others). This structure allows the sale of securities to be completed abroad with payments in hard currency, and the recorded ownership in the register of shareholders either remains the same or moves from one nominee to another.

This structure has been used for trading shares of Russian companies, MinFin bonds, and other bonds issued by the state. (However, because of restrictions on foreign ownership, state-issued short-term notes - GKOs - may not be traded in this manner.) Most registrars in Russia are willing to work with the nominee accounts system, which has been validated in the Statute on Shareholders' Registers and in the Temporary Statute on the Keeping of the Register of Owners of Inscribed Securities (No. 3, July 12, 1997) issued by the Commission on Securities and Exchanges. Under this legislation, the holder of the nominee account must inform the registrar of the name of the beneficial owner at least once a year. In practice, however, registrars often require that nominees provide information on beneficial owners more often than once a year.

A hybrid institutional market model probably will develop in Russia, assuring substantial capital market activity. Because of policy problems in Russia, the country's Depository Clearing Corporation has not yet gained the confidence of the international investment community, and its stated purpose of bringing the offshore markets onshore therefore remains unfulfilled. But the new National Registry Company, Moscow, a joint venture between the European Bank for Reconstruction and Development and The Bank of New York, shows real promise.

Russian law also does not protect the interests of a bona fide purchaser or holder in due course of securities. Under Russian law, "the holder of a security who has discovered forgery or a counterfeit security shall have the right to present to the person who transferred the security to him a demand for proper performance of the obligation certified by the security, and for compensation of losses" (Civil Code, Article 147, Paragraph 2). This provision suggests that claims can be brought against any holder of a security, even a holder in due course.

IMPACT OF NEW JOINT-STOCK COMPANY LAW

Effective January 1, , the Federal Law on Joint-Stock Companies reaffirms the regime already mandated under an earlier order, Decree 601, although it does dispense with several of the technical burdens of the older measure. As was the case under Decree 601, the new joint-stock company regime is rigid and complex and allows for relatively little flexibility and delegation of authority, especially for US business people, who are accustomed to a flexible regime, and is therefore to be avoided for wholly owned subsidiaries and other entities where possible. In Article 5 of the Law on Joint-Stock Companies, the authors were unable to avoid the onerous Civil Code requirement that each branch office and its local address be set forth in the company charter, which therefore must be amended by a three-fourths shareholder vote each time a new office is opened.

On the other hand, the new law does contain a number of useful innovations, and constitutes a more modern and complete regime for the publication of financial information, corporate governance (including detailed provisions for annual and general shareholder meetings), and company capitalization, including convertible instruments. Article 27 skirts provisions of the new Civil Code and provides a basis for companies to authorize shares for future issuance in addition to those issued and outstanding. If this approach is not invalidated as contrary to the Civil Code, it should provide boards of directors and management needed flexibility for expanding a company's equity base. Also, unless limited in the charter, bond-issuing authority resides in the board of directors. Chapter VI details the procedures for maintenance of the company share register, mandating an independent registrar for companies with more than 500 shareholders (Article 45.2).

GOVERNMENT SECURITIES MARKET

Every Wednesday 60 dealers participate in the auction of short-term government obligations (GKOs) in the form of three-month Treasury Bills. Six-month T-bills are also issued, and plans are in the works to begin issuing one-year bills and three-year notes. GKOs valued at $36 billion are currently in circulation, and the daily volume in secondary trading is now about $300 million. Real returns on GKOs over the past year have been extraordinary, given the ruble's recent stability. The rates of return are now coming down.

Stocks. Stock trading in Russia has already gone through one *boom-and-bust* cycle. But long-term growth is likely, as newly-privatized enterprises, starved of capital, prepare to offer new issues. By international standards, the asset valuations of these companies, as reflected in market capitalization's, are low. Trading in the shares of banks and newly-privatized companies is largely an over-the-counter practice at present. Even if the newly-privatized companies increase the pool of stocks through new issues, it seems likely that secondary trading in these issues will gravitate to the over-the-counter market as well.

Today, a modem financial regulatory system is taking shape in Russia. The importance of this phenomenon, and the significance of the anticipated flow of current, accurate financial information to the capital markets, is being promoted at Russia's very highest levels.

TRANSFERRING OWNERSHIP OF SECURITIES

Certified Shares

Issuing of Shares: A closed joint-stock company (abbreviated "ZAO" in Russian) may issue certificates, since all joint-stock companies are authorized to do so, but given the restrictions on transfer, such certificates would not be transferable by endorsement, in contrast to the certificates issued by an open joint-stock company (an "OAO"). As a result, in practice ZAOs do not issue certificates.

Transfer: Under Article 28 of the Law on the Securities Market, evidence of tide and ownership of issued securities is denoted in documentary form by the share certificate. Although this provision appears clearly to state that tide inheres in the certificate itself, which implies that transfer of legal title may be effected by endorsement only, Article 29 provides that transfer of tide is accomplished when the purchaser of a certified security is registered and receives a new certificate following the establishment of the purchaser's personal account.

Registration of Transfer: Under the Commission of Securities and Exchanges' July 12, 1997 Temporary Statute (Article IV), upon the transfer of ownership of certified shares, the registration procedure requires the seller and the buyer of the shares (or the buyer alone) to provide the registrar with the following:

An executed transfer order

The endorsed share certificate(s)

The stock purchase agreement, if the sale was not conducted through and registered by a professional market participant

Any relevant judgment or certificate of inheritance if the shares are being transferred under a court decision or by operation of law, including, for example inheritance law.

The Temporary Statute specifically provides that the registrar may not request notarization of signatures on the transfer order or on the share certificate. Within three

For additional analytical, business and investment opportunities information,
please contact Global Investment & Business Center, USA
at (202) 546-2103. Fax: (202) 546-3275. E-mail: rusric@erols.com
Global Business E-Books on Line: http://world.mirhouse.com

days of receipt of these documents, the registrar must register the transfer of ownership of the shares, open a new personal account in the name of the buyer (if he did not have one previously), and issue new stock certificate(s).

Uncertified Shares

Transfer: In the case of uncertified securities, Articles 28 and 29 of the Law on the Securities Market provide that title is evidenced by an entry in the register, and the transfer of such securities is effectuated by making the relevant entries in the buyer's and seller's personal accounts in the register. The list of required documents is similar to those required to register the transfer of certified shares, but legal tide to uncertified shares is established by book entry only.

Since it issues shares, a ZAO must have a shareholder register. In practice, however, very few closed joint-stock companies keep a register, since the number of shareholders is usually small and this requirement is new. A ZAO may, in theory, have an independent registrar maintain the register, since the legislation on shareholder's registers applies to closed, as well as to open, joint-stock companies, but no ZAO is required to do so (only companies with more than 500 shareholders must appoint independent registrars, and a ZAO may not have more than 50 shareholders). In practice, since closed joint-stock companies were not required to have registers prior to the introduction of the new joint-stock company law, all transfers of shares in closed companies were done by amending the charter, which contains the list of shareholders, and registering these amendments with the Registration Chamber, just as transfers of partnership interests are registered. Currently, despite the enactment of the new Joint-Stock Company Law, this practice continues, and it is likely to do so until all existing ZAOs reregister their charters under the new law.

There is yet another complication: under Article 15 of the RSFSR Law on Foreign Investment (July 4, 1991), the participation of a foreign investor in a company must be reflected in the company's charter. This law does not distinguish between open and closed companies, and compliance of open companies is impossible. However, some foreigners who buy into Russian closed joint-stock companies feel that their interests are better protected if their ownership is reflected in the company's charter.

Registration of Transfer: As mentioned above, an extract from the shareholders' register is a document confirming the registration of the ownership or nominal holding of the shares of joint-stock companies, and is not itself a security. Therefore, the transfer of shares does not require the transfer of an extract nor does the transfer of an extract trigger the transfer of ownership of the shares.

Table 9. Rating of Russian Financial Instruments by Return

Instrument	Annual return (%) at the	Annual return (%) at the	Rank at the beginning of	Rank at the beginning of 1997

	beginning of	beginning of 1997		
Savings bonds	104	33	1	2
GKO and Federal Loan bonds	70-90	30-35	2	3
Ruble deposits 1 month	40-80	20-30	3	1
Ruble deposits 3 months	48-96	30-40	3	1
Hard currency deposits 1 month	6-30	8-11	4	4
Hard currency deposits 3 months	8-30	10-14	4	4
US Dollar	23	21	5	5

The inflation rate in was 22% annually.
** The rating does not include gold, considered an untested financial instrument, and equities.

SECURITIES MARKET REGULATIONS

The most important legal instrument in securities' regulation in Russia is currently Resolution No. 78 of the Government of the RSFSR dated December 28, 1991. The document, also known as Resolution 78, approves the Regulations on Issuance and Circulation of Securities and Stock Exchanges. Resolution 78 actually dates back to the end of the Soviet era and remained in effect in the newly formed Russian Federation. The Ministry of Finance is the primary enforcer of both Resolution 78 and the securities markets in general - the banks have a smaller role.

The other major regulator in the securities market is the newly created Commission for Securities and Capital Markets (the "Commission"), which has a government ministry status and is subordinated directly to the federal executive branch. The Commission has been assuming an increasingly important role in securities regulation at the expense of the Ministry of Finance. The Commission's mandate is to be the primary regulator of financial markets, including the activities of traders in securities. All draft legislation in securities regulation is subject to the preliminary approval of the Commission. A new law on the regulation of the securities market is expected to be introduced in . This piece of legislation will further reduce the role of the Ministry of Finance and replace Resolution 78.

TYPES OF SECURITIES

Resolution 78 defines "securities" as monetary instruments confirming a property right, or a loan. The definition does not take into account promissory notes, insurance policies, and certain types of bank deposits. Under Resolution 78, shares in joint-stock companies, bonds, government obligations and related derivatives are all regulated securities.

All joint-stock companies' shares must be issued in registered form while bonds may be issued in bearer form. The former requirement for registration is one of the major pitfalls in Russian securities law. Since share registration is left up to the individual issuer and all shareholder rights are contingent on registration, maintenance of one's registration is an important concern of shareholders. Given the practical difficulties of ensuring registration (e.g. travel to remote regions of Russia to visit the issuer's registrar), only large and well connected shareholders can afford to maintain and defend their registrations.

PARTICIPANTS

Resolution 78 defines participants in the securities market as follows:

"Issuers" are legal persons - including foreign - and state bodies - including local - that have the right to undertake financial or other obligations in their own name;

"Investors" are natural and legal persons - including foreign (if in compliance with the laws of their place of origin) - who acquire securities on their own behalf; and

"Investment institutions" are natural and legal persons - including foreign - who may act as financial intermediaries - brokers -, investment advisers, investment banks, or investment funds. Banks may perform the role of investment institution, subject to the Law on Banking.

BASIC REQUIREMENTS

Foreign investors who intend to register Russian legal entities (joint-stock companies of the open or closed type) should be aware of prospectus requirements for the distribution of shares in such companies. According to the Ministry of Finance's Instruction No. 2 dated March 3, 1992, an issuer must register a prospectus in the following situations:

- An **"open"** distribution of securities to an unlimited group of potential investors; and

- A **"closed"** distribution of securities of a value in excess of 55 million rubles or to more than 100 investors.

Closed distributions of securities in an amount less than 55 million rubles to fewer than 100 investors are exempt from the prospectus requirement. However, if a closed joint-stock company later increases its charter (share) capital beyond 50 million rubles, or increases the number of its shareholders to more than 100, then the later transaction is subject to the prospectus requirement.

FOREIGN INVESTMENT IN RUSSIAN SECURITIES AND STOCKS

The acquisition of shares in Russian joint-stock companies by foreign investors requires the consideration of the following Russian legislation:

Article 35 of the Law on Foreign Investment which provides that foreign investors have the right to acquire securities of enterprises located in Russia and that any such acquired securities must be registered with the Ministry of Finance.

Article 147 on the Regulations of Joint-Stock Companies attached to Decree No. 601 of the Council of Ministers of the RSFSR which requires the consent of the Ministry of Finance for the acquisition of more than 15 percent of shares by any person other than the company's founders. As stipulated in Article 147, the acquisition of more than 50 percent of a company's shares also requires the consent of the Ministry of Finance and the Anti-Monopoly Committee.

Article 49 of Regulation 78 which provides that after acquiring more than 15 percent of the shares of a securities issuer, a legal entity or a group of legal entities associated through contractual or property arrangements has the obligation, within five days, to notify the Ministry of the Economy and the Ministry of Finance. An exception remains in effect for a joint-stock company's founder at the time of the firm's creation.

Article 18 of the Russian Federation Law No. 948-1 "On Competition and Restriction of Monopolies in Goods Markets" requires the prior approval of the Anti-Monopoly Committee (AMC) if an investor having assets 100,000 times bigger than the minimum monthly salary in Russia (55,000 rubles as of September 1997) purchases more than 20 percent of the shares in a company. A notice to the AMC is also required if the purchaser has assets amounting to more than 50,000 times the Russian minimum monthly salary.

A Central Bank Letter dated January 31, 1997 which requires non-residents to obtain Central Bank licenses if they pay shares in Russian company with hard currency. By implication, the purchase of Russian companies' securities for rubles should not require a Central Bank license. However, to pay in rubles, a foreign investor should have a bank account in Russia. For details on how to open such accounts and the restrictions on their use, refer to the section on Banking.

SECURITIES TAX

Under Federal Law No. 158-FZ dated October 18, 1997, all issuance of securities, except the primary issuance (on the foundation of the company), are subject to tax at a rate of 0.8 percent of the nominal (or face) value of the securities. The issuer must pay the amount of the tax on the Tax Inspection simultaneously with the registration of the issuance of the securities. In the event that the registration of issuance is rejected, the amount of the tax is not refundable. The tax on secondary transactions with securities has been abolished.

REGISTRATION OF SHARES

Under the Council of Ministers of the RSFSR's Decree No. 601, all shares must be inscribed in the register of shareholders maintained by each joint-stock company. If shareholders are unregistered, they essentially have no rights. As of today, there is no requirement for a centralized share registry body. Nevertheless, a consortium of Russian and Western institutions is currently working on developing such a body in order to maintain shareholders' rights. One has to keep in mind that making and maintaining the registration is of primary importance.

Under Presidential Decree No. 784 adopted August 1997 (Decree No. 784), access to the register must be provided for inspection by the registrars of open joint stock companies (OJSC) to those shareholders having one percent or more of the OJSC's common shares. The decree stipulates that shareholders should be able to consult the register within one working day after their application has been submitted. It is interesting to note that the procedure for making such a request has not been determined yet. Two restrictions apply to the registrar: 1) only one of them can be appointed to any OJSC; 2) the registrar is prohibited from being a shareholder. Clearly, however, the one percent requirement is not of assistance to small portfolio investors.

SHAREHOLDERS RIGHTS

Decree No. 784 also established new rights for OJSCs' shareholders. Shareholders in a OJSC who do not participate in shareholders' meetings or who vote against resolutions passed at such meetings have the right to require the OJSC to evaluate and purchase their shares if decisions are taken to undertake corporate reorganizations, purchase or sell a majority of assets of the OJSC, amend the OJSC's constitution to limit the amount of shares/votes that a shareholder may hold, or increase an OJSC's charter (share) capital by way of new share issuance without granting rights of first refusal to existing shareholders. Decree No. 784 further states that shareholders' statutory rights of participation in shareholders' meetings cannot be restricted by the general meeting of shareholders, the board of directors or other bodies or persons.

BANKING AND HARD CURRENCY OPERATIONS

The banking sector in Russia has been one of the most dynamic in the new private sector economy. In March 1997, there were approximately 2,600 private banks ranging from large full service institutions in Moscow and St. Petersburg to small regional banks providing fairly limited services in a single town or region. A small number of foreign banks made up that number also. Foreign investors find that the banking procedures in Russia are significantly more bureaucratic - and thus complex - than their Western counterparts.

The Russian government strictly controls the use of non-Russian convertible - "hard" currency. Over the past few years, the general trend has been to gradually narrow the scope of permissible transactions in hard currency on the Russian territory, after an initial period of comparative freedom in 1991. Russian enterprises, private citizens and foreign legal entities and citizens are currently permitted to maintain hard currency accounts at Russian banks and to hold currency themselves. However, the Russian Government has increasingly restricted the role of hard currency in commercial dealings between enterprises and individuals in order to bolster the role of the ruble as Russia's medium for transactions.

BANKING REGULATIONS

In December 1990, the Russian Parliament adopted the following laws: "On the Central Bank of Russia" and **"On Banks and Banking Activity".** These legislation established the basis for a two-tier banking system in Russia consisting of the Central Bank of the Russian Federation (the Central Bank), the main state regulatory body responsible for the supervision of banking institutions, and private commercial banks. According to the laws, all of these entities are authorized to perform banking operations.

The Central Bank, which is responsible for the registration of commercial banks, issues the necessary operating licenses as well as licenses authorizing hard currency transactions. "On Banks and Banking Activity" is the main law governing the operations of commercial banks. The legislation sets out a comprehensive list of operations that Russian banks can perform. Banking transactions often involve numerous restrictions and onerous documentary requirements. These administrative problems are due, in great part, to the Russian banking regulations' objectives. The goals of the regulations are to facilitate the collection of tax revenues by the government and provide the normal bank support required for businesses to operate.

BANKING ACCOUNTS

When it comes to opening and utilize bank accounts, Residents and non-residents face different treatments under Russian banking law. Under Russian law, "residents" are legal entities registered under Russian legislation (e.g. stock companies) regardless of nationality of ownership. "Non-residents" are legal entities established in foreign jurisdictions which act through branches or representative offices in Russia.

Opening a bank account in Russia is a complex procedure. The necessary documents for Russian residents are substantial and often require the display of a certificate of business registration in Russia, a certificate of registration with the tax inspection, notarized incorporating documents (in case of a foreign legal entity) as well as documents evidencing the nomination of the principal officers of the enterprise.

RESIDENTS ACCOUNTS

Residents are entitled to use the full range of banking services, including the opening of ruble current accounts and foreign currency accounts.

For additional analytical, business and investment opportunities information,
please contact Global Investment & Business Center, USA
at (202) 546-2103. Fax: (202) 546-3275. E-mail: rusric@erols.com
Global Business E-Books on Line: http://world.mirhouse.com

The rules affecting the currency dealings of residents depend, to a large extent, on the identity of the entities engaged in such dealings. The general rule, with certain limited exceptions, is that transactions between Russian residents within the Russian Federation are to be carried out in rubles - although in practice prices are often quoted in other currencies such as dollars. For transactions between legal entities valued at more than two million rubles (approximately $450 as of September 1997), the monetary transfer must be done through the banking system (i.e. it may not be carried out in cash). Cash payments in dollars between legal entities in the Russian Federation are prohibited.

A Russian resident's entity receiving hard currency as export income from outside Russia must convert 50 percent of its receipts into rubles within 14 days.

Hard currency bank accounts within Russia may only be used for specific purposes. Russian enterprises may pay for foreign goods purchased abroad in hard currency without Central Bank approval. Hard currency may not be used by resident Russian entities to pay Russian or foreign employees' salaries or other compensation if such employees are located within the Russian Federation. Hard currency may also be used to pay for foreign business travels up to a (rather low) limit on a per diem basis. Otherwise, all transactions involving hard currency accounts within the Russian Federation require Central Bank approval.

NON-RESIDENTS - HARD CURRENCY ACCOUNTS

Non-resident legal entities may open hard currency accounts in Russia. Hard currency payments for Russian goods may be transferred into the Russian Federation without restriction. Rubles obtained outside of Russia may not legally be transferred into Russia. In legal terms, a Central Bank license is required for hard currency transactions connected with the movement of capital into or out of Russia. However, contributions to the charter capital of new Russian enterprises have not generally been submitted to the Central Bank for approval - the validity of this practice is currently the subject of debate. Any hard currency loan to a Russian entity with a term in excess of 180 days requires the approval of the Central Bank.

NON-RESIDENTS - RUBLE ACCOUNTS

Non-residents may open ruble accounts with Russian banks. Those accounts, contrary to resident's ones, are subject to some limitations.
There are two types of non-resident legal entity ruble accounts:
"T" or ruble current accounts; and
"I" or ruble investment accounts.

"T" ACCOUNTS

"T" accounts may be used only for the purpose of making payments related to import-export operations and financing the activity of branches and representative offices in Russia. If a non-resident enterprise does not have a branch or representative office in Russia, it is entitled to carry out current ruble payments through accounts opened with non-resident banks on the condition that settlements be made through ruble correspondent accounts of these banks opened with Russian commercial banks.

Certain types of payments may be made to **"T"** accounts; they include payments from residents for goods and services delivered in Russia, proceeds from sales of foreign currency in the internal currency market, ruble loans granted by both resident and non-resident banks, rental payments from residents, payments from other **"T"** accounts including those opened in the names of other non-residents, and transfers from an **"I"** account held by the same person.

Certain types of payments may be made from **"T"** accounts; they include payments to residents for delivery of goods and services, payments connected with making bank deposits, payments under purchase and sale agreements for debt securities, payment of taxes, duties and other obligatory charges imposed by the government authorities, payment of current expenses incurred by branches and representative offices of a non-resident of Russia, and payments to "T" accounts of other nonresidents.

"T" accounts may neither be used to buy foreign currency nor to transfer funds to "I" accounts. Cash ruble amounts may be withdrawn from a "T" account by a branch or representative office of a non-resident legal entity in amounts necessary to pay salaries and finance current expenses within the limits established by the parent entity.

"I" ACCOUNTS

Non-residents will generally use "I" accounts to accumulate ruble proceeds from the sale of foreign currency in the Russian internal currency market, dividend payments from shares, proceeds from the sale of assets of liquidated enterprises, and proceeds from the sale of shares.

The amounts accumulated in "I" accounts may be used to buy foreign currency in the internal currency market of Russia, to acquire assets including privatized property (excluding securities), to purchase securities denominated in foreign currency, or shares and state securities denominated in rubles which remain outstanding for more than one year after the date of purchase, and to make payments to a "T" account held by the same person.

All operations with "I" accounts must be carried out on a non-cash basis. Cash withdrawals from "I" accounts are not allowed. Amounts kept in an "I" account may not be used to make loans or investments in bank deposits, deposit certificates, bonds (including state bonds) or other debt securities with the exception of those listed above.

Russian commercial banks are responsible for the supervision of "I" and "T" accounts and must file reports on the state of such accounts with the Central Bank. By law,

For additional analytical, business and investment opportunities information,
please contact Global Investment & Business Center, USA
at (202) 546-2103. Fax: (202) 546-3275. E-mail: rusric@erols.com
Global Business E-Books on Line: http://world.mirhouse.com

commercial banks may demand documents or information from the holders of such accounts for the verification of transactions.

RUSSIAN ACCOUNTING SYSTEM *(GENERAL OVERVIEW)*

During the Soviet era, the function and rules governing accounting were fundamentally different from those of market economies. The primary objective of the Soviet accounting system was to provide state economic planners with statistical information rather than to generate financial information of value to the management of business enterprises in a market economy. Post-Soviet reforms have shifted the emphasis in Russian accounting from planning to reporting for tax purposes. Consequently, Russian accounting retains a very different orientation from accounting systems such as international accounting standards (IAS) and generally accepted accounting principles (GAAP) employed in Western countries.

The basic framework for the present Russian accounting system resulted from the adoption by the Russian government of new regulations on accounting in 1992. The implementation of these new accounting rules became mandatory on January 1, 1993. The new rules are applicable to all Russian legal entities including joint venture enterprises with foreign investment. On July 14, 1997, the State Duma passed special legislation "On Accounting Bill", a law providing, for the first time, legal guidelines for the accounting profession in Russia; these guidelines include the necessary requirements for one to be qualified as an accountant.

It is interesting to note that most Russian bookkeeping entries are still performed manually on government approved, pre-prepared forms. These printed forms constitute a journal sheet where individual transactions are recorded. Memoranda sheets are then used to combine forms and for subsequent ledger entries. Double entry accounting is used and financial statements are prepared on the basis of various ledgers and journals.

Large accounting firms familiar to Western investors are active in Russia and provide the usual range of audit, taxation, and management consulting services. Those firms also provide Russian companies with legal advice, a service usually not offered in Western countries. Many joint ventures with western investment operate on dual accounting systems; financial statements are prepared under Russian and Western accounting rules in order to satisfy both Russian and Western investors' reporting requirements. Accounting firms usually maintain a significant numbers of expatriates and Russian-qualified auditors to provide both services. A corps of young, Western-trained Russian accountants will, in the coming years, likely replace foreign staff in many functions.

STATUTORY REQUIREMENTS

As a general rule, financial statements calculated under Russian accounting rules with the appropriate State Tax Inspection office have to be filed by any legal entity that is subject to Russian profits tax.

The required financial statements in Russian accounting are the balance sheet, the profit and loss account and the accompanying notes which together set out the financial position of the enterprise, including its retained earnings and the changes in its financial position. The balance sheet is the key financial statement, it contains information on source and application of funds and the financing of assets. The large amount of information contained in these documents often makes the understanding of Russian balance sheets difficult for those familiar with western accounting materials.

Some of the main statutory requirements of the present Russian accounting system are:

-an approved "chart of accounts" (that include bookkeeping entries made in accordance with government regulations);

-mandatory preparation of financial statements and their accompanying schedules on government-approved forms;

- appointment of a chief accountant for the enterprise who is legally responsible for maintaining the enterprise's books and preparing the financial statements in accordance with Russian law;

- maintenance of all accounting records in the Russian language;

- recording of all accounting entries in Russian rubles - all foreign currency transactions must be converted into rubles, generally at the exchange rate prevailing at the time of the transaction; and

- use by all enterprises of the calendar year as the enterprise's fiscal year.

ACCOUNTING STANDARDS

On January 1, 1997, the Russian Ministry of Finance's Order No. 100 dated July 28, 1994 setting forth regulations establishing certain basic accounting standards will take effect. It is interesting to note, however, that the methodology for implementing the new standards is not yet in place. The basic standards in Russian accounting that will be familiar to Western investors include:

- **valuation of assets at historic costs,**
- **balance sheet continuity;**

- **valuation of foreign currency assets in rubles as of the date of the balance sheet,**
- **substance to prevail over form; and**
- **consistency in application of accounting principles over time.**

SPECIFIC ACCOUNTING ISSUES

The following is a brief summary of Russian accounting principles concerning certain issues:

Sales: Sales can be recorded on an accrual basis if an invoice or equivalent has been issued or if cash has been received. The latter approach is more common. Foreign currency sales must be converted into rubles, generally at the exchange rate prevailing at the time of the transaction.

Cost of sales: Costs are generally recorded in the period during which supporting documents for expenditures, such as invoices, are received. Consequently, material costs may not be recorded if the supporting documentation has not been prepared.

Profit: Profit is calculated by rolling over balance sheet accounts to generate "balance sheet profit". As such, profit calculation simply constitutes further information appended to the balance sheet.

Mandatory conversion requirement for hard currency receipts: Under Russian law, at least 50 percent of foreign currency receipts must be converted into rubles within 14 days of the receipt at the exchange rate established by the Central Bank of Russia and recorded as such in the accounting records.

Subsidiaries and investments: Enterprises are not required to prepare consolidated financial statements with information on subsidiaries. Further, investments are included in the balance sheet at the lower of cost or market value.

Property, plant and equipment (PPE) and depreciation: PPE is recorded initially at historic cost and is afterwards re-valued periodically according to formulas set out in government regulations. The last revaluation took place on January 1, 1997. Depreciation is also based on rates established by the government; rates that may differ significantly from the expected useful life of the PPE.

Liability funds: Under Russian law, several balance sheet funds are mandatory; they include the "charter fund", which consists of the initial charter contributions of the founders and the subsequent retained earnings, the reserve fund (to cover exceptional losses) and special purpose funds (e.g. social expenses, bonuses etc.)

Inflation: Inflation accounting remains relatively undeveloped in Russia. Partial measures to take inflation into account have been attempted, including the periodic revaluation of the book values of PPE discussed above.

Contingent liabilities: Russian accounting regulations require neither accrual nor disclosure of contingent liabilities.

Deferred taxation: Since Russian financial accounting parallels Russian tax accounting, accounting profit is the same as taxable profit. Consequently the issue of deferred tax does not arise.

Reporting: Russian enterprises must file both quarterly and annual financial statements. The annual filing to the state tax inspection must be made by April 1 of the year following the financial year (calendar year).

PROPERTY AND OWNERSHIP

Private property, in general, is protected by law. The ownership of real or immovable property, such as buildings, structures or other structures, is distinct under Russian law and is governed by a separate and less restrictive legal regime than the one for land. Land ownership remains one of the most controversial areas in Russian property law. Limitations on the absolute ownership of land were abolished by the Russian Constitution of 1993. However, recent constitutional authorization for full-scale, private ownership of land has not been implemented. Currently, the Russian Parliament is considering a draft of a comprehensive law on land ownership rights (the Land Code). Until this legislation is enacted however, land ownership rights will remain obscure for foreign investors.

In general, however, under Russian law, ownership of land is distinguished from ownership of real or immovable property such as buildings, structures, and other structures, which is governed by a separate, and less restrictive legal regime. Ownership rights over land are generally limited to the upper layer of soil (not the subsoil), plant life and self-contained bodies of water within the property boundaries. The owner of a parcel of land has the right to use his property as he wishes, unless such use violates the norms stipulated in the applicable Russian legislation. Subsoil use is strictly regulated by a separate legislation (see the section on mineral rights). Agricultural land is subject to a regulatory regime different from the industrial or urban land ones.

The basic Russian legislation governing land ownership permit legal entities to exercise lesser kinds of property rights, such as lease and rights of use, rather than absolute ownership. Due to the ineffective system of enforcement of contractual rights in the domestic court system and the lack of a codified system of rights and obligations governing landlord-tenant relations, leases for land and apartments are usually much simpler than in the West. Russian leases tend to reflect the importance of the personal relationship between the landlord and the tenant - the best guarantee of a peaceful tenancy in Russia at this time.

A system of land ownership rights' registration and of land transactions is under development in the Russian Federation. Existing legislation provides for the registration of legal title and other transactions, including mortgage for a land plot or other immovable property, in the district where the property is located. The procedure for title registration varies a great deal depending on the type of property. Russia is moving closer to a uniform system of land title and land transaction registration. There are, however, various practical barriers to progress; they include poor communications infrastructure, lack of disclosure and arbitrariness on the part of local authorities.

For additional analytical, business and investment opportunities information,
please contact Global Investment & Business Center, USA
at (202) 546-2103. Fax: (202) 546-3275. E-mail: rusric@erols.com
Global Business E-Books on Line: http://world.mirhouse.com

The Moscow regional government's policy will, rather than sell property, grant leases through a tender system for a maximum of 49 years. Short term leases of up to five years will be granted as well. A recent presidential decree provides that the owners of privatized immovable property in the Moscow area acquire an automatic 49-year lease for the land upon which such immovable property is located.

SECURED TRANSACTIONS

The Law on Collateral, introduced in 1992, provides coverage for secured interests on real estate or personal property. On January 1, 1997, the new Civil Code, containing several provisions that partially modify certain technical provisions of the Law on Collateral, came into effect. These two pieces of legislation provide the legal framework for secured interests in Russia.

The Law on Collateral permits the creation of security interests - including intellectual property, securities and present and future rights - over real estate or personal property. The only significant restriction under Russian law is that in order to create a secured interest over a property, the property rights must be transferable to another person . However, the right, especially of foreigners, to own land is either severely restricted or non-existent.

Foreign investors should pay particular attention to secured transactions of state-owned enterprises' property. These transactions may be subject to certain obligations under privatization legislation. Russian legislation governing secured interests provides the parties involved with substantial freedom of choice concerning contractual terms. In general, if a document creating a secured interest is correctly drafted, executed and registered under Russian law, it will take priority over subsequent ones. However, the effectiveness of the current legal framework is unclear - the creation and enforcement of secured interests in the Russian Federation have, to this date, taken place rather seldom.

When it comes to bankruptcy, provisions relating to secured transactions included in the new Civil Code might pose a problem to the potential investor. The law "On Insolvency" (Bankruptcy) established that secured interests (claims to specific collateral) outranked all others. It is interesting to note that the treatment of secured creditors in Canada is very similar. However, the new Civil Code subordinates secured claims to two similar classes: 1) those concerning the compensation of personal injury; and 2) those relating to unpaid wages and severance pay. One has to keep in mind that the effect of this provision is still unclear given that the law has been in effect just a short time.

The system of registration is one of the main weaknesses of the Russian system governing secured interests. Secured interests must be registered if potential property is involved. For example, a secured interest in land or a right to possessing land must be registered in the local land register. A secured interest that was under state ownership must be registered with the interest privatization authorities (the State Property Fund). Ship and aircraft secured interests must be registered as well.

The only requirement concerning secured interests involving property that cannot be registered (oil rigs or other movable industrial equipment) is that the party whose property is subject to the secured interest must maintain a record of it. Any interested third party has the right, upon request, to consult the books on which a company keeps track of these particular secured interests. Furthermore, the person granting the secured interest is personally responsible for losses resulting from the absence of an adequate record or the notification of such secured interests.

Execution against property subject to a secured interest will, under Russian law, involve the satisfaction of claims in a stipulated order of priority - the actual amount of the secured interest must be satiated out of the property before other expenses, such as maintenance or legal costs, may be paid.

BANKRUPTCY: LEGISLATION & PROCEDURE

The **Bankruptcy Law**, that took effect on March 1, 1993, stipulating a judicially supervised process for dealing with bankrupt enterprises was a cornerstone in Russian business law. Given the financial condition of many Russian firms, it was necessary for the Government to devise a procedure that would deal with insolvency, in particular of state-owned enterprises. Bankruptcy legislation is incomplete, however; many rights and procedures still require clarification.

The law defines key bankruptcy terms. The definition of insolvency include both the inability to meet creditors' demands or make tax payments and the excess of liabilities over assets. Insolvency can either be declared by a court of law or by a debtor's official announcement in the course of a voluntary liquidation.

Three different, judicially supervised procedures, may apply to an insolvent debtor: 1) rehabilitation of the enterprise including possible management of the debtor's property by a trustee, 2) winding up of the enterprise's affairs and liquidation of its assets by court order according to a legally preordained division of assets among creditors, or 3) voluntary liquidation of an insolvent enterprise.

Bankruptcy cases must be brought before the Arbitration Court (*Arbitrazh),* or a specialized commercial court, with appeals to the *Supreme Arbitrazh.* A case is normally brought in *the Arbitrazh* closest to either the debtor's residence or the principal location of the debtor's business.

A Federal Bankruptcy Board has been established to supervise the reorganization or liquidation of state enterprises in the Russian Federation. The board has administrative and regulatory authority over a wide range of issues arising from the implementation of bankruptcy procedures.

FOREIGN TRADE AND CUSTOMS REGULATIONS

Russian trade procedures have largely been liberalized since 1992. During that particular year, imports were freed from administrative controls. In 1993, a system of import subsidies was phased out. Export procedures were largely liberalized in the first half of 1994 as use of export quotas and licensing system, as well as export taxes were greatly reduced. Most export quotas were eliminated in 1997. Since the beginning of , however, it appears that certain restrictions may again apply to foreign trade and customs regulation.

EXPORT AND IMPORT LICENSING AND QUOTAS

High inflation and the domestic shortages of certain goods have led the Russian Government to require import and export licenses for specific commodities. The list of specific commodities has been established by Decree No. 610 of the Russian Federation State Customs Committee amended on June 7, 1997. The decree clarifies the necessary procedures for the issuance of quotas and licenses for exported and imported goods. The list contains items ranging from nuclear and chemical materials and technologies to industrial waste products, military technologies and materials, and double application of goods and medicines.

Most export quotas were abolished by Presidential Decree No. 1007 adopted on May 23, 1994 and which took effect on July 1, 1994. The only remaining quotas are those that have been imposed according to the Russian Federation's international obligations to prevent unfair trade practices such as dumping. On March 15, 1997, the State Customs Committee of the Russian Federation revised the procedures for issuing quotas and licenses for goods exported in accordance with international obligations. The list of goods includes silicon carbide, ammonium nitrate, textile products and unprocessed aluminum. These goods can be exported in accordance to international agreements and require export licenses. While import restriction were largely abolished, the Russian Government announced in January its intention to reintroduce import quotas on some goods, including tobacco and alcohol.

On December 31, 1994, the oil-export quota system was revised by Government Decree No. 1446. This decree replaces the export quota with a system of quarterly allocations of access to pipelines. On February 28, 1997, Government Decree No. 209 established the principle of equal access to oil export pipelines. According to this decree, priority was given to Russia's few remaining international obligation.

GENERAL PROCEDURE FOR ISSUING LICENSES

Licenses are issued by the Russian Ministry of Foreign Economic Relations through its authorized representatives. After having been issued, licenses are not transferable. The kind of license issued depends on the type of product. For goods subjected to quota, a document is required to confirm the delivery of the products in accordance with the quota. If the exporter is an intermediary, an agreement for the delivery of the goods is required.

The presentation of a signed contract is essential for the issuance of a license. When the fundamental conditions of a contract are altered, the license issued in connection with the contract must be amended. "Multiple-use" or "single-use" are the two types of licenses that may be issued. The term of a single-use license may be extended. A multiple-use license is valid for one calendar year.

MONITORING THE EXPORT OF STRATEGICALLY IMPORTANT RAW MATERIALS

A list of "strategically important raw materials" was established in 1992 and amended in February 1997. It includes crude oil and petroleum products, natural gas, electricity, cellulose, non-ferrous metals, certain fertilizers, grain, soy bean and sunflower seed, fish and crustaceans, caviar and certain spirits. Furthermore, ores destined for the production of ferrous or rare metals, wood, and certain lumber products are also classified as strategically important items. Only those enterprises, either private or state-owned, that are registered and selected for such purposes by the Ministry of Foreign Economic Affairs (as "special exporters") can export strategically important raw materials.

Materials, equipment, technology and information that could be used in the manufacture of weapons are tightly controlled by a presidential decree. A list enumerating potential "dual-use" products - equipment and technology with peaceful purposes that could be used to create weapons - was also established.

CONCESSIONS FOR EXPORTERS

In the past, it was possible to obtain special concessions for a particular project on an *ad hoc* basis. Nowadays, according to the Law on Several Issues for the Granting of Privileges to Participants in Foreign Economic Activity adopted on March 13, 1997, exemptions from customs duties, VAT, and excise taxes must be established in one of the following categories: 1) the Customs Tariff Law, 2) the Tax on Value-Added Cost, 3) the Law On Excise, and 4) the Customs Code.

The Law on Foreign Investment adopted on July 4, 1991 provides that enterprises located on Russian territory may export their "own products" without limitations if their percentage of foreign participation is 30 percent. However, the term "own products" remained vague until the Russian Council of Ministers issued Decree No. 715 "On the Procedures for Determining Self-Products of Enterprises with Foreign Investment", on July 23, 1993. Under this decree "own production" requires the enterprise to 1) possess any necessary authorization to engage in the relevant activity; 2) confirm in a state-recognized audit that it owes or leases the assets being used in the production; 3) employ the personnel manufacturing the product; 4) sufficiently change raw inputs so as to have different customs classification codes; and 5) create an added value of 30 percent for the product. Enterprises dealing with oil and gas production operate under an additional set of rules (see the Regulations On the Certificate for Self-Produced Products approved on July 29, 1993 by the Russian Federation's Minister of Foreign Economic Relations).

In theory, the state have to grant "own products" certificates if the applicant is exporting his own goods and has supplied the requisite documents. In practice, "own products" certificates have become another form of licensing, which, in the past, has restricted the direct export of oil and oil by-products by non-state entities.

Applications for "own products" certificates are considered by the Russian Federation Chamber of Trade and Industry's *Soyuzexpertiza*. *Soyuzexpertiza* issues certificates for a specific volume of a particular product that are valid for a maximum of 12 months. It must act on applications within 30 days of receipt.

The enterprise must submit the following documents to *Soyuzexpertiza* in order to obtain a certificate of own production:

1. **An application to the head of *Soyuzexpertiza*.**
2. **Copies of the enterprise's charter and certificate of registration.**
3. **A certificate stating that the product has been assigned an international trade code by the State Statistical Committee.**
4. **The enterprise's annual report on production activities.**
5. **An auditor's report performed by an authorized auditing firm.**
6. **A technical study on the volume of production for the current year.**
7. **A description of the technological processes and relevant documentation.**
8. **A confirmation from the Ministry of the Economy and relevant branch ministries that the enterprise has submitted information on the volume of production for the current year.**

STANDARDS AND CERTIFICATION FOR IMPORTED GOODS

The policy of the Russian Government on standards and certification for imported goods is defined in a series of laws. These are applied to products of both domestic and foreign origin with the purpose of legally protecting life, health, the property of citizens and the environment.

Russia's national certification system - the "GOSTR Certification System"- is set out in legislation. The Russian government asserts that the system complies with the international ISO/MEC documents, including series 9000 ISO standards. The Russian certification body is the State Committee for Standardization, Metrology and Certification. The relevant rules are contained in the law "On Protection of Consumers' Rights."

Products requiring the confirmation of safety including:

1. goods for children,
2. food products,
3. goods that come into contact with food products,
4. chemical products for domestic use,
5. perfumes,
6. cosmetics, domestic electronic products, electrical measuring instruments, chemical weed and pesticides, mineral fertilizers, petroleum products, transportation vehicles, hunting and sporting weapons, and furniture.

Under the State Customs Committee Decree No. 01-12/870, which took effect in July 1997, perishable goods are to be cleared by customs and certified in a priority manner.

Both foreign and domestic goods must comply with the safety requirements set by the State Committee for Standardization, Metrology and Certification. This can be done in two ways:

1. certification that the product supplied to Russia complies with the rules of Russian certification; or

2. submission of a certificate by the exporter, obtained abroad and recognized in accordance with international, regional or bilateral agreements in Russia. This certificate is submitted to customs by the declarant or by the recipient of the goods and is reviewed before the products are cleared through customs.

SANITARY STANDARDS

Products imported into the Russian Federation must meet Russian national sanitary standards unless they have been exempted by international agreements. The State Committee for Standardization, Metrology and Certification and the State Sanitary and Epidemiological Committee are responsible for sanitary control of imports.

Certificates of hygiene must be obtained for the importation and sale on the domestic market of potentially harmful products. These certificates officially acknowledge the safety of the product and must be affixed to any good that is potentially dangerous. These requirements apply to both domestic and foreign products.

The following products must have certificates of hygiene:

raw and processed foods, food additives and preservatives, materials that come into contact with food products,

children's goods, polymers and synthetic materials for the production of children's goods; materials used in water supply, cosmetics and perfumes;

chemical and petrochemical products for industrial and household use, chemical products for the agricultural sector;

polymer and synthetic materials, yarn and threads, synthetic leathers and textiles for shoes;

Machine and engineering equipment; and

chemical substances that come into contact with human skin.

The certificate of hygiene must be obtained before the import transaction is completed. The certificate may be issued upon the presentation of a document proving that a corresponding certificate acceptable to the Russian authorities has been obtained in the country of origin, or that an analysis of the product has been carried out in the Russian Federation.

CUSTOMS REGULATIONS

The customs process is similar for imports and exports. The trader declares the imports or exports to the proper customs authority and presents a customs' declaration. The declarant, not the customs authority, must make a timely determination of the value. The customs authority will fine those who fail to present a customs' declaration. After receiving the customs' declaration, the authorities verify the declared value and must complete the registration. However, if the deadline for the registration is extended, the declarant is still responsible for any fines or penalties that may be imposed. When the customs authorities and declarant agree on a customs' value, the declarant pays the customs duty, excise duty, and Value-Added tax.

An administrative appeals process is available to the declarant who disagrees with the valuation determined by the customs' authorities. For the goods to be released, however, the declarant must pay duties based on the value determined by the customs' authorities. If the declarant does not agree with the result of the administrative appeal, the declarant can appeal to the Russian legal system. Both levels of appeal can be time-consuming and expensive.

The following documents must be submitted for customs clearances:

- **a customs' cargo declaration modeled on the document in use in the European Union;**
- **a license (for goods subject to license);**
- **a permission from the authorities (for goods under the supervision of a state body);**
- **a safety certificate (for goods where safety must be certified before entry);**
- **the transaction-identification document (for goods to be exported); and the confirmation of payment or guarantee of payment of customs duty, VAT excise duty, and customs-clearance fees.**

CUSTOMS DUTIES

Under Russian customs laws, duties apply on imports and exports. As soon as goods cross the border, they must be placed under a customs' regime. Although there are several customs regimes, goods brought into the Russian Federation by foreign companies usually fall under two categories: "release for free circulation" and "temporary import."

RELEASE FOR FREE CIRCULATION

Under the regime of release for free circulation, duty is calculated by multiplying the customs value of the goods by the appropriate duty rate. Existing customs duty rates were enacted on May 6, 1997 by the Governmental Decree No. 454. The maximum import tariff that can be imposed is 100 percent of the customs value of the goods. A duty rate of 15-20 percent is imposed on most goods considered nonessential for economic development, while rates of 25-30 percent are applied on a wide range of consumer goods. The highest duties are levied on such goods as alcoholic beverages, entertainment goods, precious metals and stones, and watches. Individuals are permitted to import duty-free goods for personal consumption up to a value of $2,000.

Russia has set goals to gradually reduce customs duties for most goods. On 1 January 1998, the maximum import tariff rate will be 20 percent. Two years later, on 1 January 2000, the import tariff is supposed go down to 15 percent. As of 1998, the average import tariff rate will be 80 percent of its existing level. In 2000, it will be 70 percent.

A fee is required from the importer for the customs clearance of the goods. Currently, the amount of the fee is equivalent to 0.15 percent of the value of the goods, of which 0.1 percent must be paid in rubles and 0.05 percent in hard currency. At the present time, with the exception of a customs fee of 0.1 percent of their customs value, goods that are in transit move freely over the territory of the Russian Federation. Finally, the importer is liable for the VAT and the special tax on goods released for free circulation.

TEMPORARY IMPORT

Temporary import status may only be applied on goods that will not be sold by the foreign company. Under the temporary import status, "full" and "partial" are the two types of exemptions from dues that are granted. No duties are charged on goods that receive an exemption. For the goods receiving a partial exemption, the importer is required to pay, each month, three percent of the amount that would have been due had the goods been released for free circulation. The duration of the temporary import status cannot exceed two years. If goods under a temporary import status are subsequently released for free circulation, the declarant must pay, in addition to the entire amount of customs duty that would have been due had the goods initially been placed under the regime of free circulation, an interest charge on the customs duty deferral.

For additional analytical, business and investment opportunities information,
please contact Global Investment & Business Center, USA
at (202) 546-2103. Fax: (202) 546-3275. E-mail: rusric@erols.com
Global Business E-Books on Line: http://world.mirhouse.com

DUTIES EXEMPTIONS

Foreign investors may be eligible for an exemption from duties on imports if they contribute to the charter capital of a newly formed Russian enterprise. This exemption only applies to import taxes (VAT and special taxes) for a one-year period beginning the day of the enterprise's registration and lasting for the period of contribution of charter capital established in the enterprise's foundation documents. The exemption does not apply to excised goods. There are other kinds of exemptions. For example, some of the equipment imported by the representative office of an accredited foreign legal entity, or by certain organizations, may be imported duty-free. Goods subjected to this exemption must be used for the own needs of that entity. Ownership or use of the goods may not be transferred. Should the accreditation period expire, all customs' duties and taxes that otherwise would have been paid upon importation will become due unless the goods are re-exported. Meanwhile, the duty-free status of some sports clubs has provided a loophole for substantial untaxed imports of automobiles, alcoholic beverages, cigarettes, and other items. In recent years, several proposals to eliminate most exemptions have been made by lawmakers.

EXPORT TARIFFS

Export duties were introduced on some non-renewable natural resources and semi-processed goods. These duties are calculated as a percentage of customs value or are based on unit weight or quantity. By January 1, , the Russian Government should have phased out export tariffs. On January 1, 1997, the export tariff on crude oil was reduced to 23 ECU per ton; it will go down to 20 ECU per ton at the beginning of April 1997.

For additional analytical, business and investment opportunities information,
please contact Global Investment & Business Center, USA
at (202) 546-2103. Fax: (202) 546-3275. E-mail: rusric@erols.com
Global Business E-Books on Line: http://world.mirhouse.com

SELECTED GOVERNMENT REGULATIONS AFFECTING BUSINESS

ANTI-MONOPOLY REGULATIONS

In order to boost free markets and competition activities in Russia, the government adopted the "Law On Competition and Restriction of Monopolistic Activities on Markets of Goods" (Competition Law). The law is aimed at restricting monopolistic activities and unfair competition, and at securing the conditions for the development and the effective functioning of markets for goods and services. The Competition Law regulates the activities of legal entities and individuals both inside and outside of the Russian Federation.

According to the law, monopolistic activities can take several forms: 1) unfair trade practices of the enterprise or Organization having a dominant market position; 2) agreements or coordinated actions between enterprises or other organizations aimed at the restriction of competition; 3) acts undertaken by state bodies aimed at the restriction imposed on the economic independence of entrepreneurs or of competition; and 4) agreements or coordinated actions between state bodies or state bodies and private organizations aimed at the restriction of competition. The law prohibits employees of state institutions from participating in entrepreneurial activities.

The Competition Law denies unfair competition in a number of ways: 1) the dissemination of false information which may be detrimental to another entrepreneur; 2) misguiding consumers about specific aspects of goods or services; 3) wrongful comparison of goods or services; 4) unauthorized use of trademarks, names of enterprises or goods, or the imitation of the form, packing or design of goods of other entrepreneurs; and 5) the acquisition, use or dissemination of technical or other information such as business secrets without the consent of the owner.

THE ANTI-MONOPOLY COMMITTEE

The establishment of the State Committee On Antimonopoly Policies Structures (Anti-Monopoly Committee), which has the power to enforce competition policies, has been provided by the law. The Anti-Monopoly Committee has branches that extend all over Russia. Each branch has its own geographic jurisdiction.

The functions of the **Anti-Monopoly Committee** are the following:

- *taking the necessary measures to prevent monopolistic activities and unfair competition;*
- *recommending to the government improvements in legislation and its implementation in the area of market development and competition;*

- *advising state institutions to undertake certain actions to develop competition and markets, including the creation of attractive conditions for foreign investment;*
- *controlling the adherence to antimonopoly requirements in cases of foundation, merger, reorganization or liquidation of organizations or companies;*
- *controlling large purchases and sales of shares that might lead to an entrepreneur's dominating position in the market.*

The Anti-Monopoly Committee is empowered:

- *to order entrepreneurs or state institutions and their executives to stop violating the antimonopoly law;*
- *to advise state institutions on the introduction of licensing procedures or bans on export or import activities of entrepreneurs that violate the antimonopoly law;*
- *to impose penalties for the violation of the antimonopoly law; and*
- *to bring actions to courts or other jurisdictional bodies, including the public prosecutor, in case the antimonopoly law is being violated.*

In order to fulfill its functions, the Committee is required to issue its operational rules and proceedings.

The approval of the Anti-Monopoly Committee is required in the following cases: 1) the foundation or merger of an Organization or company of a certain size; and 2) the acquisition of shares or participation. In other cases, simple notification may be all that is required. The Committee usually informs the applicant of its decision within 30 days.

ENVIRONMENTAL REGULATIONS

During the Soviet era, there was almost no legal framework for the protection of the environment. That change on December 19, 1991 when the "Law on Protection of the Environment" (the Environmental Protection Law) was adopted. Numerous pieces of recent legislation also deal with environmental liability. In most cases, though, they only set forth general principles. It is interesting to note that the passage of a law that would deal with environmental issues as a whole is being considered by the Duma.

The Environmental Protection Law is composed of 94 articles divided into 15 sections:

- **the basic requirements of environmental quality standards,**
- **the compensation for damages related to environmental crimes;**
- **the different environmental emergencies,**
- **the economic mechanism of environmental protection;**

- **the environmental monitoring;**
- **the environmental requirements in connection with the location, planning, construction, rebuilding or start up of enterprises, installations or other facilities;**
- **the environmental requirements pertaining to the selection of enterprises, installations or other facilities or performances;**
- **the environmental training, education and scientific research;**
- **the general principles;**
- **the international cooperation in the area of environmental protection.**
- **the liability for violations of environmental legislation;**
- **the resolution of disputes in the area of environmental protection;**
- **the right of citizens to a safe and healthy environment;**
- **the specially protected natural areas and sites;**
- **the state environmental assessments;**

According to the Environmental Protection Law, the environmental liability may fall either within the federal, regional, territorial or local jurisdiction. The Environmental Protection Law aims at parallel organizational structures at federal and regional government levels.

Compensation has to be paid for damages caused to the environment. There is no distinction in Russia between liability for on-site and off-site pollution. It is important to note that no definitions or amounts of fines have been specified. According to the current legislation - in addition to administrative fines and criminal liability -, an injured party has the right to: 1) be compensated (Article 86), 2) apply for a court injunction to prevent future harmful activity (Article 91).

The law allows relevant federal ministries - in particular the Ministry of Environmental Protection and Natural Resources - to establish the permissible pollution limits and the amount of mandatory payments required for the discharge of industrial waste. Section IV sets out the environmental quality standards but provides no quantitative guidelines. The local representative of the ministry may allow a polluter to attain Russian environmental standards over a period of several years. Mandatory payments for waste discharge do not, however, exempt polluters from administrative, criminal or civil liability for damage to the environment.

A company may also be held liable for reversing environmental damage at its own expense. The Russian Ministry of Environmental Protection and Natural Resources has the responsibility to establish certain standards for the cleanup of a particular site.

Other ministries, such as the Ministry of Health, set out standards in their respective areas of competence. If restoration is not possible, full compensation must be provided.

The civil law provides for three kinds of remedies pertaining to environmental damage:

- **compensation for damage caused to the environment as a result of an environmental offense;**
- **restoration of the environment at the defendant's expense; and**
- **termination of environmentally harmful activities being a health hazard to people or the environment.**

Russian law stipulates that local legislative bodies, the local ecological committee and the sanitary epidemiological inspection have the right to suspend the activities of enterprises which violate environmental and sanitary standards.

Under the criminal code, officials and citizens committing environmental offenses - dangerous acts violating environmental legislation and regulations, threatening the environmental security of society and causing harm to the environment and human health - are liable for criminal pursuits.

EMPLOYMENT REGULATIONS

Employees of foreign investment enterprises are subjected to Russian labor law. The Russian Federation Code of Labor Laws (the Labor Code) is the principal Russian law governing labor relations. The employment regulation framework is made out of several other pieces of legislation: 1) the 1990 RSFSR Law on Employment, 2) the 1990 Law on Trade Unions, 3) the Russian legislation on minimum wages, and 4) the 1991 Law of the USSR on the Resolution of Labor Disputes.

The employment contract of each employee must include the following items: responsibilities, salary, leave, working hours, and dispute resolution. If any inconsistencies between provisions in an employment contract and the Labor Code are present, the Labor Code takes precedence and renders the offending employment contract provisions null and void.

Under Russian law, discrimination on the basis of gender, religious belief and age is prohibited. Written reasons must be given for failure to hire a woman with a child under three years old or a single mother with children under 14 years of age.

Joint ventures, wholly owned subsidiaries, and accredited representative offices of foreign companies have the right to hire Russian citizens directly. They do not have to be hired through intermediary organizations as was traditionally required of accredited representative offices of foreign companies.

A new employee can be on probation for a maximum of three months. According to Russian law, a six-month probation can be established with the agreement of the labor union. An employee, who is under 18 years of age, either serving an apprenticeship upon finishing technical school or who has been transferred from another locality may not be on probation. If an employee has been dismissed during a probationary period, he has the right to go to court and appeal the decision.

The term of employment are usually agreed upon by both the employer and the employee; they can either be for an indefinite term - a definite term of no more than five years - or for the duration required to perform a specific task. If employment arrangements cannot be established for an open-ended period - either because of the nature of the task to be carried out, the conditions in which such work are to be done, or when it is in the interests of the employee to have such contract -, a term may be set for the time necessary to perform a specific work.

If the employment relationship is continued after the expiration of the fixed term in the contract, the labor contract is considered prolonged for an indefinite period of time.

Beside his full-time work, an employee cannot be prohibited from holding a second job. The employment contract should contain a provision making sure that the employee will devote full attention to his job during working hours, and that he will not be distracted by any other activities. An employee is violating the terms of his contract if he is unable to devote full energy and attention to his work.

An employer has to get permission from his employee if he his to transfer this particular worker to another enterprise or locality. In case of industrial emergency, employees may be transferred temporarily - up to one month - to a different firm in the same locality.

Employment duties set out in the employment contract should be reasonably broad and comprehensive. Under the Labor Code, an employer cannot require one of his employees to carry out tasks outside the scope of duties described in the contract. Changes in the employee's duties cannot be made unilaterally by the employer. If working conditions have to be changed, the employer must notify the employee two months in advance.

Russian law provides for a minimum wage. It is periodically revised to provide partial compensation for inflation.

Russian legal entities, including foreign investment enterprises, may not compensate Russian employees with hard currency.

Wages are required to be paid at least twice a month - the substantial wage arrears in many Russian enterprises notwithstanding. Income tax must be withhold by the employer and transferred from the enterprise's bank to a state budget account.

For additional analytical, business and investment opportunities information,
please contact Global Investment & Business Center, USA
at (202) 546-2103. Fax: (202) 546-3275. E-mail: rusric@erols.com
Global Business E-Books on Line: http://world.mirhouse.com

The regular workweek may not exceed 40 hours. Additional hours are considered overtime. Overtime hours may only be required in extraordinary circumstances, such as an unforeseen delay in finishing prescribed tasks and the failure of a replacement employee to show up at the designated time. Overtime is limited by the Labor Code to a total of 120 hours a year. An employee may not be required to work overtime more than four hours in two successive days. Minors, pregnant women, and women with children under the age of three cannot be required to work overtime.

Employees are entitled to take days off during the following official government holidays:

1 and 2 January	**New Year's Holiday**
7 January	**Orthodox Christmas**
8 March	**International Women's Day**
1 and 2 May	**Spring and Labor Day**
9 May	**Victory Day**
12 June	**Declaration of Russian Sovereignty Day**
7 November	**Anniversary of the October Revolution**
12 December	**Constitution Day**

Once an employee has worked five days a week for a period of eleven months, he is entitled to an annual paid leave of 20 days. Employers may not cancel accrued leave but may postponed requests for leave due to exceptional circumstances at work. An employer is prohibited from paying cash instead of granting leaves. An employee can only be paid cash if he is dismissed from the company and has not used his leave.

According to the Russian system of sick leave, the only requirement for an employee who has to miss work is to submit a medical certificate on the first working day after his absence. Provisions included in the employment contract should be a lot stricter when it comes to notification.

A woman expecting a child has the right to take a total of 140 days off - 70 days prior to the due date and 70 days after. Paid maternity leave regulations also stipulates that a new mother is entitled to 86 days off if the birth was abnormal or difficult and 110 days for multiple births. Regardless of when the birth actually takes place, the employee is entitled to the full number of days. A worker who has given birth, or the father, grandmother or grandfather who is actually taking care of the child, may request partially paid child-care leave until the child is 18 months old. The partial salary payments are made from the social insurance fund. An additional unpaid leave may be taken during the first three years of the new born child. During the entire period of paid and unpaid leave, the employee retains the right to return to her job. The full leave period is included in the calculation of the employee 's length of service.

For additional analytical, business and investment opportunities information,
please contact Global Investment & Business Center, USA
at (202) 546-2103. Fax: (202) 546-3275. E-mail: rusric@erols.com
Global Business E-Books on Line: http://world.mirhouse.com

Contributions made by the employer to the state social insurance fund cover short- and long-term disability payments. The disability payments are expressed as a percentage of the employee's individual salary.

Payments to the insurance and pension funds are made by the employer. The amount to be paid is calculated as a percentage of the employees' total remuneration - including bonuses and benefits. That particular percentage was 39 in 1997. In the event of the employee's death, benefits are payable under the social insurance regime to the next of kin. Under the law, mandatory retirement for senior citizens cannot be enforced. Amendments to the Labor Code prohibit employers from dismissing workers who have reached retirement age - 55 for women, 60 for men.

Workers are not required to form a trade union organization. If more than three employees desire to unionize, they have the right to do so. It is illegal to require employees or potential employees to promise not to unionize. In addition to individual labor contracts, employers must work out collective agreements with workers who are part of a union. The law does not require a union representative to be part of the decision-making body of the enterprise.

If no trade union organization has been formed, employment disputes are referred to the local people's court. In the event that an organization has been created, differences are initially heard by a commission on labor disputes formed by representatives of the work force and the management. If one of the parties does not agree with the decision that has been made in such a case, it is then heard by the people's court.

An employer can either issue a reproof, a reprimand or a severe reprimand to discipline one of his workers. The Labor Code does not allow an employer to deduct a certain amount of money from the employee's paycheck nor does it allow him to force the worker to take an unpaid leave. The law does provide, however, that other disciplinary actions may be taken - unpaid leave or deductions may be considered in these cases. Under the Labor Code, an employee has the right to challenge the validity of disciplinary actions taken against him.

Unless the enterprise is being liquidated, an employer does not have the right to terminate the contract of a worker who is either pregnant, has a child under three years of age, or is a single mother with children under 14. In case the enterprise goes out of business, the employer has the obligation to find his employees another job or pay them another three months' salary. Employees who are laid off for economic reasons must be given two months' notice and be remunerated with an additional one month's severance pay. Workers are entitled to draw their average salary for an additional two months while looking for a different job (bringing the total to three months' severance pay.)

The contract of an employee can be terminated on the following grounds:

For additional analytical, business and investment opportunities information, please contact Global Investment & Business Center, USA at (202) 546-2103. Fax: (202) 546-3275. E-mail: rusric@erols.com Global Business E-Books on Line: http://world.mirhouse.com

1   unsuitability (lack of qualifications or health reasons);
2.   systematic and unjustified non-fulfillment of work duties despite disciplinary measures;
3.   unjustified absences;
4.   prolonged absence due to disability;
5.   reinstatement of an employee who previously filled the position;
6.   coming to work under the influence of alcohol or narcotics; and
7.   liquidation of the employer or redundancy of the position.

Dismissal for reasons 1, 5, and 7 is permitted only if the worker, after having given his consent, cannot be transferred to a different position. In addition, the employee is entitled to two weeks' severance pay if dismissed for reasons 1 and 5, and up to three month's severance pay for reason 7.

In addition, the Labor Code contains special grounds for the dismissal of employees in position of responsibility:

- a single gross breach of work duties either by the head of the enterprise, institution, organization, or by one of his deputies;
- suspicious actions by an employee who directly handles the company's money causing the management to lose confidence in that particular worker; and
- immoral behavior by an employee charged with educational responsibilities.

On December 16, 1993, President Yeltsin issued Presidential Decree No. 2146 (the Decree) requiring foreign nationals working in Russia, unless specifically exempted by the Decree, to obtain work permits. In addition, in certain cases, employers must now obtain the authorization of the Ministry of Migration to hire these foreign nationals.

"On the Hiring and Use of Foreign Labor in the Russian Federation" sets out the regulations for the issuing of authorizations and work permits. In the Russian capital, authorizations and work permits are issued by the Migration Service of the City of Moscow.

Foreign nationals, except managers, deputy managers or chiefs of divisions, must have an authorization from the Ministry of Migration to work at Russian legal entities with foreign investment. To obtain an authorization, a Russian enterprise must submit a letter to the Migration Service setting out the number of foreign nationals the firm plans on hiring and the reason why these individuals should be hired. After making a decision, the Migration Service submits it to the Specialist on the Foreign Work Force at the Migration Service for the City of Moscow. The Specialist is the person responsible for issuing authorizations as such.

Foreign nationals employed at Russian legal entities with foreign investment are required to obtain a work permit. To obtain such document, the employers must submit, in addition to the authorization mentioned above, the following documents:

- a complete application for each foreign national;
- a cover letter mentioning the fact that the enterprise would like to obtain work permits for its foreign nationals' employees;
- a list of the names of foreign nationals employed by the firm where passport information, addresses in Russia, and positions in the company are included;
- two notarized copies of the enterprise's charter; and
- two notarized copies of the firm's registration certificate from the Moscow Registration Chamber.

For additional analytical, business and investment opportunities information, please contact Global Investment & Business Center, USA at (202) 546-2103. Fax: (202) 546-3275. E-mail: rusric@erols.com Global Business E-Books on Line: http://world.mirhouse.com

RUSSIAN TAXATION SYSTEM

Russian tax laws have changed frequently since 1991, making most of the information obsolete. In 1997, the Russian government took some important steps towards simplifying the tax system. Preliminary legislation passed by the Russian Duma in mid-1997 were aimed at reducing the number of taxes from more than 100 to 20. Local and regional taxes were especially targeted for pruning. Future tax reforms include improved collection and increased incentives for investment. In late July 1997, First Deputy Prime Minister Anatoly Chubais was appointed to head a provisional working group to reform the Russian tax system.

Under the Russian Federation's Law No. 2118-1, "Concerning the Fundamental Principles of the Taxation System in the Russian Federation," adopted on December 27, 1991, taxes are divided into the following categories: 1) federal taxes; 2) taxes of the Russian Federation's constituent republics and of territories, provinces, autonomous provinces and autonomous districts; and 3) local taxes.

FEDERAL TAXES

Federal taxes are established by legislative acts and are levied in the whole of Russia. They include the following:

1. **value-added tax;**
2. **excise duties;**
3. **tax on exchange activities,**
4. **tax on securities transactions;**
5. **customs duty;**
6. **contributions for the replacement of the mineral raw-material base;**
7. **payments for the use of natural resources;**
8. **profits tax on enterprises (incorporating the tax on excess labor cost);**
9. **income tax on physical persons;**
10. **road fund taxes;**
11. **levies on coats of arms;**
12. **government fees (or *state duties*);**
13. **tax on property inherited or received as a gift;**
14. **levy for the use of "Russia" and "Russian Federation" in a corporate name.**

Some taxes are payable exclusively to federal budgetary authorities while others, such as the profits tax on enterprises and individual income tax, are payable in part to the federal and in part to the regional or local authorities. Some federal taxes, such as government fees and those imposed on inherited property, are payable directly to local authorities.

For additional analytical, business and investment opportunities information,
please contact Global Investment & Business Center, USA
at (202) 546-2103. Fax: (202) 546-3275. E-mail: rusric@erols.com
Global Business E-Books on Line: http://world.mirhouse.com

REGIONAL TAXES

There are four types of taxes levied by the republics, territories, provinces, and districts of Russia. They are:

- **the tax on the property of enterprises (the assets tax);**
- **the income from timber;**
- **the payment for water; and**
- **the levy exacted on legal entities for educational institutions.**

The first three taxes are levied on the Russian territory as a whole. Specific tax rates are determined by regional jurisdictions, unless otherwise established by legislative acts of the Russian Federation.

The fourth tax, the educational levy, is established by legislative acts of the regional jurisdictions and is paid to the budgetary authorities of those regions.

LOCAL TAXES

Preliminary tax legislation proposed in mid-1997 sought to reduce the number of local taxes from 23, currently, to three. The most significant local taxes are:

1. **taxes on physical persons' property and land;**

2. **registration levy on physical persons who engage in entrepreneurial activities;**

3. **tax on advertising;**

4. **levy on trading rights;**

5. **levy for the right to use local symbols;**

6. **tax on the maintenance of the housing fund and social and cultural assets.**

The first three taxes are legislative acts of the Russian Federation, but the specific rates of those taxes are determined by regional and municipal legislatures. The remaining taxes are legislative acts of regional and municipal bodies.

DOUBLE TAX TREATIES

The income of a foreign legal company submitted to taxes in Russia may also be taxed in that entity's home country. Special tax rates established by treaties eliminate or greatly reduce the impact of double taxation on certain types of income.

Table 11. Russian Tax Treaties Withholding Rates, percent

For additional analytical, business and investment opportunities information,
please contact Global Investment & Business Center, USA
at (202) 546-2103. Fax: (202) 546-3275. E-mail: rusric@erols.com
Global Business E-Books on Line: http://world.mirhouse.com

Country	Dividends	Interest	Royalties	Other income
Austria	0	0	0	0
Belgium	15	15	0	0
Canada	15	15	10	0
Cyprus	0	0	0	0
Denmark	15	0	0	0
Finland	0	0	0	0
France	15	See Note 1	0	0
Germany	15	5	0	0
Ireland	10	0	0	-
Italy	15	0	0	-
Japan	15	See Note 2	1	0
Netherlands	15	0	0	0
Norway	20	0	0	0
Spain	18	0	5	0
Switzerland	-	-	0	-
UK (old)	0	0	0	0
UK (new)	10	0	0	0
USA	See Note 3	0	0	0

1. The interest's withholding rate is 10 percent, except for banks where none is required.

2. The withholding rate shown is for royalties paid for commercial property; no withholding is required on royalty payments for cultural or artistic licenses.

3. The withholding rate on dividends is five percent for shareholders that are corporations owning at least 10 percent of the payer's statutory capital. In all other cases, the withholding rate on dividends is 10 percent.

Many of double tax treaties provide for either reduced rates of withholding or a complete exemption from withholding for payments made to their residents.

To obtain tax exemptions or preferential tax rates provided by an international treaty with Russia or the USSR (if valid), a foreign legal entity must apply for treaty certification and submit the document to the entity paying the income. If a treaty certification is not presented, the entity should withhold income at the rates prescribed by the law.

The table below shows the rates under some of the treaties of Russia (and/or the USSR) that apply to dividends, interest, royalties, and other income derived from Russian sources not attributable to permanent establishment in Russia. This is not an exhaustive list of Russian or Soviet tax treaties,

CORPORATE PROFITS TAX

LIABILITY TO CORPORATE PROFIT TAX

Russian legal entities with foreign ownership and foreign legal entities with a "taxable presence" in Russia are liable for Russian profits tax. Foreign entities have a taxable presence if they are found to have a "permanent representation" under Russian domestic law. Permanent representation is similar to "permanent establishment" as defined in the OECD Model Convention on double taxation - it does not, however, include the standard exemptions found there.

While Russian legal entities are taxed on their world-wide income, foreign legal entities with a taxable presence in Russia are taxed only on profits earned through their permanent representation in Russia.

RATES

The tax rate varies according to the location of the taxpayer. Currently, the maximum rate is 35 percent. It comprises a federal and a regional element. The federal rate is set at 13 percent. The regional rate varies, but the maximum is 22 per- cent for most entities, and 30 percent for banks and insurance companies. The exact regional rate is determined by the government of each particular region. The rate in Moscow, for example, is the maximum 22 percent, for an overall rate of 35 percent.

TAXABLE BASE

The two components of the taxable base are: the profit from sales of goods and services and the net income from non-trading operations such as leasing income and capital gains. The profit is calculated by deducting the costs - material production costs, depreciation at statutory rates, salaries, payroll taxes and administrative expenses - included in the Russian Cost of Production Statute. However, there are limitations on the deductibility of certain types of expenses, notably loan interest, advertising expenses, training costs and insurance premiums. Gains and losses from hard currency exchanges are not included in the taxable base.

DEDUCTIONS AND EXEMPTIONS

The basic taxable profit is determined according to the same principles than the international accounting practice. There are, however, some significant differences. For example, several of the items listed below can be deducted in the absence of the taxable profit:

1. Profits allocated to a Reserve Fund. The maximum allocation is the lower 50 percent of the enterprise's gross profit (determined before this deduction) or 25 percent of the charter fund paid in shareholders' equity.

For additional analytical, business and investment opportunities information,
please contact Global Investment & Business Center, USA
at (202) 546-2103. Fax: (202) 546-3275. E-mail: rusric@erols.com
Global Business E-Books on Line: http://world.mirhouse.com

2. Profit reinvested in capital expenditures that exceeds the total depreciation during the period. Profit used to repay bank credits can also be used to reduce taxable profit.

3. Losses from the taxpayer's main activity in the previous five years. Loss relief must be taken in equal installments during each of the five years. A relief that is not used during a particular year cannot be carried over to another year. There is no provision for enterprises to offset profits and losses of other related firms.

4. Charitable contributions up to a certain limit.

It is important to note that the last three types of deductions are restricted. The sum of these and other specific deductions provided in the Corporate Profits Tax Law cannot reduce the tax, that otherwise would have been paid, by more than 50 percent.

Under domestic legislation, interests on bank loans are deductible if they are used either to purchase current assets or to make good a shortage of working capital. Interests are non-deductible if they are used to pay loans for the acquisition of fixed assets, intangible assets or other non-current assets.

From time to time, investment is encouraged by tax exemptions provided by the law. One example is a two-year tax break applying to newly established small Russian legal entities involved either in the production and the processing of agricultural goods or in the production of consumer and medical goods and construction.

A recent presidential Decree exempted the note to enterprises with foreign investment. The Decree grants a complete exemption from profits tax to qualifying Russian enterprises with foreign investment for the first two years of operation. To qualify, entities must engage in production activities, have foreign investment amounting to more than 30 percent of the paid-in charter-fund capital (totaling at least US$ 10 million), and be registered after January 1, 1994. Partial exemptions also exist for enterprises in their third of fourth years of business.

EXECUTION OF TAX LAW

Taxation is based on profits earned during the calendar year. As far as Russian legal entities are concerned, final audited tax returns are due by March 15 of the year following the reporting one. Penalties are imposed for failing to comply with this requirement. Advance payments of profits tax should be made each month. Monthly installments are due by the fifteenth of each month and should equal one-third of the quarterly payment. Any discrepancies between the total of payments made during the year and the final profits tax calculated in the tax return must be settled by March 25 following the reporting year.

Any excess tax payment is applied to future tax liabilities or refunded, on written request, to tax authorities.

For additional analytical, business and investment opportunities information, please contact Global Investment & Business Center, USA at (202) 546-2103. Fax: (202) 546-3275. E-mail: rusric@erols.com Global Business E-Books on Line: http://world.mirhouse.com

TAX ON EXCESS LABOR COSTS

The tax on excess labor costs is governed by the same law that covers the corporate profits tax (i.e., **Law No. 2116-1 "Concerning Tax on the Profit of Enterprises and Organization",** adopted on December 27, 1991 (as amended)). If the average wage in an enterprise exceeds six times the statutory minimum wage - the minimum wage increased from 20,500 rubles in January 1997 to 60,500 rubles in December 1997 -, it is multiplied by the number of employees and is taxed at the same rate than the corporate profits tax. The tax on excess labor costs must be paid regardless of whether an enterprise is exempt from profits tax or whether, for the purposes of profits tax, it is making a loss.

This tax is to be abolished on January 1, . However, the State *Duma* has publicly acknowledged its intentions of drafting a replacement tax to make up for loss revenue. It is not yet clear what form this replacement tax will take.

The tax on excess labor costs must be paid quarterly by Russian legal entities, but only annually by their foreign counterparts.

TAXATION OF FOREIGN LEGAL ENTITIES

Foreign legal entities that receive income from sources in Russia, but not through a permanent representation, are liable to pay tax on that income. The tax must be withheld by the source of the payment. The income includes revenues from: investment such as dividends and interest; the use of copyrights and licenses; the freight charges and lease payments; the management services; and other that result from the provision or use of any kind of services in Russia that is not associated with activities carried out through a permanent establishment.

The tax rate is 15 percent for dividends and interest, 6 percent for freight and 20 percent for all other types.

Tax treaties with the Russian Federation or the former USSR (if valid) may provide exemptions from the withholding of these payments. Following the introduction of new legislation, however, any available relief is not automatically granted. In order to obtain a relief, the foreign payee must file a complete exemption application with the tax authorities. Advance relief from tax withholding can only be obtained if prior notification that the payment to be made is of a "regular and homogenous" nature has been provided to the local inspector.

COMPANY PROPERTY TAX - ASSETS TAX

This property or assets tax is a tax on the average annual balance-sheet value of fixed and intangible assets of which depreciation, inventory, work-in-process, raw materials, supplies and prepaid expenses have been deducted. Leased assets are subject to the assets tax only if the taxpayer has the possibility of purchasing the asset at the end of the lease term. Both Russian legal entities and permanent representations of foreign legal entities are subject to the assets tax. However, Russian legal entities are exempt from the tax in their first year following registration. Russian legal entities should report the net book value of their assets in accordance with the Russian statutory accounting rules. The permanent representations of foreign legal entities should report the net book value of their assets according to their country of residence's depreciation rules.

While the maximum rate is set to two percent by federal law, the actual rate is determined by the governments of the different regions. The tax rate is currently 1.5 percent in Moscow. All entities must pay the tax and file reports quarterly. For both Russian and foreign legal entities, the filing deadline is 20 days following the reporting period. For a Russian legal entity that is wholly foreign-owned, the deadline is 30 days after the reporting period.

TAXATION OF INDIVIDUALS

EXPATRIATES

Under Russian tax law, a foreign individual living in the Russian Federation for more than 183 days will be considered, for tax purposes, a permanent resident and will be subjected to taxes computed on his world-wide income. A foreign national will only be taxed on income received from Russian sources if the length of his stay has been less than 183 days - a nonresident status is still in effect in this case. The law defines "Russian income" as an amount of money paid for services within Russia. Therefore, salaries paid from abroad are considered foreign income, even if the work has been performed inside the Russian territory.

Foreigners residing in Russia are required to submit an estimation of their worldwide income, called a preliminary declaration, for the current calendar year within one month of their arrival in the Russian Federation and before April 1 of each subsequent year of residence. Based on this document, tax authorities issue a demand equal to 75 percent of the estimated tax liability for the year, payable in one, two or three installments.

A final declaration documenting the actual income must be submitted before April 1 of the year following the reporting (calendar) year and one month prior to the individual's final departure from Russia.

Russia has a progressive tax system. An annual income above 50 million rubles is taxed at the highest marginal rate of 30 percent. The tax authorities calculate the preliminary tax liability by converting the foreign currency figures into rubles at the exchange rate prevailing on the day the demand is prepared. The same process is used to calculate the final tax liability - the exchange rate prevailing in this case is the one of the last day of each month in which income is received.

Taxes can either be paid in rubles or, in certain areas such as Moscow, in foreign currency. Foreign currency payments can be made by direct wire transfer from the foreign individual's personal bank account to the Moscow State Tax Inspection's foreign-currency account.

Russia offers a number of tax breaks to foreign individuals who have dependents.

Foreign legal entities are not required to make Russian social contributions for their expatriates if they are paid from abroad.

LOCAL NATIONALS

Russian legal entities are required to withhold income tax on individual's salaries. In addition, these same entities are obliged to contribute 39 percent of gross salaries to state social programs. Four funds are the recipient of these contributions:

Pension Fund	28.0 percent
Social Insurance Fund	5.4 percent
Employment Fund	2.0 percent
Medical Insurance Fund	3.6 percent

A foreign legal entity with a representation in Russia is subject to the same employer's requirements as its Russian counterpart if its workers' salaries are paid from a Russian bank account. A foreign legal entity with a representation in Russia is not required to withhold income tax if its employees are paid from a foreign bank account, but is required to pay Russian social contributions.

The meaning of "social contribution obligations" for a foreign legal entity without a representation in Russia is not clear. It appears that those paying Russian citizens do not pay Russian social contributions.

OTHER TAXES

VALUE ADDED TAX (VAT)

TAXPAYERS

All legal entities, including foreign legal ones receiving revenue from commercial activities conducted in the Russian Federation, are liable for a value added tax (VAT). A foreign company does not need to have a permanent representation in Russia to be liable for the VAT. There is no additional registration requirement for this tax.

TAX BASE

The tax base for the VAT includes the revenues from the sale of goods and the services performed in Russia. Unlicensed loans from Russian companies, sums received as penalties resulting from the violation of agreements and imputed market price revenue from the provision of goods and services without consideration are also part of the tax base. The tax base on revenue is the amount of the commission received on markups or surcharges. As far as imports are concerned, the tax base is the customs value including both duties and excise tax.

TAX RATES

The rate of the VAT is 20 percent for all goods and services. The only exceptions to the rule are food products not subjected to excise tax and children's goods which benefit from a 10 percent rate. Revenues from the sale of goods and services at VAT inclusive prices are assessed for the purposes of the VAT at 16.26 percent and 8.85 percent respectively.

Until its abolition on January 1, , an associated "special tax" was assessed in all instances where the VAT was applied. Following the elimination of the tax, the previous State Duma discussed the idea of increasing the VAT to 21 percent. Most lawmakers, however, vigorously oppose a change of the VAT rate.

COMPUTATION

The value added tax payable to the budget is the difference between the amount of the VAT charged to customers (output VAT) and the amount of the VAT paid on purchases (input VAT). However, if the amount of the VAT paid on purchases must be included in the cost of production - that is, be deductible for the purposes of calculating taxable profit, - it has to be indicated in settlement documents such as payment orders, payment request orders and payment requests. In addition, the VAT paid on fixed and intangible assets may only be offset over six months in equal monthly installments from the time the assets are put into use or entered in the accounting books. The only exception is the VAT paid on imported fixed and tangible assets, which is reimbursable in full when the assets are put into use.

Recent legislation have been proposed that, beginning on January 1, , the VAT - which is paid on the acquisition of fixed and intangible assets - should be recovered on the date that those assets are entered into a company's accounting records. This change, which is only an intended amendment to the existing treatment of the VAT, has yet to be enacted.

Enterprises that engage in construction and installation work or contract with other organizations of the same nature must capitalize the associated VAT in the cost of the asset. In case the input VAT is not available for offset against the output VAT, the cost of the asset including the VAT is then depreciated.

EXEMPTIONS

Exemptions to the VAT fall into the following categories: revenue, exemption with credit, and exemption without credit.

Revenues excluded from the taxable base include contributions to the charter funds of Russian companies during their first year of registration, money received from a special state budget, and assets used to carry out joint activities (without the formation of a legal entity). The exemption with credit means that the input VAT that has not been offset may be claimed for reimbursement from the budget and include revenues from exported goods or services physically performed by a Russian company outside of Russia. Exemption without credit means that the input VAT cannot be reclaimed from the budget. Bank loans and the sale and distribution of securities are closely connected with the last category. Such input VAT may be deducted for the purpose of computing taxable profit. Furthermore, in accordance with the temporary import regime, several kinds of goods exempt from the VAT are allowed to be imported.

PROCEDURE FOR PAYMENT

The VAT payment schedule is as follows:

Average monthly VAT (Rubles)	Frequency of payment
More than 3,000,000	Three times a month
1,000,000 - 3,000,000	Monthly
up to 1,000,000	Quarterly

Small Russian legal entities classified as "small enterprises" may pay quarterly, regardless of the amount of the payment. Entities falling into the "small enterprises" category are those which have: 1) fewer than 200 persons in industry and construction; 2) up to 100 persons in science and scientific services; 3) up to 50 persons in sectors related to production; and 4) up to 15 persons in non-production and retail-trade sectors.

SUBSURFACE RESOURCE USE TAXES

A number of payments are provided in the Subsurface Resources Law for the use of subsurface resources. They include: 1) payments for the right to use subsurface resources; 2) contributions for the replacement of the mineral raw-material base; 3) a levy for the issue of licenses; 4) an excise duty; and 5) payments for the use of water and sea bed areas. A draft law "On Production Sharing" passed by the Russian Duma in mid-July 1997, if eventually implemented, would supersede many of the provisions included in the Subsurface Resources Law.

ROYALTIES

PAYMENTS FOR THE RIGHT TO EXPLORE AND APPRAISE DEPOSITS

These payments are made throughout the duration of the exploratory work. The rate of payment is calculated as a percentage of the agreed (estimated) cost of that task. The rate of payment ranges from a minimum of one percent to a maximum of two. The actual rate is determined on the results of a competitive tender or auction by the licensing authority.

PAYMENTS FOR THE RIGHT TO PROSPECT DEPOSITS

These payments are also made throughout the duration of the work. The rate is also calculated as a percentage of the agreed (estimated) cost of that task. The rate of payment ranges from a minimum of three percent to a maximum of five. The actual rate is determined by the licensing authority on the results of a competitive tender or auction. Both of these payments are payable to regional and municipal authorities rather than to federal ones.

PAYMENTS FOR THE RIGHT TO EXTRACT COMMERCIAL MINERALS

Currently, two types of payments are in existence: 1) one-time payments and 2) regular payments throughout the period of extraction . The one-time payment must not be less than 10 percent of the regular payment rate as applied to the projected average annual output. The regular payment rate - determined for each deposit - must be between six and 16 percent of the value of the amount of oil produced. The value of supplies for domestic use is classified as an enterprise's regulated wholesale price of oil. It is calculated as the industrial wholesale price of which the tariffs for pumping, transshipment and delivery have to be deducted. The value of supplies to be exported is the export price less the export duty, excise duty and transportation costs.

REPLACEMENT TAX

According to the Subsurface Resource Law, users of such resources must pay contributions for the replacement of the mineral raw-material base. This payment can be deducted from the profits tax by being included in the cost of production.

The tax base for determining replacement tax is the value of production sold less the value added tax, special tax and excise duty. It is unclear whether this tax base applies to exports or whether the export tax base is the export price less export duties, excise duty and transportation costs.

LEVY FOR THE ISSUE OF LICENSES

A levy is collected by the organization issuing licenses for the right to use subsurface resources. The amount of the levy is determined on the expenses incurred in reviewing applications for the use of subsurface resources, organizational expenses, etc.

For additional analytical, business and investment opportunities information,
please contact Global Investment & Business Center, USA
at (202) 546-2103. Fax: (202) 546-3275. E-mail: rusric@erols.com
Global Business E-Books on Line: http://world.mirhouse.com

EXCISE DUTY ON NATURAL RESOURCES

Excise duty is payable, at varying rates, in rubles per ton of production. The standard base rate for oil is 14,750 rubles per ton - although different amounts have been established for individual enterprises. From time to time, the rates are increased to reflect changes in the exchange rate between the ruble and the US dollar.

EXCISE DUTY

The excise duty is an indirect duty that applies to some luxury items and other goods. Some of the items included are: wine, vodka, beer, tobacco products, motor cars, tires, jewelry, diamonds, crystal, carpet, fur, leather clothing and certain minerals.

The excise duty for goods manufactured in Russia is typically paid by the manufacturer - if the manufacturer is also the seller. Goods that are manufactured using raw materials supplied by the downstream customer are exempt from the excise duty. If the downstream customer sells manufactured goods for which he has supplied raw materials, then he is liable for the duty. The duty base on domestic goods is the cost of the goods sold. For imported goods, the duty base is the customs value. The duty rate is calculated on each specific product and varies from 0 to 100 percent.

OTHER MISCELLANEOUS TAXES

TAX ON FUELS AND LUBRICANTS

The Tax on the Sale of Fuels and Lubricants (TSFL) was introduced in December 1992. The tax is assessed on the gross income from the sale of fuels and lubricants at a rate of 25 percent - the VAT is excluded from the tax. The rate assessed on the mark-up of fuels and lubricants sold by intermediaries - supply and sales organizations - is 20 percent. The definition of fuels and lubricants include gasoline, diesel fuel, diesel motor fuel, and compressed and liquefied gas used as motor fuel. All "associations, enterprises and organizations" that sell such materials must pay the TSFL "irrespective of their form of ownership, departmental subordination and organizational and legal form." The Russian Federation Road Fund is the main beneficiary of the tax.

ROAD FUND TAXES

TAX ON ROAD USERS

This tax applies to Russian and foreign legal entities that carry out entrepreneurial activities in Russia through a permanent representation. The tax is assessed on sales. The tax rate is 0.4 percent if the goods are sold by the company and 0.03 percent if the same task is performed by traders and suppliers. The tax rates may be changed by the local parliament of the constituent jurisdiction of the Russian Federation (see Chapter 6). The tax must be honored before the middle of each month, unless the average monthly payments of the enterprise are less than 200,000 rubles, in which case the tax is payable quarterly.

TAX ON VEHICLE OWNERS

The owner - any foreign or Russian legal entity or individual - of a road vehicle is required to pay an annual fixed-rate tax that is calculated on the vehicle's engine capacity and the amount of the officially established minimum wage. In most regions this tax is payable by August 1 - the tax return should be submitted by March 15. Vehicle tax payments are deductible to calculate taxable corporate profit.

TAX ON THE ACQUISITION OF MOTOR VEHICLES

This tax applies to the acquisition of domestic or imported motor vehicles by foreign and Russian legal entities. If the type of vehicle that has been purchased is a freight car, pickup, passenger van, or motor car, the tax is 20 percent. If the vehicle purchased is a trailer or a semi-trailer, it is 10 percent. In St. Petersburg, the 1997 rate for most vehicles was two percent. According to Russian law, an acquisition can be defined by the following terms: 1) a purchase, 2) a barter, 3) a lease or 4) a capital contribution. Once the acquisition has been registered with the State Automobile Inspection (GAI), the owner has five days to pay the tax.

TRANSPORTATION TAX

The transportation tax amounts to one percent of the total wages and salaries paid by foreign and Russian legal entities. It must be honored each month at the same time than the labor payments. Quarterly reports are due within 30 days of the end of each accounting quarter. Any amounts of tax paid are deductible in the calculation of taxable corporate profit.

HOUSING AND RELATED TAXES

TAX ON HOUSING AND SOCIAL-CULTURAL FACILITIES

This tax is payable by foreign and Russian legal entities for the maintenance of housing facilities in certain localities in Russia. The 1997 rate was 1.5 percent of sales revenues in Moscow and St. Petersburg. The tax is payable by the twentieth day of the month following the reporting one. This tax calls for an annual report to be filed by March 15 of the following year for a Russian legal entity with foreign investment, or by April 15 of the following year for a foreign legal entity.

LEVY ON ENTITIES FOR EDUCATIONAL INSTITUTIONS

This tax is imposed on foreign and Russian legal entities to help meet the financial requirements of local educational establishments. As for the transport tax, this levy amounts to one percent of the total wages and salaries paid by a company. The tax is payable by the twentieth day of the month following the reporting one. Reports for this tax should be filed quarterly for a Russian legal entity without foreign investment, by March 15 of the following year for a Russian legal entity with foreign investment, and by April 15 of the following year for a foreign legal entity.

ADVERTISING TAX

This tax is levied on enterprises that incur advertising expenses. The tax amounts to five percent of the cost of advertising work and services. Tax forms and payments should be submitted quarterly. It should be noted, however, that companies may only partly deduct advertising expenses from profits tax - as these deductions are based on the level of annual sales (including VAT).

LEVY FOR USE OF THE WORD "RUSSIA"

A levy of 0.5 percent of revenue must be paid by enterprises, institutions and organizations using "Russia" or "Russian Federation" in their name. (A draft law passed by the Duma in July 1997 eliminated this tax.)

LEVY FOR USE OF LOCAL SYMBOLS

This tax on the use of symbols associated with Moscow - imposed on both foreign and Russian legal entities - is set at a rate of 50 times the minimum monthly wage. There are no clear guidelines about the payment of this tax.

LEVY ON HARD CURRENCY TRADING

This tax, imposed on both foreign and Russian legal entities on the amount of currency exchanged, is payable at a rate of 0.1 percent. The tax is withheld automatically and is not deductible from profits tax.

For additional analytical, business and investment opportunities information,
please contact Global Investment & Business Center, USA
at (202) 546-2103. Fax: (202) 546-3275. E-mail: rusric@erols.com
Global Business E-Books on Line: http://world.mirhouse.com

REGIONAL TRENDS IN FOREIGN INVESTMENTS

The division of power among the federal, regional and local levels is crucial in Russia's policy making process. While federal authorities have determined and designed the principal features of Russia's reforms, regional administrations are becoming more powerful in their implementation. The power of these authorities reflects the decentralization of political and economic decision making following the collapse of the former Soviet Union. The division of power is a complex and sensitive issue that ought to be understood and handled with carefully by prospective foreign investors.

OIL INDUSTRY: ORGANIZATIONAL STRUCTURE

INVESTMENT IN THE RUSSIAN OIL AND GAS SECTOR

This section draws extensively from the International Energy Agency (IEA) 1997 survey, *Energy Policies of the Russian Federation.* The reader is referred to that publication for a comprehensive analysis of Russia's oil and gas sectors. Russia's economic future is highly dependent on its ability to develop its energy resources. Considerable foreign capital and technology will be required for the successful development of these resources. Compared to the huge amount of financial assets needed, foreign investment in the oil and gas sectors has been relatively small (approximately $2.2 billion by the end of 1997). Major impediments to foreign investment include the lack of a comprehensive legal and regulatory framework; ill-defined property rights and physical access rights to mineral resources; a tax system that is complicated, burdensome and targets revenues rather than profits; export controls that restrict access to international markets; and pricing polices that maintain disparities between internal and external prices.

The recent adoption of the First Part of the Civil Code has been a significant factor in the creation of a more stable basis for all commercial relations. A passage of the 1992 Subsoil Law established a legal framework for the oil and gas sectors under the emerging market environment. A complementary Oil and Gas Law detailing specific licensing rules for the oil and gas sectors has yet to be passed. The enactment of the Law on Production Sharing Agreements at the end of 1997 was an important development for the oil and gas sectors.

The Law on Production Sharing Agreements sets the framework for contracts between the state and investors - domestic and foreign - for the development of energy and mineral resources. The law was initially drafted to open the way for considerable foreign investment. In its current state, however, the legislation contains a number of provisions which might be perceived as creating particular disadvantages for foreign investors in the Russian oil, gas and mineral sectors. The most notable of these shortcomings are: provisions which would appear to permit unilateral modifications of contractual agreements in the event of "changed circumstances"; the need for additional parliamentary approval of some territories subject to production sharing agreements; the possible limitations on the ability of investors to transfer or pledge property and property rights under production sharing agreements; the uncertainty regarding the Russian State's ability to waive sovereign immunity pending the adoption of further legislation; the uncertainty regarding an investor's right to seek international arbitration of certain disputes; the apparent mandatory applicability of Russian law to production sharing agreements; the applicability of Russian tax and accounting rules in determining the deductibility of business expenses; and as a result of the Law's failure to harmonize conflicting provisions of prior legislation on subsoil resources, the uncertainty regarding the legal basis for the granting of subsoil rights (i.e., by contract rather than administrative grant). One hopes that these concerns will be addresses and that a more transparent and conductive legal regime for foreign investment will be established by futures amendments to the Law on Production Sharing Agreements.

OIL PRODUCTION AND RELATED ACTIVITIES

Russia is currently the third largest oil producer in the world, behind Saudi Arabia and the United States. Compared to its 1987 peak, Russian output has plunged 40 percent in 1994 to attain 316 million tons (Mt). The IEA notes that the underlying political, economical and organizational problems associated with the ongoing economic transformation are the main factors for the decline and not the deficiencies in the oil reserve base and technology. Exploration for oil reserves has also fallen dramatically over the last few years. The number of exploratory wells drilled in 1994 was less than a quarter of those drilled in 1988. The total amount of drilling fell by 83 percent during this period. Western countries estimate that the Russian proved and probable reserves amount to 8 to 11 billion tons.

VERTICALLY INTEGRATED OIL COMPANIES

Vertical integration is an important development for the oil sector in Russia. The Government reorganized the oil industry by combining large companies - involved in crude production, refining, distribution and retailing - into one integrated structure in 1992. A number of decrees adopted in August 1997 signaled the final composition of Russia's oil companies. There are currently 13 integrated, three semi-autonomous, and several independent oil companies. The structure of vertically integrated companies is described at the end of this chapter - Table 10.

The vertically integrated companies were partially privatized during the voucher privatization program. It is interesting to note that the Government retained a majority stake in all of the oil companies. A select number of those companies have been participating in the current "loan-for shares" process that took place in late 1997. The restricted nature of the auctions drew severe criticism from both domestic and foreign sources, who claimed that the process was pre-arranged. The process essentially excluded foreigners and most of the stakes were acquired by the entities that were responsible for running the auctions: the Russian banks. The onward sale of the shares - the second part of the process - is expected to take place in late . It will be interesting to see how this will be managed. The banks' motivation behind the acquisition of oil companies' shares remain obscure. It is difficult to assess whether they are long term strategic investments or short term portfolio investment. Either of these objectives have implications for potential foreign investors.

The underlying reason for the restructuring of the oil industry was to create a competitive, decentralized oil sector. It appears, however, that integrated companies could be limiting the scope for competition and thus be in a monopolistic position. One example of this is LUKoil which possess a virtual monopoly on production, distribution and marketing in south-western Russia. The ability of integrated companies to hinder the access of smaller and foreign companies to the Russian oil sector is another factor that could potentially limit competition.

TRANS-NEFT AND TRANS-NEFTEPRODUKT

The oil-pipeline monopolies in Russia are *Transneft* and *Transnefteprodukt* - organized as joint stock companies. Even though an April 1997 Decree sets down a timetable for the issuance of preferred shares in these companies, the Russian government - which will continue to own all common stock - will retain management control. Currently, *Mintopenergo* exercises voting power over the Russian government's shares in *Transneft* and *Transnefteprodukt* and establishes, with the consent of other relevant governmental bodies, applicable transportation tariffs.

ROSNEFTEGAZSTROI

Construction activities in the oil and gas sectors is the responsibility of *Rosneftegazstroi*. Before its foundation in December 1991, its assets were controlled by the Oil and Gas Construction Ministry of the Soviet Union. *Rosneftegazstroi* is currently one of the world's largest construction companies, active not only in Russia but in over a dozen other countries as well. *Rosneftegazstroi* sold 10 percent of its shares to foreign investors in 1994 for $10 million. The company plans to sell another 30 percent to foreign investors in the future.

Rosneftegazstroi is engaged in the reconstruction and repair of many pipelines in Russia. The Russian oil and gas construction industry - previously one of the nation's most solid - is having severe difficulties. *Rosneftegazstroi*'s lack of financial resources has hindered its ability to reconstruct main gas and oil pipelines, many of which have been in use for more than 20 years. The number of kilometers of pipeline repaired annually dropped from 1,240 to less than 600 in 1994. An estimated 3,000 to 5,000 km of pipelines ought to be repaired annually to avoid increasing leakage and shut-downs.

REGIONAL ORGANIZATIONAL DEVELOPMENTS

Russia's autonomous republics have assumed a very active role regarding the ownership and management of oil enterprises on their territories. Most of the republics have already declared ownership of the oil companies on their territory and have established regional oil firms. *Rosneft*, which initially owned those assets, protested vigorously against the move. Many republics, notably Komi, Tatarstan, and Bashkortostan, have passed legislation contradicting federal privatization laws. The oil enterprises of these republics have not been included in the privatization process.

GOVERNMENT REGULATIONS

Being both shareholder and regulator, the Russian Government has numerous and often competing responsibilities and interests in the oil sector. Its ability to exercise control over the oil companies is based not only on the state's authority but also on its right to participate in the management of individual enterprises.

The government's main policy concerning the regulation and restructuring of the oil sector include:

1. **satisfying domestic demand for oil and petroleum products and ensuring that foreign economic commitments are honored; and balancing federal and regional interests;**

2. **maintaining the existing production and the technological relationships, including the integrated system of trunk pipelines, and guaranteeing unrestricted access to pipelines for producers of oil and petroleum products;**

3. **increasing efficient use of natural resources;**

4. **creating large vertically integrated companies linking upstream and downstream activities by providing financial, material and technical support.**
5.
FEDERAL MANAGEMENT SYSTEM. Several governmental bodies oversee the oil industry at the federal level. In some respects, they overlap and at the same time, as responsibilities change, are in a state of flux.

THE MINISTRY OF FUEL AND ENERGY

The authority of the Ministry of Fuel and Energy (*Mintopenergo*) over the oil industry is not precisely defined under Russian legislation. The passage of the law "On Gas and Oil" may well change that. Over the last few years, foreign investment issues in the upstream oil sector have been controlled by the authority. *Mintopenergo* exercises control over the domestic oil industry by requiring companies to supply petroleum products to certain agricultural regions that the enterprises might not otherwise want to supply. *Mintopenergo* exercises oversight for rules and access to export pipelines, although its mandate to carry out this activity is not entirely clear given the emergence of the Federal Energy Commission (see below). *Mintopenergo* also represents the state's interest in the privatized oil companies and takes part in management through representatives on the boards of directors of these companies.

THE FEDERAL ENERGY COMMISSION

The **Federal Energy Commission** (FEC) was originally established in 1992 to regulate electric utilities. On November 29, 1997, President Boris Yeltsin signed Decree No. 1194, "On the Creation of the Federal Energy Commission", which recreated the agency as the primary regulator for the energy sector. The decree stated specifically that the FEC was to be the "federal executive agency in charge of regulating natural monopolies in the following sectors: shipment of oil and petroleum products along main pipelines; shipment of gas along pipelines, and electricity and heat-energy transmission services." These activities were previously carried out by the Fuel and Energy, Economy and Finance Ministries. Implementation of the decree is pending the issuance of an ordinance by the Prime Minister to delineate the FEC's functions, structure, composition and degree of authority.

THE RUSSIAN COMMITTEE ON GEOLOGY AND THE USE OF MINERAL RESOURCES (*ROSKOMNEDRA*)

Russian Committee on Geology and Use of Natural Resources grants licenses for the use of underground resources, establishes the amount to be paid for the right to explore and mine natural resources, and organizes international tenders for the right to explore and develop natural resources.

According to the ***"Mineral Development Program Until The Year 2000,"*** *Roskomnedra* will be the governmental body responsible for geological exploration on land, on the continental shelf and in the Pacific Ocean. A federal geological service will be created comprising enterprises not subject to privatization. The financing of the geological service's activities will be drawn from the state budget. Private enterprises contracted to do a special task will also share the costs. Geological information on underground resources obtained under federally funded projects remain the property of the state. *Roskomnedra* and its territorial divisions can transfer the right to store geological information on underground resources to state or privatized entities on a contractual basis. The unauthorized use of geological information on underground resources, the refusal to provide information as required by applicable regulations, the concealment, or the unauthorized transfer of such information to third parties are punishable under Russian law. Information on underground resources, including data on the structure of territories, regions and mineral fields, projected resources, the quantity and quality of reserves will be provided to:

1. *participants of tenders on the right to use underground resources;*
2. *holders of licenses for the right to use underground resources;*
3. *enterprises authorized to conduct regional exploration and special work to the extent necessary to conduct such exploration or work; and*

4. enterprises conducting geological exploration and research financed by federal funds;

Information cannot be transferred to third parties for commercial purposes. In some cases, a fee will be charged for information on underground resources. A price will be set for information based on the cost of producing such information, its value, and other factors. The final price for such information will be established on a contractual basis with the user - except information on tracts which will be offered in tenders.

STATE COMMITTEE ON STATE PROPERTY MANAGEMENT (GKI)

While GKI is the depository of the government's shares in energy enterprises, *Mintopenergo* exercises control over such shares. Under Governmental Decree No. 96 adopted on February 10, 1994, GKI has the power to deprive federal enterprises of property if those entities do not use such property in accordance with applicable requirements. Managers of federal enterprises are prohibited from selling or leasing federal property allocated to their enterprises; contributing such property to the charter funds of other enterprises; or, using it as collateral without GKI's prior consent.

RUSSIAN PARLIAMENT

Two committees of the Russian Duma - the Economic Policy Committee and the Industry, Construction, Transport and Energy Committee - play key roles in shaping oil and gas legislation. The Natural Resources, Ecology, and Legislation committees sometimes assert jurisdiction also.

The Russian government and *Mintopenergo* play important roles in shaping oil and gas legislation. It is common practice that all draft laws be approved by the competent body or bodies before the state Duma vote on them.

Traditionally, the state Duma has taken a more conservative position on foreign investment in the energy and mineral resource industries than in any other ones. For instance, on January 23, 1997, the State Duma Committee on Property, Privatization and Economic Activity suggested that the Russian government refrain from selling its share-holdings in oil and gas enterprises at "give-away prices."

LOCAL GOVERNMENT

The Government's role *vis-à-vis* many of the autonomous republics and other federation subjects regarding the nature of the organizational changes and ownership of enterprises on their territories is rather obscure. The governments of Russia's autonomous republics enjoy a certain degree of autonomy to oversee the oil and gas industry located in their territories. Even though the local authorities have gained more powers, the federal government is still able to exercise some control over the operations of regional oil enterprise. For example, while the federal authorities no longer have the power to set export quotas, they still control access to the main pipelines.

For additional analytical, business and investment opportunities information,
please contact Global Investment & Business Center, USA
at (202) 546-2103. Fax: (202) 546-3275. E-mail: rusric@erols.com
Global Business E-Books on Line: http://world.mirhouse.com

Disputes between the federal and republics authorities regarding ownership have not been settled. Attempts to resolve these differences are made on a case-by-case basis, without a uniform federal policy. In the Komi Republic, the federal and Komi republic authorities have formally agreed to divide federal property between them equally. Other republics, except Sakha, have announced that they will not turn over to the Russian government any equity in the oil producing enterprises located on their territory.

Although the Oblasts' governments are less likely than the republic authorities to demand that the federal government hand over stakes in oil JSCs presently held by *Rosneft*, they still want a voice in the operations of these JSCs. *Mintopenergo* has already signed more than 20 bilateral agreements with various regional governments. The concerns of the regional authorities include: 1) assuring the supply of oil products to enterprises and organizations funded out of the regional budget, and 2) retaining federal non-budgetary funds constituting the main source of finance for the repair and modernization of the local oil and gas industry.

The Russian government can have jurisdiction over any energy project, including those located in the republics, if it affects "federal interests." The Russian Constitution does not provide a clear division of authority between the federal and local governments. (See Articles 71 through 79). The draft Law on Oil and Gas, currently being considered by the Russian Duma, reflects the uncertainty of the situation. It provides that: According to the **Law on Oil and Gas**, administrative jurisdictions of the Russian Republics are responsible for:

1. *drafting and implementing territorial programs for the development of hydrocarbon resources (fossil fuels);*

2. *setting conditions on the use of their share of payments and taxes from the use of underground resources, establishing the amounts of such payments and determining the forms in which they are to be made;*

3. *concluding international agreements over the use and protection of oil and gas facilities and oil transportation; and*

4. *managing relations arising from the laying of pipelines within their territories.*

According to the draft law, both the federal bodies and those of the republics are responsible for drawing up a list of property belonging to enterprises in the oil and gas and oil-transportation industries at the disposal of Russia or its constituent republics; laying down conditions and procedures for obtaining payments for the use of underground resources, and forming strategic oil and gas reserves.

While the enactment of an oil and gas law may help resolve certain jurisdictional problems, legislation establishing the boundaries of the federal and local governmental authority would further clarify them.

The passage of the **Subsoil Law** in 1992 was an important step in the institutional reform of the oil and gas sector. This particular law established the legal framework for the extraction of natural resources, including petroleum production. The law further established the "State" as the exclusive owner of all mineral deposits. The definition of the "State" remains relatively vague - one assumes that it implies the federal government. Exploration and production rights may be leased by the State by the issuance of licenses to private and state-owned entities. The legislation requires those licenses to be issued only through public competitive tenders.

Following the passage of the Subsoil Law, work proceeded on the so-called Oil and Gas Law - a legislation dealing specifically with the procedures and conditions related to the production, pricing and transport of petroleum. The law is designed to complement the Subsoil Law by establishing new and possibly more restrictive licensing and operating rules for the oil and gas industry. Oil extraction, pipeline transportation, combined oil and gas operations, geological surveying and underground storage are dealt with in details in the law. While lawmakers have worked on a draft of the Oil and Gas Law since 1991 - three versions of which have been considered by the State Duma - it has yet to be enacted.

The enactment of the **Law on Production Sharing Agreements** in December 1997 was an important development for the oil and gas sectors. The Law on Production Sharing Agreements sets the legal framework for contracts between the state and investors, both domestic and foreign, for the development of energy and mineral resources. The law was initially designed to open the way for considerable foreign investment. In its current state, however, the law contains a number of provisions that may be perceived as creating particular disadvantages for foreign investors in the Russian oil, gas and mineral sectors.

The most notable of these shortcomings are:
1) provisions that would permit unilateral modifications of contractual agreements in the event of "changed circumstances";
2) the need for additional parliamentary approval in some territories subject to production sharing agreements;
3) the possible limitations imposed on the ability of investors to transfer or pledge property and property rights under production sharing agreements;
4) the uncertainty regarding the Russian State's ability to waive sovereign immunity pending the adoption of further legislation;
5) the uncertainty regarding an investor's right to seek international arbitration of certain disputes;

6) the apparent mandatory applicability of Russian law to production sharing agreements;

7) the applicability of Russian tax and accounting rules in determining the deductibility of business expenses; and

8) the uncertainty regarding the legal basis for the granting of subsoil rights (i.e., by contract rather than administrative grant) as a result of the Law's failure to harmonize conflicting provisions of prior legislation on subsoil resources.

One hopes that any futures amendments to the Law on Production Sharing Agreements will address these concerns and establish a more transparent and conductive legal regime for foreign investment.

FOREIGN INVESTMENT IN THE OIL AND GAS SECTORS

Foreign companies have had the opportunity to invest in the Russian oil sector since the late 1980s. According to Goskomstat data, the total direct investment in the oil production (upstream) sector is approximately $1.7 billion. The relatively small amount of foreign investment in the sector has been ascribed to a number of different problems. In *Energy Polices for the Russian Federation*, the IEA found that the major impediments to foreign investment are:

• the "**lack of a comprehensive legal and regulatory framework,** which has left investors confused about the hierarchical order of rules;

• the **uncertainties in property rights and rights to mineral resources;**

• an **uncertain taxation system** that targets revenues instead of profits and endangers the economic viability of existing as well as planned projects;

    export controls restricting access to international markets, and

    pricing policies that maintained the wide disparity between internal and external prices for crude petroleum."

These problems have been compounded by more general factors: 1) macro-economic instability; 2) ambiguities regarding future reforms; and, 3) perceived confusion over authority and areas of competence between central, regional and local governments. Thus, on a risk adjusted basis, it appears that foreign companies are significantly downplaying the considerable opportunities of oil investments in Russia.

TAXATION ON CRUDE OIL PRODUCTION

The Russian taxation system for the upstream oil sector is complicated. An average of **30** different taxes and payments are collected from oil enterprises by federal and local budgets. The number of taxes imposed by some regions is even greater. The tax system has also been subject to a high degree of instability. Not only is legislation subject to frequent change, but individual tax exemptions are common.

In addition to its complexity, the Russian tax system imposes a heavy burden on the oil companies. Taxes are levied in such a way that the industry as a whole has been unable to recover capital costs. In certain case - especially during 1993 and 1994 - the tax burden amounted to over 100 percent of operation margins. This factor has limited the amount of investment in the oil and gas sectors. The current policy of the Russian Government is the reform and simplification of its tax structure. In developing its tax system for the energy sector, the IEA noted that the Government ought to have the following goals in mind:

the level of taxes should leave producers with sufficient incentives (and means) to carry out investment activity;

the level of taxes should provide reasonable revenue to the treasury of different administrative levels; but,

a limit on the number and total amount of taxes that regions may impose should be agreed upon;

the system should be stable and predictable;

taxes should be oriented toward profit and not revenue;

tax administration should be simplified, thus increasing the likelihood of compliance.

THE NATURAL GAS SECTOR

GAZPROM

Because of the dominance of *Gazprom*, the natural gas sector in Russia requires to be treated differently. *Gazprom* produces 95 percent of the country's natural gas and is the owner of all its high pressure transmission lines and associated infrastructure. *Gazprom* was formed as a *socialist concern* of the Soviet Ministry of the Gas Industry in 1989. Three years later - in November 1992 - it was transformed into a Joint Stock Company. In 1994, 60 percent of *Gazprom*'s equity was sold within Russia - both to employees of the company and to the general population. The remaining 40 percent is the property of the Russian State - a decree adopted on September 17, 1994 suggests that some of this remaining share will be sold on an accelerated timetable.

Gazprom has approximately 46 trillion cubic meters of reserves - nearly 35 per-cent of the world's total. While *Gazprom* has faced a number of challenges during the last five years, it continues to deliver this important commodity to domestic and foreign

For additional analytical, business and investment opportunities information,
please contact Global Investment & Business Center, USA
at (202) 546-2103. Fax: (202) 546-3275. E-mail: rusric@erols.com
Global Business E-Books on Line: http://world.mirhouse.com

consumers alike and accounts for a substantial share of the country's convertible currency earnings. The principal short-term problem facing the company - and for that matter the Government - is the fact that customers - including Ukraine - do not pay. In the long term, *Gazprom* has to balance the necessity of developing major supply projects with the possible changes in demand for its products. Trade-offs will be likely affected by the following factors: 1) the possibility for an early and strong economic recovery in Russia, 2) the potential for energy savings and efficiency, and 3) the changes in requirements of current and potential foreign customers in Europe and the former Soviet Union.

At the present time, formal regulation of the gas industry (and *Gazprom* in particular) is fairly light. *Mintopenergo* exercises less authority over the gas industry than it does over the oil industry, - possibly the legacy of *Gazprom*'s state monopoly over natural gas. Specific gas regulations mostly concern the setting of wholesale and retail prices for residential and industrial consumers by a government committee. The Government has apparently begun the process of setting up an independent regulatory authority that would, *inter alia,* regulate access to pipelines and tariffs to third party users.

Evidences exist that Gazprom has received favorable treatment by the Government in the past, most notably concerning taxes - although this issue is not entirely clear. By some accounts, *Gazprom* is exempt from virtually all taxes and customs duties except for the allocation of 50 percent of its foreign exchange earnings to the Government. By other accounts, while *Gazprom* was given favorable treatment in the past, the situation no longer prevails.

At the present time, *Gazprom* has come under greater political scrutiny. A decree adopted on September 1, 1997 increased excise taxes on natural gas from 25 to 35 percent. In addition, *Gazprom*'s exemption from the stabilization fund's - a fund created to enhance gas industry projects through foreign exchange earnings - taxes was canceled. To compensate for the financial loss, the Government will reduce the number of *Gazprom* customers exempt from the disconnection of services due to their inability to pay.

At the present time, foreign investors have only limited opportunity to invest in the gas sector in Russia. In terms of upstream investment, *Gazprom* has adopted the general notion that the company is capable of carrying out required projects - foreign investment are not included. However, according to IEA reports, *Gazprom* has expressed interest in retaining the services of foreign partners for the development of the *Shtokmanovskoye* held in the Barents Sea - a multi-trillion cubic meters held located 300 km offshore. Opportunities for developing gas offshore also exist in Sakhalin. Four different projects are currently under negotiation - though only one (Sakhalin-2) has signed a detailed (production sharing) agreement.

For additional analytical, business and investment opportunities information, please contact Global Investment & Business Center, USA at (202) 546-2103. Fax: (202) 546-3275. E-mail: rusric@erols.com Global Business E-Books on Line: http://world.mirhouse.com

Foreign investment is possible in the development of gas condensate - where liquids are produced prior to gas development. Gas distribution offers greater opportunities for foreign investors. Since 1990 *Gazprom* has announced a DM 1 billion loan to finance improvements of the European pipeline infrastructure. Another development is *Gazprom*'s possible venture into Italy for power generation via a 1,000 kilometers pipeline - which is currently the subject of a feasibility study. Investment is also badly needed in Russia's domestic gas pipeline network. The gas distribution system during the Soviet era was developed using imported equipment. It is thus possible that orders for foreign equipment may be forthcoming as pipelines and compressor station units are being replaced or refurbished. This was the case of an Italian joint venture which secured a loan of $1.5 billion to upgrade a number of compression stations.

It should be noted that gas distribution within Russian is carried also carried out by a large number of regional, territorial and municipal gas companies - the vast majority of which have been privatized even though they still operate under the umbrella of the former state distribution company, *Rosgazihkatsiya*. This company has signed a number of cooperation agreements with foreign entities to refurbish the distribution system and to implement gas savings and efficiency programs. The initial idea for such programs was that foreign investors would have access to a share of the gas which their projects had helped save - this gas would in turn be considered as additional exports. However, according to the IEA, it has proven very difficult to organize in practice, and investors are now looking at ways in which saved gas could be commercialized on the Russian market.

BUSINESS OPPORTUNITIES IN OIL AND GAS

Foreign investment projects in the Russian oil sector can take many forms. On one hand, there are the "mega-projects" for exploration and production in large new oil and gas fields, often involving the need to create an entire new infrastructure and requiring huge amounts of development capital. Smaller projects, on the other hand, play an active role in developing smaller fields and rehabilitating existing fields. Major opportunities to obtain supply contracts exist in some sectors for companies supplying equipment and services. These companies have the possibility to contract with national and regional geological and production associations, oil and gas joint ventures, and foreign exploration and production companies.

The appropriate structure for a project depends on its particular circumstances. As far as some major oil projects are concerned, there may be no substitute for formally approved production sharing agreements accompanied by a host of related arrangements covering the operation of owned facilities, sale and transport, etc. Such agreements, if obtainable, could offer greater security against adverse tax and regulatory measures. Thus far, smaller joint venture projects have been more common. Initially these projects took the form of "joint enterprises" under the old law of the Soviet Union on joint ventures. Under Russian law, they are taking the form of joint stock or limited liability companies.

LAWS RELATED TO NATURAL RESOURCES USE

Prospective foreign-investment projects in energy resources are subject to case-by-case governmental review. Following the adoption of Governmental Decree No. 1418, *"On the Licensing of Separate Kinds of Activities"*, on December 24, 1994, the licensing authority was divided among various federal entities:

- the Ministry of Oil and Gas licenses the storage of oil, gas and their products; the production, transmission and distribution of electrical energy and fuel energy; the assembly and repair of energy works, electrical-energy and fuel-energy equipment;

- the **Committee of the Russian Federation for Geology and Use of Minerals** licenses geological surveys, the creation and publication of geological maps as well as geological exploration, etc.;

- the **Ministry for the Protection of the Environment and the Natural Resources** of the Russian Federation licenses the use, storage, transfer, disposal, and elimination of industrial and other waste, and the conduct of expert ecological analyses and ecological audits;

- the **Ministry of Construction of the Russian Federation** licenses topographic, geodesic and cartographic works, architectural activities (together with the Union of Architects of Russia), the performance of engineering surveys for construction, and other construction related activities.

Local governments are delegated some of the licensing authority. This includes: 1) the authority to license the storage and use of oil (except certain oil reserves) and the filling of stations; and, 2) the design-prospecting work connected with land use.

Under Russian law, enterprises using natural resources or releasing pollutants must pay fines to the Government. The Russian government and its relevant agencies not only establish the amount of those fines but also create norms governing pollution control, waste disposal, and other related matters.

The **Law on Subsoil Resources** adopted on February 21, 1992 - last amended on February 8, 1997 - establishes a system of licensing and payments for the right to use subsoil resources. Licenses are issued for various activities including surveying, exploring and developing mineral deposits, as well as building and exploiting underground facilities not connected with the extraction of minerals.

In the second half of 1997, the Russian Duma was considering a number of other draft laws relating to energy and other natural resources. They include such legislation as the laws on: 1) Oil and Gas, 2) the Continental Shelf and Exclusive Economic Zone of the Russian Federation, 3) Concessions and Other Agreements, and 4) Production Sharing. Pending the adoption of that law and some other legislation, many major projects have been put on hold.

Export restrictions on energy resources

Until recently, the export of energy and mineral resources was subject to an extensive system of administrative controls, including quotas and licensing. Under this system, the only enterprises that could export "strategically important raw materials" were those licensed by the Ministry for Foreign Economic Relations. In recent months, many of these administrative controls have been eliminated. (See Russian Government Decree No. 1446 "On the Export of Oil and Oil Products from the Customs Territory of the Russian Federation," adopted on December 31, 1994.) In the past, many enterprises with foreign investment and foreign companies have found that even if legal barriers are removed, practical barriers remain - especially when it comes to exports (gaining access to oil pipelines and terminals are two prime examples).

Under current Russian legislation, quantitative restrictions on the export of goods and services, and the imposition of other non-tariff restrictions may only be established for limited purposes - including: 1) fulfillment of international obligations of the Russian Federation or 2) reasons associated with public health. (See Presidential Decree No. 245 "On The Fundamental Principles for Carrying Out Foreign Trade Activity in the Russian Federation," adopted on March 6, 1997).

Following several legislative changes, many joint ventures - which had been limited by quotas - will be able to increase the level of oil exports. Regulations preventing the dumping of Russian exports on foreign markets, controlling currencies to prevent capital flight and tax evasion, and governing the export of nuclear and military technology will remain in place. In addition, the Russian government will continue to impose tariffs on certain exports.[8]

The rationale for export tariffs is not only to generate state revenues, but also to make sales to domestic customers as financially attractive as sales to foreign customers. That is, a producer or seller making a foreign or domestic sale should be indifferent. Thus, as domestic prices for commodities - such as crude oil - rise to approximate world prices, the government should in principle reduce export tariffs. It is interesting to note that the Russian government reduced export duties on crude oil from 30 to 23 ECU per ton in January 1997. **Ministry on Oil and Power Industry** (*Mintopenergo)* has sent the government a proposal to further reduce export duties for petroleum products and make the rates seasonal, that is, lower in the summer months.

---

[8] See Supplement 7 for the basic structure of the Russian oil industry

For additional analytical, business and investment opportunities information, please contact Global Investment & Business Center, USA at (202) 546-2103. Fax: (202) 546-3275. E-mail: rusric@erols.com Global Business E-Books on Line: http://world.mirhouse.com

Mintopenergo has also proposed to reduce the duty on exports of gasoline, diesel fuel and fuel oil to the levels set out in the Table. In fact, Russia has indicated that its intentions are to eliminate export tariffs by January .

THE ENERGY CHARTER TREATY

After several years of negotiations, the Energy Charter Treaty was signed in Lisbon on December 17, 1994 by representatives of forty-one countries and the European Communities. The Energy Charter Treaty is an agreement establishing the legal framework for investment and trade in the energy sector among countries from the OECD area, the former Soviet Union and Eastern Europe. The Treaty also addresses a wide range of other subjects such as transit of energy goods, competition and the environment. The Treaty itself is a complex document containing fourteen annexes. Because of the numerous interpretations recorded in connection with its adoption, understanding the document is crucial for the analysis of its various twists.

For additional analytical, business and investment opportunities information, please contact Global Investment & Business Center, USA at (202) 546-2103. Fax: (202) 546-3275. E-mail: rusric@erols.com Global Business E-Books on Line: http://world.mirhouse.com

THE INVESTMENT PROGRAM OF THE RUSSIAN GOVERNMENT

The Russian Government's Decree No. 1016 "Concerning a Comprehensive Program for the Stimulation of Domestic and Foreign Investment in the Economy of the Russian Federation", was adopted on October 13, 1997. This "Comprehensive Program" was designed to complement two other programs of the Government of the Russian Federation: 1) "Reforms and the Development of the Russian Economy in 1997-1997", as approved by Decree No. 439 on April 28, 1997; and 2) the "Federal Investment Program for 1997", as approved by Decree No. 415 on April 25, 1997.

The "Comprehensive Program" is based on the following:

- The decline in production is practically over; investment activity must be increased in order to avoid long-term depression.

- The main legislative decisions forming the legal base for investment activity have been taken. In these conditions, the focal point is the development of procedures which regulate the implementation of those decisions. This pre-determines a short time frame (fourth quarter of 1997 and) and a relative amount of methodological materials to be developed and approved. The general logic of the Comprehensive Program is the following:

- Continuing the work that has been undertaken to improve the investment climate in Russia - the ultimate goal being an environment in which the investment process thrives. The further reduction of inflation and the re-financing rate of the Central Bank of the Russian Federation are the necessary - but insufficient - conditions to improve the investment climate. One of the central issues in improving the investment climate is to provide security guarantees to investors working in the Russian market - including personal security and protection of invested resources from non-commercial risks.

- Implementing measures directed at improving the volume of investment. The most important task is the formation of prerequisites that would turn amortization deductions of enterprises and public savings into investments.

- Increasing the return on capital investments by attaining the goals set with reduced spending in the social sphere and increasing the efficiency of investment in the production sector.

- Attracting foreign investment, ensuring the development of international economic relations and bringing in advanced scientific and technical achievements - although these are unable to compensate for the shortage of domestic investment. Foreign investment can be intensified only by increasing activities of domestic investors and by allowing foreign investors to operate under Russian domestic conditions.

The Action Plan for the implementation of the contains tasks involving the preparation of specific documents aimed at accomplishing the stated objectives. In this respect, owing to the complexity of the problem, each of the documents prepared will, as a rule, affect several areas.

CONDITIONS FOR INVESTMENTS GROWTH

The current situation in the investment sphere can be referred to the turn that the Russian economy has taken to put an end to the crisis. Characteristic manifestations of this positive process include the reduction of the budget deficit, budget financing without money emission, the deceleration of the fall in and stabilization of production against a backdrop of reduced inflation, an increase in the positive foreign trade balance, and the strengthening of the Russian ruble. As a result of the economic reforms, the ownership rights of private investors are guaranteed, price mechanisms for regulating production are starting to work, the transfer of capital via the stock market has begun, project financing is developing.

In the near future, an augmentation in the volume of capital investments will be the main lever for the modernization of production, the reduction of costs, and the renewal of economic growth. They will in turn result in an increase in the standards of living. These factors will be directed at increasing the output of competitive domestic goods and strengthening the position of enterprises on the domestic and foreign markets, and overcoming inertia in the social sector. Increased accumulation is a prerequisite for growing investment

Increased accumulation will begin from a level currently more than two times lower than in 1992. Because of the increase in complexity of production structures in 1992 and 1994, the effectiveness of capital investments - calculated on the basis of the gross domestic product - has fallen by 24 percent. It was observed, in 1997, that only a low proportion of the federal budgetary targets were being met - regarding items which provide financing for State capital investments. While the importance of internal resources is growing, enterprises finance investment by using only about one half of the amortization deductions. The situation regarding the use of profit for investment purposes is exemplified by the fact that the relevant profits tax exemption has only been enjoyed by a ratio of one in 20 enterprises. It is interesting to note that enterprises almost never reach the maximum - 50 percent - of profit used for investment purposes that is not taxable.

In the present conditions of the transition economy, the accumulation of national capital must be undertaken with the assistance of the State and private sectors of the national economy. Centralized investment resources will be used to stimulate private, domestic and foreign investment, ensuring the necessary development of the social and production infrastructure.

For additional analytical, business and investment opportunities information,
please contact Global Investment & Business Center, USA
at (202) 546-2103. Fax: (202) 546-3275. E-mail: rusric@erols.com
Global Business E-Books on Line: http://world.mirhouse.com

Alongside direct financial support allocated to projects corresponding to key growth areas of the economy, the State provides favorable conditions for investors by means of adopting and modifying the appropriate legislative and normative acts.   The rules concerning project financing provide for the possibility of selective deviation from general provisions and the granting of certain exemptions to individual investors.

Some indications of this nascent vitalization of investment activity is: 1) the increase in the proportion of long-term credits from 4 to 12 percent of the overall volume of credits granted by commercial banks in the first six months of 1997; 2) the increased activity of large domestic capital in the oil and gas, chemical and metallurgical industries; and, 3) the expansion of housing construction - which is a proven precursor to a general investment growth.

The stimulation of domestic and foreign investment is meant to increase the volume of capital investments in the Russian economy - from all sources of financing - by 4 percent in and by 7 percent in 1997.

The main source of investment in 1997 - 1997 will be the internal resources of enterprises in the State and private sectors. The internal resources of enterprises will comprise 68 to 69 percent of the total volume of capital investments in 1997 - these figures corresponds to the level seen in developed countries.

Federal budget resources will remain an important source of financing for the economy. The volume of State investment will amount to 1.5 percent of the projected gross domestic product in . Calculations show that in order to move the economy out of the crisis in , shares of State investment ought to be increased to 3 percent of the Gross Domestic Product. About 60 to 70 percent of this amount will be used to finance development in the social sphere, and 30 to 40 percent in the production sphere.

Given the absence of alternative sources of financing, State capital investments must be used primarily to accomplish the following social tasks:

- finishing the construction of housing for servicemen and reservists - expected to be 20 to 25 percent complete in 1993 - 1997 - and fulfilling the *Zhilishche (Housing)* program. In order to partly make up for delays caused in previous years, resources ought to be increased by 220 percent from 1997 to .

- undertaking measures to implement State programs to reverse the consequences of: the accident at the Chernobyl nuclear power station (15 regions); nuclear disposal at the Mayak production association; and, the effect of the Semipalatinsk testing ground on the environment. The percentage points of the fulfillment of the programs was 14 in 1993, 9.6 in 1994, and 8.4 in 1997. These figures are adding to the

For additional analytical, business and investment opportunities information,
please contact Global Investment & Business Center, USA
at (202) 546-2103. Fax: (202) 546-3275. E-mail: rusric@erols.com
Global Business E-Books on Line: http://world.mirhouse.com

already strained socioeconomic situation in areas affected by radioactive contamination.

- preventing the flooding of cities, inhabited localities and other facilities crucial to the national economy; undertaking priority measures to provide flood protection for the Caspian coast, the cities of Vladivostok, Nakhodka, Spasska Dalny, Ussuriisk, the village of Pokrovka and other inhabited localities in the Maritime Territory, water conservation measures in the destructive influence zone of the Krasnoyarsk Reservoir; and, implementing programs to improve the environment in the cities of Bratsk and Nizhny Tagil.

- supporting the construction of essential public facilities, including subway systems;

- developing fundamental science to preserve Russia's scientific, technical and intellectual potential.

It is the intention of the Government to use additional resources for the development of unique health care facilities - of federal significance - and the protection of the Russia's cultural patrimony.

The efficient development of the social and vital production sectors is impossible to achieve without federal resources. Analysts are predicting that, in - 1997, the production sector will retain its current volume of capital investment for such programs as nuclear power station safety, power engineering in the Far East and Eastern Siberia, the development of the medical industry, and other major areas such as transport, communications, the agro-industry and special complexes.

In order to create the necessary market tools to bring the economy out of the crisis, the Government is considering financing efficient investment projects by providing State support - 0.5 percent of the Gross Domestic Product - to private investors on a competitive basis (in accordance with **Presidential Decree No. 1928, "Concerning Private Investments in the Russian Federation"**, adopted on September 17, 1994); - the financing would be repayable by the conversion of the defense industry.

Sources of financing such as the secondary issue of securities and credits from commercial banks will develop significantly in the coming years. It is estimated that they will constitute about three percent of the total amount of investment in 1997.

The creation of financial and industrial groups have produced additional opportunities to attract capital for the implementation of investment projects in the Russian Federation. Financial and industrial groups pooling their resources together significantly increases the domestic investment opportunities of the group as a whole; and, given a unified technical, structural, marketing and financial policy and effective management of resources, make it possible for them to concentrate on more important areas.

The State may participate in the implementation of projects in order to increase the investment activities of financial and industrial groups. The size of the capital of the financial and industrial group determines the extent of governmental support the group will get - whether the participants have joint liability can also play a role.

A developing source of financing for capital investment is public resources which are used to enhance individual housing construction, the proportion of which will be around 7 percent of the total volume of investment in 1997.

Foreign investments will be further developed. Their share in the total volume of capital investments may grow from 3.3 percent in 1997 to 5.2 percent in 1997.

One targeted norm for the attraction of foreign investment in Russia is the increasing of its share in the total volume of capital investments to 10 percent (currently 1.8 percent). This is determined by the state of the world capital market and the high level of competition in that market.

Accrued foreign investments in the Russian economy will be a precursor for the resolution of the following socio-economic problems:

- realizing Russia's untapped scientific and technical potential, particularly at converted enterprises in the military industrial complex;
- promoting Russian goods and technologies on the foreign market;
- promoting the expansion and diversification of export potential and the development of import-substituting production in certain sectors;
- promoting the flow of capital into regions with surplus labor resources and regions with rich natural resources in order to accelerate their development;
- creating new jobs and bringing in advanced forms of production organization;
- assimilating the concept of civilized relations in the sphere of business;
- promoting the development of the production infrastructure.

The debts that various countries owe to Russia - amounting to $147 billion - is one of the potential sources for attracting investments into the Russian economy. In order for repaid debts to have a maximum impact, a significant percentage of the revenues must be used to finance expenditures associated with the technical development of the economy, and the implementation of key projects within federal sector and regional investment programs.

EFFORTS FOR ESTABLISHING BETTER INVESTMENT CLIMATE

An essential precondition for the growth of capital investment is the existence of a favorable investment climate in the Russian Federation.

For additional analytical, business and investment opportunities information,
please contact Global Investment & Business Center, USA
at (202) 546-2103. Fax: (202) 546-3275. E-mail: rusric@erols.com
Global Business E-Books on Line: http://world.mirhouse.com

The Russian Government adopted important measures aimed at improving the investment climate for domestic and foreign investors in 1994-1997. They included: 1) a reduction of the inflation rate; 2) preferential treatment for the taxation of commercial organizations with foreign investment's profit; 3) exemptions from value added tax and special tax for imported technical equipment and related spare parts; and, 4) the granting of preferential credits in foreign currency received from foreign banks and credit institutions. The restriction applying to the current number of settlement and budgetary bank accounts of enterprises, institutions and organizations has been removed. The issue on how to account for amounts of exchange rate differences arising due to fluctuations in the exchange rate of the ruble in relation to foreign currencies when enterprises determine taxable profit has been resolved. A decision has been adopted to remove the tax on expenditure on labor payment in excess of the normative level taking effect on January 1, .

From 1997 to 1997, the improvement of the macro-economic situation - resulting from the suppression of inflation and, consequently, a reduction in the interest rate for long-term credits for investment purposes - will have a decisive significance.

Ensuring that enterprises use amortization deductions for their proper purpose is essential to the creation of a favorable investment climate, The State has the right to control the charging and use of amortization as a non-taxable part of gross income. In the event that amortization is incorrectly charged or improperly used by enterprises after the expiration of the amortization deadline, the Government might withhold State credits and loans.

The increased role of amortization deductions is aided by the systematic revaluation of enterprises' fixed assets and the application of the mechanism for accelerated amortization in accordance with the Russian Federation's Decree No. 967 "Concerning the Use of the Accelerated Amortization Mechanism and the Revaluation of Fixed Assets" adopted on August 19, 1994.

Current legislative acts grant a number of exemptions from the taxation of profit of enterprises and organizations concerning the financing of capital construction. In the coming years, it will be necessary to form an optimum level of taxes, tariffs and exemptions comparable with the investment conditions in the countries with which Russia is competing on the investment capital market.

Resolving the problem of stimulating investment in the Russian economy depends to a large extent on the establishment of the Russian securities market, whose development will proceed as and when inflationary processes are overcome and production stabilizes.

For additional analytical, business and investment opportunities information,
please contact Global Investment & Business Center, USA
at (202) 546-2103. Fax: (202) 546-3275. E-mail: rusric@erols.com
Global Business E-Books on Line: http://world.mirhouse.com

The demand for shares in privatized enterprises has a significant effect on investment activity. The recent growth in the price of these shares is characteristic of joint stock companies which have a monopoly in such spheres as the oil and energy industries and communications.

The process of attracting foreign capital at a time when a significant proportion of Russian enterprises are being privatized will inevitably, in most cases, involve some of the shares in the Russian joint stock companies which own the enterprises to be sold to foreign investors.

The establishment of a favorable investment climate will be determined by the activities of executive government bodies of the Russian Federation's constituent entities in attracting domestic and foreign investments.

In organizing exhibitions, participating in federal and international exhibitions of investment projects, and undertaking publicity and information campaigns in the printed press, State government bodies of constituent entities of the Russian Federation create a favorable investment climate in the regions.

The Russian Ministry of the Economy, in conjunction with State government bodies of constituent entities of the Russian Federation and interested federal State government bodies, has developed a Plan of Action on issues relating to the attraction of foreign investment in the Russian Federation regional economies. The Plan was approved in April 1997.. The Plan of Action covers all the areas of regional investment policy and provides for specific measures aimed at attracting foreign investment in the economies of the constituent entities of the Russian Federation.

Russia's investment cooperation with neighboring countries is one of the main factors in the stabilization and further development of those nations' economy. Investment cooperation between neighboring countries cannot be undertaken successfully without a coordinated economic policy that takes into account the specialization, cooperation and production of the types of goods needed.

Capital must be attracted from member states of the CIS by means of joint State and commercial financing of investment projects, international financial leasing, and the creation of contract-based joint organizations such as consortia to engage in investment activities. It is also necessary to create the ideal conditions to attract private Russian investors to industrial establishments in member states of the Commonwealth of independent States in whose goods Russia has an interest. It would thus be advisable to develop a mechanism for investment cooperation and transition to joint financial support in conjunction countries.

It was to intensify the activities made to attract foreign investment in the Russian economy and ensure the conduct of consistent work and a coordinated State policy in

For additional analytical, business and investment opportunities information,
please contact Global Investment & Business Center, USA
at (202) 546-2103. Fax: (202) 546-3275. E-mail: rusric@erols.com
Global Business E-Books on Line: http://world.mirhouse.com

this area that the Government of the Russian Federation adopted, on September 29, 1997, Decree No. 1,108 "Concerning the Intensification of Work on Attracting Foreign Investment in the Economy of the Russian Federation".

Ensuring a favorable investment climate requires the extension of domestic conditions to foreign investors. Until recently, the establishment of join ventures was the main type of participation of foreign capital in the form of direct investment. Despite the considerable number of registered enterprises of this kind, the amount of foreign investment that has been attracted is rather low, making their role in the economy insignificant. It is necessary to improve the means for determining the share of Russian investors in the charter funds of joint ventures, and to develop a methodology for valuing buildings and installations - which are contributed as the Russian part of the charter fund of organizations with foreign investment.

Greater attempts should be made to attract foreign credits. Under those particular forms of credits - which have to be repaid - Russian companies getting the credits would not have to become dependent on their foreign counterparts.

The special-purpose bank deposits are one form of foreign credits. They provide credit for the development of Russian enterprises on condition that the amount of money that is being loaned be repaid through the supplying of goods (compensation agreements).

Transactions in which foreign companies supply machinery, equipment, technology and complete plants in exchange for counter supplies of raw materials and semi-finished goods manufactured using the supplied equipment should be encouraged.

Encouraging the return of Russian capital held in foreign banks and creating conditions that would avert the further flow of capital out of Russia are some important consideration that would, in the long term, increase the influx of investment into the Russian economy.

The concept of creating free economic zones should be used to attract foreign investors.

SUPPORT OF INVESTMENT ACTIVITY BY THE RUSSIAN GOVERNMENT

The gradual recovery of the Russian economy will facilitate the growth of accumulation in all spheres of the national economy. Furthermore, State regulations aimed at increasing the overall volume of investment provide for a certain increase in the share of centralized expenditures.

The State has undertaken the process of financing the development of a significant part of the production infrastructure. 10 percent of capital investment financed from federal budget resources are intended to be used for the construction of railways, ports, energy enterprises in Siberia and the Far East, and communications facilities.

During the period of transition to a market economy, the Government has used up to 70 percent of investment resources centralized in the federal budget to meet urgent requirements in the social sector - housing and municipal construction, health care, culture and science. The remaining 20 percent is used to stimulate private domestic and foreign investment in the production sector.

The transition from the distribution of budget appropriations for capital construction between sectors and regions to the selective partial financing of specific projects and the selection of these projects on a competitive basis is a new aspect of recent investment policy.

The transition from the automatic distribution of State capital investments to the provision of State support for private investments on a competitive basis is provided for in Presidential Decree No. 1928, "Concerning Private Investments in the Russian Federation", adopted on September 17, 1994 and in Governmental Decree No. 744, "Concerning the Procedure for Allocating Centralized Investment Resources on a Competitive Basis" adopted on June 22, 1994. In order to implement Presidential Decree No. 1928 adopted on September 17, 1994, the Ministries of the Economy, Finance, and Construction prepared and approved in December 1994 the "Method-ological Recommendations Concerning the Procedure for Organizing and Conducting Tenders for the Allocation of Centralized Investment Resources". An investment tenders commission has been established under the Ministry of the Economy. Similarly, a working group and expert council have been created to develop more effective investment projects.

The essence of this approach is to grant participants the opportunity to prove, on the basis of a business plan in which considerable space is dedicated to market research, that the product in question has a consumer with the ability to pay, and that investments will be recouped in no less than two years.

In the first six months of 1997 the Russian Federation's Ministry of the Economy received about 500 investment projects for participation in the tender - approximately 60 of them were accepted. All of these projects meet the tender's main requirement - the share of centralized investment resources in expenditures on implementing the project does not exceed 20 percent and the share of own and loaned resources (including foreign resources) of private investors comprises no less than 80 percent. In this respect, the investor's own resources (share capital, profit, amortization) is no less than 20 percent of these expenditures. Projects are appraised by two groups of specialists working independently of one another - thus allowing the best projects to be objectively selected.

The results of the first round of the tender have shown that restricted State support of effective commercial projects facilitates the attraction of private capital and will ensure production growth as soon as -1997 given a grace period of 1.5 to 1.6 years.

Two new mechanisms will be introduced in order to develop the ideas for State commercial financing of the projects on which the tender was founded: the certification of projects and the issue of State guarantees to investors.

The certification of a project confirms its quality and defines the extent of State support:

	(as a percentage of the cost of the project)
Manufacture of competitive goods (services)	50
Export of goods (services) of the processing industry	40
Import substitution (given a lower price)	30
Satisfaction of solvent demand	20

The certification of projects allows auctions to be held to attract investors. Contacts with foreign investors have shown that certification significantly increases their faith in projects. This allows capital to compete on the investment market and will enable interest rates for commercial credits to be reduced, eventually ensuring an increase in investment efficiency.

The second mechanism is to grant private domestic investors with State guarantees which include the State's obligation to return part of the invested resources in the event that a highly efficient investment program which has undergone certification is discontinued for reasons beyond the investor's control. In this respect, the investor

For additional analytical, business and investment opportunities information,
please contact Global Investment & Business Center, USA
at (202) 546-2103. Fax: (202) 546-3275. E-mail: rusric@erols.com
Global Business E-Books on Line: http://world.mirhouse.com

should grant counter guarantee obligations, including security obligations. An official procedure for granting State guarantees to investors is currently under preparation.

The main provision is for the State guarantee to cover less than 100 percent of the risk, without which banks would bear no liability for the return of the issued credit.

In order to ensure the accumulation and ongoing increase both of resources allocated from the federal budget and of contributions made by domestic and foreign commercial structures, a Fund for State Guarantees for High-Efficiency Investment Projects is currently being developed with the organization of a collateral system meeting international standard requirements.

The mechanisms under consideration allow State resources to be used with greater efficiency with respect to the attraction of private capital. For example, given a project risk rate of 50 percent, the amount of State resources required will be at least four times less (two times owing to the risk and two times owing to compensation for insurance payments based on the realization of security).

Presidential Decree No. 1929 "Concerning the Development of Financial Leasing in Investment Activity", adopted on September 17, 1994, was specifically designed to encourage private business.

The use of leasing by interested enterprises, particularly representatives of small business, allows them to employ new and advanced equipment and technology - including know-how - in production without resorting to credits. In this respect, the option to pay for the acquired equipment on an installment basis and the inclusion of all expenses associated with this in the cost of production of goods (services) allow the taxable base and tax payments to be reduced.

Leasing creates favorable opportunities for the expansion of the sales market, and for overcoming difficulties in marketing products for manufacturers of the main types of leased assets - i.e. mechanical engineering factories.

The Government of the Russian Federation's Decree No. 633 "Concerning the Development of Leasing in Investment Activity", adopted on June 29, 1997, defines the future developments that this type of activity will take. Appropriate programs are envisaged in line with that decree.

From 1997 to 1997, a consistent policy to stimulate the development of different forms of housing construction - including State, municipal and private -, and the creation of favorable conditions to attract non-budgetary sources of financing for these purposes - primarily public resources - is planned.

For additional analytical, business and investment opportunities information,
please contact Global Investment & Business Center, USA
at (202) 546-2103. Fax: (202) 546-3275. E-mail: rusric@erols.com
Global Business E-Books on Line: http://world.mirhouse.com

Incomplete residential buildings are envisaged to be included in the economic turnover. In accordance with Presidential Decree No. 1181 "Concerning Measures to Ensure the Completion of Construction of Incomplete Residential Buildings" adopted on June 10, 1994, partially completed residential buildings owned by the federal government will, in the event that the necessary financing is absent, be transferred to an investor that is financially solvent for the completion of their construction, or will be sold, exclusively on a tender basis, to be completed within the shortest possible amount of time.

The mechanism used to attract public's spare resources in order to finance housing construction is defined in Presidential Decree No. 1182 "Concerning the Issue and Circulation of Housing Certificates" adopted on June 10, 1994 and the Statute which was approved by that Decree. In 1994, the issuance of housing certificates, housing debentures and bills of exchange began in many Russian cities.

ADMINISTRATIVE AND LEGAL ENVIRONMENT FOR INVESTMENT

The creation and improvement of the legislative and normative base for investment activity in Russia, and the implementation of the necessary organizational measures are the two most important prerequisites for the implementation of the Comprehensive Program for the Stimulation of Domestic and Foreign Investments Some of the other ones include:

- stability of legislation concerning the financial, currency, tax, tariff and non-tariff regulations associated with investments;

- informing entrepreneurs well in advance of intended changes to legal norms;

- developing procedures and mechanisms to protect investors from the unlawful actions of administrative bodies.

The preparation of a draft federal law "Concerning the Introduction of Amendments and Additions to the Law of the RSFSR Concerning Investment Activity in the RSFSR" (Article 18 of the Plan of Action) is one of the main tasks waiting for lawmakers in .

The Land Code is one of the missing laws whose absence is restraining the growth rate of investments - since without the guaranteed right to use land, an influx of capital cannot be expected. A number of draft laws are currently being considered by the State Duma. One hopes that they will be adopted. By the end of 1997, draft laws aimed at protecting public investments and at preventing the illegal export of capital should be considered. The necessity to protect investments is a mandatory prerequisite for accumulating public savings, the volume of which is estimated at approximately $20 billion. Putting a stop to the flow of domestic capital abroad should be considered.

The legislative and normative acts which it is proposed to adopt in 1997 to 1997 are regarded as an instrument for the creation of a favorable investment climate in Russia in such areas as the proper use of amortization, tax incentives for the capitalization of profit, the development of a secondary securities market and the transfer of capital, insurance activity and guarantees, mortgages, preventing the flight and encouraging the return of domestic capital from abroad, attracting foreign investors. Organizational and legal support for the Comprehensive Program to encourage domestic and foreign investment will be provided within the framework of the existing system for adopting legislative and normative acts.

The placement of legislative restrictions on the export of capital and the ability to leave the price difference for goods and services exported at understated prices and imported at inflated prices in the foreign bank accounts of Russian legal entities and physical persons (Articles 2 and 19 of the Plan of Action) is essential. Appropriate drafts must be prepared by the Central Bank of the Russian Federation. In order for the adopted measures to be effective, the introduction of additional articles to the Criminal Code of the Russian Federation envisaging, in addition to fines, criminal liability for officers and private individuals who violate the law is almost imperative.

In connection with the granting of tax exemptions to investors, it is envisaged that additions and amendments will be introduced to tax legislation and normative documents regulating the relations of taxpayers and tax authorities and that a procedure will be established, for the consideration of appeals to protect taxpayers. Since current regulatory practice leads to disputes over the justification and the subject of sanctions imposed by tax authorities, a tax code regulating legal relations with tax audits is under consideration..

The concept of a nominal holder of securities is to be introduced in existing legislation in order to improve the situation regarding the registration of shareholders. A program of guarantee signatures making brokers accountable for checking their clients' identity, will be introduced, and standards for maintaining registers of shareholders will be approved.

"Concerning the Introduction of Amendments and Additions to the Law of the RSFSR Concerning Foreign Investment in the RSFSR", "Concerning Free Economic Zones", "Concerning Concession Agreements Being Concluded with Russian and Foreign Investors Concerning the Production of Sharing Agreements" are the main draft federal laws that have been developed in the sphere of international investment cooperation.

The following were envisaged in the development of these draft laws:

- the need to encourage the investment process as the main factor in the stable development of the economy;
- the promotion of the Russian economy's incorporation into the world economic system through production and investment cooperation;

- the granting of concessions to domestic and foreign investors on the basis of the results of tenders and auctions;
- ensuring national security when allowing foreign capital into the Russian economy.

The law "Concerning Production Sharing Agreements" was adopted by the State Duma and sent to the Federation Council of the Federal Assembly for consideration. The other legislation are still being considered by the State Duma.

Urgent issues concerning the creation of conditions to encourage domestic and foreign investment in 1997-1997 have been resolved in President of the Russian Federation's Decrees which are currently under preparation.

A draft President of the Russian Federation's Decree, "Concerning the Use of Amortization For Investment Provision for the Restructuring of the Economy" is in the process of being completed.

The insurance protection of domestic and foreign investors' interests in the Russian Federation is an issue that remains pertinent. The following principles for investment insurance still have to be determined to insure a good functioning of this institution:

1) a list of insured accidents where special purpose resources cannot be recouped according to the reasons due to impossibilities, upon the occurrence of which the insurer will be obliged to compensate the investor for damage to its interests;

2) the amount of insurance contributions, the procedure for concluding insurance agreements;

3) the rights and obligations of parties during the period of validity of the agreement and in the event an insured accident occurs.

The State's participation in the activity of insurance institutions must also be envisaged.

One of the most efficient investment institutions to turn citizens' savings into investments is stock investment funds which are formed in accordance with Presidential Decree No. 765 "Concerning Additional Measures to Increase the Efficiency of Investment Policy in the Russian Federation", adopted on July 26, 1997. The implementation of this Decree will allow the flow of investment into the Russian economy to be increased - primarily by mobilizing citizens' savings.

Decrees of the Government of the Russian Federation defining measures relating to the conduct of an investment policy (items 20 and 28 of the Plan of Action) are being prepared specifically to implement the Law "Concerning Mortgages" insofar as it concerns the regulation of procedures for the assessment of the real value of property

- 237 -

and its transfer to new owners, including foreign investors, in the event that borrowers do not fulfill their obligations.

In , proposals improving the securities market and the registration and depository activities (item 23 of the Plan of Action) have to be submitted in order for a Decree of the Government of the Russian Federation to be considered. Currently, both the Federal Commission for Securities and the Stock Market are affiliated with the Government of the Russian Federation. These entities, in conjunction with several Russian banks and brokerage firms, will be one of the factors in attracting foreign investors on the Russian market. The approval of standards for depository activity on the securities market is currently under consideration.

The Government of the Russian Federation's Decree No. 507, "Concerning the Attraction of Non-Budgetary Investments", adopted on May 23, 1994, approves the proposal of the Ministries of the Economy and Finance for the creation of an investment and financial consortium whose participants (commercial and investment banks) would be permitted to issue State guaranteed securities to finance investment projects. A draft decree examining the conditions under which the granting of State guarantees for the issue of securities to private investors has been prepared. This, in return, will further the growth of public trust in these securities.

Priority areas in which investment is to be encouraged must be identified in order to use foreign capital more actively. A Government of the Russian Federation's decree is envisaged for the approval of a specific list of priority sectors and industries. Depending on the specific nature of the sector and the types of activity - and their export potential -, incentives and measures to attract capital may be differentiated.

In accordance with worldwide practices, certain restrictions will be placed on foreign investment in the Russian Federation - as a country accepting foreign capital (item 11 of the Plan of Action). A list of sectors and regions which will be closed to foreign investment and/or in which investment activity will be restricted must be developed and approved at the legislative level. The need to create a legal base for the investment process increases the relevance of consolidating laws with supporting acts.

The necessity of preparing and approving six organizational and methodological documents by the end of 1997 is considered a must. The creation of a procedure for the filing of taxpayers' appeals and the prompt resolution of disputes - on which foreign investors particularly insist - until the tax code has been passed (item 6 of the Plan of Action) is particularly important. Two of the documents concern the valuation of land plots and the reflection of their value in the assets of commercial organizations (items 4 and 5 of the Plan of Action). Three documents relate to issues concerning the implementation of foreign investment.

For additional analytical, business and investment opportunities information, please contact Global Investment & Business Center, USA at (202) 546-2103. Fax: (202) 546-3275. E-mail: rusric@erols.com Global Business E-Books on Line: http://world.mirhouse.com

The regulation of investment activity on the basis of departmental decisions by controlling customs treatment is also intended. Provision will be made to further differentiate the import tariff, in particular the rates of duties applied on machinery and equipment. Lawmakers are intending to ease the import tariff on machinery which is not manufactured in Russia or is manufactured in clearly insufficient quantities. At the same time, the sectors of domestic mechanical engineering which are capable of renewing the manufacturing potential of the Russian industry will be subject to a moderate protectionist policy.

Federal departments - which have the appropriate authority - will define the procedure concerning the creation of agreements with private domestic and foreign investors regarding State support for specific investment projects. The implementation of particular projects will further increase the need to improve methods regulating business disputes and to create a range of various arbitration procedures. Arbitration procedures must be applied differently depending on the nature of the dispute.

As far as the Russian Federation is concerned, the present similarities between the Russian legal basis for investment activity and the one being used in foreign countries is a significant matter.

Considering the real process that have been made regarding the reintegration with member states of the Commonwealth of independent States (CIS) and Russia's economic and investment interests in those countries, the mutual adaptation and unification of normative and legislative acts and organizational and economic conditions regarding investment activity is taking on a decisive significance.

By being included in the international system of legal provision regarding investment activity, Russia - in addition to the adoption of several legislation - is playing an important role in the regulation of foreign investments. Russia has concluded 30 intergovernmental agreements concerning the mutual protection and encouragement of capital investments, and has become a party in two international conventions - the Washington Convention on the Procedure for Resolving Investment Disputes Between State and Foreign Entities (1965) and the Seoul Convention on the Establishment of a Multi-Lateral Investment Guarantee Agency (1985). In addition, Russia has become a member of both the International Monetary Fund and the World Bank and has signed the Agreement to the European Energy Charter. Membership of the World Trade Organization's General Agreement on Tariffs and Trade, as well as agreements with the European Community and the Organization for Economic Co-operation and Development will also enable the assimilation of Russian legal norms with those of international.

Russia has an obligation to start fulfilling the conditions stipulated in international agreements - which have been concluded or are in the process of being concluded - regarding the attraction of foreign capital into Russia: 1) the Agreement to the European

Energy Charter; 2) the WTO's General Agreement on Tariffs and Trade, documents associated with these relating to the trading aspects of investment programs; 3) agreements with the European Community on Partnership and Co-operation; 4) agreements concerning the encouragement and the mutual protection of capital investments; and, 5) agreements on the avoidance of double taxation.

FINANCIAL PRIVILEGES FOR INVESTORS

In addition to the creation of organizational and legal conditions and State support, the Comprehensive Program for Stimulating Domestic and Foreign Investment includes measures to reduce investors' costs which are not classified as direct expenditures on the implementation of specific projects. Because of this, the informational infrastructure of the investment market is being developed, tariffs for monopoly services are being regulated, and the protection of investors' property and identity is being ensured.

Investors' interests should be taken into account when preparing legislative and normative acts and departmental instructions relating to the pricing of electricity, communications and rail transport. As far as small investors are concerned, limits on payments for the lease of production premises are of prime importance.

To protect the property of investors, a unified procedure should be developed to determine the amount of damage caused by embezzlement, misappropriation and unfair competition. Improving the work that is being done by the International Commercial Arbitration Court and the Appeal Tribunal - affiliated to the Chamber of Commerce and Industry of the Russian Federation - is primordial.

In order to ensure the personal and material security of investors, special State programs concerned with the prevention of crime in vulnerable spheres of the economy and in regions of Russia with high criminal activities must be developed and implemented rapidly.

It is necessary to increase material, technical, informational and organizational support for the appropriate operational services, investigative bodies and courts.

The State ought to provide assistance to existing and newly established consulting organizations, business plan development firms and planning institutes as far as informational provision for investment activity is concerned. The collection - processing and updating of information concerning legislation -; the state of the market; the prospects for the development of the economy and individual sectors concerning

1) the plans of enterprises which are interested in attracting investments, and
2) the progress of privatization; the sale of shares; and, the production conversion are some of the

specific objectives concerned with the informational provision for investment activity. For the purpose of ensuring efficient information and consulting cooperation between potential foreign investors and Russian organizations - as well as the creation of an attractive image of Russia on world capital markets -, the Government of the Russian Federation's Decree No. 657 "Concerning the Russian Center for the Promotion of Foreign Investment Attached to the Russian Federation's Ministry of the Economy" was adopted on June 30, 1997.

A new structure - the Foreign Investment Advisory Council, comprising representatives of foreign firms engaged in large scale direct investments into the Russian economy - was created at the initiative of the Government of the Russian Federation. Its main task is to ensure a constant dialogue between the Government of the Russian Federation and major foreign investors for the purpose of developing specific recommendations relating to the improvement of the investment climate, the tax and customs legislation, and the creation of an attractive image of Russia as a host country for investment.

In order to develop the Russian economy and to advance direct foreign investments, Russia's cooperation with leading international financial organizations - primarily the international Monetary Fund, the World Bank for Reconstruction and Development, and the European Bank for Reconstruction and Development - is of primary importance.

It is necessary to organize the monitoring of the Comprehensive Program for Stimulating Domestic and Foreign Investment and the strategic modification of the measures contained therein.

The measures suggested in the draft Comprehensive Program will ensure the improvement of the investment climate in the Russian Federation and facilitate the flow of domestic and foreign investments into the Russian economy.

The effectiveness of the Comprehensive Program for Stimulating Domestic and Foreign Investment in the Economy of the Russian Federation will be ensured by the implementation of the attached Plan of Action.

PRACTICAL INFORMATION FOR CONDUCTING BUSINESS IN RUSSIA[9]

INVESTMENT AND BUSINESS CLIMATE

Russia saw a sharp increase in total investment between and 1997, rising from $ 6.5 to 10.7 billion. Direct foreign investment, as measured by the Ministry of Economy through surveys, rose from $ 2.1 to 3.9 billion. Other Russian data showed foreign direct investment in 1997 at a much higher level of between $ 6.2 and $ 6.8 billion; these data are believed to be higher because they include items such as investment in bank equity and foreign direct investment that is less than 10 percent of a company's capital. A large part of portfolio and other foreign investment, according to Russian analysts, went into government securities. This category also contains long-term, as well as short-term loans. Statistics on foreign investment can be found in Appendix D.

The Russian economy was not immune to the financial pressures which began in Asia in 1997 and continued into 1998. As of this writing, the Russian Government has pledged dramatic steps to stabilize the economy and defend the value of the ruble. The outcome of these developments will have a major impact on short-term investment in Russia, although reform trends are expected to continue in the long term.

OPENNESS TO FOREIGN INVESTMENT

While the encouragement of foreign investment is a stated Russian Government priority, there have been difficulties in creating a stable, attractive investment climate. Annual foreign investment in Russia reached $ 10.7 billion in 1997 (approximately 60 percent higher than in), of which direct foreign investment equaled $ 3.9 billion, according to the Ministry of Economy. Although the more inclusive Russian balance of payments data show foreign direct investment in 1997 to be much higher (between $ 6.2 and $ 6.8 billion), this is still considered a fairly low level given Russia's size. Foreign investors concerns about the legal system, corruption and taxation are key factors affecting foreign investment, rather than explicit Russian Government restrictions.

The 1991 investment code guarantees foreign investors rights equal to those enjoyed by Russian investors. A set of draft amendments to the foreign investment law which sets out the principle of national treatment but includes some problematic provisions, passed a third Duma reading in July 1998.

---

[9] This section basd in part on the materials of the US Department of Commerce

For additional analytical, business and investment opportunities information,
please contact Global Investment & Business Center, USA
at (202) 546-2103. Fax: (202) 546-3275. E-mail: rusric@erols.com
Global Business E-Books on Line: http://world.mirhouse.com

Russia completed the liberalization of the market for foreign investment in government securities in 1997. Non-resident investors are estimated to hold about 30 percent of the government securities market.

At this time, there are relatively few explicit restrictions on foreign direct investment. However, domestic pressures for such restrictions appear to be growing. For example, a new 1998 law on the aerospace industry limits foreign ownership to 25 percent of an enterprise. Foreign ownership in the natural gas monopoly Gazprom is limited to nine percent. Foreign investors are limited to holdings of 49 percent in insurance companies. A new law limits foreign investment in electric power giant Unified Energy Systems (UES) to 25 percent; however, because foreign holdings of UES stock already exceed this level, the Russian Government is challenging the constitutionality of the restriction and plans to draft an amendment to remove it from the law. The Duma also has been discussing a law which would explicitly restrict or prohibit investment in a number of sectors (it would follow passage of the revisions to the foreign investment law).

The Central Bank of Russia (CBR) has the right to use reciprocity as a criterion in specifying the scope of activity by foreign banks which receive licenses to operate in Russia, and is permitted to impose a ceiling on the total amount of foreign bank capital as a percentage of the total bank capital in Russia. At present, foreign banks share of the total capital is around 4.6 percent, well below the current 12 percent ceiling. In May 1997 the CBR announced new regulations requiring foreign banks to have a minimum of ecu 10 million (about $ 11.5 million) in capital and to have at least 75 percent of its employees and 50 percent of its management board to be of Russian nationality.

Current Russian foreign investment regulations and notification requirements can be confusing and contradictory. The Ministry of Finance, local authorities and/or various central government bodies all register foreign investments, depending on the particular industry concerned. Prior approval is required for investment in new enterprises using assets of existing Russian enterprises, foreign investment in defense industries (which may be prohibited in some cases), investment in the exploitation of natural resources, all investments over 50 million rubles, investment ventures in which the foreign share exceeds 50 percent, or investment to take over incomplete housing and construction projects. Additional registration requirements exist for investments exceeding 100 million rubles. Projects involving large scale construction or modernization may also be subject to expert examination for environmental considerations.

In sectors which require licensing (e.g. banking, mining and telecommunications), procedures can be lengthy and opaque. Athough the situation has improved over the past few years, foreigners encounter significant restrictions on ownership of real estate in some cities and regions in Russia.

Rules on foreign participation in privatization vary by sector and region. For example, foreign participation is sharply limited in some "strategic" sectors. In the 1997 loans-for-shares privatization program, foreign investors were banned from the oil, gas, and precious metals sectors. However, the restrictions on foreign participation in oil company privatization was lifted in 1997. Foreigners participated in the first stage of privatization of the Svyazinvest telecomm company in 1997, and in mid-1998 the government was working to eliminate restrictions on the participation of foreign investors in auction of additional government shares in the company. Foreign bidders are advised to establish contacts and work closely with local, regional and federal officials, as well as private entities that exercise ownership and other authority over firms whose shares they may want to acquire.

High and changing rates of taxation, crime and corruption problems, a fairly weak banking sector, the still developing legal system, and confusing procedures are particular problems for foreign (and Russian) business, and act as disincentives for foreign investment. Bureaucratic requirements can be confusing and burdensome to investors and bureaucratic discretion may be capricious in awarding tenders or development rights to companies. The right of ownership of real property is still being legislated, and violations of intellectual property are serious and pervasive. Delapidated infrastructure - particularly outside of the big cities - adds to the difficulty of doing business.

OIL INDUSTRY INVESTMENT

Changes in the ownership structure of the Russian oil industry have resulted in new, more market-oriented partners for U.S. firms pursuing a potential total of more than $70 billion in energy investment. While the Sakhalin-1 and -2 consortia projects, which were "grandfathered" under the 1997 PSA law are moving ahead with initial development phases on the basis of customs and tax exemptions decreed by Deputy Prime Minister Nemtsov in mid-1997, the sector remains characterized by a lack of transparency and Russian oil and gas firms' extensive political influence over the government and other economic actors. U.S. and European companies have said they will not invest without PSA or an analogous structure which would provide for a stable and transparent taxation and investment regime in Russia. Recent outspoken support for PSA by Western-partnered Russian oil companies and the government itself is a positive development with potentially decisive significance, but Russian legislators will also need to be persuaded of the importance of a workable PSA framework.

Despite the passage of a law on production sharing agreements (PSAs) in 1997, the potentially promising Russian oil and gas sector remains without a stable taxation and investment regime. The Russian Government has failed to deliver on promises to roll back excise taxes for several U.S.-partnered joint ventures, citing budgetary impact. Although Russia did prolong full access to export pipelines for these ventures effective August 1, 1998, depressed world oil prices render export access a less effective means for the companies to recoup their original investment, which have been adversely affected by the imposition by federal and sub-federal governments of more than forty new taxes since 1991. The experiences of these ventures exemplify the unstable tax environment which most Western firms insist prevents them from committing to potentially much larger investments.

Enabling legislation, intended to resolve conflicts between the PSA law and other Russian legislation, as well as a bill to amend what investors see as flaws in the PSA law, were stalled for some time; but in July 1998, the amendments to the PSA law were passed by the Duma, with enabling legislation (as well as the second and third deposit lists) on the docket for later consideration. The reorganization of the Russian Government□s PSA bureaucracy into the Ministry of Natural Resources may augur better for the future of a PSA regime, given that rivalry between the licensing agency (the Ministry of Natural Resources) and the technical agency (the Ministry of Fuels and Energy) stymied progress in the past. The recapture of line responsibility for energy issues by Deputy Prime Minister Nemtsov, a committed reformer and chairman of the government's PSA commission, may also advance PSA laws. However, the recent reassignment of PSA legislation away from the Duma□s PSA-friendly Natural Resources Committee to the Industry and Transportation Committee may complicate PSA-related legislative action after summer 1998.

Following a struggle with Russian partner Lukoil over management of the Caspian Pipeline Consortium (CPC) in late 1997, Western partners have resumed full funding of the CPC pipeline project. CPC is a $ 2 billion undertaking which will bring oil from Tengiz in Kazakhstan to an offshore terminal at Novorossiysk, Russia. Western shareholders, who assumed responsibility for financing the project in exchange for 50 percent equity, are pushing to have the first tanker loaded with crude as early as April 2001.

AGRICULTURE

Although Russian agriculture is grossly undercapitalized and in need of investment, foreign investors remain reluctant to enter into the Russian agriculture market for a variety of reasons. Most Russian agricultural sector operators seek minority partners, and few operations are available to be wholly owned by a foreign investor because of Russian concerns with food security and fear of a loss of control over domestic production. Regional administrations have added increased uncertainty to the investment climate by implementing embargoes on the movement of agricultural products out of the region after harvest, in order to ensure repayment of debts. Collective farms and state enterprises have undergone largely cosmetic reform and are now often referred to as joint stock companies. Many still operate much the same as they did during Soviet times and continue to carry social welfare responsibilities such as providing schools, medical facilities and full employment to local villages. The reduction or elimination of state subsidies has left many agricultural enterprises undercapitalized, and production is often a fraction of previous capacity. In the absence of land reform, it is difficult to obtain clear title to land and impossible to use land as collateral for loans.

REGIONAL INVESTMENT INITIATIVE

At the Gore-Chernomyrdin Commission□s February 1997 meeting, the Vice President and then-Prime Minister announced an effort to spur a climate for private investment in Russia's regions and attract foreign and domestic capital. The resulting Regional Investment Initiative is intended as a collaborative effort between the U.S. and Russian governments, regional authorities, and private sectors of both countries.

In selected regions, U.S. Government agencies work with Russian local and federal authorities to develop a set of priorities to attract investment. These priorities then serve as the framework for packages of technical cooperation, financing, and partnership activities, aimed at improving the prospects for investment and growth in these regions. Activities fall under one of three broad categories: a) joint work with the regional authorities to address key obstacles to investment; b) mobilization of finance for private sector trade and investment, particularly for small and medium-sized business; and c) promoting partnerships between U.S. and Russian regionally-based investment promotion agencies, state/oblast officials, business groups, universities and other non-governmental organizations. The initiative is now being implemented in Novgorod, the Russian Far East (with a focus on Khabarovsk and Sakhalin) and the Volga city of Samara.

CONVERSION AND TRANSFER POLICIES

The U.S. dollar is traded freely on the Moscow Interbank Currency Exchange (MICEX) and in the off-exchange inter-bank market. The official central buy and sell rates are announced by the Central Bank of Russia no later than 10 a.m. each trading day. The mid-range between the buy and sell rates serves as the "official" rate, e.g. for contract and valuation purposes, the next day. The CBR will intervene to limit fluctuations of the currency exchange rate at MICEX and in the interbank market.

On January 1, 1998, the CBR redenominated the ruble, dropping three zeroes off the previous values, i.e., 1000 old rubles equal 1 ruble at the redenominated rate. Old and new notes are circulating simultaneously in 1998, with the old notes gradually removed from the system as they come to the Central Bank in the normal course of business. The CBR established an average target ruble exchange rate for 1998-2000 of 6.2 rubles/dollar (replacing the crawling bank exchange mechanism used in recent years). The implicit target for 1998 is 6.0-6.2 and 6.3 for 1999-2000, with flexibility to float 15 percent in either direction. However, as of this writing, observers of Russia□s economy differ over whether a devaluation is likely.

The ruble is a freely convertible currency for current international transactions. These transactions include trade in goods and services, profit repatriation and normal short-term banking and credit facilities. At the end of 1997, the CBR ended the remaining restrictions on repatriation of earnings from non-resident investment in short-term government securities (referred to as ⬚GKOs⬚). The Russian government maintains some capital controls on long-term lending and borrowing (more than 180 days).

The ruble is the only legal tender in Russia. Non-residents can open ruble accounts at authorized resident banks. "T-accounts" are for servicing import and export operations, and "I-accounts" are used for investment activities (e.g. profits and dividend transfer and privatization activities). Non-resident banks may open correspondent ruble accounts to service trade operations, and non-resident natural persons may also open ruble accounts.

Residents may open foreign exchange accounts. Balances in these accounts may be used for all current accounts transactions (imports/exports) and for capital transaction excepts those specified by the CBR as requiring a license. For example, foreign exchange credits of more than 180 days to Russian legal entities requires CBR approval. Some investors report long delays in obtaining necessary licenses from the CBR (e.g. to import foreign exchange needed for direct investments or to loan the ruble counterpart of these funds to the target firm) for direct investment projects. The CBR has indicated its intention to streamline the licensing process.

EXPROPRIATION AND COMPENSATION

The 1991 investment code prohibits the nationalization of foreign investments except following legislative action and where deemed to be in the national interest. Such action may be appealed to Russian courts, and are to be paid with prompt, adequate and effective compensation. The current Russian leadership is unlikely to actively nationalize or expropriate foreign investment. However, in several cases, local government interference or failure to uphold court rulings in favor of Western investors appears tantamount to expropriation. The U.S. Embassy is tracking a small number of cases in which foreign companies are seeking compensation for loss of an investment or property. Legal proceedings are pending in some of these cases. To date, there has not been a confirmed payment in these cases.

DISPUTE SETTLEMENT

Russia has a body of conflicting, overlapping and rapidly changing laws, decrees and regulations which has resulted in an ad hoc and unpredictable approach to doing business. Independent dispute resolution in Russia can be difficult to obtain; the judicial system is still developing. Regional and local courts are often subject to political pressure.

Most Western attorneys still refer their Western clients who have business disputes in Russia to arbitration in Stockholm, Geneva or other courts abroad. A 1997 law now allows foreign arbitration awards to be enforced in Russia even if there is no reciprocal treaty between Russia and the country where the order was made; however, enforcement of such foreign awards is not mandatory. Given the possibility that court officials and law enforcement agencies may be more attentive to decisions issued by Russian (as opposed to foreign) courts, companies facing disputes may find it worthwhile to consider the alternatives available in Russia. One choice is the Arbitration Court of the Russian Federation, which is part of the court system. It has special rules for disposition of property before trial, so that assets cannot be concealed before the court has heard a claim (a common problem), as well as for the enforcement of monetary awards through banks. Additionally, the International Commercial Arbitration Court at the Russian Chamber of Commerce and Industry will hear claims if both parties consent. Applications can be made by parties to foreign trade agreements and by companies with foreign investments. A similar arbitral court was recently set up in St. Petersburg.

Despite these new developments and avenues, enforcement of foreign as well as domestic arbitral decisions still requires action from Russian courts and follow-up by a nascent marshal corps that has yet to prove its effectiveness -- a major weakness in the system. The U.S. Embassy is aware of several cases in which, following lengthy litigation in international and/or Russian courts, and despite favorable decisions and court orders for financial restitution, foreign investors continue to await compensation from former partners or customers who have failed to make contractually-agreed payments. In any event, U.S. companies are strongly advised to examine dispute resolution options before signing sales contracts or investment agreements in Russia. U.S. companies should not plan on litigating commercial disputes with Russian entities in U.S. courts (whose decisions have no legal standing in Russia), unless the Russian entity itself -- not merely its subsidiaries or affiliates -- is known to maintain assets in the U.S. against which judgements may be executed.

PERFORMANCE REQUIREMENTS AND INCENTIVES

Provision of investment incentives has been problematic in Russia, as the Government's interest in attracting investment has been tempered by its precarious financial situation, concern about special privileges given to foreign investors, and interest in complying with the rules of the World Trade Organization (which Russia is seeking to join) and other international economic institutions. Investment incentives set out in the 1991 investment law, including certain tax benefits, have never been implemented, or have been largely eliminated or superseded by subsequent laws and decrees.

In January 1998, the Russian Government adopted a decree allowing tariff breaks for large investments in the auto industry (where investments exceed $ 250 million and the projects reach 50 percent domestic content levels within five years). These incentives need to be approved by the Russian Federal Assembly. There are also proposals (including draft amendments to the 1991 Foreign Investment Law which were approved by the Duma in July 1998) to provide short-term tax breaks for foreign investments exceeding $ 100 million. However, in the face of severe fiscal shortfalls, Russia's government is under strong pressure to curtail existing tax incentives and to avoid offering new ones.

Performance requirements are not generally imposed by Russian law, and are not widely included as part of private contracts. They have appeared in the agreements of large multinational companies investing in natural resources, and in amendments to production sharing agreement legislation. One Russian Government decree, Number 716 (promulgated on July 17, 1998) requires Russian airlines to purchase domestically produced aircraft in order to receive waivers of customs duties for certain imported aircraft, a development with potentially-significant impact on the export (via sale or lease) of American aircraft to the Russian market, where aircraft duties are a prohibitive 30 percent.

RIGHT TO PRIVATE OWNERSHIP AND ESTABLISHMENT

Both foreign and domestic legal entities may establish, purchase and dispose of businesses in Russia. Investment in sectors affecting national security (e.g., defense enterprises insurance, banking and natural resources) may be limited.

PROTECTION OF PROPERTY RIGHTS

The constitution and a presidential decree issued in 1993 give Russian citizens general rights to own, inherit, lease, mortgage, and sell real property (usually not including the land on which it stands); however, legislative gaps and ambiguities impede the general exercise of these rights. Russia does not yet have a land code to regulate land use and ownership.

Thus far, Russian law and practice appear to restrict or prohibit foreigners from owning real estate. The presidential decree of 1993 gave joint ventures with foreign participants the right to own real property, and a privatization decree issued in 1994 permitted foreign owners of privatized companies to receive title to enterprise land; however, such rights have not been codified and legislation regulating land use currently being considered by the Federal Aassembly could prohibit foreigners from owning land outright.

Although a presidential decree permits the ownership and sale of land, including agricultural land, the Duma maintains that the decree is unconstitutional. Uncertainty about more general rights to land title and mineral rights will persist until the Duma and president agree on clear and comprehensive legislation to regulate land use and ownership. Meanwhile, some regional legislatures are attempting to fill in the gap. In 1997 and 1998, Saratov and Samara oblasts approved laws allowing the free trade of land in their regions.

For additional analytical, business and investment opportunities information, please contact Global Investment & Business Center, USA at (202) 546-2103. Fax: (202) 546-3275. E-mail: rusric@erols.com Global Business E-Books on Line: http://world.mirhouse.com

INTELLECTUAL PROPERTY

Since 1991, Russia has enacted several laws strengthening the protection of patents, trademarks and appellations of origin, and copyright of semiconductors, computer programs, literary, artistic and scientific works, and audio/visual recordings.

The patent law, which accords with the norms of the World Intellectual Property Organization, includes a grace period, procedures for deferred examination, protection for chemical and pharmaceutical products, and national treatment for foreign patent holders. Inventions are protected for 20 years, industrial designs for 10 years, and utility models for five years. The law on trademarks and appellation of origins introduces for the first time in Russia protection of appellations of origin and provides for automatic recognition of Soviet trademarks upon presentation of the Soviet certificate of registration.

The law on copyright and neighboring rights, enacted in August 1993, protects all forms of artistic creation, including audio/visual recordings and computer programs as literary works for the lifetime of the author plus 50 years, and is compatible with the Bern convention. The September 1992 law on topography of integrated microcircuits, which also protects computer programs, protects semiconductor topographies for 10 years from the date of registration.

Russia has acceded to the Universal Copyright Convention, the Paris Convention, the Bern Convention, the Patent Cooperation Treaty, the Geneva Phonogram Convention, and the Madrid Agreement. Under the U.S.-Russian Treaty on Mutual Protection of Investment (not yet ratified by Russia), Russia has undertaken to protect investors' intellectual property rights. The U.S.-Russia Agreement on Trade Relations mandates protection of the normal range of literary, scientific and artistic works through legislation and enforcement.

While the Russian government has passed respectable laws to protect intellectual property, enforcement of those laws has been a low priority. A new criminal code went into effect in January 1997, which for the first time applies criminal penalties to IPR violations. However, there are shortcomings in this law that need attention. In 1997, Russia was elevated to the Priority Watch List under Special-301 provisions of the U.S. Trade Act, a status which it retained in 1998, primarily for failing to adequately protect pre-existing U.S. copyrighted works and sound recordings still under protection in the U.S. Marketing of pirated videocassettes, recordings, books, computer software, clothes and toys is pervasive, and is likely to remain so until tougher action is taken to enforce the laws. Annual losses to foreign and Russian manufacturers, authors, inventors and others are estimated to be in the hundreds of millions of dollars.

TRANSPARENCY OF THE REGULATORY SYSTEM

The legal system in Russia is in flux, with various parts of government struggling to create new laws on a broad array of topics. In this climate, negotiations and contracts for commercial transactions are complex and protracted. Russia has implemented only part of its new commercial code, and investors must carefully research all aspects of Russian law to ensure that each contract conforms with Russian law and embodies the basic provisions of the new, and where still valid, old codes. Contracts must likewise seek to protect the foreign partner against contingencies which often arise.

Keeping up with changing laws, decrees and government resolutions is a challenging task. Uneven implementation of laws creates further complications; various officials, levels and branches of government interpret and apply regulations with little consistency; and as is true with respect to arbitral cases, prompt enforcement of court decisions is a more general problem as well. Finally, as described in Chapter IV, the tax system, beyond causing headaches for exporters, poses vastly more aggravation for investors.

Legal requirements may be less burdensome than reaching final agreement with local political authorities. Registration can be a lengthy, bureaucratic process, particularly where natural resources or defense production are involved. Corruption is widespread and the fears of some Russian officials that foreigners will acquire Russian assets too cheaply can impede bureaucratic approval. Environmental impacts are cited more often now by Russian officials at federal and local levels as considerations in the approval process for investments.

CAPITAL MARKETS AND PORTFOLIO INVESTMENT

Russia has moved a long way very quickly to establish an operational capital market, although in 1998 the financial crisis in Asia spread to Russia and put the capital markets under great stress. Market capitalization of Russia□ securities market at the end of 1997 was estimated at $67 billion (making it one of the hottest emerging securities markets in the world that year), with roughly 50 stocks traded regularly. However, by mid-1998, that value had fallen to $45 billion (nearly fifty percent below its September 1997 peak).

The Federal Commission for Securities Markets (FCSM), created in 1994, has become fully operational as a market supervisor and has worked with the Central Bank to delineate supervisory authority. The FCSM has also begun to perform checks on registrars and participants and to institute examinations for professional qualifications. Russia's securities markets are still evolving. The FCSMs re-licensing provisions, minimum capital requirements and the need for greater efficiency reduced the number of licensed registrars and professional market participants. The Moscow stock exchange was created, corporate share trading took hold on the Moscow Interbank Currency Exchange (MICEX) and new debt and collective investment instruments were launched, broadening the range of potentially viable trading and investment mechanisms.

Economic growth, transition to business transactions based upon money rather than monetary surrogates or barter, building value in enterprises, improved respect for shareholders rights and disclosure are important requirements for future robust investor interest in Russia's securities market.

CRIME AND CORRUPTION

The rise of organized crime (and crime in general) has received wide media attention since the breakup of the Soviet Union. Corruption, a sometimes-related but also separate problem, has also become a factor against which businesses need to be on-guard. While organized crime is not new to Russia, recent years have seen an increase in the range and frequency of criminal activity. Unfortunately, legal and judicial reforms have not kept pace with criminal advances. Many Russian entrepreneurs in a survey reporting that they must pay kickbacks and protection to stay in business.

U.S. firms have also identified both crime and corruption as obstacles. Some anecdotal evidence suggests that these problems may be growing in terms of both the number of instances and in the size of bribes sought. Russia has laws and regulations against bribery and other forms of corruption, but penalties are often insufficient deterrents. In general, companies having the most success in avoiding or countering crime have planned well, verified the bona fides of potential partners, and have thoroughly researched appropriate local laws -- good business practice in any case. Keep in mind that American business people can be held liable for the actions of their Russian partners. U.S. firms planning to open offices in Russia should consider the full spectrum of security issues before establishing operations. This includes the possible hiring of guard services, installation of technical security systems, systematic evaluation of the reliability of Russian partners and associates, and frank discussion with employees on the need to provide full information on any criminal extortion attempts. U.S. companies should prepare contingency plans to counter compromise of commercial information and human resources, and conduct frank and open discussions with local employees about company policy on such matters.

BILATERAL INVESTMENT AGREEMENTS

Russia inherited from the Soviet Union 14 bilateral investment treaties (BITs) with Austria, Belgium and Luxembourg, Great Britain, Germany, Italy, Spain, Canada, the People's Republic of China, Korea, the Netherlands, Finland, France and Switzerland. They were ratified in 1989-90 and came into force in 1991. Russia has since negotiated another 32 such accords, of which 16 have been ratified - with Greece, Cuba, Romania, Denmark, Slovakia, the Czech Republic, Vietnam, Kuwait, India, Hungary, Albania, Norway, Yugoslavia, Italy and Lebanon. The U.S.-Russia BIT (officially called the

For additional analytical, business and investment opportunities information,
please contact Global Investment & Business Center, USA
at (202) 546-2103. Fax: (202) 546-3275. E-mail: rusric@erols.com
Global Business E-Books on Line: http://world.mirhouse.com

Treaty on Mutual Protection of Investment), signed in 1992, has never been ratified by Russia and has not entered into force.

OPIC AND OTHER INVESTMENT INSURANCE PROGRAMS

In June 1992, the U.S. Overseas Private Investment Corporation (OPIC) was authorized to provide loans, loan guarantees and investment insurance against political risks to U.S. companies investing in Russia. OPIC generally insures against three political risks: expropriation, political violence and currency inconvertibility. In 1994, to meet the demands of larger projects in Russia (and worldwide), OPIC raised the amount of insurance and the amount of support -- to $ 200 million in each case -- which it can commit to an individual project (a total of $ 400 million). OPIC also makes equity capital available for investments in Russia by guaranteeing long-term loans to private equity investment funds. There are currently six OPIC-backed investment funds which concentrate on Russia, the other NIS and the Baltics, and another four funds which are global in scope. Through the end of FY 1997, OPIC had committed $ 3.26 billion in insurance, finance and opic-backed investment funds to over 125 projects in Russia. In December 1994, OPIC also committed to provide up to $ 500 million to support defense conversion projects. Russia is a member of the Multilateral Investment Guarantee Agency (MIGA).

LABOR

The Russian labor market is fragmented, characterized by limited labor mobility across regions, and consequent wage and employment differentials. In Moscow, unemployment is very low, and monthly incomes are at least three times higher than the national average. Overall unemployment, as measured by ILO standards, remains above 9 percent, with underemployment adding another 5-7 percent;, but is estimated as high as 40 percent in some depressed regions.

Labor mobility continues to be restricted by an underdeveloped housing and mortgage market, housing shortages in many cities, and difficulties in obtaining government-mandated residency permits. Utility and other costs for existing housing are disproportionately low relative to incomes, also making workers loathe to move. The lack of labor mobility across regions significantly impacts wage rates and employment; but labor mobility across professions and within regions is common as workers adapt to the needs of a market economy. Workers in Russia are generally highly-skilled and well-educated.

Wage arrears, which currently total around $ 10 billion, are the primary irritant in labor-management relations. Despite significant wage debts, which sometimes reach over six months pay, strikes have not been as frequent in late 1997/early 1998 as in the preceding 12 months. Workers have increasingly used methods other than strikes to

For additional analytical, business and investment opportunities information,
please contact Global Investment & Business Center, USA
at (202) 546-2103. Fax: (202) 546-3275. E-mail: rusric@erols.com
Global Business E-Books on Line: http://world.mirhouse.com

call attention to their plight. Enterprises that pay wages in full and on time generally have smooth labor-management relations.

The union movement is dominated by the Federation of Independent Trade Unions of Russia, which inherited the property of its Soviet predecessors. Trade unions outside this confederation have found it harder to operate as wage arrears hinder the ability of would-be members to pay union dues.

The Russian government generally adheres to ILO conventions protecting worker rights, though enforcement remains an issue. In addition to wage arrears, worker safety is a major unresolved issue, as enterprises are often unable or unwilling to invest in safer equipment or to enforce safety procedures.

FREE ECONOMIC ZONES

Federal legislation on the development of free economic zones (FEZs) is no longer a Russian priority. In 1997, a bill that attempted to unify tax holidays and other concessions for FEZs across Russia passed parliament only to be vetoed by the president. Previously-established FEZs, including the high-profile Kaliningrad FEZ, have generated little new investment. More recently, with the onset of the financial crisis and the Government's drive to boost duty collection, FEZs have been blamed for losses to the budget. The Government has turned to the model of small-scale, more easily monitored "free customs warehouses" (see Chapter VI above) as possible alternatives.

LEADING PRODUCTS FOR EXPORT & SECTORS FOR INVESTMENTS

The Russian market for a wide range of very big ticket items is unique. No other economy has experienced so large and sudden a change in direction in modern history, save for Russia itself. The disruption and economic decline of most of the 1990's denied enterprises the resources to replace aging capital equipment. In many cases the enterprises remain seriously uncompetitive, and ultimately unviable. However, through the chaos there have emerged some survivors, increasingly strong firms with good management and strong positions in their markets. In other cases the strengthening economic reform process is forcing major industrial restructuring which, when completed, will create enterprises which are viable in a market economy and for which there will be clearly identifiable income streams – in cash. Examples of these are some firms in the extractive industries and the so-called 'natural monopolies' – the electric and gas utilities and the railways.

The disruption to Russia's economic system has been so great, as to render data on market size and other basic indicators, where they exist at all, of little practical use. (Note: Rather than provide inaccurate or misleading data on the leading sectors, we have simply not listed anything.) What is known is that the pent-up demand for a wide range of capital equipment is enormous. Should Russia's economic growth continue - and the scenarios under which it will continue grow more numerous - then at some point, major purchase contracts will be signed. Many major deals are already in the offing, with European firms taking a lead.

The following pages list the best prospects for U.S. exports and investment.

AIRCRAFT AND PARTS

A) Rank of Sector: 1
B) Name of Sector: Aircraft and parts
C) ITA Industry Code: AIR

The year 2000, was the first time in a decade that Russian airlines experienced growth in passenger and cargo transportation, a sign of the economic growth that Russia has experienced since early 1999. Cargo and mail traffic on both international and domestic routes, grew by 9.2% to about 0.54 million tons. Industry experts estimate that by 2010, Russia's existing aircraft fleet will not be able to satisfy the country's transportation needs and must be replaced. The continuing high price of aviation fuel is impressing upon operators the need to invest in more fuel-efficient equipment. Within the last year, the Russian fleet declined by 11%, reflecting the growing age of aircraft, with 75% of the Russian fleet now in operation for more than 10 years. More than 95% of the fleet currently in use was designed during 1960-1980. The majority of aircraft now operating will find it increasingly difficulty to meet international standards and will needs refurbishment or replacement.

Only 4% of the existing Russian aircraft fleet meet the new international noise requirements and only an additional 20% of the fleet can be upgraded. Five types of Russian aircraft built after 1990 may be allowed to fly to Europe (IL-96, Tu-214, YaK-42, Ty-154M and IL-62) in accordance with noise requirements.

The civil aviation sector dropped dramatically in the 1990s falling from production of 500 airplanes and 215 helicopters in 1990 to only 14 and 40 respectively in 1998. After 1998, production of civilian aircraft dropped to 7 airplanes in 1999 and 4 in 2000. The Russian aircraft industry consists of about 300 design bureaus, plants and research facilities, and includes 10 major aircraft designers and over 20 major manufacturing facilities. It suffers from a lack of financing for aircraft construction and needs significant restructuring. Currently, the Russian government is discussing possible measures to revitalize the industry, including consolidation of the industry through mergers and providing state guarantees for aircraft leases.

Major partnership arrangements are being established with European and U.S. firms. Such cooperative projects with foreign companies should provide capital needed to sell newly designed aircraft in domestic and international markets. However, limiting this potential is a 1998 law that restricts foreign ownership in aerospace companies to 25%. Large purchases of imported commercial aircraft by Russian airlines are currently blocked by tariff barriers and a lack of financing. A 20% tariff makes importing aircraft prohibitive unless a waiver is granted.

Over the long run, the Russian market presents significant opportunities for U.S. aerospace trade and investment. U.S. commercial aircraft and U.S. aircraft makers (such as Boeing, United Technologies, General Electric, Lockheed Martin, and Raytheon) are engaged in joint production projects and component supply. Many U.S. companies are working with Russian partners on joint projects ranging from supply of fasteners and avionics to joint production of jet engines. Best prospects for U.S. firms include exports of components for engines and avionics to Russian manufacturers. These components will enable Russian producers to bring their products up to world standards.

Types of aircraft	2001	2002-2005	2006-2010
Passenger aircraft (US$ million)	200-250	650-800	1000-1200
Cargo aircraft (US$ million)	100	100-120	300-400
Total per year (US$ million)	*300-350*	*750-900*	*1200-1500*

Source: Scientific and Research Institute for economics of the aviation industry.

OIL AND GAS EQUIPMENT AND SERVICES

A) Rank of Sector: 2
B) Name of Sector: Oil and Gas Equipment and Services
C) ITA Industry Code: OGM,OGS
(HS categories 381510, 382440, 382490, 7304, 730421
820719, 8413, 841370, 841940, 8421, 842519, 8426, 843010, 8430498020,
8430498010, 8431, 843143, 843149, 8481, 9026, 9027, 9032)

Oil and gas field machinery, production and exploration services and pipeline engineering are expected to continue in first place among U.S. exports to Russia. The country's oil industry continues to prosper from the sustained high price for oil. A relative degree of stability in the domestic market has allowed the Russian major oil companies to devote their energies to better managing their assets, and grow their businesses both within Russia and abroad. These firms are increasing their capital expenditures on upstream development and rehabilitation equipment and services to the highest level in the last decade.
In more technologically sophisticated applications, locally produced equipment is unable to compete with Western-made equipment.

Russian oil industry experts anticipate that major oil development projects (in the Sakhalin, Tyumen, Yamal Peninsular, and Timan-Pechora areas) under Production Sharing Agreement (PSA) terms will proceed during the next 2 - 3 years, providing funds and catalyzing technological upgrades for oil and gas field development on a large scale. With the start of Russian gas market liberalization local oil companies increasingly show interest in adding gas reserves to their existing gas portfolios to further increase gas production and development.

The best prospects for U.S. equipment and services are horizontal drilling equipment, offshore development technologies and equipment, work-over, rehabilitation/reconditioning equipment/services, and maintenance and idle wells re-commissioning services and equipment.

(in US$ millions)	1999 actual	2000 actual	2001 estimate
A. Total Market	986	1,300	1,950
B. Total Local Production	515	710	1,200
C. Total Exports	168	185	250
D. Total Imports	639	775	1,000
E. Total Imports from the U.S	210	420	630

NOTE: The above figures are based on Russian Customs and U.S. Department of Commerce data and unofficial estimates.

TELECOMMUNICATION EQUIPMENT

A) Rank of Sector: 3
B) Name of sector: Telecommunication Equipment
C) ITA Industry Code: TEL

Russian telecommunications industry has been growing faster than the economy in general. Telecommunications companies upgrade existing networks and purchase new equipment to introduce value-added services. 60% of telecommunications equipment used in Russia is imported. Foreign competition is stiff and domestic production is picking up. The Russian Ministry of Communications (MinCom) is pressuring international companies to bring assembly/production to Russia.

Best sales prospects for U.S. companies include digital switches, equipment for high-speed Internet access, voice over Internet telephony, multimedia, wireless local loop, and wireless services.

(in US$ millions)	1999 actual	2000 actual	2001 estimate
A. Total Market	N/A	N/A	N/A
B. Total Local Production	N/A	N/A	N/A
C. Total Exports	247	280	310
D. Total Imports	1,275	1,315	1,330
E. Total Imports from the U.S	202	213	235
F.Total Services Market Size	4,100	5,640	6,768

Note: The above figures are based on the Russian Customs statistics and may be an underestimate of U.S. imports. Due to their corporate structure some U.S. equipment manufacturers ship product from their European warehouses. Russian Customs may attribute such shipments to Europe rather than the United States despite the U.S. origin of the product.

DRUGS AND PHARMACEUTICALS

A) Rank of Sector: 4
B) Name of sector: Drugs and Pharmaceuticals
C) ITA Industry Code: DRG

The economic crisis sharply reduced the Russian pharmaceutical market in 1999. According to industry specialists, the market shrank to just $1.7 billion in 1999 compared to $3.1 billion in 1997. The situation improved significantly in 2000 when the market recovered to $2.3-2.4 billion. Pharmaceutical industry analysts predict that the market is expected to fully recover from the crisis in 2003-2004.

In 2000 domestic pharmaceutical output grew 38 percent compared with 1999. The majority of Russia's 500 pharmaceutical producers are small companies. They generally operate outdated equipment, can hardly invest in research and development, and do not meet GMP standards. The product range manufactured by Russian producers is dominated by traditional, typically low-end drugs such as painkillers and herbal preparations based on the use of traditional technologies. Lack of pharmaceutical substances (80 percent of locally made pharmaceuticals are made from imported chemicals), strong side effects and low-quality packaging are the main problems of local manufacturers. Many advanced therapeutic treatments are not produced at all and are only imported. These include cancer and asthma drugs, insulin, etc.

The crisis consolidated the distribution sector. The number of distributors dropped from 3,700 in 1997 to 2,000 in 2000.

Russia's imports in 2000 amounted to $1,245.0 million, or about 60 percent of the total market. Some 65% of all imports come from Western Europe, the United States, Canada, and Japan. The ten top foreign suppliers of pharmaceuticals to Russia in 2000 included Aventis Pharma, Novo Nordisk, Sanofi-Synthelabo, GlaxoSmithKline, Eli Lilly, F. Hoffman-La Roche Ltd., Gedeon Richter Ltd., Pharmacia & Upjohn, Novartis and KRKA D. D.

Best prospects for U.S. exports include cardiovascular, cancer, asthma, neurological and hormonal drugs, insulins, antibiotics, analgetics, vitamins, and psychotropic drugs. Another promising sub-sector is food additives. They must pass only clinical tests and do not require often long and expensive registration and certification that drugs and pharmaceuticals normally do. Despite introduction of obligatory state registration for a number of biologically active supplements, the market for such products continues to grow rapidly and opens up good potential for U.S. companies. The total market of food additives amounted to $1.9 million in 1999.

(in US$ millions)	1999 actual	2000 actual	2001 estimate
A. Total Market	1,700	2,300	3,000
B. Total Local Production	N/A	N/A	N/A
C. Total Exports	69.2	79.8	85
D. Total Imports	854.9	1,245	1,300
E. Total Imports from the U.S	70	100	120

BEAUTY AND HEALTH PRODUCTS

A) Rank of Sector: 5
B) Name of sector: Cosmetics and toiletries
C) ITA Industry Code: COS

The Russian beauty and health products market has been one of the fastest growing industry markets in Russia. Annual growth rates of the market currently amount to 20 percent in comparison to 6 percent in Western Europe. It is also one of the most advanced and mature product markets in Russia. The total size of the Russian beauty products market, according to a number of independent beauty industry analysts is estimated at 3-4 billion dollars.

For additional analytical, business and investment opportunities information,
please contact Global Investment & Business Center, USA
at (202) 546-2103. Fax: (202) 546-3275. E-mail: rusric@erols.com
Global Business E-Books on Line: http://world.mirhouse.com

The 1998 economic crisis served as a spur for a number of Russian beauty product manufacturers, who as a result of the devalued ruble managed to increase their market share. Local manufacturers currently supply over 65 percent of the total market, taking advantage of the sharp rise in prices of imported Western cosmetics. Since then the quality of locally produced skin and hair products has improved considerably, although not yet reaching the standards of comparable foreign brands. Foreign-made skin and hair care products, including American brands, continue to have good market potential in Russia. Domestic production of make-up, perfume and nail products cannot compete in quality with well-known foreign brands. This highly competitive market is dominated by imported products.

Imports of beauty and health products come mainly from France (31%), Germany (21%), U.K. (15%), and Poland (7%). The U.S. share of the import market is 5%. The best sales prospects include professional skin and hair care products, hair color, professional and mass market make-up, perfumes, spa products, nail care products.

(US$ millions)	1999 actual	2000 actual	2001 estimate
A. Total Market	NA	NA	4,000
B. Total Local Production	NA	NA	NA
C. Total Exports	NA	170	190
D. Total Imports	800	900	1,100
E. Total Imports from the U.S	NA	47	55

Source: Customs Export-Import Statistics and unofficial estimates.

MEDICAL EQUIPMENT

A) Rank of Sector: 6
B) Name of sector: Medical Equipment
C) ITA Industry Code: MED

The medical equipment and supplies market equipment in Russia has been growing rapidly during the last two years. The total market currently amounts to about $2 billion. Imports continue to play a significant role, despite the significant increase in local production since the August 1998 crisis. Currently high-tech medical devices dominate imports, while only a few years ago most imports were relatively inexpensive low-tech medical devices and equipment. Russia still produces few high-end medical equipment items, including computer tomographs, ultrasound equipment, x-ray equipment, etc.

For additional analytical, business and investment opportunities information, please contact Global Investment & Business Center, USA at (202) 546-2103. Fax: (202) 546-3275. E-mail: rusric@erols.com Global Business E-Books on Line: http://world.mirhouse.com

Imports of medical equipment and supplies come mainly from Germany, the United States, Italy, the United Kingdom, Switzerland, Sweden, and Eastern Europe. The best sales prospects for U.S. medical equipment are for clinical laboratory equipment and test kits, dental equipment and supplies, and radiology, diagnostic, sterilization, intensive care for newborns, ultrasound, and home health care equipment.

Russia's 1,100 medical equipment manufacturers produce some 7,000 types of medical devices. 32 specialized manufacturers now control 60 percent of the total output. A significant portion of high-tech medical equipment is still developed and produced at defense enterprises, which have traditionally had access to advanced technologies. According to different estimates, local production supplies 40-60 of the total medical equipment market. Only 25 percent of medical equipment produced in Russia can compete internationally.

In the last two-years, because of the change in demand from imported to locally produced medical devices and supplies as well as some types of equipment, a significant number of Russian enterprises managed to strengthen their positions and increase their share in the market. Some recently developed medical equipment and devices manufactured in Russia are now successfully competing with their Western equivalents within the country due to high technical standards and relatively low price. These products include certain types of laser equipment, scanning probe microscopes, devices used for magnetotherapy in dentistry, knee joint implants, artificial heart, lung and kidney devices, three-channel microprocessing electrocardiographs, and endoscopes. Also, Russian computer specialists develop advanced software used by Western companies developing new sophisticated medical equipment. Generally, locally made medical equipment is 3-5 times less expensive than similar Western equipment, although it is often inferior to Western medical equipment in terms of design, efficiency and after-sale services.

(US$ millions)	1999 actual	2000 actual	2001 estimate
A. Total Market	N/A	N/A	N/A
B. Total Local Production	N/A	N/A	N/A
C. Total Exports	19	96	110
D. Total Imports	980	1,040	1,100
E. Total Imports from the U.S	170	190	210

Note: The above figures are based on Russian Customs and unofficial estimates.

For additional analytical, business and investment opportunities information, please contact Global Investment & Business Center, USA at (202) 546-2103. Fax: (202) 546-3275. E-mail: rusric@erols.com Global Business E-Books on Line: http://world.mirhouse.com

PLASTICS AND PLASTIC PROCESSING

A) Rank of Sector: 7
B) Name of sector: Plastics Production Machinery and Plastic Materials/Resins
C) ITA Industry Code: PME, PMR

The production of resins and plastics in Russia has increased by almost 10% since 1997, though total production remains insufficient for the market. Due to limited production of quality, domestically produced plastics, there is great demand for imported polystyrene products in radio-electronics, household electrical appliances, packaging, toys, and automotive parts.

There is an even greater demand for shape retentive (strike resistant) polystyrene, foam-polystyrene insulation sandwich panels, and polypropylene. Because of high costs and obsolete, inefficient equipment, Russian manufacturers produce insignificant amounts of these materials. Therefore, domestic production does not satisfy demand, and opportunities exist for U.S. exporters. Plastic material imports represent 2.3% of Russia's total imports.

The beverage processing and packaging industry is producing ever-larger quantities of bottled drinking water. The market is expected to grow 20% per year over the next five years. Therefore, one of the best prospects is plastic packaging and pre-forms for water bottling.

(in US$ millions)	1999 actual	2000 actual	2001 estimate
A. Total Market Size	N/A	N/A	N/A
B. Total Local Production	N/A	N/A	N/A
C. Total Exports	N/A	N/A	N/A
D. Total Imports	800	1,000	1,000
E. Total Imports from the U.S	N/A	N/A	N/A

Source: Russian State Statistics Committee

FOOD PROCESSING AND PACKAGING EQUIPMENT

A) Rank of Sector: 8
B) Name of Sector: Food Processing and Packaging Equipment
C) ITA Industry Code: FPP

For additional analytical, business and investment opportunities information, please contact Global Investment & Business Center, USA at (202) 546-2103. Fax: (202) 546-3275. E-mail: rusric@erols.com Global Business E-Books on Line: http://world.mirhouse.com

Consumer purchasing power is increasing in Russia, particularly in the major population centers of Moscow and St. Petersburg. This is bringing a shift in shopping habits away from the purchase of basic commodities in street markets towards a the purchase of processed and packaged foods in supermarkets. In addition, the on-going land reform process is encouraging more efficient farming, as farmers become entrepreneurs. This in turn is spurring demand for more modern processing and packaging equipment for the full range of food products. This includes small-scale, inexpensive machines for farmers, local food processors, food wholesalers and supermarkets. Large companies express interest in more sophisticated high-tech equipment. Already many Russian processed food products match imports from Europe in terms of quality and packaging, and are exceptionally competitive in terms of price. Some demand is driven by large western food companies, such as Pepsico, Mars/Masterfoods, Nestle, Danone, Coca-Cola, and many others, for their local Russian production plants. Some demand is from Russian producers aiming to replace aged equipment in order to improve product quality and competitiveness.

Major Russian food processing and packaging equipment trade shows are growing in terms of participants, including foreign suppliers. Recent Moscow trade exhibitions showed significant interest for reconditioned machinery and equipment. Promising sub-sectors include milling, refining, extracting, canning, filling, bottling, labeling and marking equipment and materials, as well as machinery to produce processed food, dairy products, frozen food, soft drinks, and beverages.

(in US$ millions)	1999 actual	2000 actual	2001 estimate
A. Total Market Size	N/A	N/A	N/A
B. Total Local Production	N/A	N/A	N/A
C. Total Exports	42.1	25.6	28.0
D. Total Imports	442.7	371.3	460.0
E. Total Imports from the U.S	9.9	8.9	9.8

NOTE: The above statistics are unofficial estimates based on Russian Customs data.

COMPUTERS, PERIPHERALS AND COMPUTER SOFTWARE

A) Rank of Sector: 9
B) Name of sector: Computers, Peripherals, Computer Software
C) ITA Industry Code: CPT, CSF, CSV

The computer market provided some of Russia's best prospects for U.S. companies. In 2000, Russia was the fastest growing computer market in Europe, at least in terms of units sold. The total market amounted to $1.3 billion. The main trends of the last year were growth of laptop and server market, a significant decline in PC sales prices, expansion of distributors to the regions and a formation of a new sector for PDA. IBM, Compaq, Sun Microsystems and Hewlett Packard are present at the Russian market and their products are available either directly or through representatives or distributors. However, in 2000 foreign suppliers faced considerable competition from local Russian companies. Corporate sales currently represent the most attractive market for U.S. exporters. The primary demand for the server market comes from governmental institutions and related large state-run enterprises such as the Central Bank, Gazprom and energy companies. Retailing is not highly profitable at the moment, although it might become more attractive should consumers' purchasing power accelerate. Industry experts forecast 10-15% growth for the entire computer hardware sector in value in 2001.

Russia's offshore software development industry is growing at an estimated rate of 50 percent a year. Value estimates for the industry range from $80 million to $120 million in 2000. Extensive pirating and highly skilled inexpensive local software development limit the potential for packaged software application sales and corresponding IT services support. Nevertheless, annual turnover of Russian software market in 2000 was about $600 million. The most popular software is expected to be sold in Russia is general business administration, operating systems, data base management and communications.
Internet in Russia is not widespread at present but this sector remains one of the promising new markets for American firms. By industry projections it will hit 6 million registered users by the end of 2001 and Internet retail will be the promising investment area.

Consistent with the Russian IT market's strong focus on hardware the best opportunities for sales of U.S. manufactured products in Russia appear to be:
- Laptops and notebooks
- High-performance PC servers
- Multimedia PCs to be used for Internet surfing

(in US$ millions)	1999 actual	2000 actual	2001 estimate
A. Total Market Size (PCs)	N/A	N/A	N/A
B. Total Local Production	N/A	N/A	N/A
C. Total Exports	66	38	45

For additional analytical, business and investment opportunities information,
please contact Global Investment & Business Center, USA
at (202) 546-2103. Fax: (202) 546-3275. E-mail: rusric@erols.com
Global Business E-Books on Line: http://world.mirhouse.com

D. Total Imports	185	202	250
E. Total Imports from the U.S	50	55	60

Note: The above figures are based on Russian Customs and U.S. Department of Commerce data and unofficial estimates.

AUTOMOTIVE PARTS & SUPPLIES

A) Rank of Sector: 10
B) Name of sector: Automotive Parts and Services Equipment
C) ITA Industry Code: APS

Of 24.5 million vehicles on Russia's roads, 19.5 million are cars and 40% of them are at least 10 years old. Analysts estimate both the OEM market for new vehicles and the aftermarket for automotive parts, expendable supplies, accessories, and equipment to be $3-6 billion. While Russian suppliers have a relative strangle hold on the OEM market for new vehicles, the aftermarket is receptive to U.S. products. Many U.S. brands are well known and highly regarded throughout the country.

In 2000, car ownership exceeded 130 vehicles per 1,000 inhabitants, a 120% increase over 1993's rate of 59 cars per 1,000. In the same period, the number of imported cars jumped 300% from 594,000 to 2.4 million. Annual car sales have also surged from 800,000 to 1.6 million in the eight years leading up to 2000. Authorized dealers reported sales of about 50,000 new foreign cars in 2000, while unauthorized dealers and individuals imported approximately 150,000 vehicles, many of them used.

There are several projects underway to assemble foreign cars in Russia. Ford's new plant in a St. Petersburg suburb should begin operation in late 2001. Ford states that annual production of its Focus model will start at 20,000 units. GM has formed a joint venture with Russia's automotive giant AvtoVAZ to produce a small, Chevrolet branded SUV based on AvtoVaz's Niva design. Initial output of 75,000 vehicles per year should start in the city of Togliatti in late 2002.

The Russian government supports projects which create local jobs and is considering special tax incentives for investors in the automotive sector. Moreover, the European Bank for Reconstruction and Development (EBRD) will consider co-financing automotive component production in Russia. U.S. automotive firms have significant opportunities to supply components to such projects.

(in US$ millions)	1999 actual	2000 actual	2001 estimate
A. Total Market Size	N/A	N/A	3,000

For additional analytical, business and investment opportunities information, please contact Global Investment & Business Center, USA at (202) 546-2103. Fax: (202) 546-3275. E-mail: rusric@erols.com
Global Business E-Books on Line: http://world.mirhouse.com

B. Total Local Production	N/A	N/A	N/A
C. Total Exports	N/A	N/A	N/A
D. Total Imports	N/A	N/A	850
E. Total Imports from the U.S	N/A	N/A	120

LEADING AGRICULTURAL SECTORS

1. POULTRY

U.S. chicken leg quarters continue to dominate the Russian import market for poultry meat. While the price of all meat products grew at a rapid pace during the first half of 2001, imported poultry products continued to enjoy a competitive position in the market. Animal health issues in Europe precipitated import restrictions on EU poultry, beef, and pork during the first half of 2001, increasing demand for U.S. poultry and meat products. Consequently, U.S. exports of poultry to Russia have returned to pre-1998 crisis levels, and the import value is expected to surpass US$ 1.0 billion this year. However, as consumers turn toward imported U.S. poultry, the Russian government perceives a threat to its domestic poultry industry. Consequently, considerable uncertainty about the future of poultry meat imports exists, as renewed rumors of new import quotas and an antidumping investigation against U.S. poultry circulate in the press and among traders.

(in US$ millions)	1999 actual	2000 actual	2001 estimate
A. Total Consumption	860	980	1,100
B. Total Local Production	400	410	420
C. Total Exports	2	2	2
D. Total Imports	400	500	680
E. Total Imports from the U.S	340	400	540

NOTE: The above figures are based on Russian Customs, U.S. Department of Agriculture data, and unofficial estimates.

2. BEEF

The problem of supplying Russian consumers with sufficient quantities of meat is expected to lead to greater opportunities for U.S. beef in the near future. Although domestic meat production appears to be stabilizing, it remains limited and unable to satisfy domestic demand. Currently, about 20 percent of the total volume of red meat consumed in Russia is imported. In 2002, beef imports are expected to increase 20 percent as growing consumer incomes stimulate demand that cannot yet be met by local production. During the first five months of 2001, Russia increased meat imports from countries outside the former Soviet Union. During that period, Russia imported 236,700 MT of red meat from non-FSU countries or some 130 percent more than imported from these countries during the same period of the previous year. Although European countries historically are the principle suppliers of beef to the Russian market, livestock disease problems in the EU and other supplying countries have helped alternative suppliers. This pattern is expected to continue as domestic processors are building new relationships with alternative suppliers of raw material. Without export subsidies, European exporters will experience more competition in the Russian market. In particular, inexpensive cuts of U.S. meat exports (e.g. beef trimmings) are increasingly popular with meat processors.

(in US$ millions)	1999 actual	2000 actual	2001 estimate
A. Total Consumption	2,500	2,400	2,750
B. Total Local Production	2,220	2,160	2,100
C. Total Exports	1	1	1
D. Total Imports	548	400	650
E. Total Imports from the U.S	5	6	7

NOTE: The above figures are based on Russian Customs, U.S. Department of Agriculture data, and unofficial estimates.

3. PORK

Despite the aftermath of the economic crisis of 1998, Russia remains one of the top ten export destinations for U.S. pork. The elimination of EU subsidies on pork and the problem of livestock diseases in Europe are making U.S. pork once again competitive in the marketplace. As the combination of these problems has led to increased domestic meat prices, Russian processors are keen to locate sources of the least expensive products. U.S. pork trimmings and picnics are becoming increasingly popular as ingredients for sausage makers. In the last two years, Russian per capita consumption of pork has remained fairly steady due in large part to U.S. and EU food aid shipments. However, imports are now expected to increase due to improved economic conditions. The greatest export opportunities in the near future consist of unprocessed and semi-processed pork products for further processing. Russia's largest processors of meat are based in Moscow and St. Petersburg. They manufacture up to 60 varieties of sausage. Fresh pork market sales will be targeted to retail stores, restaurants, hotels, and other food service providers in major cities and regions where incomes are high and where there is greater market diversification.

(in US$ millions)	1999 actual	2000 actual	2001 estimate
A. Total Consumption	1,910	1,765	1,785
B. Total Local Production	1,500	1,515	1,535
C. Total Exports	1	1	1
D. Total Imports	410	250	250
E. Total Imports from the U.S	42	42	35

NOTE: The above figures are based on Russian Customs, U.S. Department of Agriculture data, and unofficial estimates.

4. SEAFOOD

Russia's imported seafood products offer some unique opportunities for U.S. exporters. Although, in 2000, total domestic consumption of seafood products in Russia did not increase as much as expected, an improving Russian economy is positively affecting demand. Semi-ready products like fillets, fish stick, canned fish, and vacuum packed fish are gaining in popularity. This trend will continue as the economy grows. Despite lower consumer spending in Russia, expensive fish items have been marketed to hotels, restaurants, and supermarkets targeting foreigners and wealthy Russians who can still afford these items and prefer high quality imported fish products. When normal trade patterns resume, there will be significant growth opportunities for a variety of processed seafood products including canned, pickled, bottled or smoked items. Canned products are especially popular in Russia as they provide longer shelf-life and are easier to handle and store. However, in the short term, suppliers of inexpensive canned seafood products stand to benefit in the Russian market, as 60 percent of Russian consumers of canned fish products have incomes of less than 1000 rubles ($35) per month. Scandinavian and French fish products continue to dominate the market with a wide and interesting assortment of products and aggressive marketing. Current economic conditions indicate that U.S. exporters will experience some difficulty in the short term competing with cheap imported fish products from nearby countries.

(in US$ millions)	1999 actual	2000 actual	2001 estimate
A. Total Consumbtion	2,500	2,560	2,600
B. Total Local Production	2,900	2,761	2,700
C. Total Exports	239	300	300
D. Total Imports	150	140	130
E. Total Imports from the U.S	17	18	20

NOTE: The above figures are based on Russian Customs and U.S. Department of Agriculture data and unofficial estimates.

5. DAIRY PRODUCTS

The value of U.S. dairy exports to Russia has shown consistent growth since 1997. With the help of the U.S. food aid program, the value of U.S. dairy exports reached US$ 24 million in 2000 or 74 percent more than exported to Russia in 1997. As a consequence of the aid program, Russian dairy processors have become acquainted with the high quality of U.S. non-fat dried milk powder and are seeking to further relationships with U.S. exporters as the price is competitive for the Russian market. Recently, prices for domestic dairy products grew in response to an increase in raw milk prices, making U.S. product better situated to become price competitive. In 2001, U.S. exports of non-fat dry milk powder to Russia are expected to at least equal the level of the previous year. The 1998 financial crisis still affects the Russian market as foreign suppliers have found new markets for dairy products and are not anxious to return to Russia despite an improving situation. BSE and foot-and-mouth disease led to a reduction in the EU cow herd size and, consequently, reduced dairy exports to Russia. However, local producers cannot easily increase milk production to cover a shortage of butter and cheese products in the market.

DAIRY PRODUCTS (DRY MILK)

(in US$ millions)	1999 actual	2000 actual	2001 estimate
A. Total Consumption	91	68	61
B. Total Local Production	30	29	22

C. Total Exports	1	1	1
D. Total Imports	62	40	40
E. Total Imports from the U.S	29	18	20

EDIBLE NUTS

Te market for edible nuts in Russia is developing, driven by both increases in consumer demand, which reflects the growing purchasing power of the Russian population, and rapidly increasing needs of the confectionary industry. Commercial nut production takes place only on a limited area in the Northern Caucasus region of Russia, while the remainder is collected from forests. Post estimates total domestic production, including from forests, at US $ 10.0 million, and its value growth reflects price increases rather than an increase in production volume. Thus, increases in nut consumption in coming years will depend upon imports. Improved consumer purchasing power will stimulate a fast restoration of imports of nuts to the pre-crises level, which averaged US$ 40 million in CY 1996 and 1997. Post estimates that U.S. imports of high quality nuts will quite likely exceed the 1998 level of US$ 10.0 million within the next 5 years.

(US$ millions)	1999 actual	2000 actual	2001 estimate
A. Total Consumption	21	27	31
B. Total Local Production	10	11	12
C. Total Exports	0	0	0
D. Total Imports	10	15	19
E. Total Imports from the U.S	3	4	5

7. WHEAT

Russia is expected to produce 38.5 million metric tons (MMT) of wheat this year, which, although substantially larger than the two previous years, represents an average harvest. Despite the larger crop, rising demand in the Russian Far East (particularly in the grain deficit regions of Siberia, the Far North, and Far East) should continue to result in increased wheat purchases. Although many of these regions are short of cash, a transportation cost advantage should allow U.S. products to move into that region. In addition, recent food aid shipments have heightened interest in purchasing U.S. wheat commercially. Of special interest to exporters is the rapid expansion of pasta production, especially for low-cost instant noodles, which could lead to imports of U.S. durum wheat. The growth of U.S. wheat exports to Russia in 2001, however, will be tempered by the absence of food aid shipments.

(US$ millions)	1999 actual	2000 actual	2001 estimate
A. Total Consumption	2,597	3,671	3,550
B. Total Local Production	2,325	3,445	3,600
C. Total Exports	48	42	100
D. Total Imports	320	268	50
E. Total Imports from the U.S	97	55	30

NOTE:
1. The above figures are based on Russian Customs, U.S. Department of Agriculture data, and unofficial estimates. 1999-2000 figures reflect input of U.S. food assistance program.
2. Value of total local production in 2000 increased due to over 60 percent increase in wheat prices. Although value of local wheat production in 2001 is estimated only slightly more than in 2000, the volumes are forecast to be greater and prices lower.

8. CORN (FEED)

The growing Russian poultry and livestock industries will require quality feed if they are to be competitive and profitable. The dominant market share enjoyed by U.S. corn exporters and expected expansion in domestic poultry production should be the basis for greater market opportunities for our feed grain exports. Although current trade is boosted by donations and sales on concessional terms, effective promotion and an improving economy should allow U.S. exports to Russia to remain high even after trade returns to commercial terms. Cooperation between the Feed Grains Council, US Poultry and Egg Export Council (USAPEEC) and the US Meat Export Federation (USMEF) in providing technical assistance to the livestock and poultry sectors can provide an additional strategic marketing advantage for U.S. feed grain exporters. Additionally, the restoration of GSM-102 credit facilities should help improve access to credit for Russian buyers and support expanded U.S. exports.

(US$ millions)	1999 actual	2000 actual	2001 estimate
A. Total Consumption	215	254	196

For additional analytical, business and investment opportunities information, please contact Global Investment & Business Center, USA at (202) 546-2103. Fax: (202) 546-3275. E-mail: rusric@erols.com
Global Business E-Books on Line: http://world.mirhouse.com

B. Total Local Production	123	153	186
C. Total Exports	0	0	0
D. Total Imports	92	101	10
E. Total Imports from the U.S	80	81	5

NOTE: The above figures are based on Russian Customs, U.S. Department of Agriculture data, and unofficial estimates. 1999-2000 figures reflect food assistance sales to Russia.

9. SOYBEAN COMPLEX

With the increased priority put on the recovery of the livestock industry by the Russian and regional governments, domestic meat production is expected to expand. Thus, the need for raw materials to produce quality feedstuffs is expected to grow. This is especially true of protein-rich components such as soybeans. Cooperation between the American Soybean Association, USAPEEC and USMEF in providing technical assistance to the livestock and poultry sectors can provide an additional strategic marketing advantage for U.S. soybean exporters. The 1999-2000 food aid program with its concessional soybean and soybean meal shipments has helped to reestablish the position of this premium feed in the Russian regions. Soybean consumption will also be buoyed by increasing the use of soybeans in meat packing and other food processing industries that need input of alternative sources of protein. However, the issue of biotechnology as it relates to the soybean complex bears watching as Russia develops and implements regulations in this sphere. With GSM-102 credit, access to financing for Russian buyers should be wider and thereby support expanded U.S. exports.

SOYBEANS

(US$ millions)	1999 actual	2000 actual	2001 estimate
A. Total Consumption	106	68	70
B. Total Local Production	61	69	70
C. Total Exports	3	9	10
D. Total Imports	49	8	10
E. Total Imports from the U.S	45	3	5

NOTE: The above figures are based on Russian Customs, U.S. Department of Agriculture data, and unofficial estimates. 1999 figures include food aid shipments.

SOYBEAN MEAL

(US$ millions)	1999 actual	2000 actual	2001 estimate
A. Total Consumption	85	112	100
B. Total Local Production	42	75	70
C. Total Exports	0	0	0
D. Total Imports	43	38	30
E. Total Imports from the U.S	20	33	25

NOTE: The above figures are based on Russian Customs, U.S. Department of Agriculture data, and unofficial estimates. 1999-2000 figures include food aid shipments

MARKETING PRODUCTS AND SERVICES

U.S. companies have dramatically increased their presence and activity in Russia since the collapse of the Soviet Union. In illustration of this, membership in the private-sector American Chamber of Commerce in Russia (Amcham) has grown from a few dozen companies in 1994 to approximately 500 in 1998, making it the fastest-growing U.S. business chamber in the world. Amcham, with more than a dozen industry-focused committees and a newly-opened St.Petersburg chapter, has worked closely with the U.S. and Foreign Commercial Service and other private-sector associations in bringing policy issues to the attention of the U.S. and Russian governments in order to encourage improvement of Russia's commercial climate, and in calling U.S. companies attention to overlooked business opportunities in regions of Russia beyond Moscow.

The United States remains the largest single-country investor in the Russian Federation, but ranks well behind the European Community as a whole in investment in Russia, as well as in exports to Russia. Germany, with almost twice our sales ($5.2 billion versus $2.9 billion) has invested only one fourth as much as have American companies. In fact, Russia Federation has received relatively little foreign direct investment compared with Central Europe and China. Most firms have concluded that early returns are not high enough to compensate for high start-up costs and perceived risks. With few exceptions, U.S. firms investing in Russia describe their decision to do so as strategic, based on the promise of long-term advantages, rather than short-term profits.

For additional analytical, business and investment opportunities information, please contact Global Investment & Business Center, USA at (202) 546-2103. Fax: (202) 546-3275. E-mail: rusric@erols.com
Global Business E-Books on Line: http://world.mirhouse.com

Western Europe's share of exports to Russia parallels its share of direct investment in Russia: in each case, it accounts for around a third of the total. The U.S., on the other hand, accounts for only 6 percent of Russian imports but contributed 41 percent of direct investment in . There is a clear contrast between the trade-oriented policy of Western European firms vis-a-vis Russia and the approach taken by U.S. firms. Some of this is attributable to Europe□s proximity and the logistical advantages this conveys. However, anecdotal evidence strongly suggests that U.S. firms have been less active than their European competitors in marketing and building distribution networks at regional levels in Russia.

DISTRIBUTION AND SALES CHANNELS

Companies operating in America often expect well-defined distribution channels, relentless competition, and strong advertising budgets. Firms in Russia, by contrast, encounter erratic distribution, unpredictable (but often tough) competition, and word-of-mouth advertising. Although Russia boasts increasing numbers of joint ventures and Western-style stores in major cities, most goods distribution -- especially outside of Moscow and St. Petersburg -- takes place through less formal channels. Penetrating these channels is often the key to success or failure for an American company operating in the Russian market. Western companies which have succeeded have done so through a combination of improvisation and innovation, combined with a substantial investment of time and a tolerance for early mistakes. U.S. companies with a long-term market development strategy may find regional markets well worth exploring, because anecdotal evidence indicates that European products are increasingly showing up unchallenged in Russia□s regional markets.

USE OF AGENTS AND DISTRIBUTORS / FINDING A PARTNER

Both experienced exporters and those with less well-developed agent selection criteria are well-advised to cultivate personal and ongoing relations with agents, to proceed incrementally, and to retain a fall-back position should a relationship sour. Experience has shown that perhaps the highest-risk strategy is to visit Russia only once or twice, select an agent and grant him exclusive representation, then move quickly to consignment or credit sales, without establishing a consistent track record.

To succeed, U.S. companies must consider a variety of local and regional distribution alternatives. In a few product categories (i.e. apparel, packaged foods, and alcoholic beverages), foreign suppliers can choose from a small but growing number of existing Russian distributors. These Russian agents can help the foreign supplier by placing its products on store shelves, handling customs and transportation matters and (more rarely) conducting advertising campaigns. Most recently-formed Russian distributors are small-volume operations with experience limited to the main cities of Moscow and St. Petersburg, or other regional centers.

Over the last three years, many foreign manufacturers of consumer appliances and durables have moved away from using official distributors. These companies typically have replaced agency agreements with their own representation in major cities. They then sell directly to Russian importers, who take possession of goods outside Russia (in Finland, for example) and import for their own account. This affords the manufacturer greater control over prices and distribution, while avoiding potential tax and customs liabilities, as well as the uncertainties of the local commercial environment.

Meanwhile, other foreign companies have decided that the reputation of their firm and brands could suffer if they fail to ensure compliance with Russian customs regulations by acting as the importer-of-record (and in fact, some U.S. companies have met trouble as a result of false invoicing and other irregularities commited by their intermediaries). Firms which opt for direct exports will likely face lower early returns, due to reduced sales owing to duties and higher landed costs. However, for those determined to build a strong presence in Russia, this policy may be seen as an investment that will ultimately pay reputational dividends.

FRANCHISING

Franchising is little understood in Russia. Several early attempts to establish franchise distribution have foundered, due to confusion regarding ownership and the responsibilities of the parties to a franchise agreement. Some have been quite succesful, and the potential remains quite high.

DIRECT MARKETING

In major cities, telemarketing and fax marketing to business customers is common but not particularly effective. In contrast, person-to-person direct marketing works well. One U.S. firm has been successful throughout Russia in direct-marketing weight reduction products. A major U.S. cosmetics firm has launched a well-run direct marketing program, and may find similar success in fashion-conscious urban markets here. Other direct marketing channels (e.g., catalogs, internet and mail) are in their infancy. Many shippers are reluctant to send goods without prepayment, and the base of potential customers with credit cards is small. However, since catalog businesses avoid high costs of retail distribution in Russia, they have potential to capture a high profit margin, and this market segment should heat up in coming years.

JOINT VENTURES/LICENSING

Joint venturing demands meticulous planning and sustained commitment from the U.S. partner. In many cases, other forms of strategic alliance, in which the U.S. partner retains greater managerial control, are more efficient and less risky. Foreign firms have established JVs usually to market goods, and sometimes to manufacture. Goods made and/or distributed successfully by U.S.-Russian JVs range from soft drinks, ice cream and cigarettes to elevators, oil, sport-utility vehicles and jet engines. Some firms choose to create a JV to capture lower local cost structures, in effect running their business as a Russian would. High taxes and uncertainty in Russia's legal environment are barriers to greater reliance on JVs as a form of market entry by U.S. suppliers. Production of U.S. goods in Russia under license is rare, due partly to concern over quality control and intellectual property protection.

One advantage of a joint venture is that it can help a U.S. firm gain a bit of Russian identity, which can be useful in a culture where some people view foreigners with suspicion. Political pressure is mounting in Russia for domestic-content mandates for key sectors or large-scale procurements. For example, many planned foreign investments in the oil industry entail contractual commitments to use 70 percent or more Russian content. Firms that can creatively help oil producers meet Russian-content requirements for equipment and services may be in an advantageous position to serve this industry.

The idea of a joint venture is often viewed differently by Russian and American partners. U.S. businesses, especially smaller companies, often view JVs as a means of securing a local partner with experience selling in the Russian market, and may agree to a JV as the price for this expertise. Many Russian managers, on the other hand, view a foreign partner chiefly as a source of working capital, and local market development may not be as high a priority. While there are many examples of successful JVs in which both partners goals have been met, ceding managerial oversight over any aspects of a joint venture to a Russian partner who does not share the U.S. investor s objectives and expectations invites serious trouble. U.S. firms should thoroughly explore whether a potential Russian partner shares priorities and expectations before making commitments.

A frequent mistake which has often led to commercial failure and, in some cases, bitter legal disputes, is for an American to strike a JV agreement with a Russian partner after a limited history of cooperation, and then return to the U.S. as an absentee partner in the expectation that the Russian partner will manage day-to-day operations, implement a growth plan, phone the States for occasional advice, and wire home the American s agreed-upon share of the profits on schedule. This is a sure recipe for disaster. Any firm which initiates a joint venture in Russia should be ready to invest the constant personal attention of American managerial staff to keep the business on-course, both before and after the venture has achieved some success.

ESTABLISHING AN OFFICE

Foreign firms often conduct marketing activities in Russia through representative offices. Under Russian law, foreign representative offices are not considered to be Russian legal entities, although they can conduct marketing activities and sign contracts. Depending on the type of activities they conduct, foreign representative offices could be deemed to be "permanent establishments," which subjects their activities to Russian taxation. (Firms are advised to consult with an accountant and attorney.)

Representative offices may be either accredited or non-accredited. Accreditation is the more time-consuming and expensive approach, and requires the foreign firm to have a Russian Government sponsor (usually the Ministry of Foreign Economic Relations and Trade (which is scheduled to be consolidated by autumn 1998 into a newly-formed Ministry of Industry and Trade) or an industry-specific ministry. However, accreditation holds certain advantages in that the accrediting sponsor can issue invitations for foreign personnel visiting the representative office (which are necessary to obtain Russian business visas) and can assist the office in making business contacts.

Companies opening offices in Russia should register with:

-the U.S. Embassy or Consulate (for security and passport replacement facilitation if necessary);
-the local city government;
-the Russian Ministry of Finance (if you are making a major investment);
-the local inspectorate of the Russian State Tax Service;
-any ministry holding special jurisdiction over a given industry.

SALES FACTORS

U.S. firms generally find success by choosing their sales targets carefully. Because a lack of capital and poor cash flow are typical of Russian businesses, many firms find it expedient to rank potential customers based on their ability to pay. Possible candidates for export sales include:

- Russian enterprises that export for hard currency;
- development projects financed by Western sources;
- Russian enterprises with good domestic cash flow;
- regional governments in natural resource-rich areas;
- the Russian federal government;
- major modernization projects by Russian enterprises;
- the general Russian consumer market; and
- the upscale (albeit narrow) "new Russian" market.

ADVERTISING AND TRADE PROMOTION

Advertising through TV, radio, print and billboard media is now typical in the consumer goods and financial service markets. The number of Western as well as Russian advertising agencies active in Russia is growing rapidly. The regulatory environment for advertising in Russia is not well-developed, however. Additionally, advertising expenditures are not tax-deductible in Russia (although draft tax legislation under consideration in the Duma as of this writing may allow a measure of deductibility for advertising costs as soon as 1999, if enacted). Both foreign and domestic firms frequently advertise in commercially-oriented newspapers and journals in Russia, with the following among the more popular:

--Deloviye Lyudi   (monthly journal, Russian-language)
--Izvestiya   (daily paper, Russian-language)
--Kommersant   (daily paper, Russian-language)
--Delovoy Mir   (daily paper, Russian-language)
--Ekonomika i Zhizn   (weekly paper, Russian-language)
--Business MN   (weekly paper, Russian-language)
--Moscow Times   (daily paper, English-language)
--Moscow Tribune   (daily paper, English-language)
--Moscow Business Guide (monthly bus. directory, English)
--Delovoi Petersburg   (daily paper, Russian-language)
--St. Petersburg Times (daily, English-language)
--Sevodnya   (daily paper, Russian-language)

Trade exhibitions (numerous in Moscow and St.Petersburg, and increasingly common in other regional cities) can help U.S. suppliers find potential buyers and distributors, and are among the best ways for companies entering the Russian market for the first time to meet a large number of potential customers business partners at low cost. U.S. companies sometimes make substantial off-the-floor sales at Russian exhibitions. Representatives of regional governments and state enterprises from remote, poorly-supplied areas of Russia often visit trade exhibitions in major cities to purchase goods for their region or enterprises. A listing of major trade exhibitions is found in Appendix G.

PRODUCT PRICING

Pricing behavior is often counter-intuitive, and in general, price competition in the large cities is somewhat muted. The ratio of retail outlets per thousand residents in Moscow and St. Petersburg is a fraction of that found in, e.g., Warsaw or Budapest, so that competing stores often are not close enough to one another to offer consumers real alternatives. Other credible influences are instances of collusion, and the monopolistic instincts of organized crime: In one instance recently reported to the Embassy, some U.S. businesspersons who ran a succcessful business in selling photocopy machines and other office equipment at low prices reported being approached by suspicious characters who recommended that they join a cartel and sell their product at higher prices.

Regional markets are also characterized by few alternatives in outlets and little competition on price. While the market for a given imported product in Moscow or St.Petersburg may be characterized by the availability of several competing import and domestic brands, heavy advertising, consumer awareness and widespread price competition, the market for the same product in Omsk or Tomsk may differ markedly. Also, although price competition is limited in Russia compared to other countries, consumer appeal of high-priced products is very weak.

AFTER-SALE SERVICE, TRAINING AND CUSTOMER SUPPORT

After-sales service, training and customer support can be a major competitive advantage -- or disadvantage -- for U.S. firms entering the Russian market. Russian manufacturers even today are known in Russia for their almost complete lack of attention to post-sale service. For many lower-cost items, Russian buyers are accustomed to buying more of an item than they need, in order to have a supply of spare parts for do-it-yourself repairs. Similarly, Russian buyers of sophisticated equipment of all types -- from computers and process controls to medical equipment to mining equipment -- are interested in the availability of training, as their employees may never have used particular products or brands before. U.S. firms able and willing to offer even rudimentary training and support for products, particularly in remote sites, can gain a big advantage over domestic competitors. However, companies not willing to make this commitment may find themselves at a distinct disadvantage to European (or in the Far East, Korean, Taiwanese and Japanese) competitors, whose proximity affords them advantages in providing training and service.

SELLING TO THE GOVERNMENT

Regional and local authorities are potential customers for U.S. suppliers. For example, the Russian Ministry of Health and the country's more than 100 regional government administrations often buy pharmaceuticals and medical equipment to distribute to hospitals, clinics and institutes under their jurisdiction. Since local governments no longer receive subsidies from the federal government, they now have the flexibility to make purchasing decisions based on local factors and contacts. However, despite the potential for government purchases, Russia□s current fiscal situation limits the role of public-sector customers: due to the budget crunch, Russian federal agencies have been assured of receiving no more than 75 percent of their originally-authorized budgets for fiscal year 1998. Many regional governments are in no better shape, and in some depressed regions, are even worse off than the federation government in terms of spending ability.

State procurement of foodstuffs has a long tradition. The Federal Food Corporation (FFC) was created in 1997 to buy food for large cities, the far north, the military, the Interior Ministry and for emergencies. Under funding and mismanagement hampered the FFC's ability to fulfill its mandate. After being accused of misspending $460 million in its first year of operation, the FFC was replaced by a new Federal Agency for Food Market Regulations. The new agency issues tenders for procurement of foodstuffs, rather than engaging in direct purchasing, but the program remains under funded.

The Russian procurement regime is based on a law passed in December 1994. Russian officials have sought to make the law compatible with WTO standards and note that it does not prevent market access by foreign enterprises. Presidential Decree 305 of April 8, 1997 attempted to clarify the law, make the process more transparent and based on open tendering. On the other hand, the 1994 law gives preference to domestic suppliers and allows the federal government to dictate supply in certain cases. Decree 305 has not been followed up with effective legislation, which remains in a draft stage. Though it is too early to evaluate the effect of this decree -- in large part because Russian government agencies at all levels have lacked resources for significant purchases during recent years -- it is possible that foreign companies will be better able to compete for contracts previously beyond their reach.

TAXATION

Russian and foreign products alike face a 20-percent Value Added Tax upon sale in Russia (although a lower VAT of 12 percent applies for a few basic food items and children☐s necessities), so U.S. exporters should factor this into their pricing policies. Regional or municipal taxes may also apply to some transactions for some goods and services, and federal excise taxes are particularly stiff for alcoholic beverages and tobacco products.

Companies which move beyond strictly exporting into the realm of representative offices and direct investment are subject to a wide, rapidly-changing array of taxes at federal and local levels. Russian tax laws and regulations are often ambigiuous and inconsistently interpreted by authorities. Among many Russian and some foreign firms, tax evasion is common, nursing a perception among companies which respect tax laws that they are disproportionately scrutinized by Russian tax authorities simply because they have demonstrated capacity and willingness to pay. Western firms operating here are often surprised to learn that many business deductions common to the U.S. or the EU do not exist or are tightly circumscribed here (although, with proper documentation, U.S. companies may be eligible for exemption from some Russian taxes on income which is also taxed in the United States, under a bilateral treaty on avoidance of double-taxation). Although foreign firms have successfully appealed tax disputes to the courts, officials have been slow to respect court rulings. Penalties for underpayment can be draconian (often assessed at 100 percent or more of the total tax due), and a company's accounts can be frozen relatively quickly. Tax regulations and the officials who enforce them generally fail to differentiate between criminal intent versus honest errors when levying penalties.

Some measures have been taken to reduce tax burdens, including elimination of the Excess Wage Tax (from January) and exemption of inter-company loans from Value Added Tax (from April). In 1997, the Russian Government re-submitted legislation to the Duma that would comprehensively overhaul the tax system: it would lower the number of applied taxes (currently about 130) to around 30, and permit the expanded deduction of expenses from profits tax. President Yeltsin□s July 1998 veto of a law that would have lowered the corporate profits tax from 35 to 30 percent was a setback for business. Besides corporate taxes, U.S. businesspersons working in Russia are subject to Russia□s personal income tax, depending on the nature of their income and the duration of their work in Russia during a given tax year.

In 1998, Russia's drive to crack down on tax deadbeats and increase collections under pressure of Russia's budget deficit has spawned numerous anecdotal accounts of what Western companies regard as harrassment by federal and local tax inspectors and Russia's Federal Tax Police. Firms are advised to familiarize themselves with Russian tax requirements, and companies with tax questions should seek the counsel of professional tax specialists who are experienced in Russia.

NEED FOR LOCAL ATTORNEYS, ACCOUNTANTS AND OTHER SERVICES

In Russia, commercial regulations are contained in thousands of presidential, governmental and ministerial decrees. Often, these decrees and laws overlap or conflict. Determining tax obligations is a tedious task. Russian accounting rules differ markedly from Western standards, and while the Russian Government has made coversion to International Accounting Standards a priority, the process is at an early stage. U.S. firms should use experienced, locally-based (Western or Russian) specialists familiar with issues faced by Western firms operating in Russia. The Commercial Sections at the U.S. Embassy and consulates maintain and can make available upon request lists of local attorneys and accounting firms.

While professional services in Russia are expensive, companies which shun this investment from the outset of their work here do so at their own peril. In Russia□s commercial arena, when tax and legal problems are concerned, an ounce of prevention can be worth a pound of cure. Seeking seasoned advice early on can save both aggravation and money down the road.

TRADE REGULATIONS IMPORTANT FOR BUSINESS ACTIVITY

For additional analytical, business and investment opportunities information,
please contact Global Investment & Business Center, USA
at (202) 546-2103. Fax: (202) 546-3275. E-mail: rusric@erols.com
Global Business E-Books on Line: http://world.mirhouse.com

TRADE BARRIERS

In 1994, import duties were increasing to a trade-weighted average of 11 percent. In March 1997 these rates were revised to raise the floor (except for a small list of zero-duty goods) to five percent and lower the ceiling (except for a few luxury goods) to 30 percent. In , the Government raised tariffs on alcoholic drinks and chicken, resulting in an average weighted tariff of 14 percent, as calculated by the IMF. A three-percentage point tariff increase on all imports was enacted in July 1998 as a revenue-enhancing measure. Although this import surcharge has been presented as a temporary measure, it is unclear when it might be revoked.

Besides tariffs, there are two other types of charges applied to imports: excise tax and value-added-tax (VAT). Excise tax applies to a number of luxury goods, alcohol, cigarettes and autos, and varies from 20 percent to 570 percent on a price- exclusive basis. The VAT rate is now 20 percent, with the exception of foodstuffs (for which VAT is 12 percent), and is applied to the import price plus tariff plus excise tax.

CUSTOMS VALUATION

Customs duties are payable on the customs value of goods in hard currency or rubles at the current exchange rate. The customs value is generally considered to be the CIF price of the goods imported. A customs processing fee of 0.15 percent of the goods☐ actual cost is also levied. According to customs regulations, customs processing should take no longer than one month. If goods are refused by Russian Customs, regulations call for their return to the country of origin.

IMPORT LICENSES

Import licenses are required for importation of various goods, including ethyl alcohol and vodka, combat and sporting weapons, self-defense articles, explosives, military and ciphering equipment, radioactive materials and waste including uranium, strong poisons and narcotics, and precious metals, alloys and stones. Most import licenses are issued by the Russian Ministry of Foreign Economic Relations and Trade (MinFERT) or its regional branches, and controlled by the State Customs Committee. Licenses for sporting weapons and self-defense articles are issued by the Interior Ministry.

RUSSIAN EXPORT CONTROLS

Presidential Decree 245 of March 1997 lifted the need for MinFERT permission to export "strategically important raw materials," such as oil and gas, non-ferrous metals, fertilizers, cellulose, grain, fish products, and electric power. The decree also abolished the list of "special exporters." However, export of oil and gas is controlled in a practical sense by the Ministry of Fuel and Energy's granting of access to the export pipeline. Also, weapons, military equipment and dual-use materials and technology continue to require export licenses. Exports of "strategically important raw materials" still require registration with MinFERT.

UNITED STATES EXPORT CONTROLS

Certain high-technology or dual-use (civilian and military) products are be subject to United States Government export restrictions, possibly including requirements for pre-license chacks and/or post-shipment verifications. In addition, in July 1998, President Clinton banned U.S. exports to seven Russian enterprises suspected of collaboration with Iran in the development of ballistic missile and/or nuclear weapons capabilities. Prospective exporters with questions are advised to contact the Export Counseling Division of the U.S. Department of Commerce Bureau of Export Administration (contact information is found in Appendix E of this report).

IMPORT/EXPORT DOCUMENTATION

Importers are required to complete a Russian customs freight declaration for every item imported. The declaration form consists of 54 paragraphs and should be completed in the Russian language for presentation to Customs authorities. Certificates of origin and conformity (see "Product Standards" below) should also be presented at customs. Exporters are required to complete an export declaration and, if necessary, present the appropriate export license at customs. In addition, currency control authorities require the issuance of a "passport" for both exports and imports to ensure that hard currency earnings are repatriated to Russia and transfers of hard currency payments for imports is for goods actually received and properly valued.

TEMPORARY ENTRY

Temporary imports by foreign companies which are accredited with Russian government authorities are exempt from customs duties. This applies to goods imported only for company use and for one year only. Companies not accredited with Russian government authorities are charged 3 percent of the total cost of the product on a monthly basis. In this case, total cost equals original product price plus all import taxes.

PRODUCT STANDARDS

Many products imported for sale into the Russian Federation are required to have a certificate of conformity issued by the Russian State Standards Committee (GOSSTANDART). GOSSTANDART tests and certifies products according to Russian Government standards, rather than other widely-accepted international standards (e.g., the ISO-9000 system). GOSSTANDART and its authorized agents are the chief sources for certification in Russia. However, other agencies are involved in certification of certain products, including the Ministry of Agriculture (food products), the Ministry of

Health (medical devices and pharmaceuticals), the State Communications Committee (telecommunications equipment and services), the State Mining and Industrial Inspectorate GOSGORTECHNADZOR (equipment for the mining, oil and gas industries) and others.

Testing protocols from the IECEE (electrical equipment) and the IECQ (electrical components), both of which fall under the International Electrotechnical Commission, from Underwriters Laboratories, and other bodies are accepted by GOSSTANDART and help to expedite certification by the Russian agency. The certificate of conformity is valid for 3 years and must accompany every shipment. Copies of the certificate are acceptable if original seals of the U.S. company holding the original certificate accompany the copy. Russian retailers are obliged to have on hand certificates for all imported products sold in their stores; violation of this requirement can bring penalties of up to the equivalent of $10,000.

PRODUCT LABELING

New regulations on labeling for non-food products came into force on July 1, 1998, augmenting food labelling requirements which took effect previously. Companies are advised to check their compliance with these requirements before shipping products. Regulations can be obtained from Russia□s State Committee on Standardization and Metrology, also known as Gosstandart (see contact information in Appendix E).

FREE TRADE ZONES/WAREHOUSES

There are no actual free trade zones in Russia. There are some free economic zones designed to encourage investments in specific areas, as well as free customs zones and free warehouses. Customs duties do not apply in free customs zones and free warehouses. Some production and wholesale transactions can take place within these zones, but not retail sales. The storage period is not limited. Free customs zones and free warehouses are located in customs areas (airports, seaports, railway and truck terminals).

MEMBERSHIP IN FREE TRADE ARRANGEMENTS

Russia does not participate currently in any free trade arrangements, although it is attempting to finalize a customs union with members of the CIS. Russia has an association agreement with the European Union (effective December 1997), proposes to join the World Trade Organization, and currently receives MFN treatment and GSP status from the United States.

For additional analytical, business and investment opportunities information,
please contact Global Investment & Business Center, USA
at (202) 546-2103. Fax: (202) 546-3275. E-mail: rusric@erols.com
Global Business E-Books on Line: http://world.mirhouse.com

TRADE AND PROJECT FINANCING

BANKING SYSTEM

After private banks were allowed beginning in the late 1980s, their number in Russia reached a peak of over 2,500 in 1997. Although there are over 1,600 licensed banks, the sector has been in a period of consolidation since mid-1997. Bank lending has been limited, due to weak credit analysis, lack of international accounting practices and ineffective bankruptcy laws. Almost 23 percent of the financial institutions are rated in critical condition, and while these banks account for only 2.9 percent of total banking assets, there is growing concern that a devaluation could undermine many smaller, weaker banks in Russia, along with a few of the larger ones.

Russian banks remain small by world standards (Sberbank, the largest, had a capital base of $1.3 billion in January , ranking it below the world's top 500 banks). Most Russian banks are much smaller; about 80 percent have capital of only $1 million or less, and only 4 percent have capital greater than $5 million. The large majority of small banks are reliant on highly specialized transactions or perform treasury functions for small enterprises. The largest banks offer a full range of modern banking services. However, commercial lending remains a small share of business, and long-term lending (over 1 year) accounts for less than 10 percent of credits. Most business is focused on trading of various types of securities, foreign exchange dealing, and to a lesser degree in project and trade finance. Almost 800 banks have a license to deal in foreign exchange, including 270 banks which possess a general license.

The relative stability of the ruble, lower inflation and falling yields in government securities market have limited commercial banks' profit-making opportunities during the past few years. At the same time, capital inadequacy, a continuing enterprise payment arrears problem, real estate problems, and a pervasive lack of banking experience have put strains on the banking system and prompted predictions of a major shakeout in the industry. Based on past experience, few creditors of failed banks recover much, if any of their deposits.

In 1993, Citibank and Chase Manhattan Bank became the first U.S. banks to receive general licenses to open subsidiaries in Russia. The new commercial banking bill, which took effect in January , explicitly permits foreign banks to establish full-service subsidiaries in Russia, though it gives the Central Bank of Russia (CBR) the ability to use reciprocity as a criteria for granting approval. Republic National Bank of New York has taken advantage of the new law to obtain a license and recently began full-service operations. More recently, American Express has received permission to open a representative office in Russia.

CURRENCY CONTROL AND REGULATION ISSUES

Regulations that took effect in January 1994 ban the use of foreign currency in cash transactions. Under these regulations, businesses in Russia are no longer permitted to accept cash payments in dollars or other hard currency. Non-cash transactions (e.g. credit/debit cards and checks) are not affected by the new regulations, so establishments that previously accepted payment via credit cards continue to do so. Stores that sell imported goods are still allowed to mark prices in dollars. At the time of purchase clerks convert the dollar price into rubles. Through the exchange rate they employ, merchants pass on the additional costs they will incur when they convert the rubles back into hard currency to restock inventories. Russian resident entities are still required to convert 50 percent of their foreign-currency revenues from exports into rubles. The foreign currency must be sold through MICEX or authorized foreign exchange dealers.

In an effort to limit outflow of capital, the CBR introduced a computerized export control system to monitor the flow of goods out of the country and the flow of hard currency back in. The system, which unites for the first time banking and export controls, requires exporters to obtain a special "passport" from a commercial bank, which enters the trade in a computer database. Customs agents register the actual export of the goods in the database and the commercial bank completes the cycle by entering receipt of the payment. Strategic exports, including energy and several types of metals, were subject to the new regime as of January 1, 1994. The system took effect for all other types of goods on March 1, 1994.

Effective January 1, , the CBR, in an effort to disrupt the use of illegitimate contracts for imports into Russia (and resulting capital flight from Russia), instituted an "import passport" system in addition to the already existing export control system. The system requires issuance of a "passport" by the importer's bank for payment against a specific import contract. The importer will have 180 days either to document the entry of the goods with the Russian Customs Service or return the hard currency issued in payment. Failure to comply with this regulation may make the importer liable for a hard currency penalty in the amount of the payment.

GENERAL FINANCING AVAILABILITY

The financing environment in Russia continues to improve with the growing Westernization of the economy; however, high domestic interest rates continue to limit Russian enterprises□ access to working capital. While the Russian banking system as a whole is inexperienced in project financing, a number of Western investment banks and venture funds are operating locally. In addition, a number of bilateral and multilateral financing programs provide more opportunities for traders and investors. The use of limited recourse project financing remains hampered by the immaturity of commercial legislation, including contract enforcement, asset title, the rights of debt and equity holders, performance responsibility of contractors and dispute settlement, among others.

For additional analytical, business and investment opportunities information, please contact Global Investment & Business Center, USA at (202) 546-2103. Fax: (202) 546-3275. E-mail: rusric@erols.com Global Business E-Books on Line: http://world.mirhouse.com

HOW TO FINANCE EXPORTS; METHODS OF PAYMENT

Companies new to exporting to Russia should insist on payment in advance for goods and services. This is, in fact, the normal procedure in Russia for most transactions. Letters of credit are issued by Russian banks only in those cases where the Russian customer can deposit the requisite funds in its account ahead of time, and Western banks generally will only confirm letters of credit on that basis as well. Once a firm has established a strong relationship with a Russian trading partner, the U.S. firm may consider extending short-term credit as a way to bolster sales volume. This should be done with caution, and after careful evaluation.

For some large transactions, where up-front payment from Russian buyers may be impractical, financing may be provided by a bank, export credit agency or venture fund. In cases where lease transactions are appropriate, exporters should insist on three to four months' lease payment upon delivery.

Perhaps as many as twenty private Russian banks now offer forfaiting and factoring services. However, the volume and value of transactions using these techniques have yet to attain levels at which they are either profitable or self-sustaining. Given the endemic non-liquidity in the Russian economy, cross-border leasing may become an important alternative to export sales. At present, less than five percent of imported equipment is leased, including equipment for the aerospace, energy, transportation, pharmaceutical, forestry and fishing industries.

COUNTERTRADE AND PROMISSORY NOTES

Because of low liquidity throughout the Russian economy, many U.S. and other foreign companies which pursue business here are surprised to learn that, in some industries and regions, upwards of seventy or eighty percent of economic activity is conducted on a non-cash basis. In many transactions, goods or services are sold for other goods which can be used directly
-- or more typically, sold -- by the original seller, who may have better access to cash-paying third-party customers than the original customer which made the payment-in-goods. While such barter deals can be more complex than cash transactions, U.S. firms should not dismiss them out-of-hand, for they can be just as profitable, and can help a company win a market foothold which it might not otherwise obtain. As in cash transactions, however, companies are advised to stay closely engaged in all aspects of the deal, to ensure that the payer meets commitments on schedule.

Promissory notes (in Russian, veksels), denominated in rubles, are often offerred by Russian companies or government entities in lieu of cash. While many veksels are issued by reliable companies, others are issued by firms with no credit records, or worse. U.S. companies are advised not to accept promissory notes as direct payment, but may find it worthwhile to rely on Russian banks or ⬜veksel brokers⬜ as intermediaries who will accept the final risk of the promissory notes and ensure that the U.S. exporter is paid in cash.

THE U.S. EXPORT-IMPORT BANK

The U.S. Eximbank initially began lending to support U.S. exports to Russia in 1992, offering loans based on sovereign guarantees from the Russian Government. With Russia's tightening budget constraints increasingly limiting the Russian Government's willingness and ability to offer sovereign guarantees over the past several years, Eximbank has sought more creative ways to finance transactions. Eximbank's Oil and Gas Framework Agreement relied on pledges of exported oil to guarantee loans, and Exim has supported eight transactions for the oil sector, worth more than $1 billion. Russia's Gazprom withdrew from a similar arrangemnet in 1997, citing concerns over possible U.S. sanctions. Eximbank has also explored cooperatitve financing with major Russian banks on a small scale, and is also considering work with local governments in Moscow and St.Petersburg. Companies which wish to investigate whether Eximbank financing may be available for particular transactions should contact Eximbank directly (contact information is found in Appendix E of this report).

PARTIAL LIST OF PRIVATE COMMERCIAL BANKS

The Russian banking system is undergoing a period of change, during which significant disruptions may occur. The Financial Institutions Development Project (FIDP), financed by loans from the World Bank and the EBRD and grants from the European Union and the Japanese Government, aims to promote a stable and efficient banking system. The FIDP is administered by representatives of the Russian Ministry of Finance, the CBR, the Ministry of Economy, and the Council of Ministers. Banks are "accredited" to the FIDP based on recommendations of the World Bank and EBRD, and an analysis of bank financial statements prepared according to International Accounting Standards (IAS) by one of the major international accounting firms resident in Russia. While the information accumulated in the accreditation process is confidential, any foreign firm wishing to establish a banking relationship with an FIDP bank is free to request copies of their IAS financial statements. The following banks are currently accredited by the FIDP, and should be able to provide IAS financial statements prepared by Western auditors upon request:

Moscow Banks: Alpha Bank, Bank Vozrozhdenie, Inkombank, Konversebank, Kredit Moskva, Moscow Industrial Bank, Avtobank, Bank Imperial, Mezhkombank, Bank Menatep, Mosbusinessbank, Uneximbank, Stolichniy Savings Bank, Bank Moskovskiy Delovoi Mir, Most Bank, Neftekhimbank, Probusinessbank, Rossiskiy Kredit and Toribank.

Regional Banks: Bank Petrovskiy (St. Petersburg), Promstroibank (St. Petersburg), Bank St. Petersburg (St. Petersburg), Dalrybbank (Vladivostok), Dalnevostochniy Bank (Vladivostok), Nizhnegorodskiy Bankisrskiy Dom (Nizhny Novgorod), Uralpromstroibank (Yekaterinburg), Omskpromstroibank (Omsk), Investbank (Kaliningrad), Bashprombank (Ufa) and Kuzbassotzbank (Kemerovo).

BUSINESS TRAVEL

BUSINESS CULTURE AND CUSTOMS

One challenging aspect of doing business here is bridging the substantial cultural gulf between Russians and Americans. Russian business culture is different, and visitors should not assume that Russians with who they are dealing have adopted or understood American business practice. For example:

-Russian decision-making is still highly centralized in most organizations.

-While Americans prefer to base their business relationships on legally-binding contracts, many Russians still doubt the value of their business laws and courts. In contrast, many Russian business dealings are based on strong personal relationships, with contracts considered merely a formality.

-Many Russians want to keep wealth and business deals secret.

-Westerners may think "win-win," while Russians may think "win-lose."

TRAVEL ADVISORY AND VISAS

The State Department issues travel advisories when political unrest warrants. Travel to Chechnya and surrounding regions is extremely dangerous due to continued political tension in the area. Two U.S. citizens have disappeared in Chechnya and remain missing; and local separatists have taken hostages on several occasions. Public gatherings and demonstrations occur frequently in Russia, particularly in Moscow. Although such demonstrations are usually peaceful, travelers are urged to exercise caution in areas where large groups are gathered.

Travelers may need to cross great distances, especially in Siberia and the Far East, to obtain services from Russian Government organizations, the U.S. Embassy in Moscow or U.S. consulates in St. Petersburg, Yekaterinburg or Vladivostok.

All Americans traveling to or transiting through Russia by any means of transportation must have a passport and visa. Travelers who arrive without a passport or entry visa may be subject to large fines, days of processing requirements imposed by Russian officials, and/or immediate departure by route of entry (at the traveler's expense).

For additional analytical, business and investment opportunities information, please contact Global Investment & Business Center, USA at (202) 546-2103. Fax: (202) 546-3275. E-mail: rusric@erols.com Global Business E-Books on Line: http://world.mirhouse.com

Visas, other than for transit purposes, are issued based on support from a Russian individual or organization - the sponsor. It is very important to know who your sponsor is and how he or she can be contacted, as Russian law requires the sponsor to apply for replacement, extension or changes to your visa. The U.S. Embassy and Consulates cannot act as a sponsor. Tourists should contact their tour company or hotel in advance for information on visa sponsorship.

All foreigners must have an exit visa to depart. For short stays, the exit visa is issued along with the entry visa. For longer stays, the exit visa must be obtained by the sponsor after the traveler's arrival. All travelers who spend more than three days in Russia must register their visa through their hotel or sponsor. Visitors who overstay their visa's validity, even for one day, or neglect to register their visa, may be prevented from leaving. Errors in dates or other information on the visa can occur, and it is helpful to have someone who reads Russian check the visa before departing the United States. Travelers should have all points of entry and all itinerary points in the Russian Federation printed on their visa, in order to avoid potential difficulties in registering their visas and lengthy delays in travel. Due to the possibility of random document checks by police, U.S. citizens should carry their original or photocopies of the passports and registered visas. Failure to provide proper documentation can result in detention and/or heavy fines.

Americans can receive assistance from the Russian Embassy□s Consular Division. The Consulate moved in early 1998, and is now located at 2641 Tunlaw Road, NW, Washington, DC, 20007. The Russian Consulate can be reached at (202) 939-8907 or fax 202-483-7579. Travelers can also receive assistance from the Russian Consulates in New York, San Francisco or Seattle.

Russian Holidays

January 1	**--New Year's Day**
January 7	**--Christmas (Orthodox)**
March 8	**--International Women's Day**
May 1	**--International Labor Day**
May 2	**--Spring Day**
May 9	**--World War II Victory Day**
June 12	**--Independence Day**
November 7	**--Revolution Day**
December 12	**--Constitution Day**

When holidays fall on weekends, Russian authorities announce during the week prior to the holiday whether the holiday will be celebrated on the preceding Friday or following Monday.

For additional analytical, business and investment opportunities information, please contact Global Investment & Business Center, USA at (202) 546-2103. Fax: (202) 546-3275. E-mail: rusric@erols.com Global Business E-Books on Line: http://world.mirhouse.com

TRANSPORTATION

Air travel within Russia is occasionally erratic, but is increasingly on-schedule, and the overall quality of service continues to improve. Russian-based airlines (such as Transaero) certified to operate internationally usually meet higher standards than domestic-only carriers. Moscow has four major airports which ring the city. Most international flights enter Moscow through Sheremetyevo II, although Transaero has a direct flight to Sheremetyevo I from Los Angeles. Travelers may continue to other Russian cities from any of the other three airports. Travel time to the departure airport can be as much as an hour and a half from Sheremetyevo II, and ample time must be allowed for passport control, customs clearance and baggage retrieval. St. Petersburg's airport (Pulkovo) has two terminals: Pulkovo I (domestic flights) and Pulkovo II (international flights).

A good way to get around Russia is by train. Between cities as close as St. Petersburg and Moscow, travelers can generally ride overnight trains, although occasional incidents of theft and other crimes on trains have made this mode less safe, especially for unaccompanied passengers. Inclement weather, erratic maintenance and a culture of aggressive driving make road conditions throughout Russia highly variable. Drivers and pedestrians should exercise extreme caution to avoid accidents, which are common. Traffic police sometimes stop motorists to extract cash "fines," and bandits occasionally prey on travelers, especially in isolated areas.

In Moscow and St. Petersburg, the metro (subway) is an efficient and inexpensive, if crowded, means of transport. Signs are in Russian, so it is helpful to learn the Cyrillic alphabet before you come. Marked taxis are increasingly present in Moscow, but not in other cities. US&FCS recommends that short-term business travelers consider renting a car and driver for extensive excursions, or hire taxis through their hotels for shorter jaunts.

CRIME AGAINST PERSONS

Recent police statistics for Moscow report an overall decline in crime, though drug-related crimes, murders, and kidnappings have increased, and street crime, sometimes violent, remains a continuing problem. The crime rate in Moscow is still below that of many major U.S. cities, and the rate is generally much lower in regions of Russia outside major cities (however, terrorist activity is a threat in and around Chechnya, including the adjacent republics of Dagestan and Ingushetia).

In Moscow, the most prevalent crime is theft, primarily from hotel rooms and train compartments, and by pickpockets and bands of street criminals. While there is little overt anti-American sentiment in Russia, Westerners are often targeted because of their perceived wealth, and street criminals operate in areas frequented by tourists and business travelers. Most foreigners are easily identifiable on Russian streets. In April 1998, a series of violent attacks in Moscow by gangs of skinheads against persons of

African and Asian origin led to issuance of a travel warning to American citizens cautioning them of the possibility of such attacks.

To reduce the risk of personal crime, U.S. businesspeople should be alert to their surroundings and guard belongings in hotels, restaurants and other high-density tourist areas. Do not assume that you can blend in on the street. Do not leave valuables in hotel rooms -- keep your passport and visa with you at all times, and retain copies in separate locations in case of loss or theft of the originals. Be alert to theft and assault in metro stations, on metro trains, and on inter-city trains (when traveling on overnight trains, secure the door to your compartment with some sort of jamming device). While many Muscovites flag private hacker vehicles for rides, this is a risky form of transport that should be avoided, and travelers are advised to use only marked taxis. Finally, American business people who utilize local services for banking, security and medical treatment should limit the information provided to the minimum required, as reports have been received indicating that some individuals working in these sectors have passed confidential credit/financial, banking and medical information to organized crime gangs who use it to make extortion threats against foreigners.

**For additional analytical, business and investment opportunities information,
please contact Global Investment & Business Center, USA
at (202) 546-2103. Fax: (202) 546-3275. E-mail: rusric@erols.com
Global Business E-Books on Line: http://world.mirhouse.com**

SUPPLEMENTS

STRATEGIC STATISTICS

KEY ECONOMIC INDICATORS

(Millions of U.S. Dollars unless otherwise indicated)

	1997	1998	1999 1/
Income, Production and Employment:			
Nominal GDP 2/	2,522	2,685	4,600
Real GDP Growth (pct)	0.6	-4.6	1.5
Per Capita Personal Income (US$)	922	610	466 4/
Labor Force (000s)	72,000	72,000	73,700
Unemployment Rate (pct)	11.2	13.3	12.4
Money and Prices (annual percent growth):			
Money Supply Growth (M2)	30.6	3.2	48.8 4/
Consumer Price Index (percent increase)	11	84.3	45.0
Exchange Rate (Ruble/US$ annual average)	5.785	9.705	24.429
Balance of Payments and Trade:			
Total Exports (FOB)	85.0	71.3	31.1 5/
Exports to U.S.	4.5	5.7	3.8 6/
Total Imports (CIF)	52.9	43.5	14.5 5/
Imports from U.S.	4.1	3.6	0.9 6/
Trade Balance	32.1	27.8	16.6 5/
Balance with U.S.	0.4	2.1	2.9 6/
Current Account	3.5	2.4	12.6
External Public Debt	123.5	147	159.7
Debt Service Payments/GDP (pct)	1.4	3.7	5.9 4/
Fiscal Deficit/GDP (pct)	6.7	3.2	3.8 5/
Gold and Foreign Exchange	17.8	12.1	11.8 3/

For additional analytical, business and investment opportunities information, please contact Global Investment & Business Center, USA at (202) 546-2103. Fax: (202) 546-3275. E-mail: rusric@erols.com Global Business E-Books on Line: http://world.mirhouse.com

Aid from U.S. (US$ millions) 7/	492	639.4	1,937.1
Aid from All Other Sources	N/A	N/A	N/A

1/ 1999 data has been provided for the last available period (9/99) unless otherwise noted. The Russian Ruble was re-denominated on January 1, 1998 by dropping three zeros off the value of the currency. All data in ruble terms have been adjusted to "new rubles" for comparability.
2/ Billions of Russian Rubles.
3/ Data for January-October 1999.
4/ Data for January-August 1999.
5/ Data for the period January-June 1999.
6/ U.S. Commerce Department data for the period January-August 1999.
7/ USG Assistance (by fiscal year) including food assistance, not including donated humanitarian commodities shipped by USG. Military assistance included $389.4 million in Department of Defense funds, largely for strategic weapons destruction programs, plus IMET and FMF programs, from which only $228,000 was spent in FY99.

SELECTED U.S. AND RUSSIAN CONTACTS

RUSSIAN GOVERNMENT AGENCIES:

*Ministry of Trade and Industry:
Yuri Dmitrievich Maslyukov, Minister-Designate
18/1, Ovchinnikovskaya Nab., Moscow
Tel: (095) 220-1064; Fax: (095) 220-1684, 231-9220
*Note: The Russian Government announced that in August 1998, the Ministry for Foreign Economic Relations and Trade would be abolished, and that some of its functions would be assumed by a new Ministry of Trade and Industry. Mr. Maslyukov was appointed by President Yeltsin in July 1998.

Ministry of Finance:
Mikhail Mikhailovich Zadornov, Minister of Finance
Ulitsa Ilyinka 9, Entrance 1, Moscow
Tel: (095) 298-9130; Fax: (095) 925-0889

Ministry of Fuel and Energy:
Sergei Vladimirovich Generalov, Minister of Fuels and Energy
7, Kitaigorodskiy Proyezd, Moscow 103074
Tel: (095) 220-4659; Fax: (095) 975-2045 (International Dept.)

Ministry of Agriculture and Food:
Viktor A. Semyonov, Minister of Agriculture and Food
Orlikov Pereulok, 1/11, Moscow
Tel: (095) 207-4243; Fax: (095) 207-8362

State Customs Committee:
Vitaly G. Draganov, Chairman, State Customs Committee

1a, Komsomolskaya Ploshchad, Moscow 107842
Phone: (095) 975-1918; Fax: (095) 975-4823

State Committee for Standardization, Metrology and Certification
(GOSSTANDART):
Gennady Petrovich Voronin, Chairman
9, Leninskiy Prospekt, Moscow 117049
Phone: (095) 236-6208, -4044; Fax: (095) 236-6231, 237-6032

Russian Copyright Agency:
Georgiy Artashessovich Ter-Gazariyants, Chairman of the Board;
Vadim Serafimovich Dunin, Head of Foreign Relations Department
6a, Bolshaya Bronnaya Ul., Moscow 103670
Phone: (095) 203-2996, -4599; Fax: (095) 200-1263

Committee for Patents and Trademarks (Rospatent):
Alexander Dmitrievich Korchagin, General Director
2/6 Cherkasskiy Pereulok, Moscow
Tel: (095) 206-6203; Fax: (095) 923-4093

State Investment Corporation:
Yuriy Vladimirovich Petrov, Chairman
35, Myasnitskaya Ul., Moscow 103685
Phone: (095) 925-6796; Fax: (095) 207-6936
Regional Governments:

Moscow City Administration:
Iosif N. Ordzhonikidze,
Deputy Mayor and Minister for External Relations
13 Tverskaya Ulitsa, 103032, Moscow
Tel: 095-229-6360; Fax: (095) 883-6208

Moscow Registration Chamber:
Vladimir Ivanovich Sobolyev, Chairman
Mokhovaya Ul., 11, Bld. 8-E, Moscow 103009
Tel/Fax: (095) 202-2787;

Roald Nestorovich Lebedinskiy,
Dir., Registration/Accreditation (information in English)
Tel: (095) 132-0500

Tatyana Kuzminichna Nikanorkina, Expert
for Registration of Companies with Foreign Capital
(information in Russian)

Tel: (095) 202-4042

St. Petersburg City Administration:
Gennady I. Tkachev, Chairman, External Relations Committee
1, Smolniy, St. Petersburg 193060
Phone: (812) 276-1204; Fax: (812) 276-1633

Ilya I. Klebanov, First Vice Governor
Chairman, Cmte. on Economy and Industrial Policy
16 Voznesensky Prospect, St. Petersburg, Russia 190000
Phone: (812) 315-5152; Fax: (812) 319-9292.

Igor Yu. Artemiev, First Vice Governor
Chairman, Committee on Finance
16 Voznesensky Prospect, St. Petersburg, Russia 190000
Phone: (812) 319-9308; Fax: (812) 319-9967.

Leninrad Oblast Administration:
Inna L. Bigotskaya, Chief of Protocol Department
External Relations Committee,
67, Suvorovskiy Prospekt, St. Petersburg 193311
Phone: (812) 274-4859; Fax: (812) 274-2463.

Mark A. Vybornov, Chairman,
Committee on Foreign Economic Relations and Investments
67, Suvorovskiy Prospekt, St. Petersburg 193311
Phone: (812) 278-5587 or 274-4742; Fax: (812) 274-5986.

Yekaterinburg Oblast Administration:
Igor Ivanovich Arzyakov, Dir., Foreign Relations Department
1, Oktyabrskaya Ploshchad, Yekaterinburg 620031
Phone: (3432) 51-54-97, 58-96-56; Fax: (3432) 51-98-70

Yekaterinburg City Administration:
Vladimir I. Lomovtzev, Dir., Foreign Relations Department
1, Oktyabrskaya Ploshchad, Yekaterinburg 620031
Phone: (3432) 51-13-07, 51-43-83; Fax: (3432) 51-90-05

Primorskiy Territorial Administration:
Andrey Gennadyevich Zagumyonnov, Chairman
Committee for Foreign Economic Relations and Regional Trade
 of the Dept. for Foreign Economic Relations and Tourism
22 Svetlanskaya ulitsa, 690110, Vladivostok

Phone: (4232) 22-08-52
Fax: (4232) 22-10-19

Khabarovsk Territorial Administration:
Sergey I. Lopatin, Chief, Foreign Economic Relations Dept.
56 ul.K.Marksa, Khabarovsk
Phone/fax: (4212) 32-41-21

Sakhalin Regional Administration:
Vitaly Nikolaevich Elizariev, Director
Department of Foreign Economic Relations
32 Kommunisticheskiy prospect, "Sakhincenter", office 236
693000 Yuzhno-Sakhalinsk 693000
Phone: (4242) 72-74-94
Fax: (4242) 72-74-93; International fax: 7 509-95-1236

State Duma (Lower chamber of Parliament):

--Cmte. on Budget, Taxes, Banking and Finance:
Alexander Zhukov, Chairman
2, Georgiyevskiy Pereulok, Moscow
Tel: (095) 292-3618; Fax: (095) 292-5601

--Cmte. on Property, Privatization and Economic Activity:
Pavel Grigoryevich Bunich, Chairman
2, Georgiyevskiy Pereulok, Moscow
Tel: (095) 229-9559; Fax: (095) 229-6996

--Cmte. on Industry, Construction, Transport and Energy:
Vladimir Kuzmich Gusev, Chairman
2, Georgiyevskiy Pereulok, Moscow
Tel: (095) 292-0365; Fax: (095) 292-3763

TRADE ASSOCIATIONS/CHAMBERS OF COMMERCE IN RUSSIA:

American Chamber of Commerce in Russia (Amcham)
Scott M. Blacklin, President
Kosmodamianskaya Nab. 52, Building 1, 8th floor, Moscow
Phone: (095) 961-2141; Fax: (095) 961-2142

American Chmbr. of Commerce in Russia, St. Petersburg Chapter:
Slava Bytchkov, Executive Director
25, Nevsky pr., St. Petersburg, 191186
Tel: (812) 326-2590; Fax: (812) 326-2591

St. Petersburg International Business Association (SPIBA)
Anna Kessner, Executive Administrator
27, Naberezhnaya Moiki, 5th Floor, St. Petersburg, 191186
Tel: (812) 325-9091; Fax: (812) 325-9933

Vladivostok International Business Association (VIBA)
Andrew Wilson, President
c/o U.S. and Foreign Commercial Service, Vladivostok
32 Pushkin Street, Vladivostok, Russia 690000
Phone: (4232) 300-093; Fax: (4232) 300-092
e-mail: csvlad@online.ru

Council for Trade and Economic Cooperation (CIS-USA)
Boris Petrovich Alekseyev, President
3, Naberezhnaya Shevchenko, Moscow 121248
Phone: (095) 243-5514, -5470; Fax: (095) 230-2467

Russian Chamber of Commerce and Industry
Stanislav Alekseyevich Smirnov, President;
Yuriy Nikolayevich Denissenkov, Head,
Sergey B. Kulyba, Expert on Accreditation, Protocol Department
6, Ilyinka Ul., Moscow 103684
Phone: (095) 929-02-86,-60,-61,-62,-63; Fax: (095) 929-0356

Primorskiy Territory Chamber of Commerce
Vladimir Borisovich Brezhnev, Chairman
13a Okeanskiy prospekt, Vladivostok
Phone: (4232) 26-96-30
Fax: (4232) 22-72-26

Khabarovsk Territory Chamber of Commerce and Industry
Mikhail Kruglikov, President
113, Shevronova Ulitsa, Khabarovsk 680000
Phone: (4212) 33-03-11, 33-11-30; Fax: (4212) 33-03-12

U.S. GOVERNMENT PERSONNEL HANDLING BUSINESS ISSUES IN RUSSIA:

U.S. EMBASSY IN MOSCOW:

--John Peters, Minister Counselor for Commercial Affairs
U.S. and Foreign Commercial Service
Bolshaya Molchanovka 23/28, Moscow 121019
Phone: (095) 967-3414; Fax: (095) 967-3416
Satellite phone: 7 (502) 224-1105;
Satellite fax: 7 (502) 224-1106

--Michael Matera, Minister Counselor for Economic Affairs
21, Novinskiy Bulvar, Moscow 121099
Phone: (095) 956-4220; Fax: (095) 956-4146

--Asif Chaudry, Minister Counselor for Agricultural Affairs
21, Novinskiy Bulvar, Moscow 121099
Phone: (095) 956 4103; (502) 221 1245
Fax: (095) 975 2339; (502) 224 1356

--James Waller, Treasury Attache
21, Novinskiy Bulvar, Moscow 121099
Phone: (095) 956-4258; Fax: (095) 956-4146

--U.S. Agency for International Development
Office of Privatization and Economic Restructuring
U.S. Embassy, Moscow
21 Novinskiy Bulvar., Moscow 121099
Phone: (095) 956-4281

U.S. and Foreign Commercial Service, St. Petersburg
James McCarthy, Principal Commercial Officer
25, Nevsky prospekt., St. Petersburg, Russia 191186
Tel: (812) 326-2560; Fax: (812) 326-2561/62

American Business Center, St. Petersburg
Zhanna Agasieva, Assistant Manager
25, Nevsky prospekt, St. Petersburg, Russia 191186
Tel: (812) 326-2570; Fax: (812) 326-2571

U.S. and Foreign Commercial Service, Vladivostok
Richard Steffens, Principal Commercial Officer
32 Pushkin Street, Vladivostok, Russia 690000
Satellite phone/fax: (509) 851-1211
Phone: (4232) 300-093; Fax: (4232) 300-092
e-mail: csvlad@online.ru

American Business Center, Vladivostok
Inna Nazarova, Assistant Manager
2, Batareynaya Ul., Vladivostok
Satellite phone/fax: (509) 851-1212
Phone: (4232) 25-46-25; Fax: (4232) 25-46-61

U.S. Consulate-General in Yekaterinburg
Alexander Deyanov, Commercial Assistant
15A Gogol Street, Third Floor
Yekaterinburg, Russia
Phone: (3432) 564-619; Fax: (3432) 564-515
Phone: (3432) 564-736 (Foreign Commercial Service)

Federal Aviation Administration (FAA)
Dennis B. Cooper, Senior Representative
American Embassy, Brussels
27 Boulevard du Regent, B-1000 Brussels, Belgium
Phone: 322 508-2700; Fax: 322 230-06428
Phone: (095) 956-4036; Fax: (095) 956-4293

WASHINGTON-BASED U.S. GOVERNMENT CONTACTS FOR RUSSIA:

Business Information Service
 for the Newly Independent States (BISNIS)
Anne Grey, Director
U.S. Department of Commerce, Rm.7413, Washington, D.C. 20230
Phone: (202) 482-4655; Fax: (202) 482-2293

U.S. Export-Import Bank
David Fiore, Loan Officer
811 Vermont Avenue, N.W., Washington, D.C. 20571-0999
Phone: (202) 565-3815; Fax: (202) 565-3816

Overseas Private Investment Corporation
Peter Ballinger, Manager, NIS Investment Development
1100 New York Avenue, N.W., Washington, D.C. 20527

Phone: (202) 336-8618; Fax: (202) 408-5145

U.S. Trade and Development Agency
Daniel Stein, Regional Director
U.S. Department of State, SA-16, Rm.301
Washington, D.C. 20523-1602
Phone: (703) 875-4357; Fax: (703) 875-4009

U.S. Department of State, Office of Russian Affairs
Thomas K. Huffaker, Chief Economist
2201 C Street, N.W., Washington, D.C. 20520
Phone: (202) 647-6747; Fax: (202) 736-4710

U.S. Department of Commerce -- Market Access and Compliance
Russia and Independent States Division
Jack Brougher, Director,
U.S. Department of Commerce, Rm.3318, Washington, D.C. 20230
Phone: (202) 482-3952; Fax: (202) 482-3042

U.S. Agency for International Development
Office of Privatization and Economic Restructuring
Washington, D.C. 20523
Phone: (202) 736-4410

U.S. Department of Agriculture
Russian Area Officer
14th St. and Independence Avenue S.W., Washington, D.C. 20250
Phone: (202) 720-3080

U.S. Bureau of Export Administration
Export Counselling Division
U.S. Department of Commerce, Rm.3898, Washington, D.C. 20230
Phone: (202) 482-4811; Fax: (202) 482-3911

Special American Business Internship Training Program (SABIT)
Liesel Duhon, Director
U.S. Department of Commerce, Rm.3006, Washington, D.C. 20230
Phone: (202) 482-0073; Fax: (202) 482-4098

U.S.-Based Multipliers and International Organizations
with Interests in Russia:

U.S.-Russia Business Council
Eugene K. Lawson, President

1701 Pennsylvania Ave., N.W. Suite 650, Washington, D.C. 20006
Phone: (202) 956-7670; Fax: (202) 956-7674

Russian-American Chamber of Commerce
Deborah Palmieri, President
6200 South Quebec St., Suite 210, Englewood, Colorado 80111
Phone: (303) 689-8642; Fax: (303) 689-8762

Foundation for Russian-American Economic Cooperation
Carol Vipperman, President
1932 First Avenue, Suite 803
Seattle, WA 98101
Tel: (206) 443-1935; Fax (206) 443-0954

National Association of State Departments of Agriculture
Richard Kirchhoff, Executive Vice President
1156 15th Street, N.W. Suite 1020, Washington, D.C. 20005
Tel: (202) 296-9680; Fax: (202) 296-9686

The World Bank
Thomas Kelsey, U.S. Department of Commerce liaison
1818 H Street, NW, Washington, DC, 20433
Phone: (202) 458-0118; Fax: (202) 458-0118

International Finance Corporation (IFC)
Mark Constantine
1850 Eye Street, NW, Washington, DC 20433
Phone: (202) 473-9331; Fax: (202) 676-1513
Moscow Office: Roger Gale
6, Neglinnaya St., Moscow
Tel: 7-095-928-5328; Fax: 7-095-927-6832

International Bank for Reconstruction and Development
U.S. Department of Commerce Liaison
  to the U.S. Executive Director's Office
1818 H Street, N.W., Room D-13004
Washington, D.C. 20433
Phone: (202) 458-0118; Fax: (202) 477-2967

Office of Multilateral Development Banks,
  U.S.& Foreign Commercial Service
U.S. Department of Commerce, Room H-1107
Washington, D.C. 20230
Phone: (202) 482-3399; Fax: (202) 273-0927

European Bank for Reconstruction and Development (EBRD)
One Exchange Square, London EC2A 2EH, United Kingdom
Dean Peterson, U.S. Department of Commerce Liaison
Tel: 011-44-171-338-6569; Fax: 011-44-171-338-6487

MARKET RESEARCH

A comprehensive and up-to-date listing of market research reports prepared by the U.S. & Foreign Commercial Service in Russia is available on the NTDB (National Trade Data Bank). The following listing is of key publications from 1998, and publications under consideration for 1999:

SECTOR ANALYSES (ISAS):

Advertising
Agricultural Machinery and Tractors
Automotive Aftermarket
Aviation Industry
Computer and Office Equipment
Construction Equipment in Northwest Russia
Construction Materials and Services on Sakhalin Island
Construction Materials in the Urals Region
Consumer Goods (General)
Consumer Appliances
Cosmetics
Electronic Components
Financial Services and Insurance
Food Processing and Packaging Equipment
Food Processing Equipment in the Urals Region
Furniture Manufacturing in the Urals Region
Hotel and Restaurant Equipment
Internet Services
Laboratory Diagnostic Equipment
Metallurgy in the Urals Region
Meters and Controls for Heating and Ventilation
Mining Equipment Interior Building Products
Packaging Equipment
Petroleum Markets (Retail)
Pharmaceuticals
Satellite Equipment and Services
Transportation Services
Travel and Tourism Services (Russian Far East)

COMMODITY REPORTS AND MARKET BRIEFS:

Annual Marketing Plan Information Report (annual)
Livestock (annual and semi-annual)
Poultry (annual)
Fresh Deciduous Fruit (annual)
Agricultural Situation Report (annual)
Seafood (annual)
Sugar (annual and semi-annual)
Foreign Buyer List Annual Report
Dairy (annual)
Planting Seeds (annual)
Forest Products (annual)
Grain & Feed (annual)
Oilseeds and Products (annual)
Cotton (annual)

PRODUCTS EXPORTED FROM RUSSIA

EXPORT PRODUCTS	COMPANY EXPORTER	INDUSTRY
agricultural equipment	TEMP	Metallurgy Industry. Machine-Building Industry. Power Industry
agricultural machinery	RUSICH	Metallurgy Industry. Machine-Building Industry. Power Industry.
aluminum	KANDALAKSHA ALUMINUM PLANT	Metallurgy
aluminum scrap, non-ferrous metal scrap	VOLGOVYATSKVTORTSVETMET	Metallurgy Industry. Machine-Building Industry. Power Industry
aluminum, copper alloy	VERKH-NEYVINSKIY PLANT OF NONFERROUS METALS	Metallurgy Industry. Machine-Building Industry. Power Industry.
Amino plast	KHIMPLAST	Textile industry
ammonium hydroxide, methanol, carbamate resin, ammonium nitrate	AKRON	Chemical Industry
asphalt paves	STROITELNIYE MASHINY I MEKHANIZMY	Machine Building Industry
appliances	NEFTEAVTOMATIKA	Metallurgy Industry. Machine-Building Industry. Power Industry.

aromatic principle	AROMASINTEZ	Chemical Industry
art crafts	IVKOLOR	Consumer Goods, Furniture, Household & Cultural Products
artificial corundum, ammonium chloride, sulfur anhydrite, ammonium sulfate	KORUND	Chemical, Pharmaceutical & Microbiology Industry
auto and tractor parts	MICHURINSK AUTO PARTS PLANT	Metallurgy Industry. Machine-Building Industry
auto parts	AVTOZAPCHAST	Metallurgy. Machine-Building Industry
auto parts	SMOLENSK ASSEMBLY PLANT	Machine Building Industry
auto parts	MICHURINSK PUMPS MANUFACTIRING PLANT	Metallurgy Industry. Machine-Building Industry
automatic control appliances	TSVET	Metallurgy Industry. Machine-Building Industry. Power Industry
base plates	LESNOYE	Forestry & Timber Processing Industry
basic matrix crystals	PROTON	Radio-Electronic Industry
bearings	IZHEVSK BEARING PLANT	Metallurgy Industry. Machine-Building Industry. Power Industry.
bicycles	VELOZAVOD	Metallurgy Industry. Machine-Building Industry. Power Industry
binoculars, medical equipment	SALAVAT PLANT OF OPTIC APPLIANCES	Metallurgy Industry. Machine-Building Industry. Power Industry.
biological preparation	MAYKOP MEDICAL & SPECIAL TECHNOLOGY PLANT	Chemical, Pharmaceutical & Microbiology Industry
biologicals	POKROVSKIY BIOLOGICALS MANUFACTURING PLANT	Food Industry. Tobacco Industry
blank metallurgical parts	BARRIKADY	Metallurgy. Machine-Building. Power Industry
boards	ZEYALES	Forestry & timber processing, Pulp & paper industry
boards	UOYAN LUMBER COMPANY	Forestry & timber processing industry. Pulp &

For additional analytical, business and investment opportunities information,
please contact Global Investment & Business Center, USA
at (202) 546-2103. Fax: (202) 546-3275. E-mail: rusric@erols.com
Global Business E-Books on Line: http://world.mirhouse.com

		paper industry. Publishing & printing industry
boards	RIKID-NT	Forestry & timber processing industry. Pulp & paper industry. Publishing & printing industry
boards	SEVERGAZLES	Forestry & Timber Processing Industry
boiler incrustation cleaning equipment	ZEVS-TEKHNOLOGII	Machine Building Industry
boilers	BORISOGLEBSK BOILER WORKS PLANT	Chemical, Pharmaceutical & Microbiology Industry
boilers, pumps	BIYSK BOILER MANUFACTURING PLANT	Metallurgy industry, Machine-building industry, Power industry
bolts & nuts	MAYKOPNORMAL	Forestry & Timber Processing Industry. Pulp & Paper Industry. Publishing & Printing Industry.
books	YANTARNIY SKAZ	Publishing & Printing Industry
books	ZAURALYE BUBLISHING COMPANY	Forrestry and timber processing industry. Pulp and paper industry. Publishing and printing industry
borers	SVERDLOV - MACHINE TOOL MANUFACTURING PLANT	Machine-Building Industry
boron, sodium borane	AVIABOR	Mining Industry
bottling and capping equipment, automatic packaging machines	PLANETA-NMZ	Machine-Building Industry
brakes	TRANSPNEVMATIKA	Metallurgy Industry. Machine-Building Industry. Power Industry
brandy	DERBENT COGNAC MANUFACTURING PLANT	Food & Food Processing Industry. Tobacco Industry
brochures, books	BICHURA REGIONAL PUBLISHING COMPANY	Forestry & timber processing industry. Pulp & paper industry. Publishing & printing industry
bronze cast	RENESANS	Metallurgy Industry. Machine-Building Industry. Power Industry.

brown coal	BORODINSKIY OPEN-CUT MINE	Mining industry
brown coal	VAKHRUSHEVUGOL	Mining Industry
bulbs	LISMA-BNIIS IMENI A.N. LODYGINA	Electrical Ingineering Industry
buses	KURGAN BUS MANUFACTURING PLANT	Metallurgy Industry. Machine-Building Industry. Power Industry.
buses	PCHELKA	Metallurgy Industry. Machine-Building Industry. Power Industry.
buses	PAVLOVSKIY AVTOBUS	Metallurgy Industry. Machine-Building Industry. Power Industry
buses, steel sheets	SEMYONOV FITTINGS MANUFACTURING PLANT	Metallurgy Industry. Machine-Building Industry. Power Industry
buses, trucks	SEMAR	Automobile Industry
butter	INSIDE	Food & Food Processing
butyl acetate, solvents	DMITRIYEVSKIY CHEMICAL PLANT	Chemical Industry
cabels	PROVOD	Metallurgy. Machine-Building. Power Industry
cables	RYBINSKKABEL	Electrical-Engineering Industry
calcium phosphate	FOSFATY	Mining Industry
candies	OZYORY FOOD ENTERPRISE	Food Industry. Tobacco Industry
canvas, flax fabric	VYAZNIKI FLAX PROCESSING PLANT	Textile Industry
caoutchouc	OMSKIY KAUCHUK	Chemical, pharmaceutical & microbiology industry
car & truck tires	VOLTAYR	Chemical, Pharmaceutical & Microbiology Industry
car engines, motorcycle parts	ZAVOLZHYE ENGINE PLANT	Metallurgy Industry. Machine-Building Industry. Power Industry
carbamide	VNESHTREIDINVEST	Mining Industry
carbon brashes, electrodes	ELEKTROUGLI	Electrical Engineering Industry
carboxymethyl cellulose	KAMSKIY	Chemical, pharmaceutical,

	CARBOXYLMETHYLCELLULO SE PLANT	and microbiology inndustry
cars	PATRIOT	Automobile Industry
cars	BRONTO	Metallurgy. Machine-Building Industry
cars	TYUMENNEFTESPECTRANS	Metallurgy industry, Machine-building industry, Power industry
casein	BELOGORSK DAIRY FACTORY	Food & tobacco industry
casein	MOLOKO	Food & Food Processing Industry. Tobacco Industry.
casein	PETMOL	Food & Food Processing Industry
casein	ZVENIGOVO DAIRY FACTORY	Food & Food Processing Industry. Tobacco Industry
casein	VYAZNIKI DAIRY PROCESSING PLANT	Food Industry. Tobacco Industry
casein, dry milk	NADEZHDA	Food & Food Processing Industry. Tobacco Industry.
casein, dry milk	SUZDAL DAIRY PLANT	Food Industry. Tobacco Industry
caterpillar-tracked sranes	CHELYABINSK MACHINERY PLANT	Metallurgy Industry. Machine-Building Industry. Power Industry.
cement slate shingles	VOLNA	Building materials industry
centrifugal pumps	KAMENSKIY METAL-WORKS PLANT	Metallurgy industry, Machine-building industry, Power industry
ceramic tiles	VELOR	Building Materials Industry
chains	KRASNIY YAKOR	Metallurgy Industry. Machine-Building Industry. Power Industry
champagne	KORNET	Food Industry. Tobacco Industry
champagne, vodka	NIZHNIY NOVGOROD CHAMPAGNE MANUFACTURING FACTORY	Food & Food Processing Industry. Tobacco Industry
chandeliers, glass products	ZAVOD KVARTSEVOGO STEKLA	Consumer Goods Industry
cheese, casein	ORENBURGMOLOKO	Food, food processing and tobacco industry

For additional analytical, business and investment opportunities information, please contact Global Investment & Business Center, USA at (202) 546-2103. Fax: (202) 546-3275. E-mail: rusric@erols.com Global Business E-Books on Line: http://world.mirhouse.com

chemical analysis equipment	SLAVGOROD RADIO APPLIANCES PLANT	Metallurgy industry, Machine-building industry, Power industry
chemical equipment	KOMSOMOLETS	Metallurgy Industry. Machine-Building Industry
chemical industry equipment	STARAYA RUSSA CHEMICAL MACHINERY BUILDING PLANT	Machine-Building Industry
chemical industry equipment	MORSHANSKKHIMMASH	Metallurgy Industry. Machine-Building Industry
chemikal fibers	KURSKKHIMVOLOKNO	Chemical, Pharmaceutical & Microbiology Industry
chrome leather	BOGORODSK LEATHER PROCESSING PLANT	Clothing Industry. Footwear & Tanning Industry
cigarettes	ALVIS	Food, food processing and tobacco industry
clothes	YUNONA TEXTILE FACTORY	Textile industry
clothes	DELFIN	Clothing Industry
clothes	KOVDORCHANKA	Clothing Industry
clothes	MAYAK	Clothing Industry. Footwear & Tanning Industry
clothes	RADUGA	Clothing Industry. Footwear & Tanning Industry
clothes	VOLZHANKA	Clothing Industry. Footwear & Tanning Industry.
clothes	ODEZHDA CLOTHING FACTORY	Clothing and footwear industry
clothes	ISKRA	Clothing Industry. Footwear Industry
clothing	RABOCHAYA ODEZHDA	Clothing Industry. Footwear Industry
coal	KUZBASRAZREZUGOL	Mining industry
coarse calico	ARKHIPOVKA WEAVING PLANT	Textile Industry
coarse calico	VYCHUGSKAYA MANUFACTURA	Textile Industry
coats, suits	ELEGANT	Clothing Industry. Footwear Industry
colophony, lumber	SVERDKHIMLES	Forrestry and timber processing industry. Pulp and paper industry.

For additional analytical, business and investment opportunities information, please contact Global Investment & Business Center, USA at (202) 546-2103. Fax: (202) 546-3275. E-mail: rusric@erols.com Global Business E-Books on Line: http://world.mirhouse.com

		Publishing and printing industry
combined fodder, oil cake	FERMER	Food & Food Processing Industry. Tobacco Industry.
communication equipment	ELECTRONIC EQUIPMENT RESEARCH LABORATORY	Metallurgy industry, Machine-building industry, Power industry
communication equipment	MIKROKOM	Chemical, Pharmaceutical & Microbiology Industry
compressors	KOMPRESSOR	Machine-Building Industry
compressors, gas turbines, steam turbines, steel cast	NEVMASHREGULIROVANIYE	Machine-Building Industry
computer parts	FOLKOM HOLDING-TSENTR	High-Tech Products, PC, Research
computer programes	ELVIS-PLYUS	High-Tech Products, PC, Research & Design Services
computers, home electric appliances	RYAZAN INDUSTRIAL-ENGINEERING PLANT	Electrical-Engineering Industry
concrete-mixing machines	TUYMAZY CONCRETE HAULERS MANUFACTURING PLANT	Metallurgy Industry. Machine-Building Industry. Power Industry.
condensers, air conditioners	GYUNTNER-IZH	Metallurgy Industry. Machine-Building Industry. Power Industry.
condensers, thyristors	UPI-REZONANS	Metallurgy Industry. Machine-Building Industry. Power Industry.
confectionary	KARAVAY	Food, food processing & tobacco industry
confectionary	NIZEGORODSKAYA KARAMEL	Food & Food Processing Industry. Tobacco Industry
construction glass	AMURENERGO	Metallurgy, machine-building & power industry
construction lime, molybdenum, coal	PRIARGUNSKOYE MINING COMPANY	Mining industry
construction tools	INSTRYMENT	Machine Building Industry
containers, dump cars, electrical loaders	VAGONOSTROITEL	Machine-Building Industry
control panel, technological prices control equipment	SMOLENSK NUCLEAR POWER PLANT	Power Industry

control panels	NOEZ	Metallurgy. Machine-Building. Power Industry
conveyer belts, rubber	KRASNIY TREUGOLNIK	Rubber & Plastic Industry
copper-nickel-zinc alloy plates	KIROV NONFERROUS METALS PROCESSING PLANT	Metallurgy Industry. Machine-Building Industry. Power Industry
corn starch	BORISOGLEBSK STARCH MANUFACTURING PLANT	Food Industry. Tobacco Industry
cosein	KOZMODEMYANSKIY DAIRY FACTORY	Food & Food Processing Industry. Tobacco Industry
cosein	MASLODEL	Food & Food Processing Industry. Tobacco Industry
cotton and flax fabric	KINESHMA TEXTILE FACTORY	Textile Industry
cotton fabric	TOMNA	Textile Industry
cotton fabric	SOLIDARNOST	Textile Industry
cotton fabric	IZMAYLOVSKAYA MANUFACTURA	Textile Industry
cotton fabric and yarn	CHITA WORSTED & CLOTH MANUFACTURING FACTORY	Textile industry
cotton fabric, linen	KARABANOVSKAYA TEKSTILNAYA MANUFAKTURA	Textile Industry
cotton fadric	ROSTEKSTIL	Textile industry
cotton fiber, unbleached cotton	KRASINETS	Textile Industry
cotton products	OKTYABR	Clothing Industry. Footwear & Tanning Industry
cotton yarn	PETERBURGSKIY TEKSTIL	Textile Industry
cotton yarn	PROMTEKSTIL	Textile Industry
cow hide, sheet glass	BLAGOVESCHENSK CONSTRUCTION MATERIALS PLANT	Building materials industry
crabs & fish	SEA FISHERY FLEET BASE	Food & tobacco industry
craft-paper, paper bags	MARIYSKIY PULP FACTORY	Forestry & Timber Processing Industry. Pulp & Paper Industry. Publishing & Printing Industry.
crane trucks	AVTOKRAN	Machine Building Industry
cranes	UFAKRAN	Metallurgy Industry.

For additional analytical, business and investment opportunities information, please contact Global Investment & Business Center, USA at (202) 546-2103. Fax: (202) 546-3275. E-mail: rusric@erols.com Global Business E-Books on Line: http://world.mirhouse.com

		Machine-Building Industry. Power Industry.
cranes	GAZAKS	Metallurgy. Machine-Building Industry
cranes, winches	UKHTA MACHINE-BUILDING PLANT	Machine-Building Industry
crushers	STROMMASHINA	Machine Building Industry
curtain lace	GORNO-ALTAYSK CURTAIN FATORY	Textile industry
cutters, files	SERPUKHOV SOLID ALLOY TOOLS PLANT	Machine Building Industry
diagnostic preparation	NIXHNIY NOVGOROD PHARMACEUTICAL PLANT	Chemical, Pharmaceutical & Microbiology Industry
diesel boats, bicycle parts	VOLGA SHIP YARD	Metallurgy Industry. Machine-Building Industry. Power Industry
diesel engines, pumps	RUMO	Metallurgy Industry. Machine-Building Industry. Power Industry
diesel fuel, engine oil, fuel oil	NEFTEORGSINTEZ	Mining Industry
diesel fuel, gasoline, fuel oil	OMSK OIL REFINERY	Mining industry
disintegrating machines	DROBMASH	Metallurgy Industry. Machine-Building Industry. Power Industry
distilled alcohol	PETROVSKIY DISTILLERY	Food Industry. Tobacco Industry
dolomite	KOVROV QUARRY	Mining Industry
dough mixing machines	GORKOVSKIY EXPERIMENTAL MACHINERY PLANT	Metallurgy Industry. Machine-Building Industry. Power Industry
drilling machinery	RUDGORMASH	Metallurgy Industry. Machine-Building Industry
drinking water filters	EKOMASH	Machine Building Industry
drive belts, conveyer belt	PLOSREMVIS	Chemical Industry
dry milk	MELEUZ DIARY-PROCESSING PLANT	Food, food processing and tobacco industry
dry milk	KIROVSKIY DAIRY FACTORY	Food & Food Processing Industry. Tobacco Industry
dry milk	KOLOKO	Food & Food Processing

For additional analytical, business and investment opportunities information, please contact Global Investment & Business Center, USA at (202) 546-2103. Fax: (202) 546-3275. E-mail: rusric@erols.com Global Business E-Books on Line: http://world.mirhouse.com

		Industry. Tobacco Industry
dry milk	NIZHEGORODSKIY DAIRY PLANT	Food & Food Processing Industry. Tobacco Industry
dry milk	GLAZOVMOLOKO	Food, food processing and tobacco industry
dry-cargo ships, lumber ships	YANTAR	Machine-Building Industry
Dump trucks	DAVYDOVO	Automobile Industry
electric appliances	IMPULS	Electrical Engineering Industry
electric appliances	ELECTRIC APPLIANCES ASSEMBLING PLANT	Chemical, Pharmaceutical & Microbiology Industry
electric appliances	OPTRON	Metallurgy. Machine-Building. Power Industry
electric bulbs	SVET	Metallurgy Industry. Machine-Building Industry. Power Industry.
electric engineering equipment	LYSKOVO ELECTRICAL ENGINEERING PLANT	Electrical Ingineering Industry
electric engines, power circuit breakers	KARPINSK MACHINERY BUILDING PLANT	Metallurgy Industry. Machine-Building Industry. Power Industry.
electric furnaces	SIBELECTROTERM	Metallurgy industry, Machine-building industry, Power industry
electric heaters	TECHNOLIGA	Machine Building Industry
electric heaters	START	Machine Building Industry
electric motors	TECHNOLOGICAL EQUIPMENT	Metallurgy industry, Machine-building industry, Power industry
electric motors	ELECTRIC MACHINERY BUILDING PLANT	Electrical Engineering Industry
electric motors	VLADIMIR ELECTRIC MOTOR PLANT	Machine Building Industry
electric motors, pumps	EVESTUR	Metallurgy Industry. Machine-Building Industry. Power Industry.
electric power	KOLSKAYA NUCLEAR POWER PLANT	Power Industry
electric power	KOLENERGO	Power Industry
electric power	MTSENSK POWER	Power Industry

	NETWORKS	
electrical appliances	A.A.KULAKOV PLANT	Machine-Building Industry
electro-analysis appliances, process control appliances	LENDIS GIR LTD	Electrical Engineering Industry
electrodes	ELECTROD	Metallurgy Industry. Machine-Building Industry. Power Industry.
electronic components	SIMMETRON	Electrical Enginiring Industry
electronic components	ANGSTREM	Radio-Electronic Industry
electronic display boards	INFOTEKH	Electrical Engineering Industry
electronic measuring appliances, micro-processing equipment, strain gages	ELEKTROPRIBOR	Electrical Engineering Industry
engine oil	BALTIC PETROLEUM	Chemical Industry
engine wheels	USSURIYSK TRAIN DEPOT	Metallurgy, machine-building & power industry
equipment for chemical industry	PERVOMAYSKKHIMMASH	Chemical, Pharmaceutical & Microbiology Industry
equipment for oil and gas pipelines	PROMARMATURA	Metallurgy industry, Machine-building industry, Power industry
ether, polymethyl methacrylate	ORGANIC GLAS MANYFACTURING PLANT	Chemical, pharmaceutical, and microbiology inndustry
ethyl acetheten	KARBOKHIM	Chemical, Pharmaceutical & Microbiology Industry
explosives	KRASNOURALSKIY KHIMZAVOD	Forrestry and timber processing industry. Pulp and paper industry. Publishing and printing industry
eye glasses	YEVROOPTIKA	Consumer Goods, Furniture,Household & Cultural Products
fellings	YURYEVETS WOOD PROCESSING PLANT	Forestry & Timber Processing Industry.
felted fabric	BORSK TEXTILE FACTORY	Textile Industry
ferrite products, microwave ovens	DOMEN	Machine-Building Industry
ferrous metal cast	NIZHNIY NOVGOROD	Metallurgy Industry.

For additional analytical, business and investment opportunities information, please contact Global Investment & Business Center, USA at (202) 546-2103. Fax: (202) 546-3275. E-mail: rusric@erols.com Global Business E-Books on Line: http://world.mirhouse.com

products	MACHINE BUILDING PLANT	Machine-Building Industry. Power Industry
ferrous metal products, dry-cargo ships, aluminum ingots	KRASNOYE SORMOVO	Metallurgy Industry. Machine-Building Industry. Power Industry
ferrous metals scrap	MAGADANAVTORMET	Metallurgy, machine-building & power industry
fiber glass fabric, baalt fiber	SUDOGODSKOYE STEKLOVOLOKNO	Chemical Industry
film, tannin	KAZAN INSTITUTE OF PHOTOFRAPHIC EQUIPMENT	Chemical, Pharmaceutical & Microbiology Industry
filter cloth	KRASNIY MAYAK	Textile Industry
filtering catroard	KOSINO PAPER FACTORY	Forestry & Timber Processing Industry. Pulp & Paper Industry. Publishing & Printing Industry.
filters	SHAKHUNYA CHEMICAL PLANT	Chemical, Pharmaceutical & Microbiology Industry
finished boards	POTEKHINSKIY LUMBER COMPANY	Forestry & timber processing, Pulp & paper industry
finished boarda	YEROFEYEVSKIY LUMBER COMPANY	Forestry & timber processing, Pulp & paper industry
finished boards	LESNIK	Forestry & timber processing, Pulp & paper industry
fire alarm systems	TENZOR	Machine Building Industry
fire extinguishers	SPETSTEKHIKA	Chemical, pharmaceutical, and microbiology inndustry
fish products	ECOPASIFIC	Food & tobacco industry
fish products	VESTARUS	Food & tobacco industry
fish products	RADUGA	Food & tobacco industry
fish products	AKVA	Food & tobacco industry
fish products	KHOLKAM	Food & tobacco industry
fish products	ENERGIYA	Food & Food Processing
fish products	MURMANSK TRAILING FLEET	Food & Food Processing
fish products	MURMANKOMPENSIM	Food & Food Processing
fish products	MURMAN	Food & Food Processing
fish products	PRILUKI	Food & Food Processing

fish products	BELOMORSKIY RYBAK	Food & Food Processing
fish products	UDARNIK	Food & Food Processing
fish products	MURMANRYBPROM	Food & Food Processing
fish products	NORD-WEST	Food & Food Processing
fish products	SEVERRYBKHOLODOFLOT	Food & Food Processing
fish products	SEVRYBPROMRAZVEDKA	Food & Food Processing
fish products	SMENA	Food & Food Processing
flax fabric	YAKOVLEVSKIY FLAX PROCESSING PLANT	Textile Industry
flax fabric	SMOLENSK FLAX PROCESSING PLANT	Textile Industry
flax fabric	MELENKI FLAX PROCESSING PLANT	Textile Industry
flax fiber	STARORUSSKIY - FLAX PROCESSING PLANT	Textile Industry
flax fibers	YURYEVETS FLAX HACKLING AND SPINNING FACTORY	Textile Industry
flax yarn	TEKHNOTKAN	Textile Industry
flour mills	ELEVATORMELMASH	Metallurgy Industry. Machine-Building Industry
footwear	KALIF	Clothing Industry. Footwear Industry
footwear	KIROV SYNTHETIC LEATHER MANUFACTURING FACTORY	Clothing Industry. Footwear & Tanning Industry
footwear	KLIANT	Clothing Industry. Footwear Industry
forge work, electrodes	NIZHEGORODSKIY TEPLOKHOD	Metallurgy Industry. Machine-Building Industry. Power Industry
frozen fish	MAGADAMRYBPROM	Food & tobacco industry
fruit concentrate, food processing equipment	DZERZHYNSKIY DAIRY FACTORY	Food & Food Processing Industry. Tobacco Industry
furniture	VOLZHSK WOOD PROCESSING PLANT	Forestry & Timber Processing Industry. Pulp & Paper Industry. Publishing & Printing Industry.
furniture	NOVOSIBIRSKMEBEL	Building materials industry
furniture	MEBELEKSPORT	Metallurgy Industry. Machine-Building Industry

furniture accessories	OLANK	Metallurgy Industry. Machine-Building Industry. Power Industry.
furnniture	ROSMETALL	Metallurgy. Machine-Building Industry
gardening tools	TAURAS-FENIKS	Chemical Industry
gardening tools	MEKHINSTRUMENT	Metallurgy Industry. Machine-Building Industry. Power Industry
gardening tools	IZHEVSK ELEKTROMEKH ZAVOD	Metallurgy Industry. Machine-Building Industry. Power Industry.
gas bombs	URALVAGONZAVOD	Metallurgy Industry. Machine-Building Industry. Power Industry.
gas lasers, control boards	PLAZMA	High-Tech Products, PC, Research
gas-flame machinery	NARVAL	Machine Building Industry
gauze	GORODISHCHI FINISHING FACTORY	Textile Industry
German silver products	MSTERSKIY YUVELIR	Consumer Goods, Furniture, Household & Cultural Products
glass blocks, construction glass	SIMVOL	Building Materials Industry
glass bottles	PROTON	Forestry & Timber Processing Industry.
glass bottles	KRASNOYE EKHO	Building Materials Industry
glass dishes	KRASNIY OKTYABR	Building Materials Industry
glass dishes	URSHELSKIY GLASS-MAKING PLANT	Building Materials Industry
glass dishes, bottles	DALSTEK	Building materials industry
glass products	GUS-KHRUSTALNIY GLASS PRODUCTS	Mining Industry
glue	POLITERM	Forestry & Timber Processing Industry. Pulp & Paper Industry. Publishing & Printing Industry.
glue, turpentine, colophony, ether, pine oil	ORGSINTEZ	Chemical, Pharmaceutical & Microbiology Industry
grain processing	MELINVEST	Metallurgy Industry.

equipment		Machine-Building Industry. Power Industry
granite blocks	KASHINA GORA	Building Materials Industry
graphite products	GRAFI	Chemical Industry
graphitized electrodes, powdered graphite	MOSCOW ELECTRONIC PLANT	Chemical Industry
guns	IZHEVSK MACHINE SHOP	Metallurgy Industry. Machine-Building Industry. Power Industry.
gypsum products	DEKOR-1	Mining Industry
hand tools	SARATOV PLANT OF ELECTRIC APPLIANCES	Metallurgy. Machine-Building Industry
hand tools	ELEKS	Metallurgy. Machine-Building. Power Industry
heating appliances, converters	RADIKON	Machine Building Industry
heating equipment	MAGADAN MACHINE PLANT	Chemical, pharmaceutical & microbiology industry
Heat-resisting materials	SUKHOLOZHSKIY FIREPROOF PRODUCTS MANUFACTURING PLANT	Building Materials Industry
helicopter parts	MAGADAN PLANE REPAIRING PLANT	Metallurgy, machine-building & power industry
helicopters	KUMERTAU AVIATION PLANT	Metallurgy Industry. Machine-Building Industry. Power Industry.
hide	BOGORODSK LEATHER FACTORY	Clothing Industry. Footwear & Tanning Industry
hide, sheepskin, fur	NELLI	Clothing Industry
hides	MYASOKOMBINAT i K	Food & Food Processing Industry. Tobacco Industry
hides	NIZHEGORODSKIYE KOLBASY	Food & Food Processing Industry. Tobacco Industry
hides	ANNINSKIY MEAT PACKAGING PLANT	Food & Food Processing Industry. Tobacco Industry.
high voltage appliances	HIGH VOLTAGE RESEARCH CENTER	Electrical Engineering Industry
horse shoes, nails	YAMNOVO METAL WORKS PLANT	Metallurgy Industry. Machine-Building Industry. Power Industry
household chemicals	ORGSINTEZ	Chemical, Pharmaceutical &

		Microbiology Industry
hydraulic engines	OMSKGIDROPROVOD	Metallurgy industry, Machine-building industry, Power industry
hydraulic generators, turbo-generators, electrical equipment	ELEKTRONIKA	Electrical Enginiring Industry
hydroautomatics	MOSGIDROPRIVOD	Machine Building Industry
hydrogen peroxide, acetone, braking fluids	SINTEZ	Chemical, Pharmaceutical & Microbiology Industry
I	LAZERON-MEDTEKHNIKA	Metallurgy, machine-building & power industry
image convertors, TV picture tubes	MOSCOW BULB MANUFACTURING PLANT	Electrical Engineering Industry
incandescent lamps	MALOVISHERSKIY GLASS-MAKING PLANT	Consumer Goods, Furniture,Household & Cultural Products
indicators, light diodes	PROTON-OPTOELEKTRONIKA	Radio-Electronic Industry
industrial electric appliances	METRAN	Metallurgy Industry. Machine-Building Industry. Power Industry.
industrial electric equipment	NIZKOVOLTNIK	Metallurgy Industry. Machine-Building Industry. Power Industry.
industrial fasteners & holders	NORMAL	Metallurgy Industry. Machine-Building Industry. Power Industry
industrial waste processing equipment	EKONTEKH	Chemical Industry
iron	VYCHUGA MACHINE-BUILDING PLANT	Machine Building Industry
iron cast	SKOPINPROMINDUSTRIA	Metallurgy
iron cast	LITEYSHCHIK	Metallurgy. Machine-Building. Power Industry
iron cast	RUSLICH	Metallurgy Industry. Machine-Building Industry. Power Industry.
iron ore	OLENEGORSK MINING ENTERPRISE	Mining Industry
iron ore pellets, steel	RUDPROM	Mining Industry
TV Tubes	EKRAN	Forestry & timber processing industry. Pulp &

For additional analytical, business and investment opportunities information, please contact Global Investment & Business Center, USA at (202) 546-2103. Fax: (202) 546-3275. E-mail: rusric@erols.com
Global Business E-Books on Line: http://world.mirhouse.com

		paper industry. Publishing & printing industry.
kitchen utensils	TRUD	Metallurgy Industry. Machine-Building Industry. Power Industry
knifes	INTERCOUT TURBI SERVIS	Machine Building Industry
labels	SETO-ST PUBLISHING COMPANY	Forestry & timber processing, Pulp & paper industry
lactose, casein	BLAGOVESHCENSK DIARY FACTORY	Food & tobacco industry
ladels	BELGOROD REGIONAL PUBLISHING COMPANY	Publishing & Printing Industry.
laser devices	LAZERNIYE KOMPLEKSY	High-Tech Products, PC, Research & Design Services
laser equipment	PLYUS	High-Tech Products, PC, Research
lathes	YEYSK MACHINE BUILDING PLANT	Metallurgy. Machine-Building. Power Industry
lathes	KRASNIY PROLETARIY	Machine Building Industry
lathes, milling machine, wood working machinery, measuring appliances	DELFIN	Machine Building Industry
lathes, special technological equipment	FINA-S	Machine Building Industry
leather	BOGORODSK INDUSTRIAL TRADING CENTER	Clothing Industry. Footwear & Tanning Industry
leather and rubber products	KORTIZ	Clothing Industry. Footwear Industry
leather products	KHROMTAN	Clothing Industry. Footwear & Tanning Industry
leather products	KOZHEVNIK	Clothing Industry. Footwear and Tanning Industry
leather semifinished products	A.RADISHCHEV	Footwear & Tanning Industry
leather shoes	MENDE-ROSSI	Clothing Industry. Footwear & Tanning Industry.
light diodes	PLANETA-SID	Electrical Enginiring Industry
light filters	STARSTEKLO	Building Materials Industry
linen	VYCHUGA WEAVING AND	Textile Industry

	SPINNING FACTORY	
linen, underwear	KRESTETSKAYA STROCHKA	Clothing Industry
looms	PEREVOZ FLAX PROCESSING PLANT	Textile Industry
looms, furniture, clothes,refrigerators	SIBTEKSTILMASH	Metallurgy industry, Machine-building industry, Power industry
low voltage equipment	PUSHKINO ELECTROMECHANICAL PLANT	Electrical-Engineering Industry
low voltage equipment	VELAN	Chemical, Pharmaceutical & Microbiology Industry
lubricants	AVIATEKHMAS	Chemical, Pharmaceutical & Microbiology Industry
lumber	KAVKAZSKIY LES	Forestry & Timber Processing Industry. Pulp & Paper Industry. Publishing & Printing Industry.
lumber	TYNDALES	Forestry & timber processing, Pulp & paper industry
lumber	SELENGALES	Forestry & timber processing industry. Pulp & paper industry. Publishing & printing industry
lumber	SUGOMAKSIY LUMBER COMPANY	Forrestry and timber processing industry. Pulp and paper industry. Publishing and printing industry
lumber	IGIRMA-TAYRIKU	Forestry & timber processing industry. Pulp & paper industry. Publishing & printing industry
lumber	KAMCHATLES	Forestry & timber processing, Pulp & paper industry
lumber	KLYUCHI LUMBER COMPANY	Forestry & timber processing, Pulp & paper industry
lumber	LUMBER COMPANY	Forestry & timber processing, Pulp & paper industry
lumber	KEMSKIY LUMBER COMPANY	Forestry & Timber

lumber	LUZA TIMBER PROCESSING FACTORY	Forestry & Timber Processing Industry. Pulp & Paper Industry. Publishing & Printing Industry.
lumber	DVINA	Forestry & Timber Processing Industry
lumber	PECHORLESPROM	Forestry & Timber Processing Industry
lumber	APSHERONSK	Forestry & Timber Processing Industry. Pulp & Paper Industry. Publishing & Printing Industry.
lumber	KANSK WOOD PROCESSING PLANT	Forestry & timber processing industry. Pulp & paper industry. Publishing & printing industry
lumber	LODEYNOYE POLE WOOD PROCESSING PLANT	Forestry & Timber Processing Industry
lumber	ZEBERS	Forestry & Timber Processing Industry. Pulp & Paper Industry. Publishing & Printing Industry.
lumber	SHAP	Forestry & Timber Processing Industry. Pulp & Paper Industry. Publishing & Printing Industry.
lumber	ISTRA LUMBER COMPANY	Forestry & Timber Processing Industry.
lumber	VETLUZHSKIY LUMBER COMPANY	Forestry & Timber Processing Industry. Pulp & Paper Industry. Publishing & Printing Industry.
lumber	KRONA	Forestry & Timber Processing Industry. Pulp & Paper Industry. Publishing & Printing Industry.
lumber	ARYEVSKOYE LUMBER COMPANY	Forestry & Timber Processing Industry. Pulp & Paper Industry. Publishing & Printing Industry.
lumber	NOVGORODSKIY LES	Forestry & Timber Processing Industry
lumber	MSTALES	Forestry & Timber Processing Industry

lumber	DAKAR	Forestry & timber processing industry. Pulp & paper industry. Publishing & printing industry.
lumber	CHAIKOVSKIY LUMBER COMPANY	Forrestry and timber processing industry. Pulp and paper industry. Publishing and printing industry
lumber	SARS LUMBER COMPANY	Forrestry and timber processing industry. Pulp and paper industry. Publishing and printing industry
lumber	SEVERNIY LUMBER COMPANY	Forestry & timber processing, Pulp & paper industry
lumber	SAKHALINLESPROM	Forestry & timber processing, Pulp & paper industry
lumber	SAKHAJINLESPROM	Chemical, pharmaceutical & microbiology industry
lumber	KARPINSKIY LUMBER COMPANY	Forrestry and timber processing industry. Pulp and paper industry. Publishing and printing industry
lumber	SEROVLES	Forrestry and timber processing industry. Pulp and paper industry. Publishing and printing industry
lumber	YUSHALINSKIY LUMBER COMPANY	Forrestry and timber processing industry. Pulp and paper industry. Publishing and printing industry
lumber	OREKHOVO	Forestry & timber processing industry. Pulp & paper industry. Publishing & printing industry.
lumber	YAKSHUR-BODYINSKIY LUMBER COMPANY	Forrestry and timber processing industry. Pulp and paper industry. Publishing and printing industry

lumber	SAPROFIT	Forrestry and timber processing industry. Pulp and paper industry. Publishing and printing industry
lumber	VOLOGDALESPROM	Forestry & Timber Processing Industry
lumber, boards	MAYAK	Food, food processing and tobacco industry
lumber, cross ties	KHAKTEKHLES	Forestry & timber processing industry. Pulp & paper industry. Publishing & printing industry
lumber, finished boards	ZEYA TIMBERHANDLING PLANT	Forestry & timber processing, Pulp & paper industry
lumber, paper wood	TYUMENAGROLESPROM	Forestry & timber processing industry. Pulp & paper industry. Publishing & printing industry.
lumber, paper wood	TAGILLES	Forrestry and timber processing industry. Pulp and paper industry. Publishing and printing industry
lumber, paper wood	LOBVA	Forrestry and timber processing industry. Pulp and paper industry. Publishing and printing industry
lumber, paper wood	MELEKH	Forestry & Timber Processing Industry.
lumber, parquet	REY-AM	Forestry & Timber Processing Industry.
lumber, pulp and paper	SAKHALINLESPROM	Ore & mining industry
lumber, saw logs, stock timber	KARELLESPROM	Forestry & Timber Processing Industry
lumber, stock timber	AGROSTROYKONSTRUKTSIYA	Construction Materials Industry
lumber, timber	VYATKA-VUD	Forestry & Timber Processing Industry. Pulp & Paper Industry. Publishing & Printing Industry.
lumber, tock timber	ROSLAVL LUMBER COMPANY	Forestry & Timber

		Processing Industry.
machinary for plant growing, molk processing equipment	AGROMEKH	Machine Building Industry
machine-building products	SELMASH	Machine Building Industry
machinery , stock timber, lumber, scrap metal	SAMUS SHIP-YARD	Metallurgy industry, Machine-building industry, Power industry
machinery parts	KORVET	Metallurgy Industry. Machine-Building Industry. Power Industry.
magnet	POZ-PROGRESS	Metallurgy Industry. Machine-Building Industry. Power Industry.
magnet	MAGNETON	Metallurgy
magnetic circuits	PRECISION ALLOY INSTITUTE	Machine Building Industry
magnets	ELMAT	Consumer Goods, Furniture, Household & Cultural Products
maps	KARTOGRAFIYA	Publishing & Printing Industry
margarine	SOYUZMARGARINPROM	Food, food processing and tobacco industry
masticated rubber for cables	IKM	Chemical Industry
matches	BELKA	Forestry & Timber Processing Industry. Pulp & Paper Industry. Publishing & Printing Industry.
matches, cast steel	ISKRA	Forestry & timber processing, Pulp & paper industry
mchinery, nonferrous metals cow hide	CHITA MACHINERY PLANT	Metallurgy, machine-building industry
measuring appliances	ELECTRONIKA	Electrical Engineering Industry
measuring appliances	SUROVATIKHA COMMUNICATION EQUIPMENT PLANT	Radio-Electronic Industry
measuring instruments	M.V. FRUNZE PLANT	Radio-Electronic Industry
medical equipment	VELKONT	Machine-Building Industry
medical equipment	BIOSIGNAL	Medical Equipment Industry

medical equipment	BIOSPACE	Machine Building Industry
medical equipment	SAPFIR	Medical Equipment Industry
medical equipment	DOSCHATOYE MEDICAL EQUIPMENT MANUFACTIRING PLANT	Metallurgy Industry. Machine-Building Industry. Power Industry
medical equipment	VORSMA MEDICAL EQUIPMENT PLANT	Medical Equipment Industry
medical equipment	MEDICAL EQUIPMENT RESEARCH INSTITUTE	Metallurgy industry, Machine-building industry, Power industry
medical equipment	NOVOANNINSK MEDICAL EQUIPMENT PLANT	Metallurgy. Machine-Building Industry
medical equipment, solar batteries	KVANT	Medical Eguipment Industry
medicine	FITON	Food, food processing & tobacco industry
medicine	DIAGNOSTICHESKIYE SISTEMY	Chemical, Pharmaceutical & Microbiology Industry
medicine	NIZHNIY NOVGOROD PHARMACEUTICAL PLANT	Chemical, Pharmaceutical & Microbiology Industry
medicine	IRBIT PHARMACEUTICAL PLANT	Chemical, pharmaceutical, and microbiology inndustry
membrane pumps	AGAT	Metallurgy. Machine-Building. Power Industry
metal cutting machinery	KOLOMNA HEAVY MACHINERY PLANT	Machine Building Industry
metal cutting machinery	TEKHNIKA	Machine Building Industry
metal dishes	STEMA	Chemical, pharmaceutical, and microbiology inndustry
metal products	KURGAN PLANT OF ELECTRIC APPLIANCES	Metallurgy Industry. Machine-Building Industry. Power Industry.
metal products	MOSCOW PLANT OF SOLID-STATE ALLOYS	Matallurgy
metal rolling, steel wires	PROMMETIZ	Metallurgy Industry. Machine-Building Industry. Power Industry.
metal scrap	VTORMET	Metallurgy Industry. Machine-Building Industry. Power Industry
metal sheaths	METALLORUKAV	Metal-Working Industry

metal strip, gardening tools	METALLOIZDELIYA	Metal-Working Industry
metal structures	CHELYABINSK PLANT OF METAL STRUCTURES	Metallurgy Industry. Machine-Building Industry. Power Industry.
metal structures	ZARUBEZHSTROYMONTAZH	Metallurgy. Machine-Building. Power Industry
metal structures	ELEVATORMELMASH	Metallurgy Industry. Machine-Building Industry. Power Industry.
metal structures	SAMARA PIPELINE EQUIPMENT MANUFACTURING PLANT	Metallurgy. Machine-Building Industry
metal structures	STALKONSTRUKTSIYA	Metallurgy. Machine-Building Industry
metal structures, pumps	TESEY	Machine Building Industry
metal tanks, fuel-metering appliances	SHTRIKH	Machine-Building Industry
metal tare	MIKROMETR	Chemical, Pharmaceutical & Microbiology Industry
metal working tools	METALLIST	Metallurgy Industry. Machine-Building Industry. Power Industry
metal working tools	STAVROPOL TOOLS MANUFACTURING PLANT	Metallurgy. Machine-Building. Power Industry
metal works	PROMMETIZ	Metallurgy Industry. Machine-Building Industry. Power Industry.
metal-cutting tools	TERMODISK	Metallurgy Industry. Machine-Building Industry. Power Industry
metal-cutting tools	TVER ZAVOD 1 MAYA	Machine Building Industry
microwave ovens	MAGNETRON	Metallurgy. Machine-Building Industry
milk processing equipment	KURGANSELMASH	Metallurgy Industry. Machine-Building Industry. Power Industry.
milling machines	ZEFS	Metallurgy Industry. Machine-Building Industry. Power Industry
mineral furtilizers	ALMAZ	Chemical, Pharmaceutical & Microbiology Industry
mineral water	NARZAN	Food & Food Processing

		Industry.
mineral water	YESSENTUKI MINERAL WATER BOTTLING PLANT	Food & Food Processing Industry. Tobacco Industry
mineral water	MINVOGYI ZHELEZNOVODSKA	Food & Food Processing Industry.
mining equipment	ALEKSANDROVSK MACHINE-BUILDING PLANT	Metallurgy Industry. Machine-Building Industry. Power Industry.
mirrors	ALMAZ	Building Materials Industry
misical instruments	SHUYSKAYA GARMON	Consumer Goods, Furniture, Household & Cultural Products
monitors, TV sets	MONITOR	Radio-Electronic Industry
motorcycles, cars, sport rifles	IZHMASH	Metallurgy Industry. Machine-Building Industry. Power Industry.
motorcycles, parts, tractor parts	ZAVOD DEGTYARYOVA	Machine Building Industry
natural gas	GAZPROM	Oil & Gas Industry
needles	NIZHNIY NOVGOROD MEDICAL EQUIPMENT PLANT	Medical Equipment Industry
news papers, magazines	WRITER'S PUBLISHING COMPANY	Publishing & Printing Industry
newspaper paper	VOLGA	Forestry & Timber Processing Industry. Pulp & Paper Industry. Publishing & Printing Industry.
nickel, cobalt	YUZHNO-URALSK NICKEL PROCESSING PLANT	Chemical, pharmaceutical, and microbiology inndustry
nickel, cobalt, copper	SEVERONIKEL	Chemical Industry
equipment	BOLSHERECHENSKAYA AGROTEKHNIKA	Metallurgy industry, Machine-building industry, Power industry
equipment	BIYSK TOBACCO FACTORY	Food & tobacco industry
equipment	BARNAUL COTTON FACTORY	Textile industry
equipment	ZEYA CONFECTIONERY PLANT	Food & tobacco industry
equipment	BLAGOVESCHENSK SHIPYARD	Metallurgy, machine-building & power industry
equipment	SVOBODNENSKYI MEAT-PASCKING PLANT	Food & tobacco industry

equipment	AMURENERGO	Metallurgy, machine-building & power industry
equipment	EMSOTEKH	Electric Engineering Industry
equipment	BELOKATAY DAIRY FACTORY	Food, food processing and tobacco industry
equipment	BASHLESPROM	Forestry and timber processing industry. Pulp and paper industry. Publishing and printing industry
equipment	STERLITAMAK SPIRIT PLANT	Food, food processing and tobacco industry
equipment	RON-TELECOM	Metallurgy Industry. Machine-Building Industry. Power Industry.
equipment	MAGNITOGORSK FISH-PROCESSING PLANT	Food, food processing and tobacco industry
equipment	PROTEKS	Metallurgy Industry. Machine-Building Industry. Power Industry.
equipment	CHITA COMMERCIAL MACHINERY MANUFACTURING PLANT	Metallurgy, machine-building industry
equipment	ONIKS	Food, food processing & tobacco industry
equipment	TAMBOV RAILROAD CARS REPAIRING PLANT	Metallurgy Industry. Machine-Building Industry
Tobacco	TAKF	Food & Food Processing Industry. Tobacco Industry.
Timber	CHISTOPOL CHEMICAL PLANT	Forestry & Timber Processing Industry. Pulp & Paper Industry. Publishing & Printing Industry
Textile	VYSHNEVOLOTSKIY TEKSTILSHCHIK	Textile Industry
Rubber	METAPLAST	Rubber & Plastic Industry
Building materials	TRIALEV	Building Materials Industry
equipment	AVTOSVET	Electrical Engineering Industry
equipment	KAUSTIK	Chemical, Pharmaceutical & Microbiology Industry

For additional analytical, business and investment opportunities information, please contact Global Investment & Business Center, USA at (202) 546-2103. Fax: (202) 546-3275. E-mail: rusric@erols.com Global Business E-Books on Line: http://world.mirhouse.com

equipment	SPEKTR	Chemical, Pharmaceutical & Microbiology Industry
non-ferrous metals cast	KRASNIY VYBORZHETS	Metallurgy
nonrefined copper	SVYATOGOR	Mining Industry
notebooks, waste paper	ZEYA PUBLISHING COMPANY	Forestry & timber processing, Pulp & paper industry
nuts, bolts, steel wires, fastening products	ETNA	Metallurgy Industry. Machine-Building Industry. Power Industry
office accessories	PERSEY-MOSKVA	Chemical Industry
office paper	PAPIRUS	Pulp & Paper Industry
office paper	PROFIT	Pulp & Paper Industry
oil	MAYSKVNESHINTERPRAYZOIL	Mining industry
oil, oil products	YUNKO	Oil Refining & Gas Processing Industry
oilcloth	MSTERA OILCLOTH MANUFACTURING FACTORY	Textile Industry
ore enriching equipment	TRUD	Metallurgy industry, Machine-building industry, Power industry
organic fertilizers	SAPROPEL-NERO	Chemical Industry
packing paper	PISHCHEVIK	Food & tobacco industry
paint brushes	KHUDOZHESTVENNIYE KISTI	Consumer Goods, Furniture, Household & Cultural Products
paint brushes	NIZHNIY NOVGOROD BRUSH MANUFACTURING PLANT	Metallurgy Industry. Machine-Building Industry. Power Industry
paint, varnish, dye	PIGMENT	Chemical, Pharmaceutical & Microbiology Industry
paper	SEGEZHABUMPROM	Pulp & Paper Industry
paper dishes, cardboard products	ST.PETERSBURG CARDBOARD FACTORY	Pulp & Paper Industry
paper products	KONDROVOBUVPROM	Pulp & Paper Industry
paper scrap	OMSKVTORRESURSY	Forestry & timber processing industry. Pulp & paper industry. Publishing & printing industry.

For additional analytical, business and investment opportunities information,
please contact Global Investment & Business Center, USA
at (202) 546-2103. Fax: (202) 546-3275. E-mail: rusric@erols.com
Global Business E-Books on Line: http://world.mirhouse.com

paper scrap	URALUPAKOVKA	Forrestry and timber processing industry. Pulp and paper industry. Publishing and printing industry
paper waste	PRIAMURYE PUBLISHING COMPANY	Forestry & timber processing, Pulp & paper industry
paper wood	KADALINSKIY LUMBER COMPANY	Forestry & timber processing industry. Pulp & paper industry. Publishing & printing industry
paper wood	KOMSOMOLSK WOOD PROCESSING PLANT	Forestry & Timber Processing Industry.
paper wood	IVLESPROM	Forestry & Timber Processing Industry.
paper wood	IVLESPROM	Forestry & Timber Processing Industry.
paper wood	KUYBYSHEV WOOD PROCESSING PLANT	Forestry & Timber Processing Industry.
paper wood	SHUYALES	Forestry & Timber Processing Industry
paper wood	LUNDANKA LUMBER COMPANY	Forestry & Timber Processing Industry. Pulp & Paper Industry. Publishing & Printing Industry.
paper wood	ALMEZH LUMBER COMPANY	Forestry & Timber Processing Industry. Pulp & Paper Industry. Publishing & Printing Industry.
paper wood	VERKHNEKAMSK LES	Forestry & Timber Processing Industry. Pulp & Paper Industry. Publishing & Printing Industry.
paper wood	LOTOSHINO LES	Forestry & Timber Processing Industry.
paper wood	VOLOKOLAMSK LUMBER COMPANY	Forestry & Timber Processing Industry.
paper wood	KERZHENETSLES	Forestry & Timber Processing Industry. Pulp & Paper Industry. Publishing & Printing Industry.
paper wood	MUKHTOLOVO LUMBER COMPANY	Forestry & Timber Processing Industry. Pulp &

		Paper Industry. Publishing & Printing Industry.
paper wood	NIZHNIY NOVGOROD LUMBER COMPANY	Forestry & Timber Processing Industry. Pulp & Paper Industry. Publishing & Printing Industry.
paper wood	NIZHEGORODLES	Forestry & Timber Processing Industry. Pulp & Paper Industry. Publishing & Printing Industry.
paper wood	VOGULKA LUMBER COMPANY	Forrestry and timber processing industry. Pulp and paper industry. Publishing and printing industry
paper wood	KAMESHKOVO LUMBER COMPANY	Forestry & Timber Processing Industry.
paper wood	VLADIMIR LUMBER COMPANY	Forestry & Timber Processing Industry.
paper wood	INTERMESHCHERALES	Forestry & Timber Processing Industry.
paper wood	PETUSHKIINTERLES	Forestry & Timber Processing Industry.
paper wood	KIRZHACH LUMBER COMPANY	Forestry & Timber Processing Industry.
paper wood	MALENKI LUMBER COMPANY	Forestry & Timber Processing Industry.
paper wood	INTERLES-SELIVANOVO	Forestry & Timber Processing Industry.
paper wood	ALEKSANDROV LUMBER COMPANY	Forestry & Timber Processing Industry.
paper wood	MONZENSKIY LUMBER COMPANY	Forestry & Timber Processing Industry
paper wood	CHAGODA LUMBER COMPANY	Forestry & Timber Processing Industry
paper wood, lumber	ERAKHTURLES	Forestry & Timber Processing Industry.
paper wood, lumber	ROSLESPROM	Forrestry and timber processing industry. Pulp and paper industry. Publishing and printing industry
paper wood, lumber	NIZHNESERGINSKIY LUMBER COMPANY	Forrestry and timber processing industry. Pulp

		and paper industry. Publishing and printing industry
paper wood, lumber	KOVROV LUMBER COMPANY	Forestry & Timber Processing Industry.
paper wood, lumber	SOBINKA LUMBER COMPANY	Forestry & Timber Processing Industry.
paper wood, lumber	ANDREYEVSK LUMBER COMPANY	Forestry & Timber Processing Industry.
paper wood, lumber	KOLCHUGINO LUMBER COMPANY	Forestry & Timber Processing Industry.
paper wood, plywood	MAYSKLES	Forestry & Timber Processing Industry. Pulp & Paper Industry. Publishing & Printing Industry.
paper wood, plywood	SYREKSKIY LUMBER COMPANY	Forrestry and timber processing industry. Pulp and paper industry. Publishing and printing industry
paper, aluminum foil	GRAF	Forestry & timber processing industry. Pulp & paper industry. Publishing & printing industry.
paper, wood laminate	SIKOL PULP & PAPER PLANT	Pulp & Paper Industry
parchment	TROITSKAYA PAPER FACTORY	Pulp & Paper Industry
parquet	YUG	Forestry & Timber Processing Industry.
parts	ZARO	Machine-Building Industry
parts	METALLIST	Metallurgy Industry. Machine-Building Industry. Power Industry.
parts to farm machinery	VOLGOGRADMOTORSERVIS	Metallurgy. Machine-Building Industry
parts to road construction machinery	ORYOL ROAD CONSTRUCTON MACHINERY PLANT	Machine Building Industry
patterned glass	STROYTEKHSTEKLO	Building Materials Industry
peat	DEMETRA	Ore & mining industry
pharmaceutical products	OKTYABR - PHARMACEUTICAL PLANT	Pharmaceutical Industry

phenol resin	TOKEM	Forestry & timber processing industry. Pulp & paper industry. Publishing & printing industry.
photoelectric appliances	MACHINE-BUILBIND SCIENTIFIC RESEARSH INSTITUTE	High-Tech Products, PC, Research & Design Services
photoresistors	ANILIN	Chemical, Pharmaceutical & Microbiology Industry
phthalic anhydride, fumaric acid	KAMEKS	Chemical, pharmaceutical, and microbiology inndustry
pigment	PIGMENT	Chemical, pharmaceutical, and microbiology inndustry
pipe fittings	VOLZHSKIY MACHINE-BUILDING PLANT	Machine Building Industry
pipe layers	INVIS	Metallurgy Industry. Machine-Building Industry. Power Industry.
pipeline equipment	KONTUR	Machine-Building Industry
pipeline reinforcement	INTERARM	Metal-Working Industry
pipeline reinforcement	KOVROV FERROCONCRETE PLANT	Building Materials Industry
pipes	BOR TIBIFORM PLANT	Metallurgy Industry. Machine-Building Industry. Power Industry
pipes, electrodes	VOZOVSELMASH	Metallurgy Industry. Machine-Building Industry
piston rings	STAVROPOL PISTON RING MANUFACTURING PLANT	Metallurgy. Machine-Building. Power Industry
plastic	KHIMPLAST	Chemical Industry
plastic compound, varnish, paint	KOTOVSK PLASTIC WORKS PLANT	Chemical, Pharmaceutical & Microbiology Industry
plastic packaging material	KONSKOR	Chemical Industry
plastic products	AKSIOMA-PLAST Ltd.	Chemical Industry
plastic products	VOLZHSKIY MACHINERY PLANT	Chemical, Pharmaceutical & Microbiology Industry
plate-bending presses	SLAVGOROD FORGE-AND-PRESSING PLANT	Metallurgy industry, Machine-building industry, Power industry
plywood	BASHLESPROM	Forrestry and timber processing industry. Pulp

For additional analytical, business and investment opportunities information, please contact Global Investment & Business Center, USA at (202) 546-2103. Fax: (202) 546-3275. E-mail: rusric@erols.com Global Business E-Books on Line: http://world.mirhouse.com

		and paper industry. Publishing and printing industry
plywood	GIGANT	Forestry & Timber Processing Industry.
plywood	KRASNIY YAKOR	Forestry & Timber Processing Industry. Pulp & Paper Industry. Publishing & Printing Industry.
plywood	ZHESHART PLYWOOD FACTORY	Forestry & Timber Processing Industry
plywood	CHUDOVO - RWS	Forestry & Timber Processing Industry
plywood	PARFINO PLYWOOD FACTORY	Forestry & Timber Processing Industry
plywood	FANKOM	Forrestry and timber processing industry. Pulp and paper industry. Publishing and printing industry
plywood	NELIDOVO LUMBER COMPANY	Forestry & Timber Processing Industry.
plywood	VOLZHSKIY LUMBER COMPANY	Forestry & Timber Processing Industry. Pulp & Paper Industry. Publishing & Printing Industry
plywood, wood laminate, felling	MUROM	Forestry & Timber Processing Industry.
polished glass, triplex, stalinite, mirrors	BOR GLASS MANUFACTURING PLANT	Building Materials Industry
polishing wheels	STANKOINSTRUMENT	Metallurgy Industry. Machine-Building Industry. Power Industry
polyethylene	IZHEVSK PLANT OF PLASTIC PRODUCTS	Chemical, pharmaceutical, and microbiology inndustry
polyethylene packaging materials	TEKHNOFILTR	Chemical Industry
polymer, polyethylene products	PLASTPERERADOTKA	Chemical Industry
polymers	TECHNICAL EQUIPMENT PLANT	Metallurgy Industry. Machine-Building Industry. Power Industry
polystyrene foam, lumber, silicate cotton	IZOTEK	Forestry & Timber Processing Industry

polystyrene, divinylbenzene	OMSKKHIMPROM	Chemical, pharmaceutical & microbiology industry
powdered quartz	VELIKODVORYE ORE MINING AND PROCESSING ENTERPRISE	Mining Industry
power machinery	SKB KOTLOSTROYENIYA	Machine-Building Industry
power switches	ELEKTROKOMPLEKS	Metallurgy, machine-building industry
printed products	NOVOYE VREMYA	Publishing & Printing Industry
printers	KOMUTATOR	Machine Building Industry
printing equipment	NEFMA	Metallurgy. Machine-Building Industry
printing products	GOZNAK	Publishing & Printing Industry
process control equipment	TVES	Metallurgy Industry. Machine-Building Industry
process controll equipment, night-vision equipment	NOVOSIBIRSK APPLIANCE CONSTRUCTION PLANT	Metallurgy industry, Machine-building industry, Power industry
pulpwood	SIVAKLES	Forestry & timber processing, Pulp & paper industry
pulpwood	TALDANSKIY LUMBER COMPANY	Forestry & timber processing, Pulp & paper industry
pulpwood	OMEGA	Forestry & timber processing, Pulp & paper industry
pumps	EVRO-AZIA	Metallurgy Industry. Machine-Building Industry. Power Industry
pumps	HYDRAULIC MACHINERY PLANT	Machine Building Industry
pumps	GORODETS SHIPYARD	Metallurgy Industry. Machine-Building Industry. Power Industry
pumps	TECHNOLOG	Metallurgy. Machine-Building Industry
pumps	ALFAELECTRO	Metallurgy industry, Machine-building industry, Power industry

pumps	OIL EXTRACTING MACHINERY PLANT	Metallurgy Industry. Machine-Building Industry. Power Industry.
pumps, electric appliances	ELECTROAPPARAT	Metallurgy Industry. Machine-Building Industry. Power Industry.
PVC resin, caustic	KAPROLAKTAM	Clothing Industry. Footwear & Tanning Industry
quartz generators, quartz filters	MORION	Machine-Building Industry
radio equipment	MUROM RADIO PLANT	Radio-Electronic Industry
radio lamps, electronic indicators	SOYUZ	Chemical, pharmaceutical & microbiology industry
radio stations, radio buoys	YAROSLAVL RADIO PLANT	Radio-Electronic Industry
radios quartz generator	OMSK APPLIANCES RESEARCH INSTITUTE	Metallurgy industry, Machine-building industry, Power industry
rail road containers	ABAKANVAGONMASH	Metallurgy, machine-building industry
railroad and highway machinery	ISTYE MACHINERY PLANT	Machine Building Industry
railroad equipment	KUSHVA TRANSPORTATION EQUIPMENT PLANT	Metallurgy Industry. Machine-Building Industry. Power Industry.
railroad machinery	TULAZHELDORMASH	Machine Building Industry
railroad track switches	ZHELDORREMMASH	Machine Building Industry
ready-made windows	ARKTIK TIIVI	Forestry & Timber Processing Industry
reaping machine	SIBSELMASH	Metallurgy industry, Machine-building industry, Power industry
refined copper, copper sulphate, nickel	KYSHTYM ELECTROLYTIC PLANT	Chemical, pharmaceutical, and microbiology inndustry
refractory materials	SNEGIREVSKIYE OGNEUPORY	Building Materials Industry
resistors	POTENTSIAL	Metallurgy Industry. Machine-Building Industry. Power Industry
resistors	REZISTOR	Radio-Electronic Industry
resistors	ARZAMAS RADIO PLANT	Metallurgy Industry. Machine-Building Industry.

		Power Industry
resistors	ORBITA	Radio-Electronic Industry
respirators, thermoplast sheets, cerosine lamps	ZARYA	Chemical, Pharmaceutical & Microbiology Industry
rolled ferrous metals, metal girders, ferrotitanium	KULEBAKI METALLURGICAL PLANT	Metallurgy Industry
rolled metals, metal containers and tanks	STEEL CONCRETE MANUFACTURING PLANT	Building materials industry
rolled products	REZONANS	Metallurgy Industry. Machine-Building Industry. Power Industry.
roofing felt	OMSKKROVLYA	Forestry & timber processing industry. Pulp & paper industry. Publishing & printing industry.
ropes	KANAT	Textile Industry
ropes	KANAT	Textile Industry
rubber crumbs	TIRE REPAIRING PLANT	Forestry & Timber Processing Industry. Pulp & Paper Industry. Publishing & Printing Industry.
rubber products	ELF	Chemical Industry
rubber products	VOLZHSKIY TIRE REPAIRONG PLANT	Chemical, Pharmaceutical & Microbiology Industry
ruberoid	NIZHNIY NOVGOROD CARDBOARD-RUBEROID FACTORY	Forestry & Timber Processing Industry. Pulp & Paper Industry. Publishing & Printing Industry.
rubidium, cesium	SEVERNUYE REDKIYE METALLY	Mining Industry
sackcloth	MYAHKAYA TARA	Textile Industry
sandblasting machinery	SHKVAL	Machine Building Industry
saw frames	DREVMASH	Machine Building Industry
saw logs, stock timber, lumber	BELYI RUCHEY	Forestry & Timber Processing Industry
sawdust	MARIKHOLODMASH	Forestry & Timber Processing Industry. Pulp & Paper Industry. Publishing & Printing Industry.
scrap containing hard lead	METAKO	Metal-Working Industry
scrap metal	MOSVTORMET	Scrap & Waste Processing

		Industry
scrap metal	VLADVTORMET	Metallurgy
screw cutting lathe	BOGORODSK MACHINE-BUILDING PLANT	Metallurgy Industry. Machine-Building Industry. Power Industry
seeders	BELINSKSELMASH	Metallurgy. Machine-Building Industry
semiconductive appliances	ELEKS	High-Tech Products, PC, Research
shafts	BALTIYSKIY ZAVOD	Machine-Building Industry
shawls	RUSSKIY VATIN	Textile Industry
slag cotton matts	TEPLOIZOL	Building Materials Industry
smal electric appliances	KASPIYSK PLANT OF SMAL ELECTRIK APPLIANCES	Chemical, Pharmaceutical & Microbiology Industry
small electric appliances	RADIAN	Metallurgy. Machine-Building. Power Industry
soap	IRKUTSK SOAP MANUFACTURING PLANT	Chemical, pharmaceutical & microbiology industry
soap	NIZHNIY NOVGOROD DAIRY PROCESSING PLANT	Food & Food Processing Industry. Tobacco Industry
soap, glue	OKA	Chemical, Pharmaceutical & Microbiology Industry
sodium dichromate, chrom anhydrite	KHROMPIK	Chemical, pharmaceutical, and microbiology inndustry
sodium sulfate	KUCHUKSULFAT	Chemical, pharmaceutical & microbiology industry
sodium, glycerin, dichloroethane, caustic soda	KAUSTIK	Chemical, pharmaceutical, and microbiology inndustry
soybeans, hide	BLAGOVESCHENSK MEAT-PACKING PLANT	Food & tobacco industry
special clothing	PSKOVOBUV	Footwear & Tanning Industry
special technological equipment	STROYTEKHNIKA	Metallurgy Industry. Machine-Building Industry. Power Industry.
special technological equipment	LEGMASH	Metallurgy Industry. Machine-Building Industry. Power Industry
special technological equipment	IZHORSKIYE ZAVODY	Machine-Building Industry

special technological equipment	SELIVANOVSKIY MASHZAVOD	Machine Building Industry
special technological equipment	MALENKI FOUNDRY	Machine Building Industry
specialized cars	NIZHNIY NOVGOROD SPECIALIZED MACHINERY PLANT	Metallurgy Industry. Machine-Building Industry. Power Industry
specialized vehicles, antennas	PRAVDINSK PARIO-RELAY APPLIANCES PLANT	Radio-Electronic Industry
splint-slab	MEBELFORT	Metallurgy industry, Machine-building industry, Power industry
sport footwear	BASHKELME	Clothing and footwear industry
springs	BELORETSK TRACTOR PARTS PLANT	Metallurgy Industry. Machine-Building Industry. Power Industry.
stainless steel sinks	STAMOR	Consumer Goods, Furniture,Household & Cultural Products
stationery products	SVETOCH	Pulp & Paper Industry
steel	VERKH-ISETSKIY METALLURGIKAL PLANT	Chemical, pharmaceutical, and microbiology inndustry
steel cast	INSTRUMENT	Machine-Building Industry
steel concrete blocks	KHABAROVSK STEEL CONCRETE MANUFACRURING PLANT	Building materials industry
steel containers	CHEMICAL EQUIPMENT PLANT	Metallurgy Industry. Machine-Building Industry. Power Industry
steel flaps	YUGO-KAMSK MACHINE-BUILDING PLANT	Metallurgy Industry. Machine-Building Industry. Power Industry.
steel pipes, steel sheets, steel ingots	VYKSA METALLURGICAL PLANT	Metallurgy Industry. Machine-Building Industry. Power Industry
steel reinforcement	METALLURGPROM	Building materials industry
steel wire	STANDART-2	Metal-Working Industry
stick timber	IVLESPROM	Forestry & Timber Processing Industry.
stock timber	GORIN LUMBER COMPANY	Forestry & timber processing, Pulp & paper

		industry
stock timber	DALLESPROM	Forestry & timber processing, Pulp & paper industry
stock timber	DALLESPROM	Forestry & timber processing, Pulp & paper industry
stock timber	DALLESPROM	Forestry & timber processing, Pulp & paper industry
stock timber	DALLESPROM	Forestry & timber processing, Pulp & paper industry
stock timber	MARIININSKLES	Forestry & timber processing, Pulp & paper industry
stock timber	DALLESPROM	Forestry & timber processing, Pulp & paper industry
stock timber	DALLESPROM	Forestry & timber processing, Pulp & paper industry
stock timber	DALLESPROM	Forestry & timber processing, Pulp & paper industry
stock timber	AMURSKIY FURNITURE PLANT	Forestry & timber processing, Pulp & paper industry
stock timber	LAZAREVLES	Forestry & timber processing, Pulp & paper industry
stock timber	MUKHENSKOYE LUMBER COMPANY	Forestry & timber processing, Pulp & paper industry
stock timber	FURNITURE FACTORY	Metallurgy, machine-building & power industry
stock timber	LETKA LUMBER COMPANY	Forestry & Timber Processing Industry
stock timber	PRIMA KOMEKSINDO	Forestry & Timber Processing Industry.
stock timber	KRESTTSY LES	Forestry & Timber Processing Industry
stock timber	SAKHALINLESPROM	Forestry & timber processing, Pulp & paper

		industry
stock timber	BERTOZKA	Forrestry and timber processing industry. Pulp and paper industry. Publishing and printing industry
stock timber	FART	Forrestry and timber processing industry. Pulp and paper industry. Publishing and printing industry
stock timber	MENIL LUMBER COMPANY	Forrestry and timber processing industry. Pulp and paper industry. Publishing and printing industry
stock timber, lumber	UKHTUA	Forestry & Timber Processing Industry
stock timber, lumber	PIZHMA	Forestry & Timber Processing Industry. Pulp & Paper Industry. Publishing & Printing Industry.
stock timber, lumber	BISERT LUMBER COMPANY	Forrestry and timber processing industry. Pulp and paper industry. Publishing and printing industry
stock timber, lumber	SARAPUL LUMBER COMPANY	Forrestry and timber processing industry. Pulp and paper industry. Publishing and printing industry
stock timber, lumber	IKRINSKIY LUMBER COMPANY	Forrestry and timber processing industry. Pulp and paper industry. Publishing and printing industry
stock timber, saw logs	CHEREPOVETSLES	Forestry & Timber Processing Industry
stock timber, saw logs, lumber	PRIRODA	Forestry & Timber Processing Industry
storage batteries	RIGEL	Electrical Enginiring Industry
sugar	INTERSAKHAR	Food Industry. Tobacco Industry
suits	STALLES	Clothing Industry. Footwear

For additional analytical, business and investment opportunities information, please contact Global Investment & Business Center, USA at (202) 546-2103. Fax: (202) 546-3275. E-mail: rusric@erols.com Global Business E-Books on Line: http://world.mirhouse.com

		& Tanning Industry
suits, costumes	AYVENGO	Clothing Industry. Footwear Industry
suits, costumes	LODIYA CLOTHING FACTORY	Clothing and footwear industry
sulfite cellulose	ARKHANGELSK PULP FACTORY	Pulp & Paper Industry
sulfite cellulose	SYASKIY PULP & PAPER FACTORY	Pulp & Paper Industry
sulfite cellulose, bleached cellulose	VOLOSHKA PULP FACTORY	Pulp & Paper Industry
sunflower, wheat	GELIO-PAKS	Food & Food Processing Industry. Tobacco Industry.
surgical gloves	LATEKS	Chemical, Pharmaceutical & Microbiology Industry
synthetic fibers	ZARECHNIY POLYMERIC FACTORY	Textile industry
synthetic fibers	VOLZHSKOYE KHIMVOLOKNO	Textile Industry
synthetic leather	OKANIT	Clothing Industry. Footwear & Tanning Industry
synthetic resin	AVANGARD	Chemical Industry
synthetic resin, polyacrylamide, washing machines	Ya.M. SVERDLOV PLANT	Chemical, Pharmaceutical & Microbiology Industry
synthetic resin, varnish, paint	KOTOVSK PAINT & VARNISH PLANT	Chemical, Pharmaceutical & Microbiology Industry
synthetic ropes	SETKA	Textile Industry
synthetic threads	KRASNAYA LENTA	Textile Industry
tank barges, pontoons	OKA	Metallurgy Industry. Machine-Building Industry. Power Industry
tape recorders	VEGA	Metallurgy industry, Machine-building industry, Power industry
tape recorders, road construction machinery	ARZAMAS INSTRUMENT MAKING PLANT	Metallurgy Industry. Machine-Building Industry. Power Industry
technological process control and regulation units	ANALITPRIBOR	Radio-Electronic Industry

textile industry machinery	TEKMASH	Machine Building Industry
thermocouple	ETALON	Metallurgy. Machine-Building. Power Industry
thermometers	TERMOPRIBOR	Machine Building Industry
timber	BUREISKIY SAWMILL	Forestry & timber processing, Pulp & paper industry
timber	VERKHNETULUMSKIY LUMBER COMPANY	Forestry & Timber Processing Industry
timber	UMBA WOOD PROCESSING PLANT	Forestry & Timber Processing Industry
timber	KOVDORSKIY LUMBER COMPANY	Forestry & Timber Processing Industry
timber	NOVGOROD WOOD PROCESSING PLANT	Forestry & Timber Processing Industry
timber	SEVERO-SAKHALINSKIY LUMBER COMPANY	Forestry & timber processing, Pulp & paper industry
timber	SAKHALINLESPROM	Forestry & timber processing, Pulp & paper industry
timber	SAKHALINLESPROM	Forestry & timber processing, Pulp & paper industry
timber	VERKHNETYMSKY LUMBER COMPANY	Forestry & timber processing, Pulp & paper industry
timber	SOBINKA WOOD PROCESSING PLANT	Forestry & Timber Processing Industry.
timber	BABAYEVO LUMBER COMPANY	Forestry & Timber Processing Industry
timber, lumber	UST-ILIMSK LUMBER COMPANY	Forestry & timber processing industry. Pulp & paper industry. Publishing & printing industry
timber, lumber	VYKSALES	Forestry & Timber Processing Industry. Pulp & Paper Industry. Publishing & Printing Industry.
timber, lumber	KRESTETSKIY LUMBER COMPANY	Forestry & Timber Processing Industry
timber, lumber	PESTOVOKOMPLEKSLES	Forestry & Timber

		Processing Industry
tin plate	AMURSKIY KRISTAL	Food & tobacco industry
tin, indium	TIN PROCESSING PLANT	Metallurgy industry, Machine-building industry, Power industry
tires	KIROV TIRES MANUFACTURING PLANT	Chemical, Pharmaceutical & Microbiology Industry
titanium, magnezium	AVISMA	Chemical, pharmaceutical, and microbiology inndustry
tock timber	SEBEZH	Forestry & Timber Processing Industry
tools	NOVOSIBIRSK TOOL MANUFACTURING PLANT	Metallurgy industry, Machine-building industry, Power industry
toys	RUSSKOYE REMESLO	Metallurgy Industry. Machine-Building Industry. Power Industry
tractor electrical equipment	AVTOELECTROARMATURA	Electrical Engineering Industry
tractors, agricultural equipment	KURGANMASHZAVOD	Metallurgy Industry. Machine-Building Industry. Power Industry.
tractors, parts	VLADIMIR TRACTOR PLANT	Machine Building Industry
transformers	GEORGIYEVSK TRANSFORMERS MANUFACTURING PLANT	Metallurgy. Machine-Building. Power Industry
tricot gloves	ALEKSANDROVSKKOZH	Textile Industry
trucks	SHADRINSK AUTOASSEMBLY PLANT	Metallurgy Industry. Machine-Building Industry. Power Industry.
trucks	ZAVOD IMENI LIKHACHOVA	Automobile Industry
trucks, cars, auto parts	GAZ	Metallurgy Industry. Machine-Building Industry. Power Industry
trucks, trailers	AVTOPRITSEP-KAMAZ	Metallurgy. Machine-Building. Power Industry
tungsten anhydrite	NALCHIK HYDROMETALLURGY PLANT	Mining Industry
tungsten, molybdenum & tungten powder	POBEDIT	Chemical, Pharmaceutical & Microbiology Industry
tungsten-cobalt alloy, titanium-tungsten alloy	KIROVOGRAD SOLID ALLOY PRODUCING PLANT	Metallurgy Industry. Machine-Building Industry.

		Power Industry.
turbo-generators, hydro-generators	ELSIB	Metallurgy industry, Machine-building industry, Power industry
turbo-generators, turboprop engines	PRIVOD-HOLDING	Chemical, pharmaceutical, and microbiology inndustry
unbleached cotton fabric	FATEKS	Textile Industry
unbleached cotton fabric	SHUYSHIY PROLETARIY	Textile Industry
unbleached cotton fabric	TKACHESTVO	Textile Industry
underwear	TRIBUNA	Clothing Industry
vacuum pump	ARZAMAS MUNICIPAL ENDINEERING PLANT	Metallurgy Industry. Machine-Building Industry. Power Industry
varnish & paint	CHERKESSK CHEMICAL PLANT	Chemical, Pharmaceutical & Microbiology Industry
varnish, enamel	TSENTROLAK	Chemical Industry
varnish, paint	KHIMPROM	Chemical, Pharmaceutical & Microbiology Industry
vegetable oil	GEORGIYEVSKIY	Food & Food Processing Industry. Tobacco Industry
vegetable oil, tomato paste	PROVANSAL	Food & tobacco industry
vodka	SHADRINSK LIQUEUR PLANT	Food, food processing and tobacco industry
vodka	SORMOVSKIY WINERY	Food & Food Processing Industry. Tobacco Industry
vodka	VINAGROPROM	Food & Food Processing Industry. Tobacco Industry
vodka	ARZAMASSKIY LIQUEUR FACTORY	Food & Food Processing Industry. Tobacco Industry
vodka	BALZAM	Food & Food Processing Industry. Tobacco Industry
vodka and liquor products	KRISTAL	Food Industry. Tobacco Industry
vodka, liquor	MUROM LIQUOR MANUFACTURING PLANT	Food Industry. Tobacco Industry
vodka, liquor	ALKO	Food Industry. Tobacco Industry
vodka, liquor	ALEKSANDROV VODKA & WINE DISTILERY	Food Industry. Tobacco Industry
wall panels	ROS	Building Materials Industry

wall paper, tiles	ROSBI INTERNATIONAL LIMITED	Consumer Goods, Furniture, Household & Cultural Products
washig machines, vacuum cleaners	PROGRESS	Metallurgy Industry. Machine-Building Industry
washing machines	VESTA	Machine-Building Industry
washing machines	KRASNAYA ZARYA	Metallurgy. Machine-Building Industry
watches	MOLNIYA	Metallurgy Industry. Machine-Building Industry. Power Industry.
water & gas meters	BELGOROD MEASURING INSTRUMENTS PLANT	Metallurgy Industry. Machine-Building Industry
weighing machines	IGLINO WEIGHING MACHINE PRODUCING PLANT	Metallurgy Industry. Machine-Building Industry. Power Industry.
welding wire, welding equipment	PROMETEY	Machine Building Industry
wheat flour, semolina, combined fodders	KONDOPOGA GRAIN PRODUCTS PLANT	Food & Food Processing
wheels	ZAVOD IMENI VOYTOVICHA	Machine Building Industry
white pigment	LAKOKRASKA	Chemical, Pharmaceutical & Microbiology Industry
winches, pumps, boats	GOROKHOVETS SHIPYARD	Machine Building Industry
wires	UFIMKABEL	Metallurgy Industry. Machine-Building Industry. Power Industry.
wolfram concentrate	DZHIGINSKIY COMBINE	Mining industry
women's clothing	ZHENSKAYA ODEZHDA	Clothing Industry. Footwear Industry
wood craft	KHOKHLOMSKOY KHUDOZHNIK	Forestry & Timber Processing Industry. Pulp & Paper Industry. Publishing & Printing Industry.
wood crafts, plastic products	KATUSHKA	Consumer Goods, Household & Cultural Products
wood paper, lumber	YEFIMOVSKIY WOOD PROCESSING PLANT	Forestry & Timber Processing Industry
wood working machinery	KRASNIY METALLIST	Metallurgy. Machine-Building. Power Industry

wooden crafts and toys	KORALL	Consumer Goods, Household & Cultural Products
wooden toys	KRASNAYA ZVEZDA	Forrestry and timber processing industry. Pulp and paper industry. Publishing and printing industry
wood-working lathes	NOVOZYBKOV LATHE-BUILDING PLANT	Machine Building Industry
woodworking machines	KORIT	Metallurgy, machine-building & power industry
wool	NEKLYUDOVO WOOL PROCESSING FACTORY	Textile Industry
wool	NEVINOMYSSK WOOL PROCESSING FACTORY	Textile Industry
wool farbic, wool yarn	ARAMILSKIY TEKSTIL	Textile industry
wool yarn	NEVINOMYSSK WORSTED FACTORY	Textile Industry
wool yarn, cotton yarn	VERETENO	Textile Industry
woollen yarn	MODEN	Textile Industry
work clothes	TIKHVIN CLOTHING FACTORY	Clothing Industry
work clothing	INVA-BROK	Clothing Industry. Footwear Industry
yachts	EXPERIMENTAL SHIPYARD	Machine-Building Industry
yeast	BIODEN	Food & Food Processing Industry. Tobacco Industry.

For additional analytical, business and investment opportunities information, please contact Global Investment & Business Center, USA at (202) 546-2103. Fax: (202) 546-3275. E-mail: rusric@erols.com Global Business E-Books on Line: http://world.mirhouse.com

BUSINESS ACTIVITIES SUBJECT TO SPECIAL AUTHORIZATION BY THE GOVERNMENT (APPLICABLE BOTH TO LOCAL AND FOREIGN ENTREPRENEURS)

1. Activities referring to the construction of complexes in Krays, Regions, Autonomous Regions, and cities. Production of building constructions (local authorities)
2. Activity of specialized privatization investment funds and companies (State Committee for Investments)
3. Activity on servicing population and factories
4. Advertising and designing activity using city territory, buildings surfaces, streets, etc.
5. Banking operations (Central Bank)
6. Banking Operations with foreign currency (Central Bank)
7. Clearing operations (Central Bank)
8. Commodity Exchanges operations (Commodity Exchange Commission)
9. Communication services (except government systems) (Ministry of Communication)
10. Construction activities: designing, researching, investigating, contracting, assembling.
11. Construction and maintenance of nuclear and radioactive installations, technology and products, wastes of their production (Rosatomnadzor)
12. Construction, leasing, re-equipment of fishing-factories, research and fisheries patrol vessels (Roskomrybolovstvo)
13. Customs activities (State Customs Committee)
14. Customs warehouses activities (local customs)
15. Entertainment, sports and show business
16. Gambling and casino business
17. Inspection of State monopoly of alcohol products
18. Insurance (Rosstrachnadzor)
19. Inter-mediation in securities transactions (for companies with foreign participation) (Ministry of Finance)
20. Investment companies, financial brokers, investment consulting (Ministry of Finance)
21. Investment Funds operations (Ministry of Finance)
22. Investments abroad (not identified)
23. Land designing and surveying (Roscornzem)
24. Maintenance of engineering systems, territory improvement, maintenance of residential and nonresidential accommodations, town roads and bridges (local authorities)
25. Maintenance of refueling stations
26. Medical practice (except treatment of infection and oncology patients) (local authorities)
27. Organization of employment of Russian citizens abroad

28. Organization of local lotteries
29. Pawnshop operations
30. Pharmaceutical activity (License commission of the Ministry of Health, local authorities)
31. Private detective and security services (Ministry of Internal Affairs)
32. Private notary activity (Ministry of Justice)
33. Production and import of securities blanks (Ministry of Finance)
34. Production and sale of homemade products and other goods on public catering factories, including public servicing (local authorities)
35. Production and sale of perfumery and cosmetic products
36. Production and wholesale trade of other alcohol products
37. Production of food
38. Production, storage and wholesale trade of ethyl alcohol (except crude alcohol, produced from the wastes of main production)
39. Public showing of movie and video films
40. Publishing activity
41. Reconstruction and restoration of monuments and buildings of historical and architectural value (local authorities)
42. Reproduction and museum exhibits copy making
43. Sale of goods (services) for foreign currency on the Russian territory (Central Bank)
44. Sale of wine, liquor and vodka products (local authorities); sale of tobacco products; retail trade in temporary shops - including individual trade - except sale of agricultural products
45. Stock Exchange operations (Ministry of Finance)
46. Stocking up and sale of medical herbs
47. Tourist and excursion activity
48. Transportation of goods and passengers by road, freight forwarding activity, loading and unloading operations, storage services
49. Transportation, expedition and other activities connected with transportation process, repair and maintenance of automotive means of transportation (Russian transport inspection)
50. Use of natural resources, mining (Roskomzem)
51. Use of underground space construction and repair of underground communications (local authorities)
52. Veterinary activity (State veterinary department)
53. Veterinary practice (Local authorities)

SUPPLEMENT 2. INTERNATIONAL TREATIES. COUNTRIES WITH MOST FAVORED NATION STATUS

1. Afghanistan
2. Albania
3. Angola
4. Argentina
5. Australia
6. Austria
7. Bangladesh
8. Belgium
9. Benin
10. Bolivia
11. Bosnia-Herzegovina
12. Botswana
13. Brazil
14. Bulgaria
15. Burkina Faso
16. Burundi
17. Cabo Verde
18. Cambodia
19. Cameroon
20. Canada
21. Chad
22. Chili
23. China
24. Colombia
25. Congo
26. Costa Rica
27. Croatia
28. Cuba
29. Cyprus
30. Czech Republic
31. Denmark
32. Djibouti
33. Ecuador
34. Egypt
35. Equatorial Guinea
36. Ethiopia
37. Finland
38. France
39. Gabon
40. Gambia
41. Germany
42. Ghana
43. Great Britain
44. Greece
45. Grenada
46. Guinea
47. Guinea-Bissau
48. Guyana
49. Honduras
50. Hungary
51. Iceland
52. India
53. Indonesia
54. Iran
55. Iraq
56. Ireland
57. Israel
58. Italy
59. Jamaica
60. Japan
61. Jordan
62. Kenya
63. Korea(North)
64. Korea(South)
65. Kuwait
66. Laos
67. Lebanon
68. Liberia
69. Libya
70. Luxembourg
71. Macedonia
72. Madagascar
73. Malaysia
74. Mali
75. Malta
76. Mauritania
77. Mauritius
78. Mexico
79. Mongolia
80. Morocco
81. Mozambique
82. Myamnar
83. Nepal
84. Netherlands
85. New Zealand
86. Nicaragua
87. Niger
88. Norway
89. Pakistan
90. Panama
91. Peru
92. Philippines
93. Poland
94. Portugal
95. Qatar
96. Romania
97. Rwanda
98. Salvador
99. San Tome and Principe
100. Sierra Leone
101. Singapore
102. Slovak Republic
103. Slovenia
104. Somalia
105. South African Republic
106. Spain

For additional analytical, business and investment opportunities information, please contact Global Investment & Business Center, USA at (202) 546-2103. Fax: (202) 546-3275. E-mail: rusric@erols.com Global Business E-Books on Line: http://world.mirhouse.com

107. Sri Lanka	116. Uganda
108. Sudan	117. United States of America
109. Sweden	118. Uruguay
110. Switzerland	119. Venezuela
111. Syria	120. Vietnam
112. Tanzania	121. Yemen
113. Thailand	122. Zaire
114. Tunisia	123. Zambia
115. Turkey	124. Zimbabwe

BILATERAL INVESTMENT PROTECTION TREATIES

1. Austria*	17. Korea (South)
2. Belgium*	18. Kuwait
3. Bulgaria	19. Luxembourg*
4. Canada*	20. Netherlands*
5. China*	21. Norway*
6. Cuba	22. Poland
7. Czech Republic	23. Portugal
8. Denmark	24. Romania
9. Finland*	25. Slovenia
10. France*	26. Spain*
11. Germany*	27. Sweden*
12. Great Britain*	28. Switzerland*
13. Greece	29. Turkey*
14. Hungary*	30. United States of America
15. India	31. Vietnam
16. Italy*	

* The treaties were signed by the Soviet Union and are to be resigned by Russia.
** The treaties have been agreed upon and will be signed in the near future.

BILATERAL TRADE TREATIES

1. Albania	21. Cayman Islands
2. Algeria	22. Chili
3. Angola	23. China
4. Anguilla	24. Colombia
5. Antigua and Barbuda	25. Congo
6. Antilles (Netherlands)	26. Cook Islands
7. Argentina	27. Costa Rica
8. Aruba	28. Cuba
9. Bahamas	29. Cyprus
10. Bahrain	30. Dominica
11. Barbados	31. Dominican (Rep.)
12. Belize	32. Ecuador
13. Bermuda	33. Egypt
14. Bolivia	34. Fiji
15. Bosnia-Herzegovina	35. Gabon
	36. Gambia
16. Brazil	37. Ghana
17. British Virgin Islands	38. Grenada
18. Brunei	39. Guatemala
19. Cote d' Ivoire	40. Guyana
20. Cameroon	41. Honduras

For additional analytical, business and investment opportunities information,
please contact Global Investment & Business Center, USA
at (202) 546-2103. Fax: (202) 546-3275. E-mail: rusric@erols.com
Global Business E-Books on Line: http://world.mirhouse.com

42. Hong Kong
43. India
44. Indonesia
45. Iran
46. Iraq
47. Jamaica
48. Jordan
49. Kenya
50. South Korea
51. North Korea
52. Kuwait
53. Lebanon
54. Libya
55. Macedonia
56. Malaysia
57. Malta
58. Mauritius
59. Mexico
60. Micronesia
61. Mongolia
62. Montserrat
63. Morocco
64. Namibia
65. Nauru
66. Nicaragua
67. Nigeria
68. Niue
69. Oman
70. Pakistan
71. Panama
72. Papua New Guinea
73. Paraguay
74. Peru
75. Philippines
76. Qatar
77. Saint Helena
78. Saint Kitts and Nevis
79. Saint Lucia
80. Saint Vincent and the Grenadines
81. Salvador
82. Saudi Arabia
83. Senegal
84. Seychelles
85. Singapore
86. Slovenia
87. Sri Lanka
88. Surinam
89. Swaziland
90. Syria
91. Thailand
92. Tonga
93. Trinidad and Tobago

COUNTRIES EXEMPT FROM RUSSIAN IMPORT TARIFFS

1. Afghanistan
2. Bangladesh
3. Benin
4. Botswana
5. Burkina Faso
6. Burundi
7. Bhutan
8. Cabo Verde
9. Cambodia
10. Central African Republic
11. Chad
12. Comoros
13. Equatorial Guinea
14. Ethiopia
15. Guinea
16. Guinea-Bissau
17. Haiti
18. Kiribati
19. Laos
20. Lesotho
21. Liberia
22. Madagascar
23. Malawi
24. Maldives
25. Mali
26. Mauritania
27. Mozambique
28. Myanmar
29. Nepal
30. Niger
31. Rwanda
32. Samoa
33. San Tome and Principe
34. Sierra Leone
35. Solomon Islands
36. Somalia
37. Sudan
38. Tanzania
39. Togo
40. Tuvalu
41. Uganda
42. Vanuatu
43. Yemen
44. Zaire
45. Zambia

FREE TRADE AGREEMENTS

For additional analytical, business and investment opportunities information, please contact Global Investment & Business Center, USA at (202) 546-2103. Fax: (202) 546-3275. E-mail: rusric@erols.com
Global Business E-Books on Line: http://world.mirhouse.com

1. **Armenia**
2. **Azerbaijan**
3. **Belarus**
4. **Moldova**
5. **Kazakhstan**

6. **Kirgizstan**
7. **Tadzhikistan**
8. **Turkmenistan**
9. **Ukraine**

GOVERNMENT ORGANIZATIONS RESPONSIBLE FOR FOREIGN INVESTMENT

Ministry of the Economy of the Russian Federation (Minekonomiki of Russia)

Formulation and implementation of the State Policy for attracting foreign investment.

Coordination of the activities of the federal bodies regarding cooperation with foreign investors.

Establishment of free economic zones.

Arranging for and holding international tenders and bidding.

Arranging for Concession agreements and deals on production sharing.

Central Bank of the Russian Federation (Bank of Russia)
Administration of Exchange Control over Capital Transactions

Governing bank transactions with foreign capital.

Licensing of capital transactions in foreign currencies - including long-term credits.

Ministry of Finance of the Russian Federation
Department of Securities

Licensing the activities of financial and of the Russian Federation investment companies.

Governing the participation of foreign investment projects.

Ministry of Finance of the Russian Federation
Department of Tax Reforms

Drafting taxation laws and regulations.

Designing procedures for tax laws to be enforced.

State Property Committee (Goskomimushestvo of Russia - GKI)
Administration for Foreign Investment

Formulation of options for participation of foreign investors in privatization.

Administration of foreign investors participation in privatization.

Russian Fund for Federal Property (RFFP)

Arranging for and holding investment and monetary auctions in the privatization process of state property.

Control over the implementation of investment programs.

State Taxation Service of the Russian Federation (Gosnalogslujba of Russia)
Administration for Foreign Economic Relations and International Taxation

Explanation of the enforcement of tax laws.

Control over the implementation of tax laws.

State Customs Committee of the Russian Federation (SCC of Russia)

Arranging for the customs legalization of foreign economic transactions.

Customs regulation of foreign economic transactions.

Control over the use of customs incentives.

State Registration Chamber of the Ministry of Economy of Russia

Registration of ventures with foreign investments.

Accreditation of the missions of foreign companies.

Support in obtaining visas.

Foreign Investment Promotion Center (FIPC) of the Ministry of Economy of Russia

Informational and advisory services for foreign investors.

Dissemination of investment information - including information on investment projects in the Russian Federation.

Assistance to businessmen in their quest of investment opportunities and particular partners.

Coordination of the activities of the overseas investment offices.

Investment offices of the FIPC

Dissemination of investment information, including investment projects in the Russian Federation.

Promotion of investment projects in and offers of Russian enterprises.

For additional analytical, business and investment opportunities information, please contact Global Investment & Business Center, USA at (202) 546-2103. Fax: (202) 546-3275. E-mail: rusric@erols.com Global Business E-Books on Line: http://world.mirhouse.com

Advisory services for potential investors.

Federal Center for Project Financing

Investment consulting.
drafting of business plans.

INTERNATIONAL AGREEMENTS - BILATERAL INVESTMENT PROTECTION TREATIES AND OTHER INVESTMENT LEGISLATION[10]

As of June 1997, there were 11 bilateral investment protection treaties (BITs) in the Russian Federation. Most of these treaties were concluded by the former Soviet Union but are recognized by Russia as the USSR's legal successor. Additional treaties are under negotiations

The BITs are reciprocal treaties between Russia and individual foreign states that provide legal guarantees to investors from treaty states in Russia as well as to Russian investors in treaty states. Such guarantees normally pertain to the transfer of funds related to foreign investment activities, expropriation and similar measures, losses as a result of armed conflict and civil disturbance as well as the legal succession of investment insurance agencies (subrogation). Under these treaties, foreign investors are assured of either:

1) "national treatment" - treatment no less favorable than the one accorded to Russian investors;
2) "most favored nation treatment" - treatment no less favorable than the one accorded to investors from any third country; and,
3) "full protection and security".

Furthermore, they provide international arbitration for the resolution of disputes arising under the treaties. Such recourse applies to disputes between the contracting states ("state-to-state disputes") and disputes between protected foreign investors and the host state ("investor disputes").

The treatment of "indirect" and "creeping" expropriations are some of the important differences between BITs - even though most of them have similar provisions. In several BITs, transfer guarantees are subject to qualifications.

Under the "umbrella clause", any obligation toward a protected investor that is not fulfilled is considered a violation of the BIT. In this way, investors can obtain treaty protection of their contractual rights against Russian agencies.

---

[10] For the complete texts of legislation, please contact Russian Info&Business Center, Inc. at (202) 546-2103

In theory, differences among the BITs should not work against the investor. Because of the most favored nation treatment (MFN) provisions, investors from any country that has concluded a BIT with Russia can invoke in their favor the guarantees under any treaty between Russia and any third country. Thus, German investors in Russia are entitled to all the guarantees provided in the BITs of Russia with Austria, Canada, China, etc. The MFN provisions link all the Russian investment related treaties into a comprehensive network establishing the highest level of protection and investor freedoms envisaged under any one of these treaties.

MULTILATERAL CONVENTIONS

Russia is a member of several multilateral conventions which have the potential to affect the legal protection of investors on its territory. They include:

1 the 1988 **Multilateral Investment Guarantee Agency Convention** (the MIGA Convention) that facilitates the insurance against non-commercial risks in all signatory countries of investors from those countries;

2. the **Convention on the Recognition and Enforcement of Foreign Arbitrage Awards** signed in New York on June 10, 1958 (the New York Convention); and

3. the **Cooperation Agreement between Russia and the European Union.**

Other important conventions such as the one governing the settlement of investment disputes between states and nationals of other states - signed in Washington on March 18, 1965; the Convention on the International Center for the Settlements of Investment Disputes (ICSID Convention); and, the Energy Charter Treaty - signed in Lisbon on December 14, 1994 have not yet been ratified. The latter applies only to investments in the energy sector but lays out detailed standards for investment protection that reflect investment principles recognized internationally. Foreign investors may find this a useful reference in their negotiations with Russia.

RUSSIAN DOMESTIC LAWS

As of June 1997, most guarantees concerning foreign investment were embodied in the Foreign Investment Law. Foreign investors are assured of the following in Chapter 2 of this law:

1. Treatment no less favorable than that accorded to domestic investors (Article 6). Such national treatment, however, is subject to exceptions which may be established by domestic law, notably in the area of ownership or leasing of land and acquisition of rights to natural resources (Article 38) and in connection with privatization (Article 37).

For additional analytical, business and investment opportunities information, please contact Global Investment & Business Center, USA at (202) 546-2103. Fax: (202) 546-3275. E-mail: rusric@erols.com Global Business E-Books on Line: http://world.mirhouse.com

2. Protection against nationalization, confiscation and illegal actions of state bodies and officials (Articles 7 and 8). Nationalization and confiscation measures require enacting legislation by Parliament - in case of confiscation by Parliament, the president or the government is responsible. Such procedures can be contested in Russian courts and must be accompanied by prompt, adequate and effective compensation. However, this guarantee does not explicitly extend to cases of so-called "indirect" and "creeping" expropriation, which are the main concern of investors. Russian authorities compute the amount of compensation after the official announcement of confiscation. However, the value of the affected property may already have been largely discounted in anticipation of the measure.

3. Transfer abroad of investment proceeds in foreign currency (Article 10). One has to keep in mind that 50 percent of the revenues from Russian exports must be converted into rubles at the official exchange rate.

4. Reinvestment or other use inside Russia of investment proceeds in local currency (Article 11). While the conversion of local currency proceeds is not guaranteed by the Foreign Investment Law, investors can buy hard currency for rubles through banks or currency exchanges; and

5. Recourse to Russian courts and, in some instances, arbitration proceedings for the settlement of investment disputes (Article 9). However, according to international treaties, foreign investors are entitled to international arbitration. Investors from countries that have a BIT with Russia have access to international arbitration while investors from other countries do not.

Although the investment protection guarantees of the Foreign Investment Law overlap with those found in the BITs of Russia, the latter are frequently more comprehensive, avoid technical loopholes and can be enforced through recourse to international arbitration and diplomatic protection. Article 5 of the Law is particularly important. It provides that international treaties apply directly to foreign investments in Russia and take precedence over domestic law in cases of conflict. However, the latter rule may be subject to question if a conflict arises between an international treaty's provision and the Constitution of Russia.

ECONOMIC STABILIZATION TOOLS

Russian legislation provides a number of stabilization mechanisms in order to limit the damage a foreign investor may suffer in a deteriorating investment climate. The **Foreign Investment Law** includes a provision that postpone for one year the enforcement of a law or any legal act that deteriorates the conditions of preexisting foreign investments. **Presidential Decree No. 1466 "On the Improvement of Work with Foreign Investment"**, adopted on September 27, 1993 provides that legal acts will not be applied to already existing wholly or partly foreign-owned enterprises for a period of three years if they introduce changes for the worse. The law provides that they will apply immediately if they improve the present conditions. **Presidential Decree No. 2285 "On Issues of Agreements on Production Sharing in the Mineral Resource Sector",** adopted on December 24, 1993, applies the "grandfather" clause to production-sharing agreements between foreign investors and Russian state bodies. The clause calls for the agreement to be modified in order to keep the foreign investors as a whole entity. Thus, the Russian side to the agreement is the one that solely shoulder all the losses.

While "grandfather" schemes may provide some comfort to foreign investors, they afford only limited protection. First, they do not encompass all the types of adverse legislative changes. Second, the one to three years "freezing periods" are frequently too short, especially when investment projects have considerable lead times before they yield returns. Third, and foremost, the grandfather clauses are themselves part of domestic Russian legislation. As with any other piece of legislation, they can, at any moment, be changed or repealed by the Russian legislature.

Under the Russian Constitution, considerable powers have devolved to the Federation's jurisdictions and even to its municipalities. Local legislation can affect federal legislation on the rights of foreign investors. To safeguard investors against this possibility, the two presidential decrees mentioned above have provisions that void sub-federal legislation impairing federal laws or decrees. The validity and scope of these provisions might, however, raise questions about their constitutionality.

DISPUTE RESOLUTION

As mentioned above, Russia is a member of the ICSID Convention - an important international convention for the resolution of disputes with foreign investors. This Convention was opened to signature on March 18, 1965 on behalf of member countries of the International Bank for Reconstruction and Development to provide facilities for the conciliation and arbitration of investment disputes between contracting states and nationals of other contracting states. There are clear indications that Russia might adhere to the Convention in the near future. According to Article 9 of the Foreign Investment Law, "investment disputes" are to be settled by the Supreme Court or by the Supreme Arbitration Court of the Russian Federation - if no other methods of settlement are stipulated by international agreements. Therefore, the Russian Foreign Investment Law leaves a door open for the international settlement of investment disputes.

Furthermore, Russia has subscribed to several bilateral treaties on investment protection - these usually incorporate provisions on the settlement of investment disputes. Foreign investors must keep in mind that the stipulation of international treaties prevail over Russian domestic legislation. As to "other disputes" where a treaties prevail over Russian foreign interest is involved, these would typically be decided by Russian Courts, unless the parties have agreed to have them settled by arbitration.

Disputes involving an enterprise with foreign interest are usually considered, under Russian law, as disputes having an international character. Therefore, upon agreement between the parties, such disputes can be submitted for arbitration in any country. The parties are free to choose either *ad hoc* or "institutional" arbitration, and under certain circumstances they have also the choice of the substantive law.

Several Russian bodies are members of the International Chamber of Commerce - though Russia is not a member of the ICC's International Court of Arbitration. Nevertheless, ICC arbitration is increasingly being adopted involving foreign investment in Russia.

Foreign investors are advised to pay particular attention when choosing the most appropriate provision for arbitration in their contractual relationships with Russian partners or Russian subjects, as well as in the relationships between their fully or partially owned Russian enterprise and other physical and legal persons.

Special courts have been set up in Russia to replace the previous body - State Arbitration or *Gosarbitrazh* - for the settlement of economic disputes. The jurisdiction of these courts (commonly referred to as arbitrage tribunals) should not generally apply to foreign investors and/or enterprises with foreign participation. Their jurisdiction would apply only if the disputing parties agree, or if stipulated by intergovernmental or international agreement. In certain areas - mainly administrative disputes - the competence of these tribunals is considered exclusive and mandatory.

INCENTIVES & PRIVILEGES FOR INVESTORS

Incentives are granted to producers and investors promoting the development of various regions or economic sectors. The system of incentives, however, is subject to frequent changes.

SPECIAL TAX INCENTIVES

The Foreign Investment Law (Article 28) provides that tax incentives may be granted to enterprises with foreign investments operating in priority areas and in certain regions. In practice, however, a two year tax break previously applicable to enterprises with foreign investment (three years in the Far East Region) was repealed. Special tax incentives currently available are extremely limited. At the present time, enterprises registered after January 1, 1994 are the beneficiaries - under those tax incentives - of a two year tax break (reduced to 25 percent and 50 percent of the base tax rate in years three and four, respectively) if they:

are involved in the material production activities, and;

have at least 30 percent paid in foreign equity participation - the sum must be equal to a minimum of $10 million.

Moreover, tax breaks are only available if the income from production activities during the first two years is greater than 70 percent of the enterprise's total income from all activities (90 percent during years three and four).

CUSTOMS INCENTIVES

Property imported into Russia by foreign investors as a contribution to the charter capital is exempt from customs duties upon importation (also see Chapter 5). Tariff incentives, such as return of earlier paid customs, lower tariff rates or total exemptions, apply to:

imported goods that will be contributed to the authorized capital;

certain products and exports;

property imported by foreign employees for their own needs.

With a special permission of the Russian Government, tariffs are reduced by 50 percent on certain goods imported as foreign investments if:

the foreign suppliers are, at the same time, the founders of enterprises producing similar goods on the Russian territory;

these enterprises use Russian raw materials and labor;

foreign companies invest into material production;

total investments into the enterprise are no less than US$ 100 million;

foreign contribution to the authorized capital of the enterprise is not less than US$ 10 million.

EXPORT AND IMPORT ACTIVITY

Foreign affiliates and enterprises with more than a 30 percent equity stake in Russian companies may export their products and import goods for their needs without any import or export license. Since 1994, export licenses have been required only for "strategic natural resources" products.

HARD CURRENCY RECEIPTS

Enterprises operating in Russia are obliged to exchange 50 percent of their hard-currency income into rubles on the domestic currency market. It is, however, possible to buy hard currency for import needs or for transfers abroad.

FINANCING FACILITIES

Presidential Decree No. 1928, "On Private Investments in the Russian Federation", adopted on September 17, 1994 authorizes the Russian Government to allocate 0.5 percent of its gross domestic product to finance highly efficient investment projects that have a commercial participation. The State contribution to such projects is usually 20 percent - it is no greater than 80 percent of the investment. The balance of funds in the project must be made up by private investors.

These are some of the possible forms that State participation can take in a project:

loan by the Russian Central Bank, denominated in foreign currency for a maximum of 24 months;

government purchases of equity in joint-stock companies that can be sold on the market once the project is profitable; and

special incentives for large investments when a foreign contribution exceeds 30 per- cent of share capital.

FREE ECONOMIC ZONES

Russia is eager to use free economic zones (FEZs) to encourage foreign investment. About 15 FEZs exist in Russia, the most advanced of which are in **Nachodka** - in the Far East - and **Yantar** - in Kaliningrad.

The conditions for investments in FEZs differ from zone to zone and are regulated by each zone's laws and regulations. Federal legislation regulates only the most important issues.

The incentives may be the following:

simplified registration of enterprises in the FEZs;

lower rates of taxation - they can, however, not be lower than 50 percent of the rate being applied on the Russian territory;

lower leasing rates for land and leasing terms up to 70 years;

lower tariffs on imports and exports, and expedient border procedures;

simplified procedures for the entry and exit of foreign citizens, including waiver of visa requirements.

All incentives are to be endorsed by the Russian Council of Ministers and approved by the Parliament.

Free Customs Zones and Bonded Warehouses are the two specific types of FEZs detailed in the Customs Code of the Russian Federation - adopted on June 18, 1993.

For additional analytical, business and investment opportunities information,
please contact Global Investment & Business Center, USA
at (202) 546-2103. Fax: (202) 546-3275. E-mail: rusric@erols.com
Global Business E-Books on Line: http://world.mirhouse.com

INVESTMENT PROMOTION

A system of foreign investment promotion has been established in the Russian Federation (see Appendix E). The Ministry of the Economy assumes the leading role in the promotion of foreign investment and is responsible for: drafting and implementing state policy aimed at attracting foreign investment; coordinating the activities of the federal and regional executive bodies regarding the cooperation with foreign investors; establishing free economic zones; arranging for and holding international tenders; arranging for concession agreements and production sharing deals; and, allocating loans provided by international financial organizations and foreign states. The Department for International Investment Cooperation has been established within the Ministry of the Economy for the purpose of dealing with the specific FDI promotion issues. This Department ensures the interaction with other executive bodies and deals practically with all major issues of state DFI policy.

The State Registration Chamber has been established within the Russian Ministry of the Economy. Registering ventures with foreign investments, keeping a State register of ventures, and accrediting the missions of foreign companies is authorized under the law.

Information and consultative services for foreign investors are rendered by the Foreign Investment Promotion Center (FIPC) - which is affiliated to the Ministry of the Economy.

The Federal Center for Project Financing makes pre-feasibility studies. It also makes expert analysis of international investment cooperation and the use of credits granted under the guarantees of the Russian government.

The Ministry of Finance, the State Property Committee (GKI), the Federal Property Fund, the State Tax Service, the State Customs Committee, and the Russian Central Bank also play an active role in foreign investment promotion.

ADVISORY COUNCIL ON FOREIGN INVESTMENT

In June 1994, the Advisory Council on Foreign Investment was created to promote foreign investment. It was created on the initiative of the Government of the Russian Federation and more than 20 representatives of major international corporations. The Advisory Group is chaired by Prime Minister .

Governmental Decree No. 1108 dated September 29, 1994 officially established the Advisory Group. According to the Decree the three working groups have been formed to draft proposals:

to upgrade Russia's attractiveness as an investment location, especially for foreign investors - this group is headed by the Minister of the Economy to eliminate external barriers for Russian exporters - this group is headed Deputy Prime Minister and Minister of Foreign Economic Relations, and,

to improve tax legislation and incentive measures for foreign investments - this group is headed by the Minister of Finance

Proposals and recommendations were drafted by these groups and presented to the first meeting of the Advisory Council in November 1994. Many of the recommendations have been taken under consideration by the Government and proposed to the Duma. A special plan on implementing these recommendations has been developed by the different Russian ministries involved and by representatives of the work groups. The plan includes concrete measures which could improve banking and currency regulation, introduce changes in the tax law and clarify some articles concerning tax legislation.

FOREIGN INVESTMENT PROMOTION CENTER

The **Foreign Investment Promotion Center (FIPC)** was created in June 1997 as a standard framework for the long-term attraction of foreign capital. The FIPC, in accordance with Governmental Decree No. 657, adopted on June 30, 1997, is a government body subordinated to the Russian Ministry of the Economy.

The mission of the FIPC is to attract, facilitate and increase foreign investment into the Russian Federation.

The main objectives of the Centers are:

to effectively encourage foreign investment into the Russian economy;
to study investment projects and bring together potential partners;
to make it attractive for foreign investors to establish a presence in Russia;
to advocate laws and regulations to improve Russia's investment climate;
to offer pre- and post-investment services to foreign investors;
to give support and guidance to Russian regions and to their investment promotion agencies for local industries;

In accordance with its objectives the FIPC carries out the following services:

promulgates cooperation and ensures the assistance of Russian federal and regional executive government bodies to potential investors;
assists, advises and renders administrative support to foreign companies already present in Russia;

supplies information on new investment opportunities in Russia and its Regions and markets Russian investment projects abroad through FIPC's offices in Western Europe;

provides the foreign investor with all of the basic data he requires in order to structure his project and appraise it in advance;

informs foreign investors on the changes in the Russian foreign investment legislation and consults on the existing laws and regulations concerning foreign companies activities in Russia;

identifies Russian partners for foreign firms and business people looking for partnership in Russia and its different regions;

arranges contacts and prepares the itineraries for the prospective investors visiting business locations of Russian partners;

assists in the negotiation process between foreign investors and Russian partners and holds talks with potential investors on the required conditions to attract and use foreign investment credits in Russia.

In order to fulfill these objectives, the FIPCs decided to open overseas offices in Frankfurt, Paris, London and Milan during the next two years. The first two offices - Frankfurt and Paris - started their activities in the Fall of 1997.

The European Bank for Reconstruction assists the FIPC in its activities. The FIPC has elaborated its investment promotion methodology based on the practices which have been successfully developed by such prominent investment promotion institutions as the Industrial Development Agency of Ireland and the Foreign Investment Advisory Service and Multilateral investment Guarantee Agency - both divisions of the World Bank.

According to the existing foreign investment promotional techniques, the following forms of activity will be undertaken by FIPC through its Moscow led network of offices:

advertising,

direct mailing;

investment seminars;

investment missions;

participation in trade shows and exhibitions;

distribution of literature;

one-to-one direct mailing efforts;

preparation for the visits of prospective investors;

matching prospective investors with local partners;

acquiring permits and approvals from various governmental departments;

preparing project proposals;

conducting feasibility studies;
providing services to investors after the projects have become operational.

Russian Foreign Investment Promotion Center:
Smolensky Bulvar, 3/5, Moscow, Russia,.
Tel: 7 095 245 21 71 or 7 095 246 94 39, Fax: 7 095 246 94 39.

OTHER ORGANIZATIONS

Several "joint ventures" associations and clubs are currently in existence in Russia. Two of the most prominent ones - the Association of joint Ventures and the International Associations and Organizations - unite joint ventures and 100% foreign owned enterprises from all over the country. Similar organizations exist in Moscow and St. Petersburg. The aim of these organizations is to bring together managers with similar purposes and problems, to exchange information, to support business conferences, to help in the search of partners, to provide legal support, etc.

Recently, several State and privately-owned insurance companies have begun to operate with foreign investors covering non-commercial risks. One of them is the International Agency for Insurance of Non-Commercial Risks. This Agency is supported by the Russian Government.

Foreign investors can also apply to the Russian Finance Corporation - created in April 1993. It primarily works as an agent of the Russian Government and finances investment projects with centralized finance and credit resources. The Corporation has preferential treatment when it comes to finance and foreign trade operations.

Foreign firms can also get the support from the Russian Chamber of Commerce and Industry, the Ministry of Foreign Economic Relations, various Russian-foreign associations, and others - all of them well-known in the Russian Federation Foreign Economic Relations.

LEGISLATION RELEVANT TO FOREIGN DIRECT INVESTMENT

BUSINESS AND CORPORATE LAW

Russian law is, in principle, a codified law. The new Russian Constitution, adopted by national referendum on December 12, 1993, is Russia's most important law. The second most important legislation in Russia is the Civil Code - which also contains the bulk of the basic provisions regulating entrepreneurial activities. A new Civil Code (Part 1) was adopted by the Russian State Duma on October 21, 1994. The new Civil Code repealed numerous outdated laws, such as the Law on Enterprises and Entrepreneurial Activity and the Law on Property, which contained many archaic and often contradictory provisions. In furtherance of the Civil Code, a Law on joint-stock Companies was adopted in December 1997. This law clarified outstanding areas of corporate legislation. Other legislation on limited liability companies and other business firms is still under consideration.*

THE NEW RUSSIAN CONSTITUTION

The Russian Constitution does not contain any specific provisions on foreign direct investment or foreign investors' rights. Article 62, however, provides that foreign citizens and stateless persons have the same rights and obligations as Russian citizens, except where otherwise provided by federal law or international treaty. The Constitution, furthermore, upholds certain basic principles that can affect the rights and duties of an investor:

Private property is protected by law. No one may be deprived of his property by a court decision. The compulsory expropriation of property for state needs may only be carried out if full compensation is paid in advance. (Article 35).

These components do not reflect changes introduced by the new "Law on Joint-Stock Companies" introduced in December 1997.

An individual has the right to engage in entrepreneurial and other economic activity except where prohibited by law, e.g., unfair competition and monopolistic activity. (Article 34).

The federal government has the authority to establish basic policies in the areas of banking, credits, currency, customs, ecology, economics, and finance. (Article 71).

THE NEW CIVIL CODE

The Russian system of civil legislation currently consists of a combination of acts adopted during the Soviet era and acts of more recent origin. Thus, Russia's primary sources of civil legislation are currently:

1. the First Part of the Civil Code of 1994;
2. the Fundamental Principles of Civil Legislation of the USSR and the Republics (or the Fundamental Principles); and 3. the amended RSFSR Civil Code of 1994. Much of this legislation is inconsistent. In what may complicate matters further, the State Duma is considering draft legislation on the regulation of civil relations and economic activity. In the second part of the new Civil Code, new laws on banks and banking, joint-stock companies, limited liability companies, partnerships and securities are considered. In furtherance of the Civil Code, a Law on joint Stock Companies was adopted in December 1997. This law clarified outstanding areas of corporate legislation. Other legislation on limited liability companies and other business firms is still under consideration.

The Fundamental Principles were adopted by the USSR Supreme Soviet in May 1991 and were to go into effect in January 1992. With the abolition of the USSR, the Fundamental Principles had uncertain legal effect in Russia. Thus, the old Civil Code, which had been developed in the 1960s, with a few amendments, remained in force. In response to this situation, the Russian Supreme Soviet issued a decree in 1992 giving the force of law to the Fundamental Principles in Russia, overriding many concepts from the pre-reform era that had been embodied in the old Civil Code.

The new First Part of the Civil Code was enacted on January 1, 1997. It is expected to be followed by the Second Part sometime in . If the Second Part is enacted as drafted, the new Civil Code, as a whole, will provide a modern, market oriented basis for economic activity. The Code, which draws heavily from the German Civil Code, determines the legal status of individuals and legal entities; establishes the legal basis for the exercise of property and other rights; and, provides general norms for contractual and other civil obligations. Subjects which are not covered by the New Civil Code, e.g., special provisions on contracts and the law of obligations, are still regulated by the Fundamental Principles and the old Civil Code of 1964, as amended.

BASIC CONCEPTS OF THE NEW CIVIL CODE

Under the Civil Code, foreign legal entities and individuals are to get the same kind of treatment than their Russian counterparts under Russian legislation unless otherwise provided by federal law,

The new Civil Code is based on certain fundamental principles. They include:
1) equality of all participants regulated by civil law;
2) inviolability of private property
3) freedom of contract,
4) free exercise of civil rights; and,
5) judicial protection of civil rights.

The Civil Code provides that goods, services and financial assets may move freely throughout the Russian territory. Limitations on the exercise of civil rights may only be established under federal laws, and in such cases, only to the degree necessary for the protection of the constitutional system, the health of the population, the rights and legal interests of other persons, the defense of the country, or the security of the state.

Citizens have the right to own private property and engage in entrepreneurial activity not expressly prohibited by law. A citizen may conduct entrepreneurial activity as an individual, in conjunction with others (individuals or legal entities), or through a legal entity. In order to conduct entrepreneurial activity without the formation of a legal entity, the citizen must register as an individual entrepreneur. Before individuals or legal entities engage in certain regulated entrepreneurial activities, they must obtain a valid license.

The Civil Code defines a legal entity as an Organization that owns, exercises jurisdiction over or manages property and is liable for that property. A legal entity may acquire and exercise property rights, undertake obligations, and sue and be sued in court or arbitration. It must have its own independent balance sheet and books of account.

The Civil Code puts legal entities into two categories: commercial and non-commercial organizations. Commercial enterprises, whose goal is to make a profit, can be established as business partnerships and companies, production cooperatives, and state and municipal unitary enterprises. Non-commercial organizations, which do not aim to make a profit and do not distribute any profits, may engage in profit-making activities to reach their goals. Non-commercial organizations may take the form of consumer cooperatives, social or religious organizations and associations, and charitable and other funds.

Depending on its form and the nationality of its founders, a legal entity will have foundation documents consisting of a charter and/or founder's agreement. A non-commercial Organization may operate only on the basis of its general regulations.

REGISTRATION AND TERMINATION OF A LEGAL ENTITY

According to pending legislation, the new Civil Code provides for the state registration of all legal entities with the Ministry of Justice. Until its adoption, legal entities generally will continue to be registered with local executive bodies and, if necessary under the law, the State Registration Chamber of the Ministry of the Economy. Information on the state registration of legal entities is to be maintained in a State Register accessible to the public. A legal entity is considered to be established only upon its official registration. The applicant may appeal denial of an application for registration of a legal entity in court.

The activity of a legal entity can be terminated through reorganization or liquidation. A legal entity can be liquidated upon the decision of its participants or shareholders, a body of the legal entity appointed by its participants or shareholders, or a court.

At the present time, the insolvency, or bankruptcy, of legal entities is mainly regulated by the Law on Insolvency (Bankruptcy) of Enterprises signed on November 19, 1992. Under this law, a legal entity may be liquidated in accordance with a decision of the State Arbitration Court in the jurisdiction where the legal entity is registered. **Presidential Decree No. 2264 "On Measures for the Implementation of Legislative Acts on Insolvent (Bankrupt) Enterprises"** adopted on December 22, 1993, also establishes special rules with regard to state enterprises. The new Civil Code establishes a new order to satisfy creditors of a legal entity undergoing liquidation.

For additional analytical, business and investment opportunities information, please contact Global Investment & Business Center, USA at (202) 546-2103. Fax: (202) 546-3275. E-mail: rusric@erols.com Global Business E-Books on Line: http://world.mirhouse.com

FORMS OF ENTREPRENEURIAL ACTIVITIES

Commercial activity in Russia can be undertaken through various kinds of legal entities, the most common of which are business partnership and the company. Business partnerships may take one of two forms:

1) **full partnership** - *tovarishchestvo na vere -;* and,
2) **limited partnership** - *kommanditnoe tovarishchestvo.*

Companies can take one of three forms:
1) **limited liability company**;
2) **additional liability company**; and,
3) **joint-stock company**.

FULL PARTNERSHIP

A full partnership is a legal entity formed on the basis of a founder's agreement of its participants stipulating that each participant has the right to act in the name of the partnership. The agreement usually identifies each participant's respective area of activity. A full partnership must have a registered name that includes the names of all its participants as well as the words "and Company," or the names of one or more participants and the words "full partnership." Although a full partnership usually is directed through unanimous decisions of its participants, the founder's agreement may stipulate otherwise. Each participant bears full liability for the partnerships' obligations. In its relationship with third parties, the partnership may not rely on provisions of the founder's agreement restricting the rights of its participants to act on behalf of the partnership, unless such third party knew or should have known that the participant did not have the right to act on the partnership's behalf. A person may be a participant in only one full partnership. Additional rules on full and other forms of partnerships will be established by a forthcoming law on partnerships.

LIMITED PARTNERSHIP

A limited partnership is a legal entity with two classes of participants. The first class consists of full partners who manage the partnership's activities and have unlimited liability for its obligations - At a given time, a person may only be a full partner in one limited partnership; furthermore such a person is prohibited from also being a member of a full partnership. The other class of participants consists of participant-contributors, *or Command,* who are not involved in the management of the partnership's activities and whose liability is limited to the amount they contribute to the partnership's capital. The provisions of the Civil Code on general partnerships also apply to limited partnerships, except as provided, for example, regarding rules for the name of a limited partnership.

For additional analytical, business and investment opportunities information, please contact Global Investment & Business Center, USA at (202) 546-2103. Fax: (202) 546-3275. E-mail: rusric@erols.com Global Business E-Books on Line: http://world.mirhouse.com

LIMITED LIABILITY COMPANY

A limited liability company (LLC) is a legal entity founded by one or more persons whose charter capital is divided into shares, or *dolya*, without the issuance of stock. An LLC is similar to an English Private Limited Company, a French *Societe a Responsabilite Limitee* (Sari) or a German *Gesellschaft mit Beschraenkter Haftung* (GmBH). LLC founders or participants generally are not liable for its obligations. Thus, their exposure is limited to the stated value of their shares in the company. Certain special rules, however, may expose the participants to additional financial exposure. An LLC has a relatively simple management structure. It consists of a General Meeting of Participants, which has exclusive decision-making power, and which can be either collegial or unitary. Additional rules regarding LLCs will be established by a forthcoming law.

ADDITIONAL LIABILITY COMPANY

An additional liability company (ALQ) is a legal entity founded by one or more persons whose charter capital is divided into shares, without the issuance of stock. The participants in an ALC have secondary liability for its obligations proportional to their share of charter capital. This legal form is not widely used.

JOINT-STOCK COMPANY

A joint-stock company (ISC) is a legal entity whose charter capital is divided into a specific number of shares of stock, or *aktsiya*. Shareholders in a ISC generally are not liable for its obligations, and their financial exposure is usually limited to the stated value of their stock in the company. However, they may be subject to secondary or joint and several liability for the JSC's obligations under certain circumstances. A ISC generally has a three-tier management structure:

1) a General Meeting of Stockholders, which has exclusive jurisdiction over certain decisions;
2) a council of directors or supervisory council; and,
3) an executive body, which can be either collegial or unitary.

A ISC with 50 or fewer shareholders may eliminate the latter body.

An JSC may be either open or closed. Shareholders of an open JSC may freely dispose of their stock without the consent of other shareholders. In contrast, shareholders in a closed JSC may only dispose of their stock with the permission of other shareholders in the manner provided in the JSC's foundation documents. A closed JSC may not have more than a certain number of stockholders whose number will be established by a forthcoming law.

In addition to the new Law on Joint-Stock Companies, JSCs are governed by relevant provisions of the Civil Code and by the Regulations on JSCs approved by RSFSR Decree No. 601 adopted on December 25, 1990. In addition, Presidential Decree No. 784 establishes certain provisions and procedures open to JSC designed to protect shareholder rights (see the section on securities market regulation.) These remain in effect to the extent that they are not inconsistent with the provisions of the new Civil Code and the new law on JSC.

STRUCTURE OF THE RUSSIAN OIL INDUSTRY

LUKOIL

Crude producers	Refineries	Product distributors
Langepasneftegaz	Volgograd	Adygeyanefteprodukt
Urayneftegaz	Permnefteorgsintez	Tulanefteprodukt
Kogalymneftegaz		Volgogradnefteprodukt
Nizhnevolzhskneft		Vologdanefteprodukt
Astrakhanneft		Kirovnefteprodukt
Permneft		Permnefteprodukt
Kaliningrad		Chelyabinsknefteprodukt

SURGUTNEFTEGAZ

Crude producers	Refineries	Product distributors
Surgutneftegaz	Kirishinefteorgsintez	Karelnefteprodukt
		Novgorodnefteprodukt
		Pskovnefteprodukt
		Tvernefteprodukt
		Katiningradnefteprodukt
		Peterburgneftesnab
		Kirishinefteprodukt

YUKOS

Crude producers	Refineries	Product distributors
Yuganskneftegaz	Kuybyshevnefteorgsintez	Samaranefteprodukt
Samaraneftegaz	Novokuybyshevsk	Bryansknefteprodukt
	Syzran	Oreinefteprodukt

For additional analytical, business and investment opportunities information, please contact Global Investment & Business Center, USA at (202) 546-2103. Fax: (202) 546-3275. E-mail: rusric@erols.com
Global Business E-Books on Line: http://world.mirhouse.com

		Lipetsknefteprodukt
		Penzanefteprodukt
		Tambovnefteprodukt
		Ulyanovsknefteprodukt
		Voronezhnefteprodukt

SLAVNEFT

Crude producers	Refineries	Product distributors
Megionneftegaz	Mozyr (Belarus)	Smolensknefteprodukt
		Gomeinefteprodukt
		(Belarus)
		Brestnefteprodukt
		(Belarus)
		10 other Belarussian
		distributors

SIDANKO (SIBERIA FAR EAST OIL COMPANY)

Crude producers	Refineries	Product distributors
Varyeganneftegaz	Angarsk	Sakhalinnefteprodukt
Kondopetroleum	Saratov	
Chernogorneft		
Udmurtneft		

VOSTOK OIL COMPANY (VOS)

Crude producers	Refineries	Product distributors
Tornskneft	Tomsk Petrochemical	Krasnoyarsknefteprodukt
	CombineTomsknefteprodukt	
	Achinsk	Khkasnefteprodukt
		Tuvanefteprodukt

For additional analytical, business and investment opportunities information, please contact Global Investment & Business Center, USA at (202) 546-2103. Fax: (202) 546-3275. E-mail: rusric@erols.com
Global Business E-Books on Line: http://world.mirhouse.com

ORENBURG OIL COMPANY (ONACO)

Crude producers	Refineries	Product distributors
Orenburgneft	Orsknefteorgsintez	Orenburgnefteprodukt

TYUMEN OIL COMPANY

Crude producers	Refineries	Product distributors
Nizhnevartovskneftegaz	Ryazan	Ryazannefteprodukt
Tyumenneftegaz		Kursknefteprodukt
		Kaluganefteprodukt
		Tulanefteprodukt
		Tyumennefteprodukt

ROSNEFT

Crude producers	Refineries	Product distributors
Purneftegaz	Moscow	Mosnefteprodukt
Sakhalinmor	Yaroslavlorgsintez	Yaroslavlnefteprodukt
Krasnodar	Norsi (Novo-Gorkiy)	Nizhniy Novgorodneft,
Stavropol	Yaroslavi	Arkhangelsknefteprodt
Kalm	Omsk	Beigorocinefteproduki
Dag		
Term (Bashkortostan)		

For additional analytical, business and investment opportunities information,
please contact Global Investment & Business Center, USA
at (202) 546-2103. Fax: (202) 546-3275. E-mail: rusric@erols.com
Global Business E-Books on Line: http://world.mirhouse.com

INDEX

For additional analytical, business and investment opportunities information,
please contact Global Investment & Business Center, USA
at (202) 546-2103. Fax: (202) 546-3275. E-mail: rusric@erols.com
Global Business E-Books on Line: http://world.mirhouse.com

**For additional analytical, business and investment opportunities information,
please contact Global Investment & Business Center, USA
at (202) 546-2103. Fax: (202) 546-3275. E-mail: rusric@erols.com
Global Business E-Books on Line: http://world.mirhouse.com**

Printed in the United States
5979